Making News

Making News

MARTIN MAYER

DOUBLEDAY & COMPANY, INC.
GARDEN CITY, NEW YORK
1987

Grateful acknowledgment is given to the following for permission to reprint previously published material: Excerpt from *The Image: Or What Happened to the American Dream* by Daniel J. Boorstin. Published by Atheneum. Copyright © 1962 by Daniel J. Boorstin. Reprinted by permission of the author. Excerpt from *Big Story* by Peter Braestrup. Published by Yale University Press. Copyright © 1983 by Peter Braestrup. Reprinted by permission of the author. Excerpt from *The Triumph of Politics* by David A. Stockman. Published by Harper & Row. Copyright © 1986 by David A. Stockman. Reprinted by permission of Harper & Row, Publishers. Excerpt from *Nightly Horrors: Crisis Coverage in Television Network News* by Dan Nimmo and James E. Combs. Copyright © 1985 by The University of Tennessee Press. Reprinted by permission of The University of Tennessee Press.

Library of Congress Cataloging-in-Publication Data
Mayer, Martin, 1928–
Making news.
Includes index.
1. Journalism.   I. Title.
PN4731.M3945 1987   070.4'3   86-19887
ISBN: 0-385-18983-4

for Karin of course
and also a little for the J's

Contents

PART FIVE
In Print

PART SIX
New Technologies

PART SEVEN
Conclusion

The force of the newspaper is the greatest force in civilization.

Under republican government, newspapers form and express public opinion.

They suggest and control legislation.

They declare wars.

They punish criminals, especially the powerful. They reward with approving publicity the good deeds of citizens everywhere.

The newspapers control the nation because they REPRESENT THE PEOPLE.

—William Randolph Hearst, 1898

It is my thesis, to paraphrase McLuhan, that, in a sense, the mirror has become the message: that in showing us what we are and what we are doing, in reflecting the bloat, the complexity, the contradictions of post-World War II society, *The Times* has come to fulfill a new function; it has quite literally become that Fourth Estate, that fourth coequal branch of government of which men like Thomas Carlyle spoke.

—Harrison E. Salisbury, 1980

Acting upon everybody for thirty minutes in twenty-four hours, the press is asked to create a mystical force called Public Opinion that will take up the slack in public institutions. The press has often mistakenly pretended that it could do just that. It has, at great moral cost to itself, encouraged a democracy, still bound to its original premises, to expect newspapers to supply spontaneously for every organ of government, for every social problem, the machinery of information which these do not normally supply themselves . . . The Court of Public Opinion, open day and night, is to lay down the law for everything all the time. It is not workable. And when you consider the nature of news, it is not even thinkable.

—Walter Lippmann, 1922

The fact that your voice is amplified to the degree where it reaches from one end of the country to the other does not confer upon you greater wisdom or understanding than you possessed when your voice reached only from one end of the bar to the other.

—Edward R. Murrow, 1958

Part One

INTRODUCTION: PERSONAL PRESCRIPTS

1
Qualifications

An observer standing at the corner of Paradise Avenue and Great White Throne Walk in Sorrell Hill Cemetery would have seen a human figure moving among the graves toward the Superintendent's residence. Dimly and fitfully visible in the intervals of thinner gloom, this figure had a most uncanny and disquieting aspect. A long black cloak shrouded it from neck to heel. Upon its head was a slouch hat, pulled down across the forehead and almost concealing the face, which was further hidden by a half-mask, only the beard being occasionally visible as the head was lifted partly above the collar of the cloak. The man wore upon his feet jack-boots whose wide, funnel-shaped legs had settled down in many a fold and crease about his ankles, as could be seen whenever accident parted the bottom of the cloak. His arms were concealed, but sometimes he stretched out the right to steady himself by a headstone as he crept stealthily but blindly over the uneven ground. At such times a close scrutiny of the hand would have disclosed in the palm the hilt of a poniard, the blade of which lay along the wrist, hidden in the sleeve. In short, the man's garb, his movements, the hour—everything proclaimed him a reporter.

–Ambrose Bierce[1]

No other occupation brings a man into such familiar sociable relations with all grades and classes of people. The last thing at night—midnight—he goes browsing around after items among police and jail-birds, in the lock-up, questioning the prisoners and making pleasant and lasting friendships with some of the worst people in the world. And the very next evening he gets himself up regardless of expense, puts on all the good clothes his friends have got—goes and takes dinner with the Governor, or the Commander-in-Chief of the District, the United States Senator, and some more of the upper crust of society. He is on good terms with all of them, and is present at every public gathering, and has easy access to every variety of people. Why I breakfasted with the Governor,

> dined with the principal clergymen, and slept in the station
> house.
>
> —Mark Twain[2]

> Journalists are plentiful everywhere and entertaining, too, full
> of jokes and stories. Only their jokes are not very funny and
> their stories are inexact. Their information is always incom-
> plete, because nobody ever tells them the truth about any-
> thing. Their philosophy of life and art and their technique of
> expression are incurably, dogmatically superficial. Their pri-
> vate lives are full of banal melodrama. They are, to a man,
> either dyspeptic or alcoholic or both. They must be avoided in
> bands, because they bring out the worst in one another. Singly
> they are fun but rather indigestible.
>
> —the composer Virgil Thomson, who was
> about to become music critic for the
> New York *Herald Tribune*, on
> suitable companions for young
> composers, 1939[3]

1

I am by profession a snoop; by craft, a writer; by trade, a gossip. The
preferred description in today's grandiloquent news business would probably be "investigative reporter." (Or, as the especially grandiloquent Harrison Salisbury has it, "investigative correspondent."[4]) What the term appears to mean—I can't be sure—is that I usually choose my own subjects
rather than accepting assignments from an editor. I have been at the writing
and publishing part of it a long, long time, since spring 1937, when I was
nine years old and my somewhat older PS 166 classmate Lowell Blankfort
and I wrote and published and sold for 3¢ a copy a six-page mimeographed
paper we called *The Sportsman.*[5] I think it must have been mimeographed by
Lowell's father's secretary rather than by my father's secretary, because the
"Printing offices" are listed at 44 West Eighteenth Street and my father's
office was then on Madison Avenue at Thirty-third.

This rather embarrassing document is before me as I write, Lowell
having kept it all these years and having delivered it to me just the other day
on a visit back to his native New York from his adopted San Diego. It has a
dittoed cover, a line drawing of "Dizzy" Dean (prissy quotation marks in
the original) signing an autograph, presumably for one of us. Probably for
Lowell, who had more brass and, definitely—I have just reread the stuff
after forty-eight years—more gold than I.

This proved out. In *Such Interesting People,* Robert J. Casey writes that
one of his first lessons in the anatomy of news came from Rolly Bales of the
Des Moines *Register and Leader,* who bucked back to him a six-line story he

had written from a police report about the burglary of a minister's home, from which the only object of value taken was the minister's wife's silk dress. "Mr. Bales was kind in his comment. 'We ought to have more than this,' he said. 'Novelty is what makes news and this is novelty. A minister's wife very seldom has a silk dress, a newspaperman's wife never.' "[6] (This is still true, by the way: a recent study of journalists by David Weaver and Cleveland Wilhoit of Indiana University finds that "salaries are so low that income is no longer a predictor of job satisfaction for journalists younger than 40. Instead, the relative *importance* placed on salary is related to job satisfaction."[7] At a time when graduates of education schools start their teaching careers in most cities at salaries of $15,000 or more, graduates of journalism schools who can find jobs as reporters—only about a quarter of them do—mostly start at $13,000 or less.) April Blankfort, however, can have any silk dress she likes, for Lowell became much more than a scullion newspaperman.

After working for the London *Daily Mail* in Paris and for *Stars and Stripes* in Germany, *The Wall Street Journal* and Cowles Magazines in New York, Lowell at age twenty-eight bought himself the Pacifica *Tribune* for $5,000 cash. He sold that five years later for $155,000, enough to give him a year of unremunerated travel around the world and then a stake in another paper, this one in the San Diego suburb of Chula Vista. Twenty years later, he sold this one to the Harte-Hanks chain for enough money so that he didn't feel it much (though he didn't like it either) when the swindling J. David Dominelli took him for a quarter of a million dollars in the foreign-exchange Ponzi game that trapped the liberal community of San Diego in 1984. (He later got most of it back from Dominelli's accountants and lawyers—Rogers & Wells, the firm headed by the former Attorney General under Eisenhower and Secretary of State under Kissinger, head of the investigating commission after NASA's *Challenger* disaster—thus revealing that there are unsuspected values in the tort liability system.) At this writing, Lowell and his company, Blankfort Unlimited, Inc., own major pieces of fourteen newspapers in five states (Colorado, Minnesota, Illinois and Wisconsin as well as California), and he writes for all of them on the jaunts he and his wife like to make to odd corners of the globe. Mind you, he was good then, and he's even better now.

There was no news in *The Sportsman* for people who had read the newspapers and *The Sporting News*, as Lowell and I did, but most of our classmates, of course, did not read either and our parents' friends didn't care. We did have a true beat, however, in our second paper, *The Athletic News*, published September 27, 1937, with the cover line "SPECIAL: MY SERIES PREDICTIONS BY BABE RUTH *(Written especially for the Athletic News).*" This appeared on page two, Lowell holding it as a reward for people who first read his own page-one report of the pennant race. "I think the Yankees with their superior batting power will defeat either the Cubs or the Giants," the Ruth item read. "Gehrig, DiMaggio, and Dickey will be no match for the National League pitchers." Ruth's signature appeared below this, as did an "Editor's note— The Editor wishes to thank Babe Ruth for taking time to give us this exclusive statement." Ruth was a sucker for kids, and Lowell lived in the same apartment house, on the same elevator line. Just below this direct quote, which derives added authenticity from its uncertain ("no match for"), rather boozy flavor, Lowell let himself go in a paragraph he wrote about the Newark *Bears* of the International League: "The COMPLETE Bear team is Major League material. IT WOULD BE BET-TER TO HAVE THEM IN THE BIG LEAGUES THAN SUCH TEAMS AS THE BROOKLYN DODGERS, THE ST. LOUIS BROWNS, AND PHILADELPHIA PHILLIES, WHICH NEVER HUSTLE." The difference between news and opinion was not entirely clear to us fifth-graders in 1937, and page two of *The Athletic News* seems to me a textbook case: Ruth's view of the Series was news; Lowell's view of the Newark *Bears* was opinion. We had mixed them together, in part because they looked alike.

Though we were offering *The Athletic News* at an annual subscription of 25¢, I think there was only one more issue, a twenty-page monster including two ads, from Rappaports ("Children's wear fitted for all occasions at popular prices") and from the Boys Club of West End ("Keep your children off the streets at a low cost . . ."). Lowell's file contains one further publication, from January 1939, a paper called *The Scoop,* which shows by various stigmata that it has been reached by officialdom. There are four editors now, plus a cover mention of "Principal: Bernard Colton" and "Teacher: Mr. Hammerman." The paper leads with an appalling piece about "World Democracy" by Mayer, who at age eleven held the view that "Great Britain has no centralized government, but must have the ratification of its Dominions, Australia, India and Canada, which are large enough to be countries in themselves." (Toward the end of that year, I would scandalize my Irish eighth-grade teacher by defending the Soviet invasion of Finland, but thank God I don't seem to have written it down.) There are signs that school staff rather than competent legal secretaries were involved in the production of *The Scoop*—for example, the consistent misspelling of "amateur" (as "amature") in one of Lowell's contributions.

Professionally, I started, eight years later, at the New York *Journal of Commerce* in the old World Building near City Hall. There I rewrote from wire service copy a column of general newsbriefs not unlike the one in *The Wall Street Journal,* but printed on an inside page. It was my considered belief (at age nineteen, though my employers thought I was twenty-two) that nobody in the world read that column, and after a few months I began inserting jokes; and it turned out somebody did read it, and I was given the opportunity to resign. Among my colleagues in the junior general news cadre at the *Journal of Commerce,* incidentally, were Osborn Elliott, later editor of *Newsweek* and dean of the Columbia Journalism School; and Paul

Kolton, later president of the American Stock Exchange and the Financial Accounting Standards Board; and Tom Waage, later senior vice president of the Federal Reserve Bank of New York; and a lean young man with an aquiline nose and blond hair whose name and career I have lost, who was using his desk and typewriter at the *Journal of Commerce* to advance a novel of Long Island he was writing under the title *Sex at Slurp's Point.*

We had all been hired by Heinz Luedicke, a fierce German in 1947, when few Germans were fierce—but in those days the Ridder family, which owned the *Journal of Commerce* as well as the *Staats-Zeitung* and assorted papers in the upper Midwest, was among the few. That is now, of course, the Ridder part of Knight-Ridder, the $2.5 billion media conglomerate based on the Miami *Herald* and other big-city papers scattered all around the country. But they still haven't made much of the *Journal of Commerce,* which lives these days mostly on the high quality of its shipping news reporting, available both in print and through your personal computer.

For the next year, which was not an easy year, I wrestled with my father in the garden and won the right not to go to law school; but I never worked for a newspaper again. I was the English-speaking assistant editor of a scholarly magazine of the labor movement run by a great Menshevik immigrant, former editor of the Amalgamated Clothing Workers and Steel Workers Organizing Committee newspapers, named J. B. S. Hardman (among the others who sat at his feet were Lou Harris and C. Wright Mills, then just a fat and sloppy good old boy from Texas who was politically bringing himself up to speed from very far back). J.B. ran out of money, and I became the editor of a fact-detective magazine, for which I invented, among other things, dialogue, and of a line of paperback Westerns and mysteries; and then I was associate editor of *Esquire.* Since January 1954, I have been snooping and writing and gossiping from an isolated perch. The label "solo practitioner" expresses the condition far better than "free lance," a term with connotations I dislike, especially since not all of them are wrong.

Quite apart from the fact that I sometimes take assignments from magazine editors and give speeches at bankers' conventions, I have written foundation studies on subjects supplied by the foundation and I have provided acknowledged "editorial assistance" to the authors of five books published under their names and unacknowledged assistance to the author of another. I wrote a history of the Ted Bates advertising agency on commission from the agency, which suppressed it. More: I have written a long text advertisement, not to be signed, for IBM (it was about the first cut at automating the morgue and creating a computer-based information service at the New York *Times),* and "articles," also unsigned, for an annual report of a bank, a signed description of what he and his people do all day long for the arbitrageur S. B. Lewis to give to his limited partners and employees, and a signed article (about a model owner of a franchise, a smart Greek-American New Yorker now based in Huntsville, Alabama) for the annual report of

Ramada Inns. If you equate "free lance" to "hired gun," you seem to have a case. But now, suh, you go too far, because in all these "works for hire," to use the term by which authors were horse-collared in the new copyright law, I have kept one rule inviolate: I control what I sign: my name goes only on what I believe to be true.

Bob Casey, as usual, said it best. Writing of the 1920s, he claimed that "the journalistic profession in Chicago was just about as clean as it was anywhere else. It had its own peculiar system of ethics. Numerous reporters would have looked upon burglary in quest of photographs as an extremely venial sin. Nobody thought it much of a crime to represent himself over the telephone as the coroner or the Governor of Illinois. It was perfectly all right to tap a telephone wire, or read private mail, or steal evidence or bribe anybody who would accept a bribe. Nobody thought the worse of a reporter because he occasionally kidnaped the leading character in an important story. But all of this was justifiable only in behalf of an undefinable, somewhat nebulous service to a public that had only halfheartedly asked for it—the discovery, extraction and presentation of THE NEWS. The line had to be drawn somewhere, of course, and it was drawn plainly. It was, and is, the unspoken Hippocratic oath of the newspaperman that, though he may sell out everything and everybody else in the world, he will never sell himself."[8]

Today, of course, any newspaper reporter who gave himself a false identification on the telephone would be cashiered if not castrated. ("Lying," writes Lisa Sowle Cahill, a Boston College theology professor participating in a Notre Dame seminar on journalistic ethics, "like breaking promises, is morally reprehensible."[9]) Even role playing in pursuit of information is considered bad form by the authorities: the Pulitzer Prize board refused to give the Chicago *Sun-Times* a prize for a series that grew out of the paper's operation of a bar that paid bribes to policemen and politicians and received kickbacks from suppliers. Benjamin Bradlee of the Washington *Post* and Eugene Patterson of the St. Petersburg *Times* were the leading opponents; they argued, reports David Shaw, media critic of the Los Angeles *Times,* "that newspapers cannot demand honesty of those they write about if they are less than honest themselves."[10]

Myself, I have never gone further than pretending to be an uninformed customer at a store or a bank or a finance company to find out how such customers are treated. (One wonders: Would Bradlee or Patterson find that objectionable? Are they upset when the admirable Georgie Anne Geyer, one of the earliest female foreign correspondents, recalls guiltlessly in that same Notre Dame seminar that "I masqueraded as a waitress to cover a Mafia wedding—and got a wonderful front-page story which led off, 'Gangland went to a wedding, and I went along for the ride' "?[11]) But the reason I stay clean is not that I find misidentification or role assumption objectionable. The fact is that I don't have the guts or the confidence in my ability to maintain a deception.

I envy the people who were trained to peep through the keyholes in unconventional ways, people like George Wright in Chicago, for example, who put a stethoscope to the thin walls in the criminal court building and heard the prosecutor read to the grand jury the confessions of Leopold and Loeb. There is nothing more exciting—and no element of news work more socially useful—than the discovery of information others do not wish the reporter, or the public for whom he then stands surrogate, to have. By definition, you're not likely to be able to do that in a perfectly straightforward way.

To the extent that the Woodward & Bernstein and Deep Throat business dragged children from the corner and old men from the hearth to seek careers in journalism, the instincts involved were correct (though not of course the understanding: such opportunities arrive about as often as Halley's comet). I remember from my own experience the immense excitement of having in my hands the minutes of the board meetings of the Ocean Hill–Brownsville experimental school district that provoked the 1968 teachers' strike in New York. There was nothing illegal about my access to these documents—the experiment was funded by the Ford Foundation, and I had simply called the administrator of the study and said I had to see the paper, which none of the other reporters who sought to tell this story had thought to do—but it was also quite true that the prime movers of this aggressive but ultimately sad fraud would have been horrified by the idea that a reporter could find the paper trail of their activities.

The only legitimate principle of the business seems to me the one uttered by Walter Mears, executive editor of the Associated Press, shortly after Caspar Weinberger laid into the Washington *Post* for printing what everyone in American journalism (and in Moscow) knew about the payload of a forthcoming American space shuttle. "Giving aid and comfort to the enemy," Weinberger said in his artless way. "It's their job to keep secrets," Mears said on the television show *Nightline,* to which he had been summoned from Palm Beach, where he had been trying to get a vacation. Reacting without the usual news executive's briefing session with a committee of colleagues, Mears felt a need, not to defend the *Post,* which had been clearly within its rights and indeed duties, but to apologize for the AP, which had initially, and he now thought wrongly, gone along with Weinberger's demand for self-censorship. "It's our job," he added, "to find out about them." One does not place people's lives in jeopardy (troopship movements, identities of intelligence agents, etc.), for reasons of the Golden Rule (if I was on a troopship or serving my country under cover, I'd be pretty pissed off at some reporter telling people who wanted to kill me where to find me), and what is accepted under seal of course must be kept under seal, which is of course an excellent reason not to accept information under seal. But in the end the essence of reporting is finding out what the players wish to keep secret, and why, and what the secrets mean. "News," said Lord Northcliffe, born Alfred Harmsworth, who became proprietor of *The Times* of London, "is what somebody somewhere wants to suppress. All the rest is advertising."[12]

The damnedest people seem to feel that digging out what your "sources" would rather keep from you is somehow below the dignity of a modern journalist. David Halberstam, like Cap Weinberger (and me) a product of *The Harvard Crimson*, criticizes Ben Bradlee of the Washington *Post* as "for all his modern style, of the old Chicago school: the story was everything. It made his attitude toward journalism clean, but it disconcerted many of his colleagues—well-educated, middle-class—who thought journalism had some measure of social responsibility."[13] But this is all wrong. "The Chicago school" is the only school, because it recognizes that "the story" is never the problem. One already knows "the story," at least in the sense that the possible stories are all contained on the beanstalk of hypothesis that grows rapidly and automatically (for a reporter) from the first seeds of information. One lies and cheats and steals, if one has the commitment and the guts—or if one lacks the guts one does endless legwork and homework, hoping that will substitute—to get at the secrets that explain what the story means. The reporter wants to know what is happening—I mean, really happening. The well-educated middle-class journalist with his sense of responsibility may be content to slot the public information into whatever intellectually fashionable explanation seems most attractive today. Halberstam, interestingly, knows this: in his tribute to Woodward and Bernstein, he stresses that "they covered [Watergate] not as a political story but as a police story."[14]

By contrast, Stephen Hess of the Brookings Institution, an able and perceptive observer of the press in Washington but in the end no more than a political scientist, ultimately misunderstands. "The men and women who cover the White House, State Department, and Pentagon for the major news organizations," he writes, "are not high school dropouts who began their careers filling pastepots in the city rooms of Chicago tabloids. They are very well educated . . ."[15] As well educated as Ochs or Pulitzer, neither of whom ever went to college? Or the uncredentialed editors of *The Times* of London who wrote most of the thirteenth edition of the *Encyclopaedia Britannica?* Or H. L. Mencken, who became our greatest lexicographer? (Mencken flatly refused to go to college, though his father was willing and able to send him, because he wanted to be a newspaperman: "At a time when the respectable bourgeois youngsters of my generation were college freshmen, oppressed by simian sophomores and affronted with balderdash daily and hourly by chalky pedagogues, I was at large in a wicked seaport of half a million people, with a front seat at every public show."[16]) Or Carr Van Anda, the editor of the New York *Times* who found an error in Einstein's math and deciphered the Tutankhamen inscriptions himself? He didn't have a college degree either.

Hess is not alone in this mistake. "Some of the best reporters of the past never attended college," wrote Herbert Klein, Nixon's "Director of Communications" (a term he invented) and later editor-in-chief of the Copley newspaper chain, "and one wonders what they might have accomplished with a stronger educational background."[17] But many reporters whose names are household words still don't have what Hess and Klein would consider the proper credentials. The three television news celebrities most observers would consider the most allusive and intellectual—John Chancellor, David Brinkley and Peter Jennings—are men who abandoned formal education before completing high school. And Don Hewitt of *60 Minutes* didn't go to college, preferring to earn his education as a copy boy on the New York *Herald Tribune.* Nor did Jack Nelson, Washington bureau chief of the Los Angeles *Times,* 1986 winner of the *Washington Journalism Review* award as "the best in the business." Linda Ellerbee dropped out after a year and a half, and wrote of her time at Vanderbilt before dropping out: "I am as nostalgic for the good old days at Vanderbilt as I am for the Cuban missile crisis, which also took place in 1962."[18]

Reporting as a trade cannot be practiced without a commitment to and a talent for self-education, and a high order of that commitment and talent will educate a reporter exceedingly well regardless of academic preparation. Most of us have seen situations where frauds have been perpetrated by ignorant "general assignment" reporters who don't begin to understand what they are covering. Richard Harwood of the Washington *Post* remembers his early years on the Nashville *Tennessean,* and the announcement in Washington that the atom bomb had been developed in Oak Ridge, which made it a local story. "The city editor," Harwood recalls with some affection, "told the photographer to get out there and get a picture of that atom before they split it and then the two halves of it afterwards." But the autodidacts who worked in the newsrooms half a century ago were often enough as well educated as—even better educated than—the suitably baccalaureate (and magistered or even doctored) who populate the modern newsroom. They had a habit of acquiring on their own not just information but the framework of hypotheses that made the information knowledge.

Stephen White, who spent his formative years on the New York *Herald Tribune* before moving by stages to the Sloan Foundation, wrote recently about "an editor who chose a relatively inexperienced reporter for an extremely important assignment and asked to explain his choice replied, 'He is shrewd and facile.' Shrewdness and facility are what the journalist most requires. He must begin with some, and accumulate more as he proceeds; in the end he is like a pianist who learns to play by playing the piano. Intellectually, journalism is usually a trivial pursuit. None of this denigrates either piano playing or journalism, except among those who are themselves relentlessly intellectual."[19] Like Herb Klein. No doubt the old-timers drank more, but there is high authority for the view that this did no great harm. (Joseph Pulitzer in 1902 worried that the *World* was becoming a dull paper, and summoned his editor Don Seitz to his Maine retreat. "I think," he said, "it's because nobody on the staff gets drunk. . . . When I was there someone always got drunk, and we made a great paper. Take the next train back to the city, find a man who gets drunk, and hire him at once."[20]) Anyway, they made up for that defect by taking themselves much less seriously.

"The elite press," the English newspaperman Martin Walker writes enthusiastically, "seeks to recruit from the elite universities, of Moscow, Tokyo, Oxford and Cambridge, Harvard and Yale, and the *Ecoles Normales* [sic]. Their classmates go into government, diplomacy, the academic life, the professions; the graduate journalists remain a part of that intellectual, power-broking, economic and administrative magic circle which runs the country. They spend their professional lives as journalists in explaining the decisions and options of the various segments of that magic circle to the others. They socialize, investigate, report and comment within that dominant layer of public life."[21] That's the way it looks on the worm's-eye view: they really are taking me seriously, thinks the worm. In fact, the people who have to do the world's work regard news gatherers (including their classmates) as an inescapable excrescence, to be used or confused according to need, even if their company is charming. All of them, I think without exception, share Stanley Baldwin's view that journalists enjoy "power without responsibility—the prerogative of the harlot throughout the ages." (Quoting this comment, the estimable James Deakin of the St. Louis *Post-Dispatch* notes that "those prime ministers knew their harlots."[22]) While it would be misleading to portray these links as scorpions-in-a-bottle stuff, the famous "adversary relationship" goes both ways. In any event, a reporter who loses his suspicion of his sources is not just useless but dangerous.

Some years ago, when I was pulling a laboring oar in the wretched galleys of American education, a Ford Foundation seminar at the Columbia Journalism School invited me to address a dozen or so students who were considering a career as education reporters. How do you get started covering a city school system? they inquired; and I said, Well, you nose around for the disaffected, make your own contacts with teachers and principals and assistant principals, clerks at headquarters, deputy assistant superintendents if possible, and you visit classes, and in all possible ways you make certain that your judgments are not at the mercy of the press releases and public statements of the superintendent and the Board of Education. A young lady at the table sniffed disdainfully: "You make it sound," she said, "like police reporting." I stepped onto my chair and then onto the heavy Pulitzer-donated oak table, and from this height far above their eager young faces I addressed the class and its Ford-sponsored professor, and I said, "All reporting is police reporting. If you can't live with that, you shouldn't be in this

business." They were very offended; so was Ford, then engaged in bringing
McGeorge Bundy's easy yet earnest gentility to the ghetto, the schools of
education, television, public policy, etc.

Reporting is snooping, and snooping is not a genteel activity. It is not, I
fear, entirely compatible with brownnosing to get invitations to Henry Kissinger's cocktail parties or Pamela Harriman's dinners. "So much of my life
is a fairyland," Roone Arledge of ABC News once told an interviewer.
"Anybody would want to be doing it—going to Henry Kissinger's birthday
party, election night in London."[23] The other way to look at this is Alan
Abelson's way, when the managing editor of *Barron's* wrote of "the Washington press corps, whose primary exercise is collecting handouts from
those informational soup kitchens run by government agencies and Congressional staffs. Washington newshounds, whether of the show-biz or the
print breed, are constantly sniffing around the heels of 'sources,' who occasionally throw them bones of gossip or mealy scraps of intelligence. In
return for which, the newshound will bark on command at some enemy of
the source or wag his tail at the source in living color before an appreciative
audience of millions."[24]

Casey's Chicago catalogue of crimes seems less heinous to me than
stationing a camera team in the home of the sister of a priest abducted by
Islamic types in Beirut, as CBS News did in fall 1984, to show the American
people that the poor fellow's family was happy when they thought he'd
been released and unhappy when they learned he was still in captivity.
That's not reporting: that's exploiting predictable human trauma in an already known situation: over time, it would be cheaper and every bit as
honest to keep a staff of actors at the milk barn (the converted dairy on New
York's Eleventh Avenue where CBS news shows and soap operas originate)
to play out such episodes in a studio. What is being done here is different in
kind from the disgusting but defensible practice of sending a newspaper
reporter to inform the new-made widow that her husband's car got mashed
by a trailer truck on the Interstate: this visit may yield a photograph of the
fellow before mashing, or some information about his life that is legiti-
mately part of the story. Ghoul patrol has several purposes (not least among
them, toughening up the novitiate), but it is not planned to give the house-
holder in his easy chair a truly unusual glimpse of the victim's wife coming
apart before his very eyes.

Asked to explain his philosophy of "moments" as central to television
news, Van Gordon Sauter, the plump and richly bearded then president of
CBS News, a man who has risen through the ranks of local station managers
to that eminence, sent critic Ron Rosenbaum a tape including a visit by
Charles Kuralt to the widow of a man whose death from a land mine in
Vietnam Kuralt had caught on his sound track twenty years before. "The
footage of the widow and children," Rosenbaum writes, ". . . is one of the
most genuinely shocking moments of TV I've ever seen. It happens when

Kuralt shows to the family, *for the first time,* the clip of husband and father being blown up 20 years ago. We watch them watching him die . . . there's a moment when Kuralt's 1985 camera gives us a close-up of the widow's face as she watches the 1965 clip—a moment when we hear the explosion and see her flinch as if hit by the sound of her husband being blown up." One regrets to report that Rosenbaum likes this: "It's the kind of piece," he writes, "that makes CBS News, at its best, the best there is."[25] But the fact that this is the real Kuralt and the real widow and the real children (are they? does Rosenbaum know? did Sauter know?) is totally irrelevant here. The thing isn't "news" at all; it's a staging that may or may not involve people playing themselves.

Real news has an improvisatorial excitement. What is terribly hard to convey about the life is the overwhelming excitement of participation in the process that speeds toward deadline. "You work on the four A.M. shift," says Chalky Furlong, a young man who has moved on from New York's all-news WINS to its parent company Group W, "and you watch the city start to light up. The sound starts to pick up at the station. You're part of a big on/off switch, and you're turning the city on."

Apart from intimate matters, I have known three moments of overwhelming excitement in my adult life. One was leading a group of more than five hundred parents from the district where I was chairman of the local school board to demand action from the New York City Board of Education on a site for a junior high school. One was the rehearsals for the Bernstein-Zeffirelli production of Verdi's *Falstaff,* which I attended day after day, learning how a great opera performance gets put together but, more than that, becoming absorbed in the music and the staging, the lives of the artists. I would come home every night clutching my score, and my wife Ellen would say, "Did they give you a part yet?" The third was working for a week at the New York *Daily News* with a first-class reporter named Martin Gottlieb (now at the *Times)* on a series of pieces growing out of a scandal I had uncovered as part of the work on a book, revealing safety hazards in housing built under the auspices of the New York State Urban Development Corporation, which had abused its legislated powers to circumvent state and city building codes. We closed for the early edition, of course. Gottlieb's desk, at which I sat, was virtually beside the horseshoe desk where the copyreaders on the rim cut and polished the stories handed to them by the lordly editor in the slot. People walked faster as six o'clock neared, and the clacking typewriters mingled in an increasingly frantic crescendo, and one handed the copy over, finally, in a kind of exaltation.

What drives the excitement, I think, is not the moment of production, though people involved in news are probably closer to their product than anyone else who does not work with his hands, nor the peculiar combination of deadline and ephemera that is unique to news. The consuming fire flares from a combustible element that putting a newspaper to bed shares

with my other epiphanies: the intensity of the collaboration, the perfection
of the machine that seems suddenly activated, that slots into precisely the
right place at the right time the work and thought and hopes of so many
human beings. It is an especially fierce feeling, I suspect, for a writer like
myself whose work—and whose self-image of his work—is so solitary.

2

Reuven Frank when he was head of NBC News defined "news" as
"change seen by an outsider in behalf of other outsiders."[26] As we shall see,
this will not quite do, but the outsider part of it is true enough. I claim that
advantage: I am an outsider not only to the worlds I report but also to the
world of reporters, which has become heavily institutionalized. In the next
two introductory chapters, we shall try to find the boundaries and the hori-
zons of this external world. And then we shall try to explore it.

Ideally, a book about news, like news itself, should be a succession of
narratives illuminating the business while telling the story. I have tried. Two
of the five parts and five of the twelve chapters between this introduction
and our conclusion will tell stories, and sections in the other chapters will
rise from exposition to narration in hopes of conveying a greater sense of
the meaning of this large societal enterprise, so much discussed and praised
and denounced, so little understood. For the rest, we deal because we must
with institutional structures, their origins, separate purposes, and popula-
tions—and their responses as organizations to the technologies that are
changing the procedures of news production and the habits of news consumption. In the last chapter, we meet again in hopes of answering some of
the more general questions these introductory chapters seek to ask.

2
"News" and an End to Sociology

When blessed infant truth was born
(fa la la la la la la)
He crept into a hunter's horn
(fa la la la la la la)
The hunter blew to make you wince
(fa la la la la la la)
And not a soul has seen truth since
(fa la la la la la la)

–from Carl Orff, *Die Kluge,*
very courageously written in
Munich in 1943; singing
translation by the author

What is original, distinctive, dramatic, romantic, thrilling,
unique, curious, quaint, humorous, odd, apt to be talked
about, without shocking good taste or lowering the general
tone, good tone, and above all without impairing the confidence of the people in the truth of the stories or the character
of the paper for reliability and scrupulous cleanliness.

–Joseph Pulitzer, defining
"news" for the benefit of his
new managing editor at the New
York *World,* 1910[1]

"Look at it this way. News is what a chap who doesn't
care much about anything wants to read."

–the wire service correspondent
Corker in Evelyn Waugh's *Scoop*[2]

1

Casca in Shakespeare's *Julius Caesar* was a gifted reporter of no small
imagination, who would describe to Cicero in memorable detail the incidents of the night before the Ides of March: "Against the Capitol I met a

lion,/ Who glar'd upon me and went surly by/ Without annoying me: and there were drawn/ Upon a heap a hundred ghastly women/ Transformed with their fear, who swore they saw/ Men all in fire walk up and down the streets." That would have been worth a bonus from Hearst or Pulitzer eighty years ago, and even today I can get you airtime for it, Casca, if the color plays on the tape. But when asked by Cassius to report on Cicero's speech to the Senate, Casca as an honest man could say only that "he spoke Greek." And when asked what the philosopher had said, Casca answered, "Those that understood him smiled at one another and shook their heads; but for mine own part, it was Greek to me," thereby giving the English-speaking world a phrase for incomprehension that probably survives to this day in areas where there is no Greek-speaking population to protest it.

Intelligibility comes first. If the reporter cannot at least pretend to make sense out of what he is reporting, and convince his editor or producer that he has made sense of it, it isn't "news." Thus much of what is truly most unusual and most important in the world passes unnoticed outside a small circle of initiates. The greatness of the New York *Times* derives not from its efforts at creating the "record" or maintaining an authoritative objectivity but from a century-long, oft-interrupted yet persistent struggle to acquire the expertise necessary to broaden and sharpen and add dimensions to the perceptual apparatus of the institution. (In sports, too: Meyer Berger tells the story of the formidable, chilly Carr van Anda, who in addition to everything else followed the ponies, stopping by the sports desk to inquire the author of a piece about a certain horse. The editor gave him the name, and asked why. "Just wanted to be sure," van Anda said. "I thought it was the horse wrote it."[3]) Yet it is also true that the drive toward intelligibility detours often into distortion. The first cut at imposing pattern on observation, taken under deadline pressure, rarely exposes the heart of the matter.

There is another phrase in the same linguistic bag as Casca's Greek—"It's news to me," a recipient's rather than a reporter's phrase, expressing not incomprehension but skepticism, perhaps disbelief. Placed in the past tense, however, the phrase is a confirmation, with some degree of self-deprecation: "It was news to me," I hadn't known it before, perhaps I should have known it.

One should note in passing that the converse of this statement is false: you may know it already, but for practical purposes, from the point of view of the news providers, it is still "news." What people *really* want to read about in the newspaper is their daughter's wedding. Failing that, they will settle for the *Monday Night Football* game they watched on television last night. The Miami *Herald* has purchased ten presses more than it would otherwise need to make sure that it can postpone until after the end of *Monday Night Football* the run on all twelve of its daily editions, including the one that goes the two hundred-plus miles up the Treasure Coast to Vero Beach. More seriously, Richard Salant, who was president of CBS News through most of the 1960s and 1970s, argues that television was a major factor in the success of the civil rights movement, not because viewers were strongly affected by the pictures of Bull Connor and the water hoses and the college kids with linked arms and the black children at the white schools, but because, having seen these pictures the night before, readers were for the first time willing to read the stories about such subjects in their newspapers. Certainly that works with reference to Ethiopia: the newspapers had carried quite a lot about starvation on the Horn of Africa, but nobody read it until after NBC showed the BBC film.

"News," says the Random House Dictionary. "A report of a recent event." But old things become recent, like the burial of Tutankhamen, when conditions call them forth. The reporter who digs up the fact that Gary Hart knocked a year off his age on an official document has news to sell though the incident is more than fifteen years old.

The second of several definitions of "news" offered in the OED is "tidings," and that one works. It isn't very helpful, but it works. The committed missionary on the edge of the Amazon does indeed bring "news" of Christ's birth and life and death and resurrection. Time is all over this business: *Die Zeitung, Le Temps, Il Tempo, El Tiempo, The Times.* So is novelty: *nouvelles, novità, Neues, nieuws,* news—it's one of the relatively few words where the Germanic tongue simply picked up the Latin and kept it. But the novelty is not a quality of the event itself, for news purposes. The key question is not when something happened, but when it was uncovered, from the standpoint of the recipient.

"What protrudes from the ordinary," said Walter Lippmann, but that simply shifts the definitional problem to "ordinary." Indeed, we don't need protrusion. Things that *don't* happen are news, because news relates to expectations. The rocket remains on the launch pad, the firemen do not strike though their contract has expired and they said they would. At the same time, the most predictable events get to be treated as news: daylight saving time begins tomorrow, the chairman of the Federal Reserve Board tells the appropriate congressional committee that interest rates cannot come down unless the deficit is reduced. The Statue of Liberty is repaired in honor of the hundredth anniversary of her installation, and the President hosts an event not only scheduled to the second for television with scenarios published in the paper but paid for by advertisers promised just this or that adjacency—and for a long weekend that's the front-page headline and the first five or more minutes of the network news.

Even tautology can seem newsworthy. As I write, there comes across my ken an article in the New York *Times* about a study out of Notre Dame on the marrying habits of Catholics. The population sample included 1,213 Catholics and 3,160 Protestants. "A higher proportion of Catholics than Protestants are involved in 'mixed marriages,' " the news story reports. ". . . Seventeen percent of [the] Catholics are married to Protestants, while 7 percent of the Protestants surveyed are married to Catholics."[4] As every mixed marriage involves one of each, the group with the lower population mathematically must show a higher proportion indulging—what is being said here is simply that 212 is 17 percent of 1,213 and 7 percent of 3,160—but the Notre Dame sociologists wrote it, so it's news.

And then there are incidents and people who become newsworthy, very briefly, because they are accidentally (and meaninglessly) within the cone illuminated by what Walter Lippmann called the searchlight of news. Some people like this escalation of their lives from quiet to noisy desperation, but it doesn't matter much whether they like it or not. Or you can set it up, as Bennett's *Herald* did when it sent Henry Morton Stanley to find David Livingstone, who wasn't lost, or Pulitzer's *World* did when it sent Nellie Bly off to surpass Phineas Fogg's (fictional) record of round the world in eighty days (she did). This sort of thing persists: note the chimpanzee in Dallas that picked winners of the NFL football games better than the newspaper's sports columnist and gave the ABC evening news show an easy "closer" for Monday nights (when the network wants a little something about football if possible as a lead to the game it will presently televise) for the better part of a season.

It is not even unheard of for the entire enterprise to be faked. In an affectionate reminiscence of Cissy Patterson, Joseph Medill's granddaughter, who invented the women's page and made the *Times-Herald* Washington's premier newspaper in the 1930s and 1940s (by driving the *Post* into bankruptcy, she opened the doors for the banker Eugene Meyer and his daughter Kay Graham to become newspaper people), Lynne Cheney remembered how furious Mrs. Patterson was at a radio announcer named Arthur Godfrey, who read over the air on his local early-morning show her paper's gory, detailed, supposedly "eyewitness" account of a Virginia murderer dying in the electric chair. Production schedules being what they were, this description went on the streets two hours before the execution. Godfrey kept breaking into the dramatic narrative with due amazement: "And the poor guy ain't even dead yet!"[5]

Drew Middleton of the New York *Times* remembers that in the early, boring months of what was called the phony war, in late 1939, Bob Casey, in Paris for the Chicago *Daily News,* invented an intrepid French flier who patrolled the Rhine shooting up traffic on the German side; when one of the French papers began to write about the same gallant aviator, Casey indignantly shot him down. Fourteen years later, also in Paris, a young reporter who went on to important jobs invented the nurse of Dienbienphu, and generated such editorial pressure that the French finally had to fly such a lady into the besieged city. Janet Cooke, who made up an eight-year-old heroin addict for the "Metropolitan" section of the Washington *Post,* was part of a long if not great tradition. News-gathering institutions are sitting ducks for malicious minds. Casey illustrated his argument that "editors are just as gullible as their three-cent customers" with a story from the New York days of the peripatetic reporter Frank Ward O'Malley:

"Some managing editor had been discussing with Mr. O'Malley—in a purely academic way, of course—the close relationship between truth and the news, and implying that error in the printed word could be ascribed only to the deliberate intent of the writer. Mr. O'Malley had taken the position that facts are sometimes deceptive in their very nature and that human interpretation of them is bound to have its defects. He was still brooding on this matter over a glass of beer in a saloon overlooking the broad river when his eye suddenly lighted on *La Gloire*. With no hesitation whatever he went to the telephone and called the City Press and after that most of the managing editors in New York, including his own. His speech in all instances was the same:

" 'Zees is Capitaine Rolland of *La Gloire*. Eet is not true we have ze explosions, ze fire on my sheep. Eet is not ze trut we have feefty men keel . . .' And in all cases he hung up the receiver before anyone could ask him for details.

"His telephoning finished, he returned to his beer and passed a pleasant afternoon . . . watching boatload after boatload of his colleagues being pushed away from the gangplank of *La Gloire*. . . . He was pleased to note, some hours later, that the stories of the incident in all the newspapers confirmed his theory that fact may somehow contrive to get itself all mixed up with fiction, and vice versa."[6]

And such things unquestionably persist. A New York commercial artist named Joey Skaggs strikes the news gatherers every so often with elaborate and usually successful practical jokes. In 1976, he ran an ad in *The Village Voice* for his "Cathouse for Dogs . . . get a little tail for your dog . . ." The local ABC news show was nominated for an Emmy for the program on cruelty to animals that featured an interview with Skaggs as proprietor of the Cathouse. Ten years later, he made the New York *Daily News*, the Washington *Post* and the Miami *Herald* with an alleged "Fat Squad" dieters could hire to ride herd on them around the clock and enforce their diet.[7]

All news items are necessarily in competition for attention with all other news items, and the decision on what is "news" today is a function of the intensity of the competition. Not infrequently, the real problem is the lack of competition, which of course provides opportunities for people part of whose function is to "make news": Theodore Roosevelt liked to say that he had "invented Monday": having noticed how thin and dull the papers were on Monday, he had made it his business to do or say something easily reportable on Sunday. Filling the space and the time on such occasions becomes increasingly difficult as news consumers develop ever-greater expectations of how entertaining the world should be. The historian Daniel Boorstin has noted that in the nineteenth century a man might come home from church, leaf through his Sunday paper, and tell his wife that not much happened yesterday; now he will fling the paper angrily into the corner with a comment that this is a lousy newspaper.

News judgment, obviously, is a set of opinions—they can never be more than opinions—on the relative salience of different persons and events. The internal culture of news-gathering operations, and the training of the people who rise through that culture to supervisory positions, seems to produce results that are highly similar across a wide spectrum of news organizations. "Seems," incidentally, is the word: Richard Salant when president of CBS News commissioned a content study of the three nightly network news shows, and found that the lead item was the same in all three only about 30 percent of the time; David Shaw of the Los Angeles *Times,* reputedly the only reporter in the country who has the newspaper business as his beat, did a study of 155 days' worth of his paper, the New York *Times* and the Washington *Post,* and found only 28 days when the same story led all three papers—and 33 days when there was no one story that appeared on the front page of all three. But the fact that most students of journalism believe that all the major media present "the same news" on each day may be more significant than the truth, for it means that, regardless of the individual items, they all present the same general sense of what is going on in the world.

We shall have plentiful occasion in these pages to deal with Rashomon effects (the reference is of course to the great Japanese movie in which a rape is separately portrayed from the points of view of participants and different observers). People differently placed in relation to an event do indeed see different events. And understanding that what you see is a function of where you stand is surely the beginning of Truth in the study of news qua news. But it is not, as virtually all the academics who write about these matters seem to believe, the beginning (let alone the entirety) of Wisdom.

The sociologists Harvey Molotch and Marilyn Lester see what appears in the papers and the broadcasts as simply "a battlefield of actors struggling to generate public experience." They begin with the proclamation: "Borrowing from the ethnomethodological perspective, we suspend, for strategic analytic purposes, the assumption that there is any objective reality 'out there' to be reported."[8] (I kid you not.) But then we have no theoretical framework in which to slot all those occasions when the lead in the paper and on the television news show is the blizzard or the hurricane or the drought, or the bus accident with seven dead, or the transit strike and its effect on the parking rules, or the adoption of the budget, or even, in the quintessential Rupert Murdoch headline, "HEADLESS BODY IN TOPLESS BAR!"

It is possible to make this argument less foolishly, as Todd Gitlin, ex-Students for a Democratic Society, does in his book *The Whole World Is Watching:* ". . . the schools and the mass media specialize in formulating and conveying the national ideology. At the same time, indirectly, the media—at least in liberal capitalist society—take account of certain popular currents and pressures, symbolically incorporating them, repackaging and distributing them throughout the society. That is to say, groups out of power—radical students, farm workers, feminists, environmentalists, or homeowners groaning under the property tax—can contest the prevailing structures of power and definitions of reality. One strategy which insurgent social movements adopt is to make 'news events.' "9 But if you think about it a little, that doesn't have much to do with "media" or with "liberal capitalist society." It's why Luther tacked his theses on the church door and Antony asked permission to deliver Caesar's funeral oration: finding ways to get yourself talked about is the oldest political trick. As Ernst van den Haag once wrote of a study demonstrating that people tend to marry people from similar religious, ethnic, class and income groups, it may be sociology, but it isn't news.

For our purposes, it will be enough to assert that when the residents of Harrisburg, Pennsylvania, worry about the possibility of trouble at the nearby nuclear reactor at Three Mile Island, and the owners of the reactor massage their computers to create strategic plans, both are dealing with a real nuclear installation; and there was a real accident at this installation; and various authorities and polemicists really disagree on how greatly the residents of the Harrisburg area were at risk from the accident. Real things happen to real people in real time, and news reports derive from the examination of real situations "out there." The fact is that news gatherers presenting what seem to them important stories react in similar fashion less because they stand in the same place than because they are dealing with the same realities.

The sociologist Michael Schudson calls these assumptions "naive empiricism." "Journalists before World War I . . . were, to the extent that they were interested in facts, naive empiricists; they believed that facts are not human statements about the world but aspects of the world itself. This view was insensitive to the ways in which the 'world' is something people construct by the active play of their minds and by their acceptance of conventional—not necessarily 'true'—ways of seeing and talking."10 It is hard to maintain patience with this supercilious foolishness. The results of the Battle of Waterloo? The hurricane coming onshore at Galveston? Anwar Sadat in the Knesset? These are "constructs"?

"The idea of 'news' itself," Schudson adds, in a book highly praised by such able and important sociologists as David Riesman, Daniel Bell and Morris Janowitz, "was invented in the Jacksonian era."11 One wonders what the sociologists think Shakespeare meant when he had Richard III say to Ratcliff, "How now! What news?"—and to Lord Stanley a minute later, "Stanley, what news with you?" Why do they think that Congress in 1792, in the first Post Office Act, gave every newspaper the right to send one copy free of charge to every other newspaper so the papers could learn from each other? Do they really believe that what papers would take from other papers was opinion? "For a citizen in the eighteenth and early nineteenth centuries," wrote Ithiel de Sola Pool of MIT, who was not a sociologist, "getting the news was not the easy matter it is today. The arrival in port of a ship from abroad or at an inland location of the fortnightly post riders was an event of importance. From it flowed handwritten letters, talk in coffee houses, and exchange of newspapers that caught people up on the world's events."[12] Fourteen years before Andrew Jackson became President of the United States, Rothschild had made a fortune by being the first to know the results of the Battle of Waterloo. Every literate person in the Western world knew that story, and it was the sort of story that stays in the mind of the man of affairs. That sort of "fact" is "news."

News gatherers handle this question of events as "human statements about the world" simply by gathering a number of statements from different humans, and they have done so for a long, long time. Of course each reporter has his own background, education, opinion and "apperceptive mass," as the educational psychologists called it in the old days. In Michael Arlen's fine comment, "a journalist is in some respects not unlike a novelist in that, in the end, he sees whatever his eyes tell him to see."[13] And each editor or producer responsible for the final shape of the story, in print or broadcast, has his own view of what the readership or the audience wants to know or should know about this event. Practitioners can be highly cynical about this decision making. An editor once told the young Liebling that readers were interested only in death, money and the female organ of sexual intercourse. The Australian Murray Sayle once argued that there were only two real stories in journalism: "We name the guilty men"; and a picture with the caption "Arrow points to defective part."[14] But it isn't the insiders who speak the last word.

2

The more interesting question is what the news recipients want and expect from the news they consume. Those recipients live in a condition of information overload, and their gate is strait, much more narrow than that of the reporters and editors. Moreover, most of what can cross that threshold will, one way or another, get there in a society with competing news providers. One of the few profound insights in the advertising business argues that brands do not in reality, as they do in the textbooks, find their customers; instead, customers find their brands. By the same token, people find their news. An editor, Bernard Cohen of the University of Wisconsin wrote with great precision in 1963, "may believe he is only printing the things that people want to read, but he is thereby putting a claim on their attention."[15] That's right. People find their news more easily and are more likely to talk about it (the most restrictive but perhaps the most correct definition of news is "what people talk about") when they make contact with it as a claim on their attention.

The presentation of news is a major force for cohesion in the group that receives that presentation. "When no firm and lasting ties any longer unite men," Tocqueville wrote in 1833, "it is impossible to obtain the cooperation of any great number of them unless you can persuade every man whose help is required that he serves his private interests by voluntarily uniting his efforts to those of all the others. That cannot be done habitually and conveniently without the help of a newspaper. Only a newspaper can put the same thought at the same time before a thousand readers. . . . In a democracy an association cannot be powerful unless it is numerous. Those composing it must therefore be spread over a wide area, and each of them is anchored to the place in which he lives by the modesty of his fortune and a crowd of small necessary cares. They need some means of talking every day without seeing one another and of acting together without meeting. So hardly any democratic association can carry on without a newspaper. . . .

"The extraordinary subdivision of administrative power has much more to do with the enormous number of American newspapers than has the great political freedom of the country and the absolute independence of the press. . . . the law has established in each province, each city, and, one may almost say, each village little associations responsible for local administration. The legislature has thus compelled each American to cooperate every day of his life with some of his fellow citizens for a common purpose, and each one of them needs a newspaper to tell him what the others are doing. . . . A newspaper can survive only if it gives publicity to feelings or principles common to a large number of men. A newspaper therefore always represents an association whose members are its regular readers."[16]

This is mostly right, even today, and it was extraordinarily perceptive of Tocqueville, who wrote it at a time when few newspapers had a circulation of as much as 3,000 copies—when, indeed, the muscle-powered presses on which newspapers were printed could not turn out more than one or two hundred copies an hour. The "associations" to which Tocqueville referred were townships and counties in agricultural America, and like-minded groups usually divided by social class or political allegiance in the cities. In the aftermath of the revolutionary agitation of the later eighteenth century, urban newspapers that had been largely commercial ventures by printers, who wished to antagonize as few people as possible, had become to one degree or another organs of political actors or political parties.

This was soon to change. The year of Tocqueville's publication was also the year of the launching of the *Sun,* a New York paper that was an entirely commercial venture ("It shines for all," said the slogan under the logo) and that specialized in scandal stories. The *Sun* was the first paper in America to have as many as 10,000 purchasers, and in 1835 it became the first to use a steam-driven press that could turn out as many as 4,000 copies an hour. (The London *Times* had been printed on such presses since 1814.) In 1835, too, James Gordon Bennett founded the *Herald,* the first modern newspaper, which offered up-to-the-minute real political and social news as well as a steaming diet of vice and crime. (Bennett is generally credited with the invention of the interview as a news feature; his first interview was with the madam of New York's most popular brothel.) Using improved steam-driven presses that could produce up to 8,000 copies an hour, Bennett in five years achieved an astonishing circulation of 40,000 a day (and profits approaching $100,000 a year, at a time when a skilled worker earned about $400 a year). To the extent that these remained political organs, however—and, of course, they did—their politics was essentially local, as Tocqueville predicted. Who was mayor or governor or chief of police was and maybe still is a more important matter than who was President or senator for most news gatherers and the consumers of their product.

In the cities, then, for more than a century after Tocqueville, there were multiple papers catering to significantly different "associations" of readers. In the New York of my childhood, the *Times* was read on Wall Street and in the garment district (because the *Times,* in a feature that may have been the most important innovation by Adolph Ochs when he bought the paper in the late nineteenth century, printed every day the names and locations of arriving buyers); the *Sun* by civil servants and by schoolteachers; the *Herald Tribune* on the commuter trains and by doctors; the *News* in the morning, and the *World-Telegram* and the *Post* (with their excellent sports sections) in the afternoon, by craftsmen and shopkeepers; the *Mirror* and the *Journal-American,* Hearst papers, by an underclass.

These different groups of people were primarily looking for different news, with different time frames, and the same attitudes and customs characterized the news market in other cities. Some stories have universal interest and do not become stale (NBC News has a category of film in the files labeled "AOT," for "any old time"); others are good right now and right now only, for these people and no others. The movement of the prices of options to buy or sell futures contracts for the delivery of hog bellies is not news to the cop on the beat on Chicago's Prairie Avenue, but if the cop gets ventilated by a drug dealer as he answers a call from a half-occupied tenement, the story may play well in the newspapers that are bought at the Mercantile Exchange. Moreover, if nobody picks up the story of the cop shot by the drug dealer today, it will still be good tomorrow, while the day before yesterday's price movements in the commodity markets are simply washed away, as news (chartists may keep records of them), by yesterday's prices.

Part of the folklore of the big-city reporter in the days of an active ethnic press was the man from the German- or Russian- or Yiddish-language paper who would come around and badger his English-language colleagues for the background of stories in their papers, so he could write them for his audience. The fact that the story had already been in the English-language press did not bother him: his readers didn't see the English-language press. Similarly, the late Louis Lerner, publisher of a string of Chicago neighborhood and suburban papers, recounted a tale of a big shot in a northern suburb whose son had been involved in a vehicular homicide and who called to ask Lerner not to put it in the semiweekly that served that suburb. Lerner pointed out that the story had already been on page two of the Chicago *Tribune,* and the man said, "That doesn't matter. I don't want my *neighbors* to see it."

In the world of news, one reconstructs the sound that the tree makes falling in the forest when there is no one to hear. If—only if—there is reason to believe that enough of the consumers of this particular news product will care to hear. Until fairly recently, one could have considered the governance of New York City to be primarily the task of reconciling into a single geographical association these quite different associations (plus the Germans who read the *Staats-Zeitung,* and the Jews who read the *Vorwaertz,* and the Italians who read *Il Progresso,* and the Spanish who read *El Diario,* and the Irish who read the *Irish Echo,* and the blacks who read the *Amsterdam News).* A Fiorello La Guardia could do it, partly because he had the flair for "media events" that cut across the differing news perspectives of all these audiences. Long before the word "media" was part of a politician's consciousness, La Guardia as a congressman fighting Prohibition invited reporters to watch him brew gin in his bathtub.

Today, supposedly, we have monopoly newspapers, but the supposition is misleading. The Los Angeles *Times* has in effect no competition as Los Angeles' daily paper—the competing Hearst *Herald-Examiner* sells only about one-sixth as many papers—but it reaches into only a quarter or so of the area's homes. Advertisers identify twenty-six separate markets in the Los Angeles basin and adjacent valleys, and there are at most two of them in which the *Times* is the leading paper: in Long Beach and Santa Monica and Burbank and Ontario and the many others, more people take the local paper than the *Times.* Similarly, the Staten Island *Advance* outsells the New York *Times* and the *Daily News* on Staten Island, and the Bergen *Record,* with well over 100,000 circulation, outsells the *Times* and the Newark papers in its part of the New Jersey suburbs. To the extent that competition keeps people honest in the news business, broadcasters and the national newspapers (especially *The Wall Street Journal* and to a slightly lesser extent the New York *Times)* are likely to prevent outrageous slanting of national and international news (for all the skill of its production and presentation, *USA Today,* as shameless a cheerleader for the country as local boosters would like the local paper to be for the city, is not worth much as an inducement to honesty).

Nearly everyone dislikes the fact that newspaper markets are now divided by geographical location rather than by taste in news and news treatment. But that taste usually reduced to race or class or ethnic origin or
political or religious belief. Given the human tendency to read what one
agrees with, the diversity of the press in the early twentieth century can also
be seen as one of the sources of the provincialism and intolerance and
bumptiousness that were generally perceived as prime characteristics of
what Mencken liked to call the booboisie. We shall have occasion in Chapter
12 to look at the pressures that persuade the great majority of "monopoly"
papers to cover their localities from a variety of viewpoints. For now, be it
noted that there can be great societal disadvantages to a situation where
people looking for reinforcement of their already established views can find
papers that will do just that. An excellent illustration of what makes
apartheid so awful and so intractable is the fact that the Johannesburg *Star* is
printed in two very different versions. Steve Mufson of *The Wall Street Journal* reported on the difference between the two: "On April 14, 1985,
80,000 blacks went to a political funeral in Uitenhage for 29 blacks shot
dead by police. On April 15, readers of the *Star,* Johannesburg's major daily
newspaper, could see a front-page photo of the throngs at the funeral—but
only in the "Africa" editions printed for blacks. Readers of the "city" edition for whites saw a front-page photo of a girl with a homeless dog. 'Lots of
love and attention is what this seven-month-old St. Bernard needs,' the
caption read."[17]

The crusade against the monopoly newspaper has been led mostly from
the left, but that, I think, confuses the reality. Open competition in journalism, devil take the hindmost, is at bottom a right-wing cause, as noted
almost sixty years ago by an impeccably right-wing commentator: "With the
further expansion of our ideology . . . the desire and need for new local
party papers finds expression. By dealing with daily occurrences such papers
deepen our ideology in the local area and bring us new members. . . . The
new paper will survive in competition with the older only if it satisfies the
needs of its circle of readers better than the older one. A struggle thus
develops in which both parties must put forth the maximum effort to survive. The performance of both is thus increased. *Und das ist gut so."[18]* (The
reader is encouraged to consult the note reference, which is a zinger.)

The most news-soaked community in the world is Israel, where five
times a day the national radio service broadcasts a news summary and in
offices and homes, on the streets and on the farms, people listen. Israel's is a
society still in process of creating itself, living in an atmosphere of almost
constant menace. Everywhere in the world, the basic market for news is
people who for good reason or no reason consider themselves threatened,
and like any businessman, the news provider serves his basic market first.
"For my viewers," says Ed Turner, who was recruited from the producer's
post at the *CBS Morning News* to become senior vice president of Ted Tur-

ner's nationwide Cable News Network, "news is: 'Will it get to such a state that junior will be drafted?' 'Are we all going to take dope?' 'Is my daughter pregnant?' That's not newsie's news—you have to give them awards and recognition if you want your producers to cover it." For most consumers most of the time (all bets are off when the Soviets shoot down a Korean airliner or the hydrogen bubble fills the dome in the reactor building at Three Mile Island), such stories will be local. On the desk of the general manager of the overwhelmingly local all-news WINS in New York is "the symbol of the station"—a silver-plated baby's pacifier. "We're part of people's security," says John Waugaman, who sits at that desk. "They know that if they flick the switch the light goes on, if they turn the faucet the water comes, and if they hit the button on the radio they get WINS news."

People use news for purposes of self-aggrandizement, personal (from *I'm* in that story to *I* saw that game on television) or corporate (*my* school or town or company or club has won a prize; *my* team has won a pennant; *my* political party has won an election). They use news to secure a sense of their own position, enjoying the tales of the downtrodden (I thought I was bad off because I had no shoes until I met a man who had no feet) and the reports of the alleged lifestyles of the rich and famous. They like to fantasize about celebrities and political leaders; they like to be entertained. But the great function of news in the lives of its consumers is that it helps them integrate themselves into a community beyond their immediate experience, gives them reason to hope that they know what to expect next from the world, that their lives relate to a larger whole. These tasks were performed in an earlier time by the church and its rituals (or the shaman and his superstitions), by the round of the seasons, the talk of the women at the washing pool and the men at the vendage, market days and holy days and family occasions. The coherence once supplied to groups of people by church and state and village, patronage and family, now must be achieved by individuals. The most potent tool they have for this purpose is news.

This coherence, moreover, must be a by-product: it cannot be an intended result. Thus in the Eastern bloc, where most news is purposeful, readers and viewers do tend to believe what they are told about remote peoples and places, but not what they are told about themselves and their neighbors. Propaganda may or may not convince, but it does not integrate, and in the crisis it fails. Russian newspapers, Ellen Mickiewicz of Emory University writes, devote only 15 percent of their space to "fast-breaking stories. . . . Soviet specialists are aware that once a foreign information source has put forward its story, the Soviet media have the task of breaking down that story and then building up their own."[19] One returns to Chernobyl: no amount of television footage of Kievan girls in dirndls dancing to celebrate May First could convince the Soviet public that the place was safe. By contrast, one can find communities in the liberal West where news is delivered for its own sake, with an understanding that there is a real

world out there and that the truth about it is not precisely knowable. There
some vanguard of news consumers may acquire that tolerance for ambiguity
which education in theory seeks but fails in fact to find. The subject is very
Victorian: to seek, to strive, to find but not to yield. It is also nontrivial.

3

The institution that most cuts across community lines, of course, is the
government. Peace and war, taxes, toxic wastes, student loan programs,
pronouncements on inflation—such things are urgent to large numbers of
people in many communities. Meanwhile, and most important, the government badly needs the attention of the purveyors of news. Henry Hart of the
Harvard Law School and Herbert Wechsler of the Columbia Law School
wrote in their textbook on the federal courts that "as a matter of the hard
facts of power, a government needs courts to vindicate its decisions."[20]
That's easy enough: needing courts, the government appropriates money,
builds courthouses, appoints judges, and *voilà!* The government needs news
coverage even more than it needs courts, as a matter of the hard facts of
"power," because in the absence of news it would be difficult for people to
find out what the government wants them to do, and impossible for them to
find out what the government thinks it is doing. "I was in the government,"
says James Greenfield, assistant managing editor of the New York *Times* (as
indeed he was: the flap about bringing Greenfield from the State Department to the *Times* sufficiently stimulated the bureaucratic Borgias of Forty-
third Street to become one of the more poisonous episodes in Gay Talese's
The Kingdom and the Power), "and I know that sometimes you can't do things
before the public has the supporting information." And that is not so easy,
because news judgment, as each arriviste to "power" discovers in his own
way in his own time, is not a governmental function.

   This is a deeply troubled symbiosis. In the splendid shorthand of James
Deakin, who represented the St. Louis *Post-Dispatch* at the White House for
a quarter of a century, "Government is order. Journalism is disorder. Life
imitates journalism."[21] This is significantly false, because government is
often disorderly, and news of what the government is doing is often dis-
torted by reporters' as well as bureaucrats' felt need to find logic behind
governmental activity. As Emmet John Hughes put it after a career with *Life*
magazine and a stint as Dwight Eisenhower's speech writer, "Journalistically, it is most difficult to report the details of confusion in an unconfused
manner."[22] Edward Epstein has pointed out that the leaks from the National
Security Council meetings indicting Henry Kissinger for wishing to "tilt"
toward Pakistan in its war with India were in fact provided by the Joint
Chiefs of Staff, not because they disagreed with the policy, but because they

saw a stick they could use to beat Henry. Quite apart from the question of what you say to your source tomorrow morning, it's hard to report that.

But profound truths are hidden beneath Deakin's statement. Government is statistical, and news is individual ("anecdotal," if you like). Government is, at least in theory, purposive; news is, in all but universal fact as well as in theory, reactive. Government is corporate and thus soulless, which means that its criterion for truth is simply the probability that a lie will be exposed; news is the work of people who, with few exceptions, hate mistakes, and especially hate to peddle dishonesty. One can sophisticate the conflict, as a peer of the realm is reported to have done when he was working as a press officer in the British Defense Ministry and trying to calm an irate local journalist: "You think we lie to you. But we don't lie, really we don't. However, when you discover that, you make an even greater error. You think we tell you the truth."[23] In the end, the result is the same: governments (and corporations too, of course) want news stories that make them look wise and good and far-seeing; they (again, like corporations) want to prevent stories that make them look dumb or corrupt or short-sighted. As Reagan press spokesman Larry Speakes put it, explaining why the President had decided to have even fewer press conferences than he used to have, governments, like corporations, have the right to put out only those stories that put them in a good light. Plus some disinformation about the competition, under the table.

In a study published in 1973, Leon Sigal found that 78 percent of 2,850 domestic and foreign stories that appeared on sample dates over twenty years in the New York *Times* and the Washington *Post* involved official sources. This is a little tricky, because official sources are often inescapable: if a crime is committed, a reporter pretty much has to talk with the cops, and that makes his story one with an official source. And the cumulative total is deceiving, for Sigal also found that as the years progressed more and more of each paper's contents involved "enterprise," reporters digging things up for themselves. Between 1949 and 1969, in fact, the proportion of "enterprise" stories in the *Times* rose from 21 to 39 percent.[24] Still, the fact is that news occurs where news people are looking for it and that it is most cost-efficient for them to look where the officials are. Thus Wes Gallagher, president of the Associated Press, complained in the mid-1970s that "the Washington politician's view of what is going on in the United States has been substituted for what is actually happening in the country. The two are not always the same."[25]

Within the community of officials, except when peculiarities like Joe McCarthy intrude, the news gatherers find it most efficient to concentrate on the executive branch. Al Hunt, who runs the Washington bureau of *The Wall Street Journal,* points out that television sets itself up to favor the President by stationing four reporters per network at the White House, as against only two per network for all of Congress. Whole countries are cov-

ered from their capital cities. The West Coast of Africa is covered by most of
those who cover it at all from Abidjan in the Ivory Coast—"a nice city," as a
deputy assistant secretary of state once explained to me, "and very convenient to Africa." For much the same reason, quite a lot of South America is
covered from bureaus in Rio.

Painfully often, news judgment is the servant of convenience. Nora
Ephron writes wickedly but accurately of the success of the "Godfrey Sperling breakfasts" (named for the Washington bureau chief of *The Christian
Science Monitor*) in drawing both scores of reporters and the biggest shots in
politics to the Sheraton-Carlton Hotel: "It provides a way for our politicians
to get out of bed and come to show their dependence on the press; . . .
the press reciprocates by certifying the politicians as heavyweights and con-
tenders."[26] This then becomes the norm. Walter Cronkite in his one public
outburst about what happened to his old news show was especially critical of
its producer's decision to reduce the number of "stand-up" reports from
Washington and deal with political "issues" in terms of how they "affect
people in the countryside. . . . I have a rather strong disagreement with
that," Cronkite said. "I think a lot of important stories in Washington are
not getting told because of that."[27] It's possible that Cronkite would have
been less critical had the reports from around the country been better done,
but the fact is that convenience perpetuates itself in a highly imitative business, and the old-timers come to like it that way.

"Most of us happen to be Midwesterners," said David Weir of the
Center for Investigative Reporting in San Francisco, "but there are ten
stories out of California for every one in Ohio and Michigan. One gets
intense media coverage of the coasts and the New York–Washington corri-
dor, but everything else is considered peripheral. It reminds me of a Third
World country, with a great undeveloped center, and nobody knows what's
going on there. We've done a number of stories west of the Mississippi but
not California, and they haven't been successful—crime in the Rocky Mountain states, environmentalists in Hawaii, Indians in South Dakota, we have
an uphill battle getting them published. And we raise money from California foundations." So the Center staffs California, with a small office in Washington, because everybody has to have an office in Washington.

Judgments about salience can be almost entirely individual. "I was in
Washington," says Henry Grunwald, editorial director of all Time Inc. publications and especially of *Time,* which he once edited. "I saw photographs
of the Pope talking with Agca in his cell. I called Cave [Ray Cave,
Grunwald's successor as managing editor of *Time].* He said, 'Yes, it's a
terrific cover, but what do we write about?' I was in a hurry; I said, 'Forgive-
ness,' and I hung up. So that's what we did, and we *just* got away with it."
Advertisers like to see heavy newsstand sales; news judgment at a newsmagazine involves the editor's decision (and it is a one-man decision) of what
the public wants to buy this week. That decision is guided less by market

research than by the editor's recollection of the track record of what covers have sold—muffled, sometimes, by a sense of duty straight out of *The Pirates of Penzance.*

"We did a cover on the two women candidates for the Democratic nomination for Vice President," Grunwald remembered not very cheerfully, "and we helped stimulate the debate. It sold very badly, but we had to do it. On the other hand, if you do Erma Bombeck, or ice cream, or cats [all subjects of recent *Time* covers], you know you'll sell. I get into the topic of news salience with the Third World journalists, and I keep telling them, 'You're right. But what good is it if we slap it in the magazine and nobody reads it?' The deployment of resources in a newsmagazine has to do with public attention. The appeal of Israel and Ireland goes beyond the ethnic question—there is something about those places that has captured the imagination. And it's difficult in a TV age not to try to be pretty early in covering events—or individuals. It's always a question—when is it best to hit an author or a movie star, at the time of the first big hit, or do you wait a couple of years until people are curious? Cave's theories are conditioned by his years on *Sports Illustrated:* he learned the great lesson that TV stimulates the appetite. My instinct is stronger to be first."

News administrators prize flexibility above all. "The worst correspondent," says James Greenfield of the New York *Times*, "is the guy who keeps lists. When a story breaks, it interferes with his list, and he says, 'I'm working on other things.' " But flexibility exacts a price in ignorance or money. "The British system," Greenfield continues, "is to base everybody in London and send them out. The first two days they interview other correspondents—they haven't been reading the local newspapers or going to the local cocktail parties, they don't know why they are there except that their editor sent them. As foreign editor [a post Greenfield has held], you don't want to tell people what to do; they should be telling you what's going on. Almost every year we decide we need a bigger foreign staff. Most papers are not really ready to spend money to get the news, but we are: the publisher makes this huge deposit in the bank for us every year, and we write the checks. A Lagos bureau would cost us half a million dollars a year, but we would open one—except that the government won't give us assurance we can file copy, and stay. The Third World keeps us out more effectively by denying visas than anything UNESCO can do."

There isn't much news out of the Third World because there aren't many reporters working there, but one of the reasons for that failure is that the leaders of these countries, like our own William J. Casey at the CIA (one thinks of him, jowly and spittled, dressed in a leopard skin like the Emperor Jones or Sékou Touré), want no news out of their fiefs that they don't control themselves. They would much rather have no news than bad news. Jonathan Fenby reports from his experience as news editor of Reuters in the 1970s: "Reuters was told by the authorities in Addis Ababa that the

Reuter correspondent there would be beheaded if the agency ran any information from anywhere in the world that displeased the Ethiopian government. This, and a previous experience in which the agency's correspondent was held in detention for several hours with a cocked submachine gun pointed at him, led Reuters to withdraw its correspondent. . . . A few months after the withdrawal of the correspondent, Reuters received messages expressing the dismay of the Ethiopian authorities that the agency was not represented in their country and urging that a new correspondent be sent. I declined to take up the invitation."[28]

When he wrote a book, Fenby published this story. It would have been news when it happened, when the Ethiopians solicited the return of Reuters and sovereign Reuters (doubtless wisely) refused; but he didn't publish it then.

3

Biases

In all but exceptional cases, journalism is not a first hand
report of the raw material. It is a report of that material after it
has been stylized.

–Walter Lippmann, 1922[1]

A fellow discharged his pistol in the alley adjoining the
Union Bank yesterday afternoon, and for a time succeeded in
raising quite an excitement. We feel grateful to him for giving
us an item, but if he had committed suicide, or shot some one's
cat, so that we could have spread ourselves, we would have
been even more grateful.

–Memphis *Commercial
Appeal,* April 27, 1859[2]

[John Eastman], was the last of the great personal editors.
. . . His S.O.B. list—the roster of names that in no circumstances were to find themselves in print in his paper—was one
of the longest ever seen north of the Mason and Dixon line.
He was continually adding to his file of enemies, most of
whom he had never seen. . . .
  We had a little row with City Attorney Harry B. Miller.
John thought he had been unkind to us in the matter of a libel
suit that grew out of the action of one of his assistants. Years
later Mr. Miller wanted the *Journal's* support in his campaign
for State's Attorney. He mentioned his need in an interview
that started off with smiles, handshaking and a great amount of
sweetness and light. "I think you know me, John," said the
candidate. "It's hardly necessary for me to go into my record
with you."
  "Of course not, Harry," replied John cheerily. "I've
known you for years. You're the S.O.B. who threw me down
in the Whosis case."
  I spoke of this afterward to Mr. Eastman—when the votes
were counted and Mr. Miller's defeat was comfortably assured
—and he explained his philosophy. He had lighted a cigar and
was broadly expansive and pleased with himself.

"A newspaperman can get even with anybody in the
world if he lives long enough," he said. "I just sit here quietly
with a bouquet of roses in one hand and a sockful of nightsoil
in the other. And my friends and my enemies pass under my
window."

                                                      –Robert J. Casey[3]

1

A very high fraction of the unfairness in news derives from personal
likes and dislikes. When Abe Rosenthal's friend Jerzy Kosinski was attacked
in *The Village Voice,* he put his staff at the New York *Times* to work to find
errors in the attack and discreditable reasons why the authors of it had done
their dirty work. Sidney Zion, who also works for the *Times,* but not so
steadily, describes in his memoirs a run-in with Reggie Jackson when that
ballplayer was part of the Yankees: "Jackson is reputed to be an open guy
and a good talker. But as soon as I told him who I was, he said: 'I'm afraid
of you; I won't talk to you.' . . . But I'm a Yankee fan, I said. Reggie
Jackson walked away. If a politician did that to me, I'd drop everything and
investigate him until I had enough to put him in Dannemora . . ."[4] As
A. J. Liebling put it: "Freedom of the press belongs to those who own
one."[5]

Such attitudes have a bad name, and with reason. In monopoly situations, as we learned every four years for a generation when William Loeb of
the Manchester *Union-Leader* spewed bile at candidates in the New Hampshire presidential primary, personal journalism can destroy reputations and
give life to disreputable causes. And yet, I must say, one misses it. Some
years ago, I had occasion to drive through Indiana, and you could tell when
you had moved into the market for the Indianapolis *Star* when you began to
see cars with a third headlight in the center. This was the doing of managing
editor Robert Easly, who ran the paper for something like thirty years and
retired at age seventy-seven only because remaining longer would have cut
his retirement annuity. He believed passionately that a third headlight in
the center of a car would greatly reduce night automobile accidents. The
paper's penetration of its market and its status in the community were such
that well over half the cars in and around Indianapolis had this ornament
that simply did not exist elsewhere in the United States.

The personal newspaper made possible diversity based as it should be
on taste rather than on class, occupation and ethnic status. People bought
the *World* rather than the *Times* or the *Herald Tribune* in New York for
reasons associated with Herbert Bayard Swope, as they bought the *Journal-
American* for reasons associated with William Randolph Hearst. Personal
identification, moreover, gives a paper added standing in disputes with local
advertisers and muckamucks. Local businessmen can have a profound influ-

ence on faceless professionals and corporate officers, but nobody, not even the mob, pushes Hank Greenspun around in Las Vegas.

Andrew Barnes, who was born and raised in New York and brought up professionally in Washington, reports having been surprised when he came to St. Petersburg to be editor of the *Times* at the extent to which business types considered themselves competent arbiters of what the paper should do: "When you report that the channel for the cruise ships isn't deep enough, the head of the Chamber of Commerce gets up and says, 'Why can't the St. Petersburg *Times* get behind the city?' Then when the ship goes aground you carry that, too." The St. Petersburg *Times*, a first-class paper in one of the nation's most rapidly growing urban areas, does not have to worry about whether the business community thinks well of its stories, but there are lots of others who do—independents because advertising is two-thirds of the revenues and the paper has a struggle; chain-owned because the year's profit target may be jeopardized. Richard Meeker reports that the *Long Island Press,* owned by the Newhouse interests, had a deal with advertisers that no story about a store robbery on Long Island would run in the *Press* unless it had already run in the New York City papers.[6] One notes with some pleasure that the *Press* went under, while its rival *Newsday,* though sold to a chain (Los Angeles Times-Mirror) after the death of its tough-minded founder and owner, Alicia Patterson, remains relatively trustworthy if a little bland about the troubles of Long Island, and thrives.

Because the truly local, neighborhood or suburban paper lives on ads from the little storekeeper and on local classified ("Per ton of newsprint," Knight-Ridder treasurer Robert Singleton says a little wistfully, "the classified section is the best moneymaker in the newspaper"), it can be as aggressive as it likes on the local political, environmental protection and consumer affairs scene. It's the little local papers on Long Island, where the Long Island Lighting Company has historically been the largest single advertiser, who roused the political animals first against Lilco's nuclear plant at Shoreham and then against Lilco itself, advocating a state takeover of the utility. Usually the local paper boosts the local business, because the entrepreneur who operates a local paper shares a mind-set with the entrepreneur in other commercial ventures, and the chains that specialize in small papers (Gannett, Harte-Hanks, etc.) tend to be conservative at the rightmost edge of the national consensus. Still, many of the neighborhood and even suburban papers in the bigger metropolitan areas—New York, Chicago, Boston, Philadelphia, Detroit, San Francisco—tend to be toward the left side of the consensus. Papers rarely succeed if they take political positions that are outside the consensus and insist on making their pages inhospitable to people who don't believe their "news." The statement is conjunctive: you can get away with a lot politically if you have a sense of humor.

2

Politics in its all-devouring aspect, as the source of perceptions and salience and attitudes, barely touches most American news presentations most of the time. It is, however, the meat and drink of the scholarly media/communications specialty, and most academics who write about this subject carry politics around on their shoulders like the Old Man of the Sea.

"Modern, well-groomed corruption in the guise of 'independent' journalism and entertainment," Ben Bagdikian, dean of the University of California Journalism School, wrote in 1983, "has enunciated the following judgments at the express demand of advertisers:

"All businessmen are good, or, if not, are always condemned by other businessmen. All wars are humane. The status quo is wonderful. Also wonderful are all grocery stores, bakeries, drug companies, restaurants, and laundries. Religionists, especially clergy, are perfect. All users of cigarettes are gentle, graceful, healthy, youthful people. In fact, anyone who uses a tobacco product is a hero. People who commit suicide never do it with pills. All financial institutions are always in good shape. The American way of life is beyond criticism.

"The above messages, to cite only a few, are not vague inferences. Major advertisers insist, successfully, that these specific ideas be expressed not in the ads but in the ostensibly 'independent' news reporting, editorial content, or entertainment programs of newspapers, magazines, radio, and television . . ."[7]

Quite apart from the fact that Upton Sinclair said it better and quicker sixty years ago (when he trumpeted that those "who write and distribute our newspapers and magazines . . . betray the virgin hopes of mankind into the loathsome brothel of Big Business"), one wonders what Bagdikian has been watching. Has he been lucky enough never to have seen *Dallas* or *Dynasty* or *Falcon Crest?* Has he never watched Mike Wallace or Morley Safer take apart some toxic-waste salesman on *60 Minutes* or witnessed the work of the ineffable Geraldo Rivera? Herbert Schmertz of Mobil cites "the nonprofit Media Institute" as source for a statement that "almost half of all work activities performed by businessmen [on prime-time TV] involve illegal acts."[8] It isn't the world's best source, but the estimate looks reasonable.

Bagdikian is one of the ten "media experts" who advise Professor Carl Jensen of Sonoma State University in California on his annual choice of "The 10 Best Censored Stories." Jensen feels that "much citizen alienation may be due to a lack of reliable and usable information on critical issues." The public lacks this information, he argues, because chain ownership of the press, political motivation, interlocking directorates and social-class bias censor stories that people would find interesting and informative and persuasive if the press carried them. (Interlocking directorates is a favorite whipping post: a group called Paper Tiger Television, greatly admired by the *Columbia Journalism Review*, notes the truly sinister "fact" that "something like seven of . . . thirteen board members [of the New York Times Corporation] sit on the boards of large military contractors." Just let a newspaper or broadcast news program try to get away with "something like seven."[9]

Jensen's 1984 list, generously publicized by a squib in *USA Today*, includes only one story that was not in fact prominently displayed in the newspapers I read (that story was a claim by a researcher at a study group in a British New Town that the United States and Britain were violating the Nuclear Nonproliferation Treaty by using civilian nuclear by-products in the manufacture of weapons: when Chernobyl blew, it developed that the Russians had been doing just that rather openly, apparently without violating the treaty). The looseness of the panel's connection to reality is revealed in No. 9 of the "10 Best," which is a compendium of "Three Stories That Might Have Changed the 1984 Election" (dubious dealings by Senator Paul Laxalt, authoritarian attitudes of Edwin Meese and self-dealings by USIA director Charles Z. Wick). Few people who have looked at that election can imagine that votes would have been changed by such stories if they had been trumpeted to the skies. And they were, I think, covered to the likely level of public tolerance. According to Mark Dowie in *Mother Jones*, ABC illegitimately killed an eight-and-a-half minute sensational exposé of how Wick had profited in the 1970s by the ownership of nursing homes in which old folks were horribly abused, taking two-fifths of the nightly news to rehash already published denunciations of a man in a not very important job who was already widely known as a hypocritical, egomaniacal, sycophantic stinker.

Professor Jensen has an idiosyncratic definition of censorship. It is, he writes, "the suppression of information, whether purposeful or not, by any method—including bias, omission, or under-reporting—which prevents the public from fully knowing what is happening in its society." The panel signed on to help him, and presumably accepting this definition, included in 1985, in addition to Bagdikian, George Gerbner, dean of the Annenberg School of Communications at the University of Pennsylvania, former FCC commissioner Nicholas Johnson, English-born polemicist Jessica Mitford, Mary McGrory of the *Washington Post* and Noam Chomsky of MIT. But all that these eminent media experts are saying, really, is that they would have given greater salience than the newspapers and broadcasters did to the stories they list as "censored." At least seven of the ten were on the AP and UPI wires, the L.A. *Times*–Washington *Post* service, the New York *Times* service and the KNT wire—not on some one of them, but on all of them, if only in a story that contained, for example, the CIA's denial of charges that it was training death squads in El Salvador.

The right is as paranoid and pigheaded as the left in these matters. In their book *The Media Elite: America's New Powerbrokers,* Stanley Rothman of Smith College and S. Robert Lichter and Linda S. Lichter of Columbia University make much, for example, of the fact that newspapermen consider Ralph Nader and his subsidiary pressure groups good sources of stories on consumer protection, and like to touch base with the Sierra Club and various activists (including amateurs like Robert Redford, Jane Fonda and Gary Hart) on environmental issues, while businessmen think more highly of business groups and formal government agencies as sources of information on such subjects. The authors do not mention the fact that Nader & Co. are always happy to be quoted on these subjects, while businessmen and traditional government agencies, sensing a no-win situation, rarely like to get involved.

Rothman and the Lichters also write three- and four-paragraph sample news stories (four of which are printed in their book) and measure the reactions of newspeople and businessmen to them. The stories are parodies, bearing about the same relation to real news stories as the jokes in Freud's book on jokes bear to real humor. In another test, journalists and businessmen were shown pictures and asked to write stories about them. One such picture showed two men in one kind of uniform taking away someone in another kind of uniform. A Public Broadcasting System staffer is quoted as describing the man in the middle as an army recruit being told, "There are eighteen tons of horseshit out in that field, son, and you've got one week to pick it all up." The recruit goes AWOL in this story and "later writes a tough honest novel about army life and wins a Pulitzer Prize." It is not within the repertory of responses of the authors of this study to imagine that their legs are being pulled.

Three of the supposed news stories are devoid of specific information, and all use charged language concealed by a passive tone. They deal with the areas of civil rights, energy politics and foreign bribery. The authors give only a blended figure for how many in the total sample gave "neutral" reactions to the stories, and then separate out figures for how many journalists as against how many businessmen had a "liberal" or "conservative" response. Only a snoop of a reporter would wonder whether the journalists were more likely to provide a neutral paraphrase, and whether the authors' failure to provide that information represents a fear that someone might make a rude response to their giveaway rhetorical question: "Why should journalists be any less prone to selective perception than anyone else?"[10]

For the answer, after all, is obvious, and has been for a very long time. "Printers," Benjamin Franklin wrote in 1731, "are educated in the Belief that when Men differ in Opinion, both Sides ought equally to have the Advantage of being heard by the Publick."[11] Objectivity is not really difficult to achieve, provided you really in your heart don't care which side wins the arguments. As Tom Griffith put it in 1974: "A journalist . . . learns to deaden reactions that get in the way of doing his job—a disengagement at the crucial moment from feelings people normally have. . . . He fears becoming a partisan, a crank or a bore on any subject, and thereby professionally disabled. A journalist must be more seized by journalism than by any subject it deals with. Most journalists hang a little loose in their thinking. They are fated to have to listen to both sides of every argument (and may be the last people in the country who do). They content themselves with sharp judgments about persons but only vague attitudes about correct policy."[12] Journalists are less prone to selective perception because that's their job. Social scientists are more prone to selective perception because that's how you get attention and they don't have to worry about editors.

Reporters do indeed make sure (or their editor insists) that they go and talk to people who see the world in a different lighting and from different viewpoints. This does not present problems to them, for whatever their political *instincts,* they are rarely partisan. Mostly, for better or worse, they have come to feel that it doesn't make one hell of a lot of difference who wins the arguments, that Hilaire Belloc had it about right some sixty years ago when he wrote his epigram "On a General Election":

> *The accursed power which stands on Privilege*
> *(And goes with Women, and Champagne, and Bridge)*
> *Broke—and Democracy resumed her reign*
> *(Which goes with Bridge, and Women, and Champagne).*

The sociologist Herbert Gans reported with some surprise in 1979 that "the national media, and journalism generally, appear to recruit people who do not hold strong personal values in the first place. They have no prior values about the topics which become news, nor do they always develop them about topics on which they are working. Many of the reporters and writers constantly immersed in American politics did not seem particularly interested in it apart from their work." Moreover, the choice of the most salient story of this day is not normally influenced by the political or other views of the editors: "Leads for the nightly television news, and the initial stories in the [news] magazines' domestic sections, virtually choose themselves most of the time." Professor Gans is unusual among his kind in his belief that reality matters (his books about urban renewal in Boston and the growth of the lower-middle-class suburbs of the Delaware Valley are extraordinarily informative and fair-minded). One can scarcely find a better definition of objectivity in news judgment—or a stronger assertion of the reality of the world "out there"—than his statement that leads "virtually choose themselves." And yet when he comes to generalize, Gans finds the notion of objectivity among journalists ultimately impossible to contemplate.

"Most journalists," Gans writes, "fully realize that objective methods provide no guidelines for the selection either of stories or of which facts go into stories." This is anthropomorphic of Professor Gans: he is projecting the problems of sociologists onto newspeople. Writing eight years after the government ruled cigarette advertising off the airwaves, for example, Gans illustrates the pressures on news broadcasters with the tale of "a top producer [who] chooses a story on smoking and lung cancer [and] checks whether a cigarette company is listed as one of the day's sponsors." To show that the fundamentally conservative bias of news organizations influences what they are willing to believe, he takes as his example, "most recently, the number of people killed by the postwar Communist government in Cambodia . . ."[13] In the end, Gans cannot be objective himself or accept the possibility that others may be objective, because he is politically active. He believes he can affect the political attitudes of his readers and he cares what those attitudes are. Very few news professionals believe that what they write makes much difference to their readers' or viewers' attitudes, or care very much anyway.

Walter Mears, the easygoing, ruminative political reporter who became executive editor of the AP, writes admiringly of a colleague on the Goldwater campaign of 1964 who found a way to deal with the senator's groupies' orchestrated shouts to the press corps to "tell the truth for once." He "faced down a little old lady in tennis shoes and said to her: 'Madam, the truth is not in me.' I don't know what she thought, but she stopped shouting."[14] In the end, then, the best reporters have neither Gans's problems nor the problems he attributes to them.

Any intelligent reporter with the time and the desire and the energy to work at it can present a story in such a way that people who disagree with each other about the relative importance of the facts and about their meaning will all recognize what they read or view (a portmanteau word necessarily encompassing both the words and the pictures on television) and will find their conflicting beliefs reinforced by the story. "The truth" does not often change people's minds; most of the time, they already know "the truth," and they disagree with others similarly in the know because they see things differently. I myself once wrote a book about the advertising business *(Madison Avenue, USA)* which was hailed by David Ogilvy as a defense of the business and by Cleveland Amory as an attack on it. The community of people whose activities "make news" is relatively limited on any one day, and up to a point all their viewpoints can be accommodated. The larger problem is the endless difference in situation of the members of the much larger community that consumes the news. That's where the pressure comes from, but it can be managed. "A wise publisher," says Leonard Silk of the New York *Times,* "will always say to a complaining businessman, 'I'm sorry, but I cannot control these people.' "[15]

Television news is even less likely to feel such heat. (Though pressure has been put on public affairs shows as well as entertainment. I remember from the very early days of television an NBC special on energy, a special pet of NBC president Sylvester (Pat) Weaver, where sponsorship was eventually taken by the American Petroleum Institute and much of the material on nuclear energy somehow dropped out. Airline advertisers usually can get agreement that their commercials will not run adjacent to the report of an air crash, something that disturbs Bagdikian but I must say does not bother me.)

Broadcasting started off badly in this regard in 1924, when H. V. Kaltenborn, then associate editor of the Brooklyn *Daily Eagle,* criticized Secretary of State Charles Evans Hughes on a radio broadcast for his failure to recognize the Soviet Union as the legitimate government of Russia. Hughes called AT&T, which owned the station (there were no licenses yet), and station WEAF heard from corporate headquarters that "this fellow Kaltenborn should not be allowed to criticize a cabinet member over the facilities of the New York Telephone Company." Kaltenborn lost his contract—but thought, incidentally, that the end result of federal intervention might be positive: "Before long," he wrote, presaging the arrival of licensed broadcast channels, "we are likely to witness a legal battle to compel broadcasting stations which make a practice of selling time, to sell it to all comers on equal terms. 'Freedom of the air' will come to have meaning akin to 'free speech' or 'freedom of the press.' "[16] In fact, the government and the broadcasters finally settled for enforced fairness rather than freedom, and the commercial mechanics of selling individual minutes rather than program time left the networks more completely in charge of their own news services than Kaltenborn would have expected.

Through most of the 1960s and 1970s, the president of NBC was a newsman, first Robert Kintner, then Julian Goodman, both of them men deeply sensitive to any thoughts that advertisers might dictate to news gatherers; and until 1975 at least there was only one instance in records I was privileged to examine (I was writing a history of CBS News for the network) when William Paley interfered with what was done on the evening news. (It was Watergate time: from the White House, Chuck Colson had threatened the licenses of CBS-owned stations if the network carried in the Cronkite news the second section of a two-part report on the Watergate burglars and their known friends. Solving Paley's problem upon his insistence that it was really *his,* the news division ordered producer Paul Greenberg—now in charge of the Brokaw show for NBC—to cut that second part in half.) Dealing with environmental questions, which are the true plague of news of business as seen by business, the progression has been from books to magazines to television, with the newspapers bringing up the rear: environmental stories lend themselves neatly to pictorial treatment. Strikes, as the Glasgow University Media Group in Britain bitterly and convincingly complain, tend to be covered from the point of view of an inconvenienced public—but that, after all, is who buys the papers and watches the telly.[17]

Misfocusing a story because of commercial concerns or ownership bias is in any event a subset of a larger problem, which is the ignorance of the home office and the cheerful willingness to exercise that ignorance in deciding what "points the story must contain." Mencken noted in 1941 that "in my day [pre-World War I] a reporter who took an assignment was wholly on his own until he got back to his office, and even then he was little molested until his copy was turned in at the desk; today he tends to become only a homunculus at the end of a telephone wire, and the reduction of his observations to prose is commonly farmed out to literary castrati who never leave the office, and hence never feel the wind of the world in their faces or see anything with their own eyes."[18] The man in the office, of course, was far more susceptible to pressure from the man at the desk in the corner.

Still, the spread of the portable word processor with its modem to link to the office computer has increased the likelihood that the man in the field will see his own story printed, and now the problem is most severe in television. "Correspondents," Edward Jay Epstein argues, "are under some pressure to focus their reportage on the elements of stories which best fit the needs of the organization, even if it conflicts with their own news values."[19] Cokie Roberts of National Public Radio proclaims a preference for doing pieces for *Morning Edition* and *All Things Considered* rather than for a radio or TV network, which would doubtless pay her better. "I work," she says, "at the radio-TV gallery at the Capitol, and I see the frustration of my colleagues. I'm surrounded by smart, dedicated people who can't get one-tenth of what they know on the air."[20] The problem is especially intractable when it's a foreign correspondent, and the minder in charge of such must shape the story just so in the scheduling conference to win that precious eighty seconds for his ward. A man who has headed an overseas bureau remembers complaining about the preposterous angle New York wanted on his story, and the comment of his sympathetic boss: "Look, the guys who make up this schedule never worked outside this building; they think you need a visa to go to Staten Island."

Studies about how people feel about the news services they receive usually show that they doubt the accuracy of local reporting, consider national news fairly accurate, and believe implicitly in the international reporting. This equates to a statement that the more you know about a situation, the less you trust the news reports, but the question is trickier than that. Everyone who writes for publication has burned with embarrassment about errors in his stuff, only to be congratulated quite honestly and flatteringly by readers who know something about the subject but either didn't know the matter of the specific error or (a not uncommon phenomenon) read the right spelling or the right date in place of the wrong one. What the owners of newspapers and the presidents of broadcast news divisions mean when they talk about their credibility ("Accuracy," Pulitzer liked to say, "is to a newspaper what virtue is to a woman"[21]) is the willingness of their audience to overlook the little ways the reporter got the story wrong (perhaps the same can be said of the consumer perspective on virtue). Kermit Lansner, who was once executive editor of *Newsweek*, observed in casual conversation the other day that "you and I know what a miracle it is that news reporting is as accurate as it is."

Once people begin to doubt that the reporter or the paper or the broadcaster is straight, there is always evidence of error. Every news story is full of details, from names, dates and places to antecedent events. The closer the story comes to the reader, the more likely he is to find that one of these bits is off. If the title of the father of a Sudanese general is wrong in the story from Khartoum, nobody in the United States knows (let alone cares). But if the father of the medical school valedictorian is an ophthamologist and the newspaper calls him an optometrist, someone will be damned annoyed. Couple these with an occasional, unavoidable misunderstanding— requiring intelligibility, the reporter oversimplifies or (worse) makes a leap of faith and falls into the abyss of ignorance he has tried to jump—and a kind of rage develops in the community. People, sometimes wholly innocent people, can be harmed by the publication or broadcast of news; publishing, Justice Oliver Wendell Holmes, Jr., wrote while still on the Massachusetts Supreme Court, is "very like firing a gun into the street."[22]

Important communities can come to feel that nobody in "the media" cares, as they did in the 1970s. Note, for example, *The Other Side of the Story,* an ill-tempered and ill-informed but instructive tirade by Jody Powell, Jimmy Carter's amateur press secretary. One cannot appeal, Powell writes, to a reporter's "sense of responsibility and fair play" because "evolution over the centuries has resulted in the atrophy of those character traits among reporters, in much the same manner as the legs on a snake have shrunk into two small internal bonelets entirely invisible to the casual observer."[23] Once such tripe is widely believed, people with sinister reasons for wishing a pliable news instrument gain influence not only in the executive but in the courts. The legislature becomes the bulwark of the free press, partly because reporters tend to pay attention to legislators only when legislators ask them to do so, partly because legislatures today, what with sunshine laws and open committee hearings, have virtually lost hope that they can keep secrets if they try.

One reason for confidence in the future is that legislatures were not always so friendly. Reporting from the Constitutional Convention in Philadelphia was strictly forbidden (delegates, in fact, were prohibited from taking notes for their own purposes to minimize the chance that accounts of the meetings would leak), and in the nation's early years the Congress did not permit reports of deliberations. As late as the 1920s, the Senate went into executive session to vote on presidential appointments, and nobody was supposed to know who voted how. "Paul Mallon of our Washington bureau," Hugh Baillie of the United Press wrote, "developed a source of information in the Senate, and began putting on our wire the roll calls on all important nominations. We believed that the people had a right to know how their Senators had voted on appointments. The lid blew off on President Hoover's controversial nomination of Senator Lenroot of Wisconsin to be a federal judge. Great care was taken to keep the vote private. Yet Mallon published it, as usual. There followed a Senatorial investigation, to which Mallon was hailed as a witness, to divulge—under the threatened penalties of contempt—the name of the man who had told him. . . . Mallon stood his ground. The Senatorial inquisition backfired, and the Senate changed its rules and abolished executive sessions on Presidential appointments."[24] Those who worry about access to information are right to worry, but somewhere in their consciousness they should guard and nourish an understanding that there never were any good old days.

Part Two

ITEM: TYLENOL

4

The First Word

C'est terrible, mais ce n'est pas votre faute
—Arkel, Act V, *Pelléas et Mélisande*

1

The tradition of the scoop has been cultivated more jealously and single-mindedly in Chicago than anywhere else. Even in 1982, when the local television news shows competed mostly through the amiability of their anchorites and only two rather dignified papers survived from the dozen brawling rivals that had once enlivened the city's streets (this was before Rupert Murdoch bought the *Sun-Times* and reduced its dignity quotient just a little), an interesting crime quickly brought Chicago reporters to a condition James Squires, editor of the *Tribune,* describes as "balls out." "In New York," he adds, "they're fighting in the streets and running over everybody for pictures, but they don't compete like we compete."

As a practical matter in a big city, however, this competition is almost necessarily after the fact, in the details and angles of a story subsequent to the break of the event itself. In small cities, the police radio plays softly into the editorial quarters at the paper, and a cub monitors it while doing other things. If the police dispatcher sends a cop car to a certain address where there seems to be a corpse, the paper can get a reporter to that address right on the policeman's heels. In a modern metropolitan area, there are simply too many calls, too many dispatchers within the city limits and too many suburban police departments. Even in the days before police radios, when the police fanned out from headquarters and a reporter who knew the back alleys might get to the story ahead of them, the Chicago newspapers had been forced to face the fact that they could not hope to staff up all the potential sources of the kind of news that readers—straitlaced as well as prurient—expect to find in their paper. There had to be a system by which the desk could find out what was going on even if the paper had nobody on the scene.

Given the competitive pressures in the Second City, editors could not risk the pooling procedures arranged by the reporters who covered police headquarters in the First City, where, A. J. Liebling wrote, "the men working for competing newspapers swapped news. This was a tactical necessity, for otherwise, while all the papers were competitively covering the same fairly good story, a *real* story might break and find the shacks [a term of art used for the nearby tenement apartments the papers rented as offices] stripped of reporters. One day a paper might have needed seven men to cover Headquarters properly, and another there wouldn't have been work for one. The city desks, set, as always, on keeping payrolls low, tacitly connived in the practice."[1] In Chicago, the pool would have leaked: a reporter's loyalties and ambitions would have been too strongly engaged in getting the word first to his own city desk. Indeed, the spirit of competition could go beyond such conventional desires as beating the opposition. Casey told a story of two reporters for the *Herald-Examiner* who burgled what they believed to be the home of a murder victim, looking for photographs, diaries and such. They had the wrong man. Presently, the residents returned to their apartment from the movies. The *Herald-Examiner* reporters made their escape, went to the Chicago *Tribune* building, and gave the now-unwanted photographs and diaries to a taxi driver. He should return this material, they said, to its owner, and tell him it had been handed over by two men in the lobby of the *Tribune*.

In fairness to Chicago, one should note that pools are by their nature risky, and not only in the Midwest. Robert Harris, in his splendidly funny *Gotcha!*, a book about the coverage of the Falklands War, reports that a pool report of the Argentine surrender by a group of British newspapermen somehow never got to London. It had been entrusted by landbound colleagues to Max Hastings of the *Evening Standard* for Hastings to send together with his own separate story when the helicopter disgorged him at the shipboard communications facility that was all the Royal Navy allowed its journalist guests. Hastings' copy reached his paper; the pool story for the rival papers, Harris writes, "disappeared: what happened to it remains a mystery to this day."[2]

In the 1920s, as *The Front Page* demonstrates, the Chicago courthouse and police headquarters and City Hall were still heavily staffed, covered by people who basically lived their working day in the pressrooms of their beat rather than at their offices, like today's White House and Pentagon and State Department correspondents. But even then, since you couldn't trust colleagues to cover for you, reporters relied for backup and sometimes for first approximations on a City News Bureau jointly owned by all the city's papers. CNB staffed all the frequent news sources from a roster of youngsters on their way to greater things, and distributed copy from its offices to the newspaper offices by means of pneumatic pressure through fifteen miles of brass and copper tubing under the streets of Chicago. The alumni list of this organization is dazzling, including people who later fell out of the news business, like the actor Melvyn Douglas and Kurt Vonnegut, "Yellow Kid" Weil ("briefly," the historian of the bureau writes rather stuffily, "long before his confidence games had earned him his nickname"[3]) and Clare Snively, who became chief of police of the city of Los Angeles—and also great stars of the journalistic firmament, from luminaries of the old days like O. O. McIntyre and the great Hearst editor Walter Howey and Junius B. Wood, the brilliant foreign correspondent of the Chicago *Daily News* (who allegedly knocked off an auditor querying an expense account item for breakfast caviar in Moscow with the cabled answer "Eggs is eggs"), to the more modern columnist Mike Royko and reporter Seymour Hersh.

"What each publisher probably wanted," writes Arnold A. Dornfeld, longtime night city editor and ultimately chronicler of the bureau, "was a local bureau so weak that it could be beaten out on the occasional good story by the publisher's own staff, but strong enough to prevent the other newspapers from getting scoops. This kind of unreasonable, perhaps subconscious attitude, brought pressures to bear on the bureau staff."[4] Since its reorganization as a publishers' cooperative in 1890 (it had been founded as one man's enterprise nine years earlier), the CNB (originally City Press Association) has won an enviable reputation for getting to its stories early and getting them back accurately. It has also, of course, missed a few. The most famous such miss is dealt with by Dornfeld in a quote from Joe Ator of the *Tribune:* "I remember in 1929, having my lunch interrupted to chase off on what seemed a silly City Press bulletin which said: 'Six men are reported to have been seriously injured in a fight in a pool room at 2122 N. Clark st.' It wasn't a pool room, there were seven men, not six, and they weren't seriously injured. They were blown apart with tommy guns and shotgun slugs. . . . But the address of the St. Valentine's Day massacre was correct."[5]

CNB never became a model for the news fraternity elsewhere. New York had a City News Association from 1894 to 1942, but it was essentially a semi-detached wing of the Associated Press, which eventually absorbed it. (Until the 1940s, AP could not have operated something like the City News Bureau within its customary framework; the wire service was organized as an exclusive membership corporation—an AP "franchise" was among the assets of an established paper—while the local news services were necessarily all-inclusive.) The closest relative to Chicago's CNB is a Los Angeles news-gathering co-op that has survived since the 1920s as a trade-off by which the L.A. *Times* backstops its regional editions at the price of making copy available for cheap to the many small papers in the counties and valleys that are its major competitors for retail advertising.

In Chicago, however, the City News Bureau has remained a central agency in providing that city with a diet of local news somewhat richer and gamier than other cities receive. Jointly owned now by the surviving Chicago papers, the *Tribune* and the *Sun-Times,* CNB serves nearly all the center city's commercial news outlets: the television and radio stations and the national wire services as well as the metropolitan dailies. Reporters on the papers and to a lesser extent in the broadcast studios still have beats, and go out from the office (or hang on the phone, depending) to cover the predictable stories and continuing stories on their turf, and to develop stories to which they have their own leads. But the first cut at a crime story or a fire or something peculiar at the Board of Education or the county offices, or something not in the prepared text said by a big shot at a banquet, will probably come on the wire from the City News Bureau, the work of one of its forty young and drastically underpaid reporters (their starting salary in 1982 was $175 a week).

City News is still old-fashioned enough to put its beginners on the police beat. Especially at night, when the phones have to be manned—only CNB operates a Chicago news-gathering activity twenty-four hours a day: the newspapers are dark from about three to about six, the radio stations have no writers on duty from midnight to four—cubs at CNB are not to reason why, as a normal matter, nor to investigate on the spot without very specific instructions from the office. They sit at telephones, in the bureau's new offices in a skyscraper on Wacker Drive, where teletype wires have replaced the old pneumatic tubes, or at desks set aside for them in press-rooms at police headquarters, the state and county office buildings, etc. On the late-night police beat they call in their material, and a rewrite desk takes responsibility for the final product. This is still in large part a training program—"a college newspaper run by grown-ups," as its director, Bernie Judge, formerly city editor for the *Tribune,* called it in 1983[6]—and the youngsters on the phones are careful to get the names spelled right and the addresses right, and to ferret about for details as much as one can on the telephone.

It was through this institution that word first went out that Chicagoans were dying because they had swallowed a proprietary medicine that contained potassium cyanide. In the first week that this story was before the public, it would take 21 percent of the time on the three national network nightly news shows, and it would consume more ink and newsprint than any domestic event since the assassination of President John F. Kennedy. Eight weeks later, 99 percent of Americans over the age of fourteen knew that some fellow Americans had died from taking contaminated Tylenol, more than 90 percent knew the problem had been in the capsules only—and 90 percent knew it was not the manufacturer's fault.[7] Rarely if ever has so much information about a single but complicated event been spread to and retained by so many people in so short a period of time.

The story of the Tylenol poisonings emerged through routine procedure, but developed as quickly and accurately as it did for the Chicago papers in part because of the assiduous follow-through of a single reporter, John Flynn Rooney, a handsome, dark-haired, mustachioed twenty-three-year-old CNB rookie (who was not, however, a novice in the news business, being the son of Ed Rooney, a much-liked veteran of the recently defunct *Daily News* turned journalism professor at Northwestern). Rooney was one of three City News Bureau staff assigned to police headquarters on Wednesday night, September 29, 1982. His mission was the first cut at suburban crime stories. Part of the job was following up on deaths reported by the county medical examiner. (By law, doctors must report all deaths to the medical examiner, with a certification of cause of death.) Three or four times a day, an even more absolute beginner at the head office of the bureau checked in with the examiner's office and picked up the "case names." A call was then made to a bereaved spouse or relative to see if this individual was someone important enough to justify a story from the City News Bureau. When the medical examiner did not know the cause of death (or the cause was a violent one), the name and the hospital where the death occurred were referred to the reporter responsible for that turf at police headquarters, who would check with the authorities. Every hospital had a designated spokesman, sometimes from a p.r. department and sometimes in the admitting office, whose job included answering or not answering queries from the press.

Among the names given to Rooney at about ten-thirty that Wednesday night was Stanley Janus, who had died suddenly of unexplained causes at Northwest Community Hospital in Arlington Heights, Illinois. Rooney already had a call in to this hospital about another death, and he was busy trying to learn some details on a shooting spree in the police station in Forest Park, another Chicago suburb. This was *the* story in Chicago late Wednesday night: a Puerto Rican Chicago Transit Authority employee arrested for street theft had grabbed a policeman's gun while being booked and shot three cops before being gunned down himself. He was dead; the cops were variously injured; medical reports, background on the perpetrator, the personal histories of the injured policemen were all arriving in a steady stream, courtesy of a chief of police who was happy to speak on the phone to reporters and radio announcers.

Rooney decided to hold the Janus matter until the hospital replied to his earlier inquiry. The call-back came at about eleven o'clock with word that the death Rooney was inquiring about had been natural, and Rooney asked about the Janus case. The woman on the other end of the phone thereupon read him a press release. There were three Janus cases: Adam, twenty-seven, whose equally sudden death had occurred about three o'clock that afternoon and was on a list of unfinished business that had been passed on to Rooney when he came to work; Stanley, twenty-four; and Stanley's wife Theresa, nineteen, who was in critical condition. Five other members of this working-class Polish-American family were being kept in the hospital under observation, but appeared to be in good health. Autopsies were being performed on the two brothers to determine the cause of death. Nobody at the hospital was prepared to speculate.

Rooney began calling Arlington Heights: the police, the Januses' neighbors. (Part of the training offered in a place like the City News Bureau is the destruction of the natural human reluctance to call strangers and ask them questions at an hour when most people are asleep. Harold Evans tells a nice story of the night when a London *Times* reporter awoke Lord Goodman, chairman of the Arts Council, to ask "if it were true that the Arts Council had made a grant to Bertram Mills Circus. No, Goodman had replied, but a grant had been made to the zoo to train the chimps to become night reporters on *The Times.* [8]) What he learned was that the medical examiner had sealed the Janus residence and police officers were all over the property. The medical examiner's office itself had nothing to say: these were suspicious deaths, and like all suspicious deaths they were being investigated. At a nearby desk in police headquarters the *Sun-Times* reporter noted that Rooney seemed to be working on something other than the Forest Park shootings, and asked what it was about. Rooney did not tell him, and since nobody fed "case names" to the *Sun-Times* (that was a CNB franchise), he had no way to find out. Presently he left the office to go to Forest Park to look at the police station and interview witnesses; and Rooney kept calling Arlington Heights.

Shortly before 1 A.M., a call came into the News Bureau from a tipster who said he worked at Northwest Community Hospital. The caller did not identify himself. He said that the cause of the Janus deaths had been cyanide poisoning, and that the cyanide had been mixed into the headache remedy Tylenol. Then he hung up, refusing to be questioned. By the rules of the City News Bureau, stories of this nature can be moved onto the wire only if they are confirmed by two sources, both named. Here there was one source, not named. Northwest Community Hospital said it knew nothing; the skeleton post-midnight staff at the medical examiner's office, Rooney says, "actually laughed at us. Nobody could remember the medical examiner's office laughing before."

At one o'clock Rooney's tour ended and his replacement appeared. But he remained on the phones, talking with the hospital, the police, the neighbors, the medical examiner. "Some people might have exercised discretion in who or what they called," Rooney says, "but I called everyone—I didn't know any other way. Everybody detests doing these things, but they do serve a purpose." When he left the office at about two-thirty, Rooney was not quite sure whether the tip about cyanide in Tylenol was real or a hoax. Midnight editor Rick Baert at the News Bureau thought the story was real, but was entirely unwilling to invite a lawsuit from the makers of Tylenol by putting the name of the brand on the wire. What the News Bureau sent out to its clients, at 3:01 A.M. on Thursday, September 30, was a story that there were at least two unexplained deaths and one critical illness in this Chicago

family, that several other members of the family were being held at the
hospital under observation, and that the police had sealed off the house. (A
Chicago *Sun-Times* editor, waking at six in the morning and hearing this
story read over the radio, noted the "sealed off" line and thought the cause
of death was probably furnace fumes.) At 7:33 a roundup message from the
News Bureau, for the radio news shows and the afternoon editions, added
to the list of overnight mysteries the unexplained death of Mary Kellerman,
a twelve-year-old girl, at Alexian Brothers Medical Center in Elk Grove,
another Chicago suburb. The story suggested that the Kellerman death
might be related to the poisonings that had decimated the Janus family, but
it did not indicate what that common cause of death might be.

It is a measure of the self-deprecation of the print news media that
Editor & Publisher, the trade magazine of the newspaper business, gave credit
for breaking this story to CBS-owned all-news radio station WBBM.[9] The
report in the magazine was that WBBM received its anonymous tip at 1:30,
and aired a report on the Janus deaths "20 minutes later." In fact, the radio
station had two tipsters, both hospital employees, one of whom said the
Januses had died from ingesting Tylenol, while the second reported that the
Tylenol had contained cyanide. Neither was anonymous (though both insisted their names could not be given on the air), because WBBM, 78 on
your AM dial, had an advertised policy of paying for news tips at a rate of
$78 for the best of the week, $780 for the best of a 78-day period. (And the
Tylenol tipsters won both prizes, as announced on the air November 20:
"You, too, can be a winner. Listen for more details right here on the news
station, WBBM Newsradio 78.") But the first broadcast report did not air
until eight minutes after CNB had moved its first bulletin, and what was
broadcast could fairly be categorized as less than adequate to the story.
Local news following the network on-the-hour roundup still led with the
cops shot in Forest Park, including a moment on the phone with the chief of
police. Then, at 3:09 A.M., the WBBM announcer picked up what was
obviously a new piece of paper sent in by the producer. "The Cook County
Medical Examiner," he read, "is trying to confirm the death of three people
at Arlington Heights police station yesterday. Police have not determined
the cause of death"—there was a brief caesura—"or why they were at the
Arlington Heights police station." He then moved on to other things.

It should be noted, however, that by 7:13 in the morning WBBM was
far ahead of CNB. The story then led the local news hour following the *CBS
World News Roundup* (which WBBM truncates from fifteen minutes to ten,
even though it is an owned subsidiary of the network). The copy for the
story was as follows (the dots are in the original and are stigmata of the
radio script style, not indications of elision): "Autopsies are scheduled this
morning for 27-year-old Adam Janus of Arlington Heights . . . his 24-
year-old brother Stanley Janus from Lisle . . . and a 12-year-old girl, Mary
Kellerman of Oak Grove Village . . . all of whom died of cardio-pulmo-

nary arrest . . . apparently the result of cyanide poisoning. In addition, 19-year-old Theresa Janus is extremely critical and 5 other family members were treated at Northwest Community Hospital in Arlington Heights and released. The deaths and illnesses all were traced back to a home in Arlington Heights that was ordered sealed by the Cook County Medical Examiner's office. A source has told newsradio that one family member had taken a headache remedy yesterday . . . became ill . . . and died later at Northwest Community. Other members of the family, apparently depressed by the death, took pills from the same bottle. Blood samples from each of the victims revealed the presence of cyanide. The headache remedy also was analyzed and it too contained cyanide. The question no one can answer this morning: how the cyanide got into the tablets. The source indicates the headache remedy . . . even if aged on the shelf . . . should not break down into a poison . . . certainly not sufficiently strong to kill three people."

This story was the work of Don Milemma, a fiftyish writer-announcer with a plummy, elegant voice and a rotund, inelegant appearance (one does not get dressed up to sit at a mike in a radio station). He had two details wrong, for the cyanide had got into capsules rather than tablets, and the Kellerman girl had never been in the Janus home. The second error was an interesting example of the dangers of leaping to conclusions in the newsgathering process. Milemma had spent a good deal of time between six and seven making phone calls to find evidence that the Janus and Kellerman families knew each other, and though he hadn't yet found his smoking gun he was sure it would be only a matter of time. He also knew—from the WBBM tipsters, to whom he had spoken—that the villain was Tylenol, but the time for naming names was not yet. A few months later, Rooney and CNB received the Peter Lisagor Award from Chicago's press club for the early coverage of the Tylenol story. "It's bugged me," Milemma said. "CNB didn't break that story. I broke that story. When I wasn't on the air I was on the phone. I called everybody and his mother's uncle. The sources, the police in Arlington Heights, the police in Elk Grove. If there was a base to be covered, I covered it. I've done enough death stories, I know what you do—and for me that morning, this was the only story. That was pretty unusual. For us it's not like the newspapers, where they can tell someone to take the day and just do that story."

Reports in the newspapers the next day said that the link between the Janus and Kellerman cases had been made by two rather overweight firemen, Richard Keyworth of Elk Grove and Philip Cappitelli of Arlington Heights, who were in the habit of listening to the police radio. They talked to each other on the telephone about these sad deaths in their neighborhoods, commented that both the Janus brothers and young Miss Kellerman seemed to have been taking Tylenol, and called their respective police departments to suggest that perhaps this was an angle to be explored. "Their self-appointed detective work," Andrew Malcolm of the New York *Times* reported on Saturday, "matching the characteristics of the deaths, led medical investigators in two cities to the Tylenol link." The *Tribune* was especially pleased that it had found out about these firemen before anyone else, and had a beat on their story and pictures of them in the afternoon editions on September 30.

In fact, Tylenol had been suspected in both the Kellerman and the Janus deaths before anyone thought of cyanide. Like most medications, aspirin and Tylenol can kill people. Baby aspirin and Tylenol are packaged only in small bottles to make sure the total contents are less than a fatal dose. People try to commit suicide with Tylenol, as they do with aspirin, and the results are memorably messy, because pumping the stomach doesn't always help: these are drugs that get into the bloodstream fast (which is what makes them effective analgesics). To help hospitals handle such cases, McNeil Consumer Products Company, the makers of Tylenol, funds a hot-line poison control center in Denver, staffed twenty-four hours a day. One of the few things the doctors in suburban Chicago knew about both Kellerman and Stanley Janus was that they had been taking Tylenol, and among their first thoughts was that the catastrophic event that had paralyzed the victims' nervous systems was the effect of a Tylenol overdose. The doctors on the other end of the hot line, however, said that the symptoms described were not those of Tylenol poisoning. It did seem likely that some poison was involved, of course, and in the interests of abundant caution the Tylenol doctors said they would pay the costs of studying tissues from both victims. They offered the services of a Chicago lab called Bio-Tox, which was under contract to McNeil. It was probably a telephoned report from Bio-Tox that triggered the anonymous phone call to the City News Bureau.

There was never any public mention of the Tylenol hot line: McNeil and its parent company, Johnson & Johnson, had no stake in calling attention to the fact that Tylenol had been on other occasions an agent of death, and neither the hospitals nor the medical examiner had reason to proclaim that some of the work the public assumes they do themselves is in fact done by outsiders. (Much better to have an editorial writer for the Cleveland *Plain Dealer* call it "a tribute to the sharpness of Chicago's law enforcement and medical personnel that the cause of death was so swiftly found.") It seems likely that both at the hospitals and in the medical examiner's office the low-level bureaucracy on duty in the middle of the night decided that the problems associated with the release of what would be an extremely frightening announcement should await the arrival of the bosses the next morning. And on the evidence of tipsters the people staffing the City News Bureau and WBBM would not even consider alarming the population or accepting the legal risks that might come with starting a panic. Even after the evidence improved, the news organs held back. Robert Emory of CNB came in to start his day at six in the morning, looked at the file, and immediately "went to the morgue. Routine practice. When two young men in the same family die on the same day, that's a story, even if it's a heart attack. But I knew it was Tylenol. I saw the Cook County investigator who had been to the hospital. He wouldn't confirm. I said, 'Was there a Tylenol bottle out there?' He said, 'Yeah, we've looked at some Tylenol.' "

2

Dr. Michael Schaffer, chief toxicologist for the Chicago medical examiner, came to work at eight in the morning on September 30 and found on his desk the lab reports on the Janus and Kellerman deaths. Cyanide poisoning, from potassium cyanide mixed with Tylenol. An examination of the bottles of Extra-Strength Tylenol capsules found on the kitchen table at the Janus home and in the bathroom at the Kellerman home revealed that several of the capsules remaining in the bottle (but not all of them) contained as much as half a gram of cyanide, five times a fatal dose and nearly the entire contents of the capsule. By what turned out to have been an unlucky chance, the two bottles were labeled from the same lot, MC-2880, manufactured in the McNeil plant in Fort Washington, Pennsylvania, a suburb of Philadelphia. "I thought," Schaffer says in a still awed recollection: "My God—suppose something's happened at the factory. The drugstores open at nine o'clock . . ."

A round-faced, fortyish scientist in a lab coat who came to public service from some years in the anonymity of the research division of Abbott Laboratories, Schaffer was not a man to seek publicity. His boss, Dr. Robert Stein, an avuncular, mustachioed master of the politico-scientific life of the medical examiner (an elected office in Chicago), was off on a speaking engagement; Stein's deputy, Edmund Donoghue, had not yet come to work. "I called every agency I could think of," Schaffer says. "The retail drug association, the poison control center, the state Department of Public Health, the police departments . . ." He tried to call McNeil Consumer Products, but the switchboard at McNeil put the call through to the wrong office, and then cut him off, and he decided that could wait. It did not occur to him to call the newspapers or the broadcasting stations: toxicologists do not assume responsibilities of that sort. Then Donoghue arrived and did call a press conference, for nine-thirty. It would be, the secretaries were instructed to tell the press, about the contamination of a widely used medicine: no names yet. Nobody at the medical examiner's office, of course, knew about the story the City News Bureau had moved on the wire in the middle of the night.

But then, the noise level had begun to rise. Individual reporters' contacts at the police departments and the hospitals had brought rumors of what lay behind Rooney's story. The press conference, at which Donoghue and

Schaffer shared the podium, drew about fifty people, including TV crews from all the local commercial stations. There was also a press release, in which the wrong number was given for the lot of bottles from which the contaminated capsules had come. (Because the reporters at the press conference trusted their ears, the right number got on the air and into the wire service copy and the newspapers, but the next morning a researcher who had been trained to trust the written word got the wrong one onto the *CBS Morning News.*) "Even the people involved didn't understand what they were saying," says Jack Houston, senior crime news reporter at the Chicago *Tribune.* "Schaffer announced what he called an alert on taking Extra-Strength Tylenol. I asked, 'Are you talking about a local alert or a nation-wide alert?' He paused and thought, and then said, 'I guess, nationwide.' "

Back at the newspaper offices, the Chicago city desks were already marshaling forces for what had the look of a major story. These were suburban cases: the first reporters out on the story were the juniors who worked the suburban beats. Howard Witt of the *Tribune* spent the day "following around the police officers who were trying to find out which stores the bottles had come from. I spent a couple of hours talking to people in the stores, checking disgruntled-employee angles." Among the assignments given immediately was a background report on the history, nature, usage and status of Tylenol. At the *Sun-Times,* that task went to a young consumer affairs reporter named Jim Ritter, who called Johnson & Johnson. James Murray, assistant director of public relations, took the call. He was busy, and when Ritter asked him for general background material on Tylenol he said he'd have to call back. That was fine with Ritter, who had not been told why his paper wanted the information. Then Ritter *was* told why, and he made another call. Murray heard him out, and reported what he had learned to his boss, F. Robert Kniffin, director of public relations. Kniffin called Arthur Quilty, a senior member of the fourteen-man J&J executive committee, the basic governance structure of this conglomerate corporation with annual sales of $5.4 billion. Until a few weeks earlier, Quilty had taken corporate responsibility for the McNeil subsidiary. And Quilty immediately went to the office of J&J chairman and chief executive officer James E. Burke, who was in the middle of his scheduled last-day-of-the-month casual chat about the world at large with president and executive committee member David R. Clare. The two men, both Irish and Catholic, were friends as well as allies in the sometimes complicated political battles within this de-centralized corporation. Clare was by training (at MIT) an engineer; Burke was a graduate of Holy Cross and the Harvard Business School—and, perhaps more significantly, of Procter & Gamble's real-life school of marketing. Neither man can remember what was on the table when Quilty (another P&G alumnus) came to the door of Burke's large office with its long conference table and family photos and handsome abstract art. "You're not going to believe this," Quilty began . . . but they did believe it, immediately. Nobody could have made up such a story.

Burke was then fifty-seven years old, a compact, handsome man with a florid complexion, thinning gray-and-white hair and a thoughtful manner. He works in shirt sleeves at a long table with a telephone clamped to it below the surface; the shirts have French cuffs with elegant cuff links. He exudes good health and good sense, and he is very smart. Burke had been with J&J for twenty-nine years, and had been chairman for six of them. His was a consultative leadership: he was in the habit of listening to other people's opinions rather than offering his own, and he was capable of letting his deputies take decisions with which he disagreed. The result was a forthrightness that permeated the staff level, and a pattern of information gathering that would serve J&J well in the weeks of what Burke later called "an unremitting nightmare." The product that had been attacked was the largest-selling medication in the country, accounting for 35 percent of all American purchases of analgesics. It was also the lead ewe of the J&J flock in terms of its contribution to the corporation: with only about 7 percent of total J&J sales, it generated a third of the profits. All by itself, as a single brand, Tylenol had earnings that would have placed it in the top half of *Fortune*'s five hundred largest American industrial corporations.

There was nothing Burke could do immediately. He called David E. Collins, recently appointed chairman of McNeil Consumer Products, who worked out of an office at corporate headquarters in New Brunswick, New Jersey. (J&J ran its larger subsidiaries as separate companies, each with its own chairman and president, some with their own boards of directors.) Burke told Collins what he knew, and added that the corporate helicopter was waiting to take him to Fort Washington, where Joseph Chiesa, president of McNeil, was trying to find out what if anything had happened in the factory. Collins, a youthful man with a relaxed manner whose round face was then graced with a luxuriant mustache, had started at J&J on its legal staff, and in the crisis he reverted to professional type. He put in a call to Chicago, to a lawyer named Paul Noland, his roommate at Notre Dame Law School some years before, and hired Noland and his partner Michael Carew to be J&J's eyes and ears on the scene. Collins was a native Chicagoan: he had grown up reading the Chicago papers and watching Chicago television, and he could imagine what was likely to happen down home.

Meanwhile, Quilty put in a call to Madrid, where Wayne Nelson was just checking into a hotel. McNeil and Tylenol were Nelson's babies. Another alumnus of Procter & Gamble (and another Chicagoan), Nelson had gone to Fort Washington in 1975, at the age of thirty-six, to be vice president and general manager of what had been until that time McNeil Laboratories, a supplier of prescription medicines to hospitals, and a useful but less than major player in the Johnson & Johnson story since its acquisition in 1959. Among the McNeil products the company had acquired was acetaminophen, a safe and effective aspirin substitute sold to hospitals under the brand name Tylenol, and available at drugstores by prescription. J&J had registered Tylenol with the Food and Drug Administration as an over-the-counter "proprietary" (i.e., nonprescription) medication, but had not advertised it.

Then Bristol-Myers made a splash in the analgesics market with Datril, another acetaminophen product, and J&J saw a great light. The health-and-environment worry of the 1970s had settled on the nation, and among the drugs nagged by bad publicity was aspirin (which is in fact a more serious medication, with more poorly understood and sometimes unfortunate side effects, than most users realize). McNeil Laboratories divided into McNeil Pharmaceutical and McNeil Consumer Products, and Nelson was assigned to build the Tylenol brand. As Tylenol triumphed in the market ("It was big, growing and profitable—the magic words," Nelson says in fond reminiscence), Nelson advanced in the J&J executive corps. He had been Collins' predecessor as chairman of McNeil, and only a few weeks earlier had been promoted to the status of company group chairman, with responsibilities that extended to J&J's international activities. He was in Madrid as a stopover on his way home from South Africa on his first trip in connection with his new duties, and he was debating whether he had time for a little tourism on his first visit to Spain, when the phone rang.

Nelson had reported to Quilty while chairman of McNeil, and the two men knew each other well. "Art had one simple question," Nelson recalls. " 'Is it *conceivable* that this happened at the plant?' I had put seven and a half years of my life into this product. There must have been thirty or forty seconds of silence while I went through the entire process in my mind, from the moment when the bulk granulation comes into the plant to the moment when the cartons leave it. There were only two places where anything could have happened. The first was in the mixer, where they make batches of ten million tablets or capsules, a quantity too large to blend in a poison—you could dump a fifty-five-gallon drum of cyanide into the mixer and it wouldn't make a lethal dose. After that everything was automated until the quality-control checkpoint, which was staffed by very senior people, nice old ladies who had been with the company for thirty years. At that point you *could* substitute, take a bottle off the line and put in another one. But that couldn't have happened. I told Quilty it wasn't conceivable."

Larry Foster, J&J corporate vice president for public relations, was on his last day of a summer-long leave of absence to write a biography of General Robert Wood Johnson, son of the founder of the company and its leader from 1932 to his death in 1968, when, after many years of relatively small contributions to hospitals and philanthropic causes, he left a personal fortune of more than a billion dollars to endow in his own name what immediately became the second-largest charitable foundation in the United States. Foster's arrangement was a complicated one, because he did not wish the book to be a company project, but he also did not feel he should leave his ship rudderless while off duty. He had been in the habit of calling in every day to ask his secretary if there was anything at the office he should worry about. On this Thursday morning, he heard the words "Tylenol" and "cyanide" and left for the office at once. He would not get home again until the next week. A deliberative, careful man in his fifties who had been night editor of the Newark *News* before he came to J&J, Foster heard reports on the radio while driving to the office, and watched the noon news shows on the New York television stations. There were now four dead: the Chicago medical examiner had found cyanide-contaminated Tylenol in the body of Mary McFarland, thirty-one, a divorced mother of three- and four-year-old sons, who had been dead on arrival at Good Samaritan Hospital in Downers Grove at 3:18 that morning.

Like Collins, Foster wanted his own men on the spot. He sent p.r. director Robert Kniffin to Fort Washington to direct the "very slim" p.r. staff at McNeil, and another assistant, Robert Andrews, to Chicago to gather information at the scene (but not to speak for J&J: that would have to be done at headquarters). Foster began taking telephone calls from reporters and TV story researchers, telling those who called that at present the company knew no more than they did, but would respond fully when it had the information. The secretaries in the p.r. office began a log of calls from the press that would eventually number 2,500. ("We got calls from dozens of small-town papers," Foster recalls. " 'We have a report of a Tylenol-related death here; the family that brought the patient in said they were Tylenol users. What can you tell us about what's happening elsewhere?' Remember the drama of being in a small town in Texas or Wyoming and feeling you're a part of a national story. It's perfectly understandable: that's what makes the journalism business so exciting. They felt they were caught up in a wave.") Then Burke called Foster in for a conference.

The first decision had been taken and there was some news to announce: J&J was "withdrawing" (the word "recalling" might be legally dangerous) the 93,400 bottles of lot MC-2880, which had been distributed in thirty-four states. Burke had called the Food and Drug Administration in Washington and spoken with deputy director Dr. Mark Novitch (director Dr. Arthur Hull Hayes, Jr., was in Philadelphia visiting a regional headquarters of the agency as part of an inspection-cum-encouragement program). One school of thought had argued that McNeil should make its own analysis of the retained samples from MC-2880 before calling Washington, but Burke would have none of it: if this was as bad as it looked, the company would need the FDA as a partner rather than an antagonist. The FDA already knew about the Chicago story, but it knew no more than J&J; its Chicago district people were trying to meet with the medical examiner's office and the hospitals and the police (all of whom were very busy and not at that time keen to solicit the intrusion of the feds). Burke invited FDA inspectors to join the company's own investigators in Fort Washington, and passed on for what it was worth Nelson's assurance from Madrid that the contamination could not have happened at the plant. And he pledged the FDA the full cooperation of the company, whatever the costs. Now there were some questions before the meeting on which Foster's advice was needed.

How bad was it going to be, and what could the company do to control the damage? Assuming, of course, that Nelson was right and McNeil was blameless, and also that there would be no further deaths. These were large assumptions, for the key fact that awful day at J&J, the first thing everyone involved in the meetings insists upon, was: *"We didn't know."* Even under this best-case scenario, Foster told Burke, the situation was hopeless. "Some stories are naturals," he said recently. "This one was a classic. One, a hundred million Americans used the product. Two, it was a product meant to relieve pain, not to cause death. Three, there was a mystery." In the back of his experienced mind he could already see the folkloric implications: a talismanic significance for the number 2880 (which had to be withdrawn from several state lotteries because too many people chose it), the black humor (Herb Caen of the San Francisco *Chronicle* would offer a good news/bad news story: the good news was that researchers had found a cure for herpes, the bad news was that it was Tylenol), the "copycat crimes," further contaminations of Tylenol itself and of other food and drug products, all of which would be tied back to this monstrous poisoning.

There had been some thought at the meeting that this was a McNeil Consumer Products matter; the reporters were flocking not to New Brunswick but to Fort Washington, and J&J market research, a continuous effort, had reported not long before that less than 1 percent of the public knew that Tylenol was made by the makers of Johnson Baby Products and Band-Aid bandages. ("The foundation businesses around here," Nelson says, "were sterility and motherhood. The rule was that you don't put the Johnson & Johnson name on a product that won't bring more to the name than Johnson & Johnson brings to the product.") It would be nice if those brands, and the large medical-supplies business with the hospitals, and the corporate logo, could be insulated from the Tylenol story. Foster said, No way: Johnson & Johnson was the household name. Burke already knew that (after all, the news had come through a reporter's call to New Brunswick, not Fort Washington), but there were others he had to convince.

Next question: should Burke himself be the company spokesman? It was a role he had never played; J&J historically had never sought publicity (almost alone among the large industrial companies, it had never made a presentation to security analysts). Here Foster agreed that at the beginning Burke should be protected and that he and his staff should answer what questions they could from the print press. On television, the initial spokesman would be Collins, who as a lawyer was trained to function on his feet.

Burke and Clare as the heavy hitters would be held in reserve until the company knew for sure what had happened.

Meanwhile, the decision about who would be the company's first spokesman had been taken independently at Fort Washington, *force majeure.* A mob of reporters and camera crews had gathered outside the door to the McNeil factory and offices. President Joseph Chiesa had given orders not to admit them to the building, and the situation was turning ugly. Collins, who was in Chiesa's office, was too busy asking questions himself to pay attention to what might be happening outside. On his own motion, Dr. Thomas M. Gates, medical director at McNeil, went out to talk with the reporters. Collins remembers looking out the window for no particular reason in the middle of the afternoon and seeing the mob gathered around Gates, poking microphones at him. "A great stroke of luck," Foster said some time later. "Gates could have come out of central casting. He had a great calming effect. When he said he thought this could not have happened at the plant, people believed him." Foster added Gates to the short list—previously just Collins and Chiesa—who would be offered for interview on television.

Both the public and Johnson & Johnson needed as much calming as they could get that night. The story led the CBS evening news for September 30, running as lead stories will for almost three minutes. For the next week, saving only one evening on ABC, it would lead *all* the network news shows, but on this first evening NBC and ABC were more cautious with it. They introduced it nine and twelve minutes into the show, and gave it two minutes and ninety seconds, respectively. They stayed with three deaths (though ABC anchor Max Robinson was based in Chicago: it was a matter of some amusement to the Chicago press corps that Robinson with the country's biggest story in his bailiwick did nothing personally to cover it); Dan Rather before going off the air confirmed a fourth death. CBS and NBC provided the lot number; ABC did not. There wasn't, oddly enough, a great deal of *news.* Though the local stations had taped the medical examiner's press conference—and the tape was used on other local stations all across the country—the networks were too proud to take material from their affiliates. And the statement to the press by Novitch at the FDA, noting that the problem seemed to be local to Chicago but urging that people everywhere avoid the use of Tylenol until the source of the contamination had been discovered, came too late for the nightly news shows and did not begin appearing on the air until the post-prime-time local news.

By then the story could be pieced together on available film: the news conference at the medical examiner's office; clerks taking bottles of Tylenol capsules off the shelves in Chicago-area drugstores; Novitch; Gates at the doors of the McNeil plant; comments by the stations' own pet doctors or science reporters. By the late-night news, too, yet another Tylenol-cyanide death was reported by the Chicago medical examiner: Mary Reiner, twenty-

seven, the mother of four (including a baby five days old), who had died at
9:03 that morning in Central Du Page Hospital in Winfield.

Foster had organized his staff (which was never more than eight people), and claimed helpers from Johnson & Johnson personnel around the
country, to monitor the news reports. He had the wire service tickers in his
own shop, and his people were listening to the all-news radio stations and
keeping an eye on the television sets. "All former newspaper people," he
says affectionately. "One of the things we do best around here is handle the
press. The rule was: Don't panic. We were very methodical." WABC-TV in
New York promoted its late-night news with artwork showing a Tylenol
bottle and a skull-and-crossbones; Foster called and the artwork was withdrawn. Ted Koppel's promo for that night's *Nightline,* which would feature
an interview with Novitch of the FDA, mentioned deaths from taking Tylenol "tablets"; Foster called the ABC Washington office, which found Koppel for him in less than twenty minutes. Koppel agreed that tablets were not
implicated, and the next time the promo ran Foster noted with pleasure that
the offending word was gone.

The local station night news shows were more immediately dramatic. It
was bad enough for Vivian Rosenberg on WLS-TV in Chicago to pro-
nounce the descent upon her city of "a mood of deep concern and warning
that death can be as near to us as our medicine cabinet"—and to show Mary
Kellerman's father trying to shut the door of his modest house on an ABC
reporter so he could be alone with his grief. But then there was WNBC-TV
in New York, with Sue Simmons announcing: "If you take Tylenol at all,
you are about to hear a number that might save your life." WCBS-TV in
New York sent a camera crew to the home of a very ordinary housewife in
Queens, who excitedly showed to the magic eye a bottle from the indicted
lot that she had bought because her doctor told her aspirin might be bad for
her. The reporter asked what exactly "he" [the doctor] had said, and was
corrected with the information that the doctor was a she. For KYW-TV in
Philadelphia it was a local story, and workers at the Fort Washington plant
were interviewed as they left the plant after a long day.

Not everything was negative from the J&J viewpoint. UPI moved a
late-night roundup story which mentioned that "at least three people in two
states—Nebraska and New Jersey—reportedly took capsules from the suspect lot and suffered no ill effects, authorities said." Mary Kay Ellen of the
Chicago office of the FDA came on camera and said, "The fact that McNeil
is willing to recall means they too are interested enough to just be certain it
isn't their problem." On *Nightline,* Dr. Novitch of the FDA told the nation
that "it's too early to tell, but it looks like a Chicago problem. In a couple of
days, we should know a lot more than we know now." Less then twenty-one
hours had passed, after all, since Jim Rooney organized the first story for the
City News wire.

Virtually every newspaper in the United States played the Tylenol murders in Chicago on the front page on October 1. The one major exception was the New York *Times,* which carried an AP dispatch on page twelve with only a "reefer" (a one-sentence reference to a story on an inner page) in the "Inside" box on page one. National news editor David Jones had been in Chicago that day on a routine visit to Chicago bureau chief Andrew Malcolm, and the two of them had been so preoccupied with housekeeping details that they missed the story. The *Times* hates to run wire service stuff on page one, and, said then-managing editor Seymour Topping, who was in the meeting that decided this was not front-page material, "We don't like to panic people." Anyway, Jones, who would have fought for the story in the conference, was a thousand miles away, and his deputy did not have his clout. By Friday, Malcolm was back at his post and the prejudice against scary stories had been overcome by the magnitude of national interest; and the Saturday *Times* had two pieces about Tylenol and Chicago on the front page.

Everyone was careful. Though bottles from lot MC-2880 were for sale in thirty-four states, the fact was that there were no confirmed ill effects from the ingestion of Tylenol anywhere outside the Chicago suburbs. There was enough hard news of the incidents to take the available space in the news hole. Speculation about why these crimes had been committed could wait for a day when news was less voluminous. The nationwide alarm was spontaneous and required no amplification. On the New York Stock Exchange, Johnson & Johnson was the most active stock, trading 1.2 million shares and falling three dollars a share.

5

Inside Stories

The killer, in effect, had appeared in everyone's home—
every medicine cabinet had become a potential hiding place
for some life-threatening horror.

–Loudon Wainwright, Jr.,
Life[1]

The consumer press, almost from the start, has devoted its
efforts to sensationalizing the Tylenol incident and publicizing
other product tamperings. Throughout, the press has sought
to uncover the bizarre, promote product recalls, dig up sensational angles and play up dramatic developments. . . . Indeed, the only irresponsible party in this entire episode has
been the consumer press. Late last month a crew from a local
television station came to the offices of *Chain Drug Review* to
do an interview on the analgesic situation. The reporter had
only one question: how badly have analgesic sales fallen off?"

–*Chain Drug Review*,
November 22, 1982

1

Two major elements were missing from the early stories about cyanide-
contaminated Tylenol. One was an account of the turmoil and horror at
Johnson & Johnson and McNeil, the immediate and profound involvement
of everyone on the executive level of the giant corporation. The press
couldn't present any part of this story because it wasn't privy even to the
names, let alone the activities. The inevitable result was the presentation of
victims, of government agencies working to solve a crime and of one or two
corporate "spokesmen" for a big organization that stood somehow in an
antagonist relationship to everyone else.

This sort of thing is almost inescapable, and fuels the fires lit by organizers like Ralph Nader, whose agenda of hostility to the dominance of
the economy by private corporations is quite separate from the incidents

they employ to gain public support. As the concentration on the lot number indicates, the initial assumption was that something must have gone terribly wrong in the manufacturing process. But there was of course no evidence that this was true, and by avoiding a knee-jerk public insistence that it *could not* be true—essentially because they were honest men and were living this nightmare themselves—Burke and Foster prevented an equally instinctive certainty on the other side, from those whose joy is *Schadenfreude.* (Nader inserted himself into the Tylenol story only with a comment to an inquiring reporter that the brand was now dead and could never be resuscitated.) In the Tylenol matter, the evidence built quickly and credibly that Johnson & Johnson was victim rather than villain, and both press and public attitudes toward the company in fact improved as the story played out on the world stage.

The other omission was more important and perhaps—only perhaps— more avoidable. Two weeks later, the Food and Drug Administration would give Johnson & Johnson a letter certifying that the contamination could not possibly have occurred at the McNeil plant. J&J wanted the letter as a defense against the lawsuits which had (of course) been brought against the company by the families of the victims, and (more important) needed some document of this sort if Burke was to proceed with his plans to revive the brand. The government had never issued such an absolute clean bill of health before, and the decision to do so was controversial within the agency. What tipped the scales was not the evidence from the factories (which included the fact that dogs trained to sniff cyanide had found none of the stuff) but reports from the FDA lab in Cincinnati, which had been working nonstop on cyanide and Tylenol since the first days of October. Cyanide, the scientists certified, was strongly hydroscopic—that is, it absorbed water from any substance with which it came into contact. The capsules in which Tylenol was packaged were a hardened gelatin made with water. In a matter of weeks such capsules would disintegrate from their contact with cyanide. Lot MC-2880 had been manufactured in April, and had gone into distribution in August. If the contamination had occurred at the plant, there would have been no capsules to hold the poison by the time the poor devils who bought the deadly bottles had opened them.

This would have been a complicated scientific story to mix into the sensational news of September 30 and October 1. Science, moreover, could not provide a sure guidance for consumers or storekeepers, because it remained possible, though very unlikely, that lot MC-2880 had been tampered with while in a warehouse en route to the shelves. (Very unlikely, because the little boxes in which the bottles were sold were packaged into plastic-wrapped sealed six-packs within the cartons shipped from the factory: a storekeeper, even a stock boy, finding the plastic torn around one of the boxes, would have been suspicious.) And, of course, any bottle in any retail outlet, from any lot, might have been contaminated in the store, which is in fact what had happened. But some of the panic that obsessed the country in the next week would have been averted if the government or even the company had publicly announced that any Tylenol capsules that had been in people's medicine cabinets for more than a month or so, regardless of lot number, were safe to take if the casing of the capsule was intact.

The point itself is not major, but its implications are. Second-guessing the coverage of an event is an easy sport and—given the self-righteousness of the executives of news organizations (not the grunts in the trenches, who are often self-critical)—it is an all but irresistible sport. But news is necessarily unreflective. The people involved in the story and the people covering it are as one in their inability to get below what is happening, down to the general principles that history, an easier art, will scornfully point out as the criteria that should have been employed to determine the truth that lies beyond accuracy. Nobody connected with the Tylenol horror in its first days, even those who felt a personal as well as a commercial need for self-exculpation, had the time to pause and inquire whether there might not be something below the surface of their story that was more convincing than any information that could be gained by even the most thorough exploration of the events pressing so hard for their full attention.

2

Friday, October 1, was the worst of days but also, for the beleaguered executives at Johnson & Johnson, the best of days. It was a day of two more deaths: Theresa Janus, whose condition had been hopeless from the moment of her arrival at the hospital, and Paula Prince, thirty-five, an airline stewardess, who was found dead in her Chicago apartment—she had probably died Wednesday night—with a 24-capsule bottle of Extra-Strength Tylenol beside her. The bottle had been purchased at a Walgreen's on the near North Side. J&J withdrew all Extra-Strength Tylenol capsules from sale in the Chicago area. Police cars and fire trucks patrolled the Chicago suburbs with bullhorns, calling to people not to take Tylenol; teams of social workers were organized to call on the homebound, and brochures were prepared in Spanish for the non-English-speaking. In Washington, Dr. Novitch held a press conference and opened with a statement that "the Food and Drug Administration advises consumers nationally not to buy or use Extra-Strength Tylenol until a series of deaths in the Chicago area can be clarified." Mayor Jane Byrne held a hysterical midnight press conference, live on television, during which she banned the sale of all Tylenol products—tablets and liquids as well as capsules—in her city.

Poison control centers across the country were swamped with calls from people who had been taking Tylenol from the "bad" lot, and felt sick. In Pittsburgh, Dr. Richard Moriarity, director of the local poison control center, wearily told the Pittsburgh *Press* that "if you've taken one and it's been more than two hours ago, you have nothing to worry about." It did no good: six people were admitted to hospitals in the Pittsburgh area—wisely, the *Press* did not print their names—with a history of Tylenol usage and a list of symptoms they had just heard described on the television news. No small part of the problem was the ignorance of hospital pathologists, who did not realize that everyone's blood contains a tiny element of cyanide, and that heavy smokers of cigarettes may have three or four times the normal cyanide content in their blood and still be as healthy as heavy smokers of cigarettes can be.

In a suburb of Cleveland, Margaret Dagostino, forty-nine, became the banner head in the *Plain Dealer:* "Woman Here Ill, Took Tylenol." It was a carefully written story: "A Parma Heights woman was hospitalized yesterday with a higher than normal level of cyanide in her blood after she said she had taken Extra-Strength Tylenol capsules purchased in Greater Cleveland.

"Police and hospital officials have not yet been able to determine if the capsules were poisoned. . . . Dr. Jeffrey Blumer, director of the Poison Control Center, said it was doubtful the woman's condition was directly related to the Tylenol because there were other sources of cyanide in the environment."

(But UPI would get this story wrong in a most remarkably complete and unnecessary way, and put its cockeyed version out around the country from a Cleveland dateline: "Tests completed Saturday on Tylenol capsules belonging to a suburban woman suffering from cyanide poisoning showed no traces of the painkiller [sic], but cautious authorities called the results 'inconclusive.' " The story included a comment from Dr. Theodore Marsh at Parma General Hospital that "she is very fortunate that she took such a small amount.")

In Chicago itself a nineteen-year-old waiter at a dinner theater dropped dead, and there was a bottle of Extra-Strength Tylenol in his locker with only one (clean) capsule left. Television jumped to wrong conclusions. In another Chicago suburb a woman was admitted with what looked to the locals like high cyanide levels, and the papers listed another suspected case. In Tennessee, a truck driver died in the cab of his truck with a bottle of Tylenol on the seat beside him. In Texas, an old man died in a nursing home; the family called the newspapers to report that he had been a big consumer of Tylenol. . . . Calls flooded in to New Brunswick. When the calls were stacked up, as they always were, Foster's people took the numbers and promised to call back (and always did: Foster comments dreamily on the element of pleasure, after being on the receiving end of so many late-night calls, from the experience of calling a reporter at home at five in the morning). The information from the calls was passed on to Johnson & Johnson's staff of doctors and security men, mobilized for twenty-four-hour-a-day duty, who called the hospitals and police in the reporters' home towns to see what they could learn. With Burke's entire backing, Foster told McNeil and the relevant Johnson & Johnson executives to cooperate fully and courteously with all reasonable requests from the press. "We got credit for being open," said McNeil chairman Collins, who was the most frequent spokesman. "But we had no choice. We needed the press for information, and there was no way we could ask for information for us without giving information to them."

But Friday was also the day when the greatest weight lifted from the shoulders of the embattled executives in New Brunswick and Fort Washington. The police revealed that the contaminated Tylenol Mary Reiner had taken was from lot 1910MD, manufactured in McNeil's plant in Round Rock, Texas. Foster announced that McNeil was withdrawing all 170,000 bottles of lot 1910MD. This was, as some of the McNeil people complained, a knee-jerk reaction. It was out of the ballpark of probability that Tylenol had been contaminated at two factories separated by half the country, to turn up suddenly in the Chicago area in a two-day period. Everyone in New Brunswick was still overwhelmed by the enormity of the news reports flooding into the office ("I tell you," said David Collins, "we were *scared"*), and the best recollection of the participants is that it was not until Saturday that they realized the full significance of the fact that the second lot to be implicated had been made in Texas. From this moment on, however, Johnson & Johnson could be sure that the Tylenol murders were not something its people had done, but something that had been done to them. Even then, it was considered unwise to argue the point in news releases or statements to the press or television: best to have the FDA or the local police explain to the public.

On Friday, too, the news coverage of the mystery assumed the shape it would keep for the next crucial week. The first morning, as the news reports circulated, Illinois attorney general Tyrone Fahner had convened a meeting of all interested parties—the county attorneys, the half dozen local and county police forces, the State Department of Law Enforcement, the U.S. Attorney's office, the medical examiners, the Illinois retail merchants' association. "The Chicago police didn't come," medical examiner Stein says scornfully (this meeting happened before the Paula Prince death, when Chicago was not officially involved), "because some big shot had died and everybody had to go to the funeral." The medical examiner was not invited to Fahner's subsequent meetings, which briefly influenced what was in the news over the weekend.

"This would be larger than a one-county problem," Fahner says, "and the attorney general is the only official with statewide jurisdiction. We didn't know how broad the problem was. We figured there were eleven to twelve thousand potential retail outlets for Tylenol, statewide. We were all being badgered by the press, everybody was calling to ask what everybody else was doing. There was press all around the meeting, the locals who cover the State of Illinois building. We agreed to tell them only that we were meeting to determine the size of the problem."

During the course of the day on Friday, spokesmen of one sort or another from a dozen agencies gave the press expressions of opinion about what was going on. After a brief show of reluctance while someone hunted up a plausible federal jurisdiction, the FBI threw twenty-six agents into the investigation; and the FBI detests uncontrolled publicity. James Zabel, director of the state Department of Law Enforcement, suggested that he, too, would appreciate limits on the broadcast of rumor and opinion—and, indeed, news—from those engaged in the investigation. It was agreed that the investigators would seek to coordinate their activities, and that one individual would become the spokesman for all. At six o'clock that evening, at a press conference in the state office building, Fahner announced the formation of a "Tylenol Task Force" under his direction. From now on, he added, all statements about the progress of the investigation would come from him.

The press saw this decision as self-interested, because Fahner, a youthful corporate lawyer originally from Detroit, with experience as a federal prosecutor and as director of the Department of Law Enforcement, was running for election on the Republican ticket, with voting only six weeks off. His TV commercials said he knew how to handle crime. It was his first electoral quest—he had been appointed to his post by Governor James Thompson (who was also up for reelection) after the state's previous attorney general had been sent to jail—and he had been considered a likely loser, for his opponent, Neil Hartigan, had been a popular lieutenant governor and was known throughout the state. "Tylenol Ty," as the reporters called him, would be on television morning, noon and night for the next ten days. "They set up a headquarters in Des Plaines," said Louis Lerner, proprietor of a chain of several dozen neighborhood and suburban newspapers in northern Chicago and its environs, "and there you would see Ty Fahner every day, standing out front in vest and shirt sleeves. He was running for election on Tylenol. We said he was the only person who took Tylenol that week and lived." Editor James Squires of the *Tribune* thought "one of the great mysteries was, how did Fahner go from one TV station to another? What means of transportation was he using? He'd be on all three channels at once, and the studios are in different parts of town."

Neither Fahner, who lost his election, nor the newspeople have happy memories of the ten days or so when this was the biggest story in Chicago (for the first five or six, the biggest in the country) and the state's attorney general—who in Illinois law has virtually no authority over criminal prosecutions—was the only official source for news about the investigation. By the middle of the week, Fahner had 170 people on his "Tylenol Task Force," all muzzled. (William Grigg, p.r. director for the FDA, remembers that the agency's half dozen senior investigators, sent to Chicago to help

out, refused to report to Washington on what was happening, because they
had taken Fahner's oath.) Literally scores of press and broadcast reporters
clustered around the converted garage in Des Plaines from 7 A.M., ready to
assault anyone who walked in or out the door. Dr. Arthur Hayes, then
director of the FDA, slim and slight, Woody Allen size, remembers from his
one visit that "Fahner sent four of his people out with me like football
guards to protect me, and I needed the protection."

The real problem, of course, was that the press was slavering for news,
and most of the time Fahner had no news. This was hard for the reporters to
believe, especially after the Chicago police department became involved: a
number of senior officers, confronted with a choice between accepting the
muzzle imposed by the Republican politico Fahner and maintaining their
long-standing relations with friends in the press and at the TV stations,
opted to pass on what little they knew. Hundreds of people were being
questioned, and while none of them was a "suspect," there were tidbits that
would interest the press. Individual reporters came to Fahner's press conferences primed with surmise, and were not to be put off by blanket denials or
refusals to comment. "It was very difficult," says Richard Koziol, a veteran
Tribune crime news reporter. "We were trying to put material together from
sources, and we were scared it would come out when someone asked Fahner
a question."

"The harder you tried to satisfy the media pressure," Fahner recalls,
"the worse it was. If you held press conferences at one time, TV was angry;
at another time, the print media were angry. The media acted very badly.
They'd get a rumor, and confirm the information with some low-level
source, some clerk. They'd say, 'Are we on the right track?' He would say,
'I think you are,' and they would go and print it. The papers were paranoid,
each afraid the other would get a scoop. There was a TV guy, a household
name, who called and cried, he was up for a new contract, he was in danger
of being terminated, his wife was going to have a baby, I had to give him
something. Others called and said, 'If you don't give me a scoop, I'll destroy
you, I'll fix you.' If I came out and said there was no news, they would find a
way to fill the slot. 'How many bottles did you check today?' 'What about
this thing you said yesterday?' There were fifty of them, two of them had
flown in from London, they camped out at Des Plaines from seven in the
morning.

"We were tracking leads all day, not only the real things, the three hot
bottles that turned up, but all the look-alikes, the people seen at the funerals, the people on the drugstore surveillance cameras, the phone calls, the
guy reporting cyanide in some apple cider, turned out it was a defective
bottle and the stuff had fermented. We'd hand out the assignments at seven
in the morning, try to get together at six o'clock every evening to debrief
each other. Homicide guys work exotic hours, but the FBI is a nine-to-five
operation, and so is the state department. Everybody put in double shifts.

The state brought in its heavy-duty folks. The press would grab them. We'd sit around and someone would say, 'Shall we watch TV and see what's on there about us today?' They couldn't believe all the false crap that was on the air."

Some of what Fahner said to the press was part of what the FBI or the police considered psychological warfare to shake up the criminal and tempt him to something rash. Early on, he spoke of the poisoner as a "crazed madman," because the FBI believed the crime was most likely a new form of urban terrorism (it is the Bureau's professional deformation), and someone thought that describing the Tylenol killer as crazy would "produce," Fahner says, "a statement from the FALN—'Hell, no, *we* did it.'" This produced a blast in the Washington *Post* from Dr. Thomas Szasz, the scourge of the psychiatric industry: "Instead of preparing to prosecute and convict the Tylenol terrorist, the highest-ranking law enforcement authority of the State of Illinois is diagnosing him and thus laying the ground for his insanity defense."

It was, of course, routine procedure to claim promising leads, and to outline the fingerprint tests that were being conducted on bottles and capsules, the effort to locate the source of the potassium cyanide (which is, unfortunately, in every high school chemistry lab in addition to a number of industrial shops). One of the more remarkable ventures was a suggestion—first to Mike Royko of the *Sun-Times,* the city's most popular columnist, who found he couldn't do it; then to his *Tribune* colleague Bob Greene, who did do it—that a column should be written on the great tragedy of the death of little Mary Kellerman, the only child of her parents' middle age and in many ways their reason for living, whose father had given her the pills himself when she woke with a cold and a headache. "I played the violin," Fahner says in sour recollection. The police had staked out the girl's grave; the FBI hoped that when he read the story the poisoner would come look at the grave.

But there were also some moments of plain and simple folly. One of the earliest suspects Fahner announced was a man who had been arrested for shoplifting Tylenol at a suburban drugstore in August—and two days later he had to make a further announcement that this miscreant had been convicted of that shoplifting and had been in jail ever since. One day Fahner would be promoting a "disgruntled worker" theory; the next he would say the task force was looking at trading in options on J&J stock. The police believed that one of the cases was a planned murder of the individual who was killed, and the others were the murderer's scheme for distracting investigators' attention (another professional deformation). When this leaked, the local TV stations besieged the house where Mary Reiner had lived, because there was no other possible victim to fit this theory. Her husband called Koziol of the *Tribune,* whose material he had read and respected, to ask advice on what to do: "These idiots think I killed my wife." He said he was tempted to put a blanket over his head and run to his car, hiding from the cameras, to see what they would make of it on the screen. Koziol told him to do what he could for his four motherless kids and not to think about it: the cameras would eventually go away.

It was probably the expertise and authority of the task force, however, that saved Johnson & Johnson from the one misstep Foster made through the long weeks of fast and dangerous responses to questions. On the first day, James Litke, AP bureau chief in Chicago, asked him an obvious question, to which, after checking with McNeil, he gave a flat answer: cyanide was not used in the manufacture of Tylenol. Later in the day, the answer escalated to a blanket statement that there was no cyanide in the McNeil plant—and this was untrue. In the testing lab, far removed from the area where the product was mixed and bottled, there was a 100-gram vial of cyanide used as a reagent in the chemical tests for the presence of lead in povidone, one of the ingredients that bound the powders together in the capsule.

Collins first learned about this piece of bad luck in a late-night call from one of his people in Fort Washington. He knew Noland, his lawyer on the spot, had given the Chicago medical examiner assurances about the absence of cyanide, and he called at three in the morning to tell Noland to get the truth to the investigators as fast as possible. Noland went to the state office building the next morning to tell Fahner's task force (which was in process of organization). A suspicious sergeant denied him access, but he pleaded successfully with the sergeant to get his message to the meeting.

A leak from the task force told the AP that the previous day's information from McNeil had been wrong, and an AP reporter, preparing the weekend roundup piece on the story, called Foster to check. Foster checked, incredulously, and found the story was true. It was a last straw. There really was no possibility that the cyanide in the lab (in two plants) had contaminated the Tylenol capsules, but the publication of the information might well turn what was already a near-panic into a nationwide hysteria. He pleaded with the reporter to hold the information out of the weekend story. The reporter was sympathetic and agreed to check it out with his bosses. Foster was relieved and grateful when he called back a few minutes later to say that the AP would not go with the story, on Foster's pledge that if he found anyone else had it he would call and release it. Then it developed that the Newark *Star-Ledger* also had the information.

"I had known Mort Pye, the executive editor of the *Star-Ledger*," Foster says, "since my days at the Newark *News*. I made a plausible case that this was not the responsible thing to do, and he agreed. Then Kniffin [Foster's assistant in Fort Washington] called to say that the *Times* had a scientific type in the lab probing what went on in the testing procedures, and he had been told about the cyanide by another scientific type in Fort Washington: he had asked the right question and got an honest answer. My next thought was to try to convince the *Times*. I tried to reach the reporter, but he was driving back to New York. AP deadlines are always imminent. The deadline for the bulldog edition of the *Star-Ledger* would hit while the *Times* reporter was on the road. So I called the AP and the *Star-Ledger* and told them someone else had the story, and all I could ask from them was that they use the information responsibly. Which they did, and the *Times* did, too." It was an enormous stroke of luck. If J&J had succeeded in concealing, even for a day, the presence of cyanide on the McNeil property, it would never have regained its credibility with either the press or the public.

Even so, it was a close call. His nose out of joint because his office had been excluded from Fahner's task force after its first meeting, medical examiner Stein gave a statement to the press on Saturday. With the revelation that there was cyanide on the premises, he said, he was unwilling to rule out the possibility of "factory error" in the contamination of the capsules. But the task force itself, impressed by Noland's insistence on volunteering the information before it was public—and guided by the FDA scientists, who had been sent to Chicago in part to calm public fears—brushed the story aside as an irrelevancy. And the press believed the task force.

3

The Tylenol story, said Louis Lerner of the Chicago suburban papers (and a man of parts: he was Jimmy Carter's ambassador to Norway), "was magical for the media. It tended to last. Tylenol took the place of Richard Nixon. After the election the story died, because there was nobody to hate." In the first days, there was the all but unbearable agony, the seven young people so meaninglessly struck down and the misery of the survivors. The print reporters on ghoul patrol felt themselves deeply resented, and the TV crews turned people's stomachs (especially, perhaps, the stomachs of the print reporters) by elbowing mourners aside to get pictures of the caskets and the immediate families. But the emotional side of this story was so self-evident, and so much else was going on during those first days, that the editors and the TV producers did not play the human-interest angles as heavily as media critics believed.

Patrick Malone in the Miami *Herald* on October 10 made the intelligent point that this story could dominate the news while nobody could get ink or air space for birth defects or infant deaths from maternal malnutrition. "We know the Tylenol victims," he wrote, "the Janus family and little Mary Kellerman. Television brought us the grief of their relatives in aching detail. We do not know the birth-defect victims or the people who will die for lack of an air bag. They are nameless and faceless, and they will always be so. When editors tell reporters, as they do every day, 'Let's get some real people in this story, not just numbers,' they are making political and moral decisions about what kind of people and what kind of problems should receive our attention." The rebuke is surely true in general, but not in this instance. There was some purple prose (Roger Rosenblatt in *Time:* "One shudders picturing Stanley and Theresa Janus in Chicago a couple of weeks ago, stunned over the death of Stanley's brother Adam a few hours earlier, the couple sitting in despair at the kitchen table, about to reach for the Tylenol"), but the story in the first days was driven by an immense public self-concern, and the reaction to that concern by political actors. So much was happening that there wasn't much space or time to manipulate the tear ducts.

North Dakota and Colorado banned the sale of Tylenol. Massachusetts ordered stores to remove all Tylenol capsules from their shelves. The San Francisco police warned people not to flush their Tylenol down the toilet for fear of contaminating the sewer system. At Heathrow in England and at Orly and Charles de Gaulle in France, loudspeakers blared warnings to air travelers arriving from the United States that if they had any Tylenol in their luggage they should take it to a special desk in customs to have it checked. In Italy, the state television urged everyone not to take Tylenol. The product was banned in Guatemala, the Philippines and Singapore. In Poland, with God knows what feelings of delight, the government of General Jaruzelski, noting that the Janus family was of Polish origin, warned the Polish-Americans who had retired to the old country (lured by apartment houses specially built for their use because Poland needed the foreign exchange) that if friends and family in the United States had sent them Tylenol, a product not available in Poland, they should refrain from using it.

At *Newsweek,* the Tylenol story was assigned to Melinda Beck, a young "senior editor" who was one of the six writers of the national news section. She had just returned from a lunch-break visit to her doctor for advice on what to do about a nasty sinus headache; he had suggested Tylenol, which she did not take. Even on Thursday afternoon, the editors had decided that Tylenol would be the "violin"—the lead item—in national news for this week. On Friday, editor William Broyles got on the phone to his bureau chiefs around the country to inquire about the degree of interest and concern where they lived. He had come to his editorship recently, summoned by owner Katharine Graham from the very different magazine *Texas Monthly* for reasons that never became clear in his less than two-year tenure, and he had been roundly criticized by the media fraternity a few weeks before when he played Princess Grace on his cover in the week of the massacre of the Palestinian refugees in the camps outside Beirut. For this week, the editors had decided (on Tuesday, as usual) that the cover would be the Broadway opening of the British musical *Cats.* Saturday morning, late indeed for a magazine that goes into distribution on Monday, Broyles made Tylenol the *Newsweek* cover. While shedding tears for the tragedy of the victims and the undeserved disaster at Johnson & Johnson, the reader might spare a sob for the press agent for *Cats*, who lost one of the most precious goods a press agent can achieve. Big news stories make ripples in areas totally unconnected with their provenance because there is a single pool of time and attention that runs off every day.

"I opposed it as a cover," Beck recalls, "because we couldn't push the story. On a story like this, it's hard for a newsmagazine to do its own enterprise, and it was too soon: even one more day would have helped. We tried, went to the hospitals, got details on poisons, but the newspapers had everything we could get. Unlike TV shows, we have to consider that covers are on the stands all week. I made the decision early on to write it as a detective story. The debate was on how much resonance it would have: a story must have news value seven days later to be a viable newsmagazine story. You've got to write the story so it doesn't sound wrong late the next week. There could have been more deaths. I was on the phone back and forth with the Chicago correspondents all day Saturday, I read the newspapers and the wire stories. I finished writing at one o'clock Sunday morning. It was being edited, checked and fit while I was writing, but we weren't finished until four or five."

The week to come would amply justify the judgment of Broyles and his bureau chiefs that the Tylenol story had staying power and national interest. Real events in Philadelphia, California and Wyoming and false reports and diagnoses from virtually all over kept the story on the TV news and the front pages of the newspapers, though nothing was happening. The fact that nothing was happening became rather sinister news: "The massive nation-wide campaign to keep people from taking Extra-Strength Tylenol seems to be working," Frank Reynolds intoned on ABC's *World News Tonight* on Monday night. "There have been no further reported deaths." On NBC, Tom Brokaw announced that "investigators at the local, state and federal level are worried that there may still be more contaminated Tylenol somewhere," and a Chicago camera crew from NBC caught a lady shopper saying, "I'd rather be a little sick." In Washington, the Proprietary Association, the league of manufacturers of over-the-counter drugs, met in urgent session on Monday, with the encouragement of the FDA, to design their own "tamper-resistant packages" before legislators and regulators mandated impenetrable seals on everything. (By January, they would be in trouble with the press for trying too hard: under the heading "PACKAGE OVERKILL," the Sacramento *Union* would write: "According to the Arthritis Foundation, some manufacturers have created containers extremely difficult to open by the able-bodied person, let alone the arthritic.")

Front-page attention to months-old stories of cyanide poisonings in Wyoming and Philadelphia opened up the inevitable conflict of interest between the news purveyors on one side and the company and the government on the other. In the first two days, when in fact everyone was terrified, the papers and broadcasters had "responsibly" emphasized that the poisonings seemed localized in Chicago. But insensibly, as the days passed, editors and producers acquired an interest in elements that might seem to touch the lives of news consumers in a wider catchment area. "The investigators kept saying no link, no link, but you couldn't know," says Melinda Beck, whose second-week story was even longer than the first ("I got fascinated by all the details, I kept asking for forty more lines, a hundred more lines"). There were wild cards among the sources. The Philadelphia police reopened the suicide by cyanide of a Filipino student at the Wharton School of Business, took another look at the Tylenol bottle that had been found among his effects when he had died that April, and found the capsules disintegrated and the bottom of the bottle covered with cyanide. They called a press conference to announce their discovery. "TYLENOL MYSTERY SPREADS EAST" was the headline in the Chicago *Tribune* and on the story moved nationwide by the KNT service (Knight-Ridder, New York *Daily News,* Chicago *Tribune).*

Dr. Novitch at the FDA blew his stack at the Philadelphia police and at the reporters, denouncing them for stimulating public anxiety at a time when it seemed increasingly clear that only Chicago was involved. Robert J. McCloskey, ombudsman for the Washington *Post,* wrote a column supporting Novitch's displeasure with "the attention given to the reopening of the six-month-old suicide of a University of Pennsylvania student after contaminated Tylenol was found in the student's apartment. The death was reconfirmed as a suicide," McCloskey noted, "but not before giving an impression that a nationwide Tylenol plague was threatening." But the Philadelphia story was potentially relevant (the FBI was particularly interested in the fact that analysis of the contents of the bottle indicated a hefty dosage almost identical to what had been put in the Chicago capsules), and indeed there is still a school of thought that holds that this student's "suicide" was related to a dry run for what was later carried out in Chicago. More difficult to justify was the headline treatment for the death of an adolescent in Wyoming (who had never taken Tylenol) and for the convulsions of a butcher in Oroville, California, whose Tylenol had been contaminated with strychnine rather than cyanide, a fact concealed by the banner in the *Tribune* and the users of its syndicate: "POISON-LACED TYLENOL FOUND IN CALIFORNIA."

The California story played into the hands of those who found the Tylenol poisonings useful to sell newspapers and boost ratings. It "opened up the possibility," Anne Taylor Fleming wrote in a roundup piece for the next Sunday's Los Angeles *Herald-Examiner,* "that there was a consortium of poisoners, a group of terrorists who, for whatever as yet undisclosed reason —perhaps to bring Tylenol's parent company, Johnson & Johnson, to its knees—was moving around the country poisoning people. It was that second batch raising that second possibility that was so unnerving—the possibility that terrorists were at work and that biological and chemical warfare had finally been added to their repertoire of weapons." Less visibly but more significantly, the California story also served the strategic planning of J&J's chairman, James Burke.

As early as that first Friday night, once the police had reported that a lot from Round Rock had been contaminated and the exoneration of the Mc-Neil factories had become a certainty, Burke had made a first-draft decision that J&J should pull all Extra-Strength Tylenol capsules from the market, then seek to restore the brand to the shelves in a newly designed tamper-resistant package. He worked out the costs on the back of an envelope, and came out with a ballpark figure of $100 million, which turned out to be about right. On Monday morning, McNeil announced that it had stopped making Extra-Strength Tylenol capsules. (The announcement was by Mc-Neil president Joseph Chiesa, and included a pledge from Burke that no employee would lose his job: everyone would stay on the payroll, and if worse came to worst J&J would find other things for all these workers to do. It was a big story for the Philadelphia television stations, one of which did a long interview with Chiesa for the local news. This coverage produced one of the very few instances when J&J felt the news coverage had done the company dirt. "Chiesa has a mannerism," says McNeil chairman David Collins. "When he talks, he goes like this." Collins crossed his fingers. "The TV station showed him crossing his fingers when he said nobody would be laid off, made it look as though we didn't mean it.") And Burke went to Washington, to discuss the situation with FBI director William Webster and the senior officials of the FDA and to tell them that J&J was going to pull the product, nationwide.

"I had thought both the FBI and the FDA would leap at the idea of a recall," Burke says, "but I was wrong. Webster was concerned about copycat crimes. He mentioned Halloween, which was only a few weeks away; we hadn't thought about that. He had a generalized concern that if we capitulated, whatever sick mind was doing this would be encouraged. I felt copycat crimes were more likely to occur if the brand were on the shelves." (Executive committee member Wayne Nelson felt there was also a moral obligation: "Someone was using our brand as a vehicle for murder; we had to remove the vehicle.") There was also, of course, a commercial reason: J&J could not hope to bring the brand back, which Burke clearly wished to do though he hadn't had anything like the time that would be needed to think it through, unless some way could be found to prevent a Chinese water torture of copycat crimes that would keep the name Tylenol in the papers as something to fear.

At the FDA, Burke ran into even more determined opposition. "If you recalled everything," said Dr. Hayes, remembering his time as FDA director (he later moved on to be president of the New York College of Medicine), "in a sense you set a precedent, that in a panic the knee-jerk response would be to recall. First it's Tylenol. Then somebody does it to Anacin or a mouthwash. Then it's Gerber baby foods or ketchup, and then somebody puts a hypodermic needle in a banana. Where do you stop? Are we going back to the turn-of-the-century store with all the products behind the counter?" He lit a cigarette: it was strange to see a former FDA chief smoking. "So much was riding on this," he said. "It could have been sabotage. We were in touch with the science attachés in all the embassies." Hayes was not terrified by the media: his father had been president of CBS Radio.

It was Hayes's deputy, Mark Novitch, who explained all this to the astonished Burke and a group of McNeil executives at a meeting at the FDA on Monday afternoon. The meeting dragged on into dinner hour. Frightened by the thought of what the press or the Congress might say if they accepted a meal from the makers of Tylenol, the FDA staff insisted on sending out for pizza and Coke, which they would buy. So the dozen executives and bureaucrats, doctors and scientists were chewing on cold pizza ("worst meal I ever had in my life," Burke says) when the word arrived from California.

In fact, the strychnine poisoning had occurred on Thursday, as the story of the deaths in Chicago burned up the wires, and on Friday the victim's doctor had called Johnson & Johnson to ask what he should do. His message went on the stack with all the others, and did not emerge until Monday, when a designated hitter at J&J checked with him, and the hospital, and the police. The call to Washington was to J&J's research director at the meeting, and he came back to it staring. He told Burke, who heard him through and then looked at where Novitch had been sitting. Novitch was gone; *all* the FDA people were gone: they had opposite numbers in California they had to reach immediately. It was still late afternoon in California.

Before the drugstores closed that evening in Oroville, the residents of the town were treated to the sight of bands of earnest men, some from the FDA and some from J&J (for neither had enough personnel in the area to do the whole job), taking Tylenol boxes off the shelves. They thought it had something to do with what they had been seeing on the television—as indeed it did, though only by accident. By macabre coincidence, a local butcher had chosen Tylenol as the medium for a poisoning scheme of his own, and had planted additional bottles on the shelves of the general store to cover his tracks, some days before the murderer struck in Chicago. The local police were deeply and correctly suspicious of him; but the truth would not be out for some days. Publicly, both the government and the company would advise that the cases were probably unrelated; privately, both FDA research director Joseph Hile and J&J president David Clare say, in the same words, "We were scared. We didn't know."

There are places in the world to which the arm of the news gatherer does not reach, and Oroville, California, is one of them. Nothing appeared that night on television, or the next morning in the newspapers. All Extra-Strength Tylenol capsules were gone from the stores in the Oroville area before the announcement was made on Tuesday, and the news was as managed as it could be. But for Burke, the incident in California was proof that he had been right in his decision to recall. He was amazed to learn in a long phone conversation that day that the FDA still did not agree. A statement was worked out stressing that Johnson & Johnson was moving on its own, without orders from the government, to "withdraw" some 31 million bottles from the distribution chain. The next day, the FDA reconsidered its public position, and issued a carefully limited order that the company make a "Class 1 recall" of all Extra-Strength Tylenol capsules, but only in the Chicago and Oroville areas.

News, say the philosophers, is when man bites dog. People expect the government to insist on the recall of suspect products; everyone would have been fascinated by the notion that in this case the government was leaning on the manufacturer to keep selling it. Nobody talked, so nobody knew. *Quaere,* as they say in the law schools. Should the world have known this very interesting "fact"?

Asked the question, most reporters, editors, publishers, broadcast producers and lawyers think a little and then say that the press should indeed have printed the story. It is not the function of a news medium to decide what people should or should not know; the job, except in the most extraordinary circumstances, is to relate what is happening. As Charles A. Dana of the *Sun* put it more than a century ago: "I have always felt that whatever the Divine Providence permitted to occur I was not too proud to report."[2] The assumption of a free press must be that the consumers of news can handle reality. In this instance, the disclosure that the government was against a recall might have stimulated a few more copycat crimes (which were common enough anyway: between October 1 and December 7, when the product went back on the shelves in a tamper-resistant package, the FDA logged and investigated 295 reports of contaminated Tylenol). By the same token, however, the uproar that would have followed the disclosure would have alerted more people to examine their purchases more carefully before ingesting them, which is—as Dr. Hayes said in a widely broadcast public service announcement prepared by the FDA for the television and radio stations—the only fully effective preventative for this particular disease. Myself, I can argue it either way.

To ask whether the press should carry a story, however, assumes that the press knows it. Most people, even those in the trade, seem to assume when such questions are raised that the press knows or can learn everything. This assumption is false, and the truly important question is whether the press *should* know everything. The FDA had reasons of public policy for wishing to prevent the recall of Extra-Strength Tylenol capsules, and J&J ordered them out of distribution in part for commercial reasons. But it is also true that the FDA was motivated by bureaucratic fears of the unknown, and the executives of J&J, horrified by their involuntary association with mass murder, were looking to protect the consumers of their products.

As news stories play, this one would have been negative in its implications for the agency (which would have been shown as—yet again—"failing to protect the public") and quite possibly for the company, because commentators would have been scornful of its desire to salvage its brand name. There are values for the society when a government agency can act on arguments too complicated to be fairly presented in a newspaper story (let alone a television news show)—and also when a corporation takes a long view of the quality of public trust in a branded product. Those values would have been sacrificed if the full story of this debate had been available to the public, and the countervailing values of full disclosure, while never entirely absent—Brandeis' insistence that sunshine is the best disinfectant remains a valid general principle—are in this instance something that would have to be dug up from pretty far down.

This question usually rises to the surface in matters like the invasion of Grenada, when those who opposed the invasion are furious at the government's ability to restrict news coverage while those who admired it also admire the secrecy. Even in historical focus, judgment tends to be contaminated by political opinion. Those who respect Grover Cleveland believe he was right to keep secret the operation performed on him for a cancer of the mouth early in his second term as President (it was done on a Wall Street friend's yacht, where presumably the President was taking a vacation); others consider the concealment of the operation as yet another example of Cleveland's sanctimonious hypocrisy. Supporters of Woodrow Wilson believe he and his wife were right to keep from the press the severity of the stroke he suffered in autumn 1919 and the role played by Edith Wilson in American governance during the next eighteen months; opponents believe it to be the last megalomaniac gesture that doomed the League of Nations and the Treaty of Versailles. Better to look at these matters of closely held vs. public information in the context of Tylenol, where perceptions will not be contaminated by political or social views. To limit the hunting license of the press is, I suspect, entirely undesirable. But it is not always a misfortune when the targets can successfully hide.

6

Responsibilities

One thing evident, though somewhat overlooked: the Tylenol tragedy is a reflection of American culture. We are the land of mass murders: Howard Unruh, George Banks, the Mafia wars, and so forth.

–Msgr. S. J. Adamo, columnist,
Philadelphia *Daily News*,
October 11, 1982

It began to look as though anytime anyone in Anytown USA found so much as a cinder in a box of corn flakes, the story would make the network newscasts, . . . because it fit into a news pattern. . . . Television news behaved irresponsibly in taking virtually every local case that appeared to fit the pattern and making it a national story.

–Tom Shales, TV critic,
Washington *Post*, December 9, 1982

Now the saving grace for Johnson & Johnson and all the rest of us is that over time people do tend to forget idiosyncratic phenomena, particularly when the experience is not repeated or reinforced. The forgetting is of course delayed as long as news reports keep the idiosyncratic event in the public eye without putting it in perspective and some persons meanwhile will unconsciously repress the disturbing news in an effort to retain their own sense of stability because they need it. One final observation: representatives of the media should be aware of how your own feelings influence how the subject is covered and played. Subconsciously the reporter or editor may deal with his or her own helpless feelings by repeatedly addressing the story again and again as if that will help gain mastering. It is a common human phenomenon, we see it in victims after the trauma who attempt to relive the experience. How could it be done differently? The repeated nightmare. The concept is one which in our profession we refer to, if you will pardon the jargon, as counter-transference, namely being aware of how one's own needs and reactions to the situation

bias and potentially distort our approach to it. We can over-
respond and excessively react and thus make the anxiety more
extensive and disproportionate than it needs to be. That is the
constant challenge that you have to face.

–Dr. Walter Menninger,
speaking to the Associated Press
Managing Editors convention,
November 12, 1982[1]

1

James Burke had been round the barn with the national newspapers
and wire services and TV networks once before, about eighteen months
before the Tylenol story broke, and he had scars to show for it, but also
medals. On that occasion, a stringer for the Washington *Post* and radio station WRC in that city had stumbled upon a crusader at Mount Sinai Hospital
in New York who was spending a grant from the Food and Drug Administration to prove that a lot of things you think are safe are really very dangerous. One of his pets was baby powder; he had found asbestos in it. This was
a very good story for a stringer; the *Post* published it on the front page, and
it was blared over WRC. The wire services picked it up, and the Mount
Sinai researcher got his moment in the sun from the television networks.
The problem was, the baby powder he had analyzed had been made before
World War I by a company long defunct, and there was no asbestos in any
such product now being offered to the public.

Against all professional advice, Burke had gone on the warpath in
defense of Johnson's Baby Powder. "I went to the FDA," he says. "They
were concerned with politics. Mount Sinai was worried about the hospital.
The *Post* was worried about its reputation. I argued that all of us—including
Johnson & Johnson—should worry about the public. In the end, we got a
full recantation of the story from the *Post*, the wire services and the networks. NBC sent Frank Field to film the recantation. The experience made
me feel strongly that we had an opportunity to deal with the media strongly
and up front. The Tuesday and Wednesday after I came back from Washington, I went to see the heads of the three network news divisions. I went in
alone, after calling the chairmen of the boards, all of whom I knew, just to
tell them what I was going to do—I didn't want them to do anything for
me." Burke's purpose was simply to ask the networks to be careful, to avoid
artwork and photos and language that would contribute to public panic or
tar the company with the murderer's brush. Somewhat to his surprise, the
people he saw were entirely sympathetic. "Dick Wald had been president of
NBC News in the baby powder days, and he'd been tough as nails. Now he
was at ABC. He gave me the tape recorder off his desk, insisted I take it, to

keep a record of the meetings in my office; he said the time would come when I'd want it."

Over some objections from McNeil, Burke had pulled all advertising for Tylenol. ("People," he says, "can't be persuaded when they're frightened.") But he told the agency to keep making the commercials, which had been slice-of-life interview stuff. He used the edited tapes, which were sent to him every evening to take home and run on his own videotape player, as a supplement to the formal market research conducted for Johnson & Johnson through the crisis by two separate agencies ("I like having two opinions"). The research tested the extent of consumer knowledge (amazingly high: "Ninety percent of the American public doesn't understand *anything,* but they understood this") and, of course, attitudes: how many Tylenol capsule users had sworn off the product forever, how many would take it again if they found it in the stores.

When the decision was firmly taken to return to the market with Tylenol capsules, using the original name and visual presentation (the commitments were made at a meeting on the Friday eight days after the story broke), the strategy included building back with publicity before advertising resumed. Thirty McNeil personnel were trained to do guest appearances on 103 local talk shows around the country, and Burke and president Clare were made available to the networks. This was not an easy decision: neither Burke nor Clare had ever appeared on television before, and there were areas of vulnerability. Interviewers might attack the extraordinary profitability of the product, ask how the company could justify restoring Tylenol to the shelves while the murderer was still at large, inquire why there had been no barriers to tampering before. (Until the Chicago disaster, Tylenol, like most headache remedies, had been sold in bottles with a cap that came off and on, and only a wad of cotton between the capsules and the cap. Bryant Gumble on the *Today* show had asked that question of an exhausted David Collins, and received the straightforward answer that "the concern for tampering was not, to be honest, on our minds. The idea that someone would tamper with an over-the-counter product . . . . To us, that's a new idea.") The big gamble was a decision to cooperate with *60 Minutes.* Foster opposed it; Burke overruled him.

"When I left that FDA meeting the first Monday," Burke recalls, "I went to the airport and found the company plane was going to be held in traffic, so I took the shuttle to New York. On the plane I found Alex Brody, the head of Y&R (Young & Rubicam) International, a very creative guy. Compton was the agency on Tylenol, but Y&R had the baby products and the Band-Aids. I asked him what he would do in my shoes, and he said he would go on *60 Minutes,* call them and ask them to do the story. I said, 'That's peculiar. Why?' He said they had the largest audience and a lot of credibility. 'Usually,' he said, 'they attack business, but in this case they won't.' We didn't call them, they called us, but how we would have reacted if I hadn't talked to Brody I don't know.

"Our people were scared about what would happen to us on the *60 Minutes* cutting-room floor. I went to see Mike Wallace, and he said, 'Why are you reluctant?'

"I said, 'Because I've watched your show.'

" 'Did you see the Coors show?' he said.

"I said, 'Yes. The bad guy was the unions. But you always have a bad guy. Who's the bad guy here?' I told him I would have to see his producer. [Don] Hewitt said, 'If you really believe in the marketing and selling of this product—that it was good for the public—then we can't hurt you.' In the end, the thing that persuaded me to do it was a deep gut conviction that we couldn't lose—we were right, we were victims, and people would sense it. And I felt that inherent in this story was the value of the branded product and the big corporation. A generic would simply have been withdrawn. And Tylenol *alone,* despite its profits history, would have been destroyed because no bank would have lent the money."

Foster used his log of 2,500 press queries as a mailing list for press releases as the company planned the reintroduction of Extra-Strength Tylenol capsules. Burke himself came up with the idea of the coupon ad in the newspapers good for a free bottle: "A lot of people threw their Tylenol away in the panic," he said; "let's give it back to them." The announcement of the tamper-resistant package and the marketing plans was by a teleconference to thirty cities (reporters in New York, Los Angeles, Chicago, Philadelphia and Washington could ask questions); three hundred television stations were notified by teletype that they could pick up the conference live from their local telephone company or by satellite. Among them, the stations in the top ten markets aired eighty-four segments. By the time the mostly positive *60 Minutes* show aired in December, it was frosting on the cake: Tylenol was coming back. A year after the poisonings, it had roughly regained its market share. Some months before that, Compton Advertising had sent a watercooler jug full of rotgut white wine to adman Jerry Della Femina, who had told a reporter while the poisoning was on the front pages that it would be impossible to bring back the brand; if Compton could do that, he said, he wanted them to come to his office, because they could turn the water in the cooler to wine. Unabashed, Della Femina sent back to Compton a couple of loaves of bread, to see what they could do with that. This got in the newspapers.

Other things did not get in the papers, for what had been going on behind the scenes at Johnson & Johnson was far less certain and cheerful than the public image. David Clare says, "We watched the news together, we lived together, we thought together, we fought together, week after week. My memory of the three months, September 30 to Christmas, is one of unending stresses, of attempting to help in dealing with bombs blasting all around the country—around the world, really. What do we do in Canada, in the Philippines, in Costa Rica? And you had to keep running the company in its other markets." Burke formed a Tylenol strategy committee of seven (himself, Clare, Collins, Quilty, Nelson, Foster, and general counsel George Frazza); they met every morning and almost every night for ten weeks. There was so much to do: new packaging to be designed and tested (a special group at McNeil, labeled "Machiavelli, Inc.," worked on ways to tamper with the new seals), enemies to be fended off (both Anacin III and Datril greatly increased their advertising budgets while Tylenol was quiescent), doctors and druggists to be stroked by the detail forces and the sales staff, false reports and rumors, copycat tamperings and extortion threats, all of which were taken seriously, to be investigated and discussed with at least two levels of police and the FDA. Burke commissioned his scientists at McNeil to work on ways of contaminating the tablets, which was the most common extortion threat, and one of his worst moments came when they reported that they had found one. But it involved the use of a hyperbaric chamber, which was not the sort of equipment a blackmailer was going to command.

"There are people out selling courses in crisis planning," Burke says, "on being prepared for contingencies. That's all bullshit. The fact is that in crisis situations people always behave better than you thought they would, and show greater foresight; and that's what pulls you through." What pulled Johnson & Johnson through its crisis with the news gatherers, however—and left the company with so high a reputation that the press reacted sorrowfully rather than savagely a few months later when another of its drugs, Zomax, turned out to be a menace for some users—was something rather deeper. I commented to Burke that I thought he had won his news media wars because he and his people had never publicly cried out at the injustice that had been visited upon them, never complained about the ordeal to which they were being subjected through no fault of their own. Burke was perplexed. "How could I have complained to the world that *I* was the victim?" he said. "Seven people were dead because they had taken my product."

2

On February 8, 1986, history recurred: that night, Diane Elsroth of Peekskill, New York, was dead at a friend's house in Yonkers, from a cyanide-contaminated Tylenol capsule. There were other brown, discolored capsules in the bottle. The Tylenol had been emptied out of them and a mixture of 60 percent potassium cyanide and 40 percent "inert materials" had been substituted. The word "Tylenol," broken by the two halves of the capsule, had been misaligned when the capsule was put together again. Once again much was made of the lot number, ADF 916.

The story broke on Monday, February 10. The FDA warned Yonkers residents not to take Extra-Strength Tylenol capsules; Westchester County embargoed their sale, and told people to return any capsules purchased in the last two months. A&P removed Tylenol capsules from its shelves through a twenty-six-state area. FDA agents seized all bottles of Tylenol capsules in stores within a one-mile radius of the drugstore where the contaminated capsules had been purchased. No other store had bottles from this lot, which had been manufactured in Fort Washington the previous May and shipped in August and pretty much sold out by February.

In New Brunswick, assistant p.r. director James Murray tried the tactic that had been avoided in 1982, announcing that if people had bought the bottle more than two weeks ago and the capsules were still intact, they had nothing to worry about. In Fort Washington, McNeil president Joseph Chiesa amended this statement to claim safety only after a full month. The wisdom of the original decision not to use this argument was then demonstrated when the FDA announced that, well, with this composition of potassium cyanide, which had a different "chemical profile" from the one used in Chicago, the capsule might not disintegrate for several months. That still exculpated capsules manufactured in May 1985, but now the story was *much* too complicated, and no further statements about the hydroscopic nature of cyanide were issued.

Larry Foster was on Captiva Island near Fort Myers, Florida, taking some time in the sun (and also talking to a *Wall Street Journal* reporter who had been trying to reach him for weeks to get comments on the similarities between the Tylenol tragedies and the *Challenger* disaster; Foster said he didn't think there were any). As he hung up from that call, he had another, from Murray, who had also been his source of the bad news the first time. And a few minutes later, he was on the phone with Burke.

Johnson & Johnson now knew all about cyanide and capsule contamination, and thought it knew all about the press. (This turned out not to be true: because the new Tylenol murder took place in a New York suburb, near the headquarters of the networks, the newsmagazines, the leading wire service and two of the three national newspapers, Foster felt that the pressure on him and his people for the week this story played near the top of the news was more intense and steady than it had been in 1982, when the story was really in Chicago and putatively widely diffused. The coverage of the second Tylenol poisoning, however, never achieved the dominating presence of its predecessor: it had happened before, it was a single, isolated case, and the victim's parents—her father was a state trooper—absolutely refused to be interviewed or to make public any information about their daughter.) Foster and Burke on the telephone worked up a statement that Johnson & Johnson would cooperate fully with the media and keep the public fully informed, and Foster got on the plane to return to New Jersey. There was little confusion this time, and Burke could get full value from the fact that Johnson & Johnson, with all its group presidents in the one starkly modern tower in New Brunswick, was equipped for fast reaction. The world was told that no crisis committee had been formed; a security analyst told the New York *Times* that "the company is indicating it does not anticipate a full-blown major recall."

Burke and Foster met much of Tuesday morning, and at noon they decided on an immediate news conference with Burke himself handling the questions. Between noon and four o'clock, AT&T and New Jersey Bell, working amidst one of the worst snowstorms New Jersey has ever known, set up a facility with 900 lines through which any news organization in the country could listen in, though only the reporters in attendance could ask questions. About seventy of them came, mostly from New York; something more than 700 of the call-in lines were used. Burke had relatively little news. The company had canceled all advertising for Tylenol until further notice. No decision had yet been made on whether Tylenol capsules should be recalled. The company was considering what to do next. Johnson & Johnson had never claimed that the new package was tamper-*proof*, though considerable ingenuity would have been required to violate it without leaving a telltale trace: there was a metallic seal on the mouth of the bottle and another red plastic seal molded to the cap and the bottle itself, and everything was in a glued box. Still, if J&J could put it together that way, someone with a little equipment presumably could restore the sealed appearance after contaminating the capsules.

Johnson & Johnson would of course cooperate with the investigators from the Westchester County district attorney's office who wished to inspect McNeil's Fort Washington plant, but had absolutely no reason to doubt its previous confidence that the contamination could not have occurred in the production process. J&J hoped that the FBI would enter the case (so did Carl Vergari, the Westchester County DA, whose budget would otherwise have been shot irremediably to hell). One aspect of the developing coverage of the story struck Burke as unfair, and he complained about it—the use of file footage from three and a half years before, especially footage showing supermarkets and drugstores emptying their shelves of Tylenol.

On Thursday, the news was bad: cyanide-contaminated capsules had turned up in another bottle, this one from lot AHA 90, manufactured in Puerto Rico the previous July. The bottle had been found on the shelves of the Woolworth's in Bronxville, next door to Yonkers. And this bottle was unopened and showed "no visible signs of tampering." In the case of the first bottle, J&J could feel if it could not say that the seals had in fact been removed from the bottle by the poisoner but the purchaser had not noticed. Now there was an intact bottle that a careful person could have opened without observing anything wrong—though the capsules themselves were obviously discolored, which presumably would have alerted a careful person that this stuff was dangerous. The fact that this lot had come from a different factory in a different month once again should have demonstrated that the contamination occurred on the shelf, and once again did not. DA Vergari revealed that the FBI had found no sign of tampering with the package, and announced that "in all likelihood, the probabilities are the contamination occurred sometime during the manufacturing process." Now the FBI came in with both hands, announcing that the case was being given its "highest priority."

Fourteen states banned the sale of Tylenol capsules. In Westchester itself, county supervisor Andrew O'Rourke, who would soon announce his candidacy for governor of New York State, banned the sale of all nonprescription capsules. Johnson & Johnson held another press conference with wires to all points in the country, and Burke said he still had no plans to recall nationwide. Ominously, the wire services and television news shows played up the fact that the product the year before had racked up $550 million in sales and $90 million in profits. But Burke's problem was more than money: some scores of his people had worked day and night to bring Tylenol capsules back to their leading status in the analgesics market. "They had built this business back from ashes," says Foster. "They had spent four years of time and energy and talent in rebuilding that product. It was a difficult decision to put them out of business." Burke reverted to the arguments the FDA had used against him in opposing the original recall: the Tylenol contaminations were "a national problem that affects everything people eat and drink"; to kill off Tylenol capsules would "remind the terrorist that he won." The terrorist reference was by no means unreasonable: in Westchester, especially in and around Brownsville, *all* shopping was down, as though someone had exploded a car bomb in the shopping center.

It was announced that the Illinois police had passed on to Westchester some six thousand names that had cropped up in connection with the 1982 poisonings, and that Westchester had said thanks a lot. There were new extortion stories—a twenty-two-year-old man out on bail after an arrest on credit-card fraud charges was arrested again for sending a letter demanding two million dollars from Johnson & Johnson. Copycat stories again came over the wires and onto the air. A medical technician in Texas dropped dead with Tylenol in his locker. Déjà vu was everywhere, but two incidents were novel both in substance and in their coverage. One was a man in Nashville who undoubtedly died of cyanide poisoning. He was a jeweler who bought cyanide to use in cleaning jewelry, and had bought a pound of it the day he died. (Reporters from the Nashville *Tennessean* rather than the police found the receipt for the purchase in his house, and were the first to inform J&J that Tylenol was not involved.) Why he committed suicide remained a mystery, as did the location of the block of cyanide, still very nearly a pound, he had just bought. The police dug up his garden pretty good, and couldn't find it.

The other story was far more sinister, not as an incident but in terms of the irresponsibility of the television news shows. A woman collapsed in a courtroom in downstate Missouri, remained in a coma, and was taken to Barnes Hospital in St. Louis. The next day, a source at the hospital seems to have tipped science reporter Lisa Allen of KTVI Channel 2, the ABC affiliate, that there had been Tylenol and Dexatrim capsules in the lady's purse; somebody remembered seeing her take a pill shortly before she collapsed; the doctors at Barnes were checking for possible cyanide poisoning; and the capsules had been turned over to the FDA. This ran on the five o'clock news: "Channel Two News has also learned," said anchorman Larry Connors, "that Food and Drug officials are investigating a [pause] *possible* case of cyanide poisoning that may involve Tylenol or Dexatrim capsules." By the six o'clock news this had become the lead item, presented as "what may be a case of cyanide poisoning that may involve Tylenol." Ms. Allen had conducted a telephone interview with Bill Grigg of the FDA, who said, "The woman is not dead and is not known to have taken cyanide or Tylenol." At ten o'clock, Ms. Allen was on with word that "the information is still rather sketchy. . . . What alerted local officials to the possibility of cyanide was the presence of Tylenol in her purse." A doctor at Barnes was interviewed and said, "We are running a number of tests, one of them a test for the presence of cyanide."

KMOX-TV Channel 4, the CBS affiliate (indeed, CBS owns it), had been beaten and was clearly not taking it lying down. Anchorman Julian Hunter opened the six o'clock news with word that "a downstate Missouri woman is unconscious in intensive care . . . and one of the suspected causes of her unconsciousness is some Tylenol capsules in her possession." NBC affiliate KSDK Channel 5 opened its peacock at six with news that a woman at Barnes Hospital was "apparently suffering from cyanide poisoning." That night at ten, reporter Al Naipo from Channel 5 did a stand-upper outside the hospital, and spiced it with the comment that the incident "raised the question: 'Can the deadly chemical be readily obtained?' " We then had a brief clip from an interview with "Rich Haunsom, pharmacist," behind his drugstore counter. He said cyanide was "not available at all through a pharmacy," and reporter Naipo echoed the fact that you can't buy cyanide at a pharmacy and returned us to the anchorman.

The next day, the woman died from her heart attack, hospital pathologists reported no unusual quantity of cyanide in her blood, the FDA lab in Kansas City said there was nothing wrong with the Tylenol or the Dexatrim capsules taken from her purse. In short, there was not and never had been a story. It's an interesting question whom to blame. Ms. Allen certainly had a right to offer the story to the scheduling meeting: it was not impossible that there was something to it. The Channel 2 news director cannot be faulted for putting it on the "maybe" list. The FDA *did* have possession of the capsules, and Grigg was willing to talk, though he added to his we're-looking-at-it statement a comment to the effect that, on the evidence from the hospital, the agency a couple of months earlier, before the Yonkers murder, would not have taken any interest in this woman's condition or what might have caused it. The easiest person to blame, of course, is the producer of that night's Channel 2 news, who made the decision to throw this nothing-ball at a nervous public. But the fact is that he's junior talent, and if he doesn't go with this story and the other local stations do, it may well be his ass. Nobody gets punished for zealousness.

The person who had what personal-injury law used to call "the last clear chance" to prevent the accident was the anchorman (on all three stations in this case it happens to have been a man). It's universally identified as "his" show; he gets the six-figure salary; he has to speak the misleading words. Except that he doesn't have to; he can always say, "What sort of crap is this?" and the whole make-believe structure of the phony story will vanish in a puff of smoke. But it's trouble, the reporter who has what story there is wants some airtime, the producer who wants to be sure nobody leaves him behind will protest bitterly, and after all, who cares? Who will remember? Not the least of Johnson & Johnson's contributions in the Tylenol matter is that the immense archive it built on the coverage of the story is available to improve, if anyone wishes to improve it, the institutional memory of the news gatherers.

A week after the death in Yonkers first reached the airwaves, Burke had a third and last press conference. The company would stop offering proprietary medicines in capsules, would offer everyone with a bottle of Tylenol capsules a replacement bottle of Tylenol "caplets" (tablets in capsule shape, introduced as a backup after the first incident), and would take a charge of between $100 million and $150 million against 1986 income. Capsules were relatively easy to contaminate; caplets were all but impregnable, though nobody wished to issue challenges. Consumer survey data after this episode were very different from what they had been in 1982: now that murder had struck again, people were *not* confident about the product. Though the FBI on closer examination did find that the Yonkers and Bronxville Tylenol bottles had in fact been opened and resealed (finally: "It was tremendous news for us," says Larry Foster), the public remained in a sour mood. An attempt to bring back Tylenol capsules this time would yield at least as much resentment as admiration, and much less gratitude from users. "When you're on a pedestal," says Foster, "there's a great danger that you'll be knocked off it."

As a personal matter, Burke was horrified that his product had once again become a murder weapon, and troubled by the farfetched but inescapable thought that if he hadn't rescued Tylenol in 1982 this girl might still be alive. On February 19, he was at the National Press Club for a big businessmen's conference with President Reagan (who, ever the opportunist when there's something nice to be said, departed from his prepared remarks to praise Burke for his handling of the Tylenol crisis), and a reporter (ever the opportunist in looking for something nasty) asked him whether he was sorry now that he hadn't stopped making capsules in 1982, and Jim Burke replied, "Yes, indeed I am."

Once again, of course, his instincts were correct. The Proprietary Association assembled again and noted that Johnson & Johnson had its own troubles, but that the public still liked to take proprietary drugs in capsules (thought they went down easier, and were more like "real" medicines). Tylenol's competitors continued to make headache remedies in capsule form until June 1986, when two people in Seattle suburbs died from cyanide in Excedrin and cyanide-contaminated bottles of Anacin III were found on drugstore shelves, and that was an end to it. The people who committed random murders through Tylenol capsules would no doubt find some other vehicle, but the death-dealing headache remedy would become unimaginable once again.

3

In Chicago, the story of the original seven Tylenol killings played out as a local murder mystery without a solution. Everyone continued to hold his pet theory: the FBI thought it was urban terrorism but the terrorist lost his nerve in the face of the uproar; the Chicago police feel it was a single specific murder covered over by the planting of additional poisons; a school of thought at Johnson & Johnson holds that it was a group of heartless young people who made a killing in the options market (for the stock dropped eight points before beginning to recover, giving put options, options to sell at a fixed price, a value about twenty times what a buyer would have paid for them the day before the story broke; it has to be young people, in this theory, because the trading in puts in the stock doesn't show enough activity to reward an adult). Medical examiner Stein says the poisoner will never be found: "He's dead, a suicide, having committed the perfect crime." "Son of a gun," said Richard Koziol of the *Tribune. "I* told *him* that." Koziol himself thinks there is an outside chance that the crime itself was the purest and most brainless of copycat actions. "Nobody ever published anything about it, because there was so much else to write, but a few weeks before there had been a TV show, *Hart to Hart,* in which a guy was killed by substituting poison for medicine in some capsules he was taking for heart disease."

When the searchlight moves about society looking for behavior to highlight in connection with so prominent an event, it picks up peculiarities that would never otherwise be noted—and stimulates very strange actions.

One day the news was dominated by the tale of two Kane County sheriff's deputies who had found the parking lot of a Howard Johnson's littered with broken Tylenol capsules and the resulting powder; they had touched it and gone home feeling sick, and cyanide can be absorbed through the skin. On another day there was a poor black hospital orderly who had been fired and tried to extort $8,000 from the hospital by threatening to contaminate the Tylenol; he was caught, quickly, because he had been visiting a friend who was a patient in the hospital and had asked her how to spell "cyanide," and she told the police. Three additional bottles of cyanide-contaminated Tylenol turned up, one for sale in a drugstore in Schaumburg Plaza, the nation's largest shopping center, two because people had turned them in to the police as part of a well-publicized drive by the task force to accumulate possible evidence. One of the two was handed in by a man whose signature on the receipt was illegible; nobody ever found out who it was. The other came from a woman who was identified as the wife of a state judge who was in fact living with another woman, and it took a while to untangle that.

WLS-TV got a much-admired scoop on nutty procedures at the medical examiner's office, where bottles that had been turned in were being handled in ways that would make them useless as evidence if it turned out they contained cyanide. ("They were liquefying the contents and sniffing them," Fahner says disgustedly. "Good way to get sick.") But there was never any real hope that there would be fingerprints on the capsules themselves, for anyone handling cyanide would necessarily use rubber gloves. At one point the investigators held the hope that they could "fingerprint" the potassium cyanide itself, tracing it back to its origin and thus creating a lead to a killer with access to this batch of poison. The FDA laboratory in Cincinnati set up to perform such tests, and Fahner's group gathered up the evidence. "They wanted to keep it secret," says FDA research director Joseph Hile. "If we could have traced the cyanide back to the person who put it in, they didn't want him to know. They had some samples, and arranged for one of our investigators to drive them down to Cincinnati with a screaming motorcycle escort on the Interstate. You don't do that sort of thing unobserved." But potassium cyanide is potassium cyanide, and it's too widely available; the newspapers grumbled editorially about the need for controls on the sale of poisons.

One vicious oddity remained in the news for months. The *Tribune* had the story first, from a source inside the Continental Illinois bank. Johnson & Johnson had received an extortion letter from a man who demanded that a million dollars be paid into a bank account with a specified number if the company wished to "stop the killing." The letter had been sent from New York to the J&J branch in Massachusetts, and had kicked around the corporation's internal mail for several days until a clerk noted that the envelope contained a reference to Tylenol. The bank number was that of an account owned by Frederick M. McCahey, a businessman and socialite, who had recently suffered some reverses, as they say, in his business ventures. He woke up in the morning to find police cars all over his driveway, and he had a miserable day in a precinct house.

This story was highly implausible: it was hard to imagine anyone demanding that extortion payments be made to an account that would be automatically traced—and in any event the account had recently been closed. What developed, after two days of checking around, was that McCahey had owned a travel agency that went bust, and had failed to give his employees severance pay. One of them, a woman who had made the deposits and thus knew the account number, was the wife of an accountant named Robert Richardson, a literate fellow who a few months before had contributed an op-ed piece to the *Tribune*. Richardson, who had since left Chicago, apparently with his wife, was not to be found; the police hypothesized that he had sent the letter as revenge. But they still wanted to talk to him: he was the closest thing to a real, live suspect that they had.

Then the police learned that "Richardson" was really James W. Lewis, a known sociopath from Kansas City, who had been charged there with a murder. Fahner announced a nationwide manhunt, and in Texas a woman whose son was the spit and image of the pictures of Lewis grievingly turned him in. In fact, however, Lewis was known to be in New York, whence he was sending a stream of letters to the *Tribune*. The letters indicated that he was reading the paper, and the FBI asked the *Tribune* to supply the list of outlets where it could be bought in New York; a little reluctantly, the *Tribune* complied. But staking out the newsstands did not produce Lewis. Editor James Squires suggested that maybe Lewis was using the public library, and there, indeed, the FBI found him. Score one for the press.

Lewis, it turned out, had written letters elsewhere, too, including one to the White House, threatening to bomb the place with model airplanes packed with plastic explosives and launched from the Mall with remote control. J&J's Foster recalls a sidebar from the Lewis matter as the one time he deliberately did not tell the truth to a reporter. AP's James Litke called from Chicago late at night and said, "What the hell is the Secret Service doing at the Tylenol Task Force?" Foster says, "As it happens, the FBI had told us, but they had pledged us to silence. I said I didn't know."

In June 1984, a federal court sentenced Lewis to ten years in prison for his monstrous practical joke in Chicago, a sentence that seems heavy by comparison with what the courts give armed robbers and rapists until one considers the desirability of having the Lewises of this world behind bars. U.S. Attorney Daniel K. Webb at the sentencing hearing insisted that this proceeding closed out the Tylenol case. Lewis' admission that he had sent the letter, he said, "is a confession that he did the Tylenol murders." But Webb is alone in that belief.

In West Bend, Wisconsin, state legislator James R. Lewis woke up the morning after James W. Lewis was arrested, and found his picture in the early edition of the *Wisconsin State Journal* as the Tylenol extortionist. The second edition had the right picture, and the next day's paper carried a correction, but Representative Lewis sued anyway. This may be an extreme version of the recent American insistence that bad luck must be made illegal and punishable, or it may be a reasonable response by a man who really was held up to hatred, ridicule and contempt, however briefly. In 1986 (the law's delays), Dane County circuit judge Michael Torphy found that because James R. Lewis was a public figure he had to prove actual malice by the newspaper before he could win a libel case. This may be an example of the Dickensian comment that the law is a ass, or it may be a natural induction from the fact that James R. Lewis himself had voluntarily done things that put his photograph in the files of the *Wisconsin State Journal.*

For the press, the moral question raised by the investigation of the Tylenol case was the identification of those caught in the enormous dragnet laid throughout the Chicago area. (It is by no means certain, of course, that the killer had remained in Chicago after planting the contaminated capsules.) "I'll tell you a cute story," says medical examiner Stein. "The *Sun-Times* carried a full front-page picture from the surveillance camera at the Walgreen's where the Prince girl bought her Tylenol. It showed a man with a beard, and a blonde beside him buying a box of Tylenol. I teach a class in pathology at the medical school. A student came up to me after a lecture and said, 'Do you know me?' I said, 'You're in the class here.' He said, 'I'm also the man in the picture on the front page of the *Sun-Times.* ' " The same picture, appropriately blown up, led the *CBS Evening News* with Dan Rather.

More than two hundred people were questioned by the police in connection with the Tylenol murders, and the reporters' contacts in the police departments supplied many of the names. To the annoyance of his staff, *Tribune* editor James Squires set a policy of refusing to print such names (he was also reluctant to name the stores where the contaminated Tylenol had been bought). "They were questioning everybody who moved," Squires says. "They were desperate." But the *Sun-Times* was less scrupulous, and the television stations were unrestrained. At one point, Chicago police superintendent Richard Brceczk felt it necessary to make a statement that his own definition of a "suspect" would be "someone against whom the police have tangible evidence." A couple in Wheeling, Illinois, sent a letter to all the Chicago and suburban papers:

> We wish to state that our son, Kevin, recently wanted for questioning by the Tylenol Task Force, has been absolutely cleared in every way of any involvement or suspicion in the matter.
>
> Journalism, as practiced today, apparently sees more reader entertainment value in leaving an issue in the shadow of doubt and suspicion than in reporting facts in the Light of Truth. Indeed, a statement is as necessary now as it was when the initial injustice was done through "trial by media and guilty until proven innocent" since some major papers report dropping of marijuana

charges but leave room for doubt in regard to the Tylenol situation. Therefore, we wish it made eminently clear that our son has answered all questions and been totally cleared in every way regarding the Tylenol investigations.

This letter does nothing to counteract the great volume of extremely negative and harmful publicity to which our family was subjected. By comparison, it stands as a sad but true example of the helplessness of innocent individuals in the face of powerful media coverage. . . .

Most papers printed the letter. It was interesting.

One genuine suspect did turn up: an odd fish named Roger Arnold (this name the *Tribune* printed), who was linked to the case through a chain of circumstance. He had been a dockhand for Jewel Food Stores, through which several of the hot bottles had been distributed. He knew the father of one of the victims. He was tattooed with Satanic and other deathly symbols. Someone who had worked with him when he was a bartender told the police that his apartment was full of poisons and books of instructions on how to use them. The police raided, and found a horrifying kitchen laboratory, and a dog-eared book that included a chapter on how to put poison in capsules. Among the vials was one that apparently contained cyanide (the contents were reported as sodium cyanide, rather than potassium cyanide, but no matter; later it developed that it was really a nontoxic household cleansing agent). He had fled Chicago, and when he was picked up in Florida he had an airplane ticket to Thailand in his pocket. But there was nothing whatever to tie him to the poisoned Tylenol; in fact, he had not been in Chicago on the day when, by all logical deduction, the boxes had been planted on the store shelves.

Arnold brooded over his treatment, and from the newspaper reports made his own determination of which of the men who had worked with him as a bartender was the villain who had turned him in. He killed the man. It was the wrong man. "People talk about seven victims of the Tylenol murder," says Koziol of the *Tribune.* "I like to say there were eight."

But there were of course many more than eight who suffered, including a number picked out at random by the searchlight of news. Among these might be included a woman who was living with the bartender Arnold killed, and continued to occupy the apartment. "We put in the address of the dead man as a matter of routine," says editor James Squires. "Every time we repeated the address that woman came home and found people, curiosity seekers, waiting to badger her. I made fifteen speeches to tell people to purge that address, but when we did our magazine piece on the anniversary of the murders, there it was again." Because she had been living with a man falsely suspected as a stool pigeon by a man falsely accused of the Tylenol murders, this woman had become a celebrity.

There is a price paid for a free and untrammeled press. The people who pay it are selected in a kind of reverse lottery. Very little can be done about this.

Part Three

ON THE AIR

7

The Invention of Broadcast News

. . . the first morning out of Yokohama coming out of my cabin, I was handed the day's bulletin of wireless news. I unfolded the typewritten sheet and read: "Mrs. X, of Los Angeles, girl wife of Dr. X, aged 79, has been arrested for driving her automobile along the railroad track, whistling like a locomotive." This piece of information had been transmitted through the ethereal holes between the molecules of air. From a broadcasting station more than five thousand miles away, it had come to our ship in rather less time than it would have taken the sound of my voice to travel from one end of the promenade deck to the other. The labours of half a dozen men of genius, of hundreds of patient and talented investigators, had gone to creating and perfecting the means for achieving this miracle. . . . The ether reverberated with the name of Mrs. X. The wave that bore it broke against the moon and the planets, and rippled on towards the stars and the ultimate void. Faraday and Clerk Maxwell had not lived in vain.

. . . I took the liveliest interest in young Mrs. X. After being arrested for whistling like a locomotive—whether by means of an instrument or with the unaided vocal cords was never made clear—she was bailed out of prison by her husband, the aged doctor. The time came for the hearing of her case. Mrs. X told the doctor that she proposed to forfeit her (or rather his) recognizances and run away. The doctor protested. Mrs. X then began to smash the furniture. The aged doctor telephoned for the police; they came, and Mrs. X was rearrested on charges of assault. We on the Pacific waited in a dreadful suspense. A few days later, as we were crossing the hundred and eightieth meridian, we learned to our profound relief that a reconciliation had taken place. Aged Dr. X had withdrawn his charge; the girl wife had gone home quietly. What happened about the whistling business we never learned. The anonymous powers which purvey wireless news are strangely capricious. The name of Mrs. X no longer rippled out towards Aldebaran and the spiral nebulae. In the next morning's bulletin there was a little paragraph announcing the declaration of the General Strike. And Bebe Daniels had fallen off her horse and received contusions.

–Aldous Huxley, 1926[1]

If you want it to be unique, it has to be at least a little unusual.

–William S. Paley,
remembering advice given him by his
promotion director Lou Dorfman. It
should be noted that Huxley's comments
were published two years before Paley acquired
his first interests in broadcasting.

1

The miracle of broadcast is the live event, the accurate if not necessarily truthful simulacrum of something that is happening, as it is happening. There is some question as to whether the event, put on the airwaves in sound or sound-and-picture, qualifies as "news." John Chancellor, for one, says it does not, that a report becomes "news" only on the intermediation of a "trained intelligence," and that some other word should be found for, say, the television hour exposing the President's State of the Union message as delivered to the houses of Congress and the diplomatic corps, cabinet officers and Supreme Court justices, the top-level official Washington community. You, too, are there. At its worst, it's more entertaining than reading the speech in the newspaper.

And on consideration—I was not always of this view—I think it's news. For our purposes here, the radio announcer who sets the scene and the cameraman who points the camera and zooms the lens are sufficient intermediation. It is the decision to devote the airtime on this frequency to this event that is crucial; the act of broadcasting makes the event "news." The world really did change when AT&T put together the first radio network to carry the inaugural address of Calvin Coolidge, calming the nation after the death of Warren Harding in 1923. Those of us who were young in the 1930s remember the surreal experience of the loudspeaker presenting the unique voice of Adolf Hitler far away haranguing the crowds at Nuremberg while H. V. Kaltenborn in a New York studio, hearing what we were hearing, delivered a translation over the steaming calls of *"Sieg Heil!"* from the audience.

There has to be something really happening. William S. Paley, creator if not founder of CBS and for more than half a century its *líder máximo,* a few years ago remembered a conversation with Harry Hopkins, Franklin Roosevelt's resident adviser, in spring of 1940: "Hopkins said that instead of going around the country the President wanted to make his political speeches from the White House. 'What do you think?' I said, 'It's a bad idea —crowd reaction is very important in the impact of a speech. People cheering and going whoopee make the speech exciting.' Hopkins picked up the phone and said, 'Get me Madison Square Garden' for this date and that date." Even then, almost half a century ago, political campaigning was best conducted in large part by the creation of events for broadcast. Ronald Reagan, an apt student of the Roosevelt tradition, did well with his weekly Saturday noon radio talks, timed to catch the earliest bulldog editions of the Sunday newspaper, because he has superbly developed his original talents as a radio announcer—but when it came time to campaign he generated "events." By contrast, Jimmy Carter steadily lost ground in the first months of 1980 because his Rose Garden campaign confused exploitable events with photo opportunities.

The supremacy of events is of course a function of their currency. Among the factors that made the American Civil War different from all previous wars—more political, more subject to flows of enthusiasm and despair on both sides—was the existence of the telegraph, the possibility of getting reports out to the governments, and to the public, in a matter of hours (sometimes minutes) rather than days. The rapidity of the reporting (and the Brady photographs) gave a new cast to the relationship between a wartime government and its people, though the collapse of the South in 1865 has come to mask from historians the extreme unpopularity of the war in the North and the electoral peril to Lincoln in 1864. Yet even this quantum jump was smaller than the leap from the telegraphed reports of World War I to Ed Murrow's live radio transmissions of the bombing of London in World War II, to the instant real blood-real guts-live sound that poured out of Vietnam to a consuming public in what television critic Michael Arlen called "the living room war." You are there. Damned unpleasant it is, too.

Murrow, incidentally, had also pioneered that. Going to Korea, he insisted on a "single system" camera that would catch sound as well as sight, something then very rare (all feature films and most newsreels were done with sound track added later), and very expensive in terms of extra personnel (partly because two different unions were involved: the "behind the panel" crew for CBS Television were members of the International Brotherhood of Electrical Workers, and the men who manned the single-system cameras were members of the International Association of Theatrical and Stage Employees, and all the cutting had to be done twice). There were twenty CBS people on the plane that went to Korea; "money," said William Paley, remembering not without affection all the years with Murrow and his sidekick producer Fred Friendly, "meant nothing to these fellows."

But the result was that viewers would hear the thud of real artillery and the screams of real rockets as the background to Murrow's interviews. Palmer Williams, an affable young veteran of Frank Capra's wartime film unit and John Houseman's Media Productions who organized all the details for Murrow's *See It Now,* from locations to equipment and personnel—and who later made *60 Minutes* possible as the number-two man on executive producer Don Hewitt's table of organization—remembered that "there were a number of things Murrow and Friendly had done on radio that they wanted to do on film. I'd think of a dozen reasons why it wouldn't work, and then we'd do it. I'd looked at a million feet of war film," Williams added, "but I'd never heard the real sound of the battle; it added a whole dimension to what people had done before. You'd see Murrow talking with a guy at a gun, and there would be a whump-whump-whump sound in the background. Murrow would jump and say, 'What's that?' and the boy would say, 'Oh, that's outgoing'—and you'd believe it."

Broadcasting made a great difference in the relations between the providers and the consumers of news. "When Damon Runyon and Paul Gallico started writing about the World Series," says Walter Mears of the AP, "they wrote for people in New York who first heard about it when they read what Runyon and Gallico wrote. In those days, people saw the world through the eyes of reporters. Now they see it with their own eyes, and they argue with the reporters." Not when the subject is Tylenol, of course: that was a "tell" story that left television producers scrambling for symbolic pictures. Not when it's the budget, because nobody can visualize the budget. Not when it's crime stories, because the camera gets there long after the crime. Indeed, people can argue with the reporter from what they consider their experience only in sports; space shots and moon walks (a rare situation where the news consumer and the reporter have in fact seen precisely the same thing); national rituals like State of the Union messages and conventions (where the public, if it cares, is probably better placed than any single reporter to know what is going on); election debates (which the news organizations now cover with two reports, one from someone in the hall and one from someone watching the screen); storms, maybe fires, earthquakes (the most spectacular news television I ever saw was the early-morning coverage of the Los Angeles earthquake of 1971 by the KTLA helicopter—the zoom lens revealing the cracks in the dam, the death of a pickup truck under a collapsed freeway bridge, the horror of the rubble that had been the wing of a hospital, all shown to us in the early-morning light while the ground was still rumbling and bouncing under our feet). But Mears is right, anyway: once the public has seen and heard the actors, the reporter's freedom to depict them is much restrained. By 1986, the Washington press corps almost without exception was awfully tired of Ronald Reagan, and it didn't matter.

This is not to say that the press is always right in its judgments of individuals. Elliot Richardson, talking about the Washington reporters while Nixon's Secretary of Health, Education and Welfare, made an analogy with his experience in basic training in World War II. He and six others from various parts of the country, various ethnic and educational backgrounds, various walks of life, were put into the same tent, "and we had to assign each other a personality that first day. We did, and we all kept those personalities for thirteen weeks, whether or not they had anything to do with reality." That's right: the heroes very rarely become villains in Washington (viz., for example, Congressman Richard Cheney, whose deep involvement in aspects of Watergate as a member of the Nixon staff was barely noticed because everybody liked him), and the villains never become heroes, because all information about their activities filters through the unchanging screen of a distrusted personality.

Public perception of personalities observed through the television tube is wildly unreliable, however, and reporters even when stuck with their first constructs are likely to have a much better fix on personal qualities—and the corrective can be important. Unlike Richardson's fellow dogfaces, politicians usually turn up for impalement in a reporter's butterfly collection only after they have been around for a while: the reporter can often make his judgments on better criteria than instant comfort. It is not true that no man is a hero to his valet, and in the choice of political leadership it is important to know what those who have observed the candidate at close quarters think about him. Reporters can find this out, while those who make contact with the individual through "direct experience" on broadcast channels simply cannot. The Gary Hart that voters perceived on their television screens in March 1984 was significantly different from the fellow the Senate staffs (those ultimate valets of the powerful) had watched at work on Capitol Hill, and it was not the least contribution of the press to the 1984 election that this difference was revealed.

"I did a piece on Frank Sinatra," Andy Rooney said, thinking back to the days when he was just a writer for the on-camera people. "He can disprove every detail, make even me believe that he really didn't punch that *Daily News* guy in the mouth. But the truth is that the impression the public has of Sinatra, through the media, is more accurate than the image Sinatra has of himself."

2

It did not happen all at once. Coolidge's inaugural was a service and a novelty, but not, given Coolidge, anything that was talked about. A year later, however, live coverage generated a gag line of the sort that flies about the nation. "The embattled Democrats," Frederick Lewis Allen wrote, "met at Madison Square Garden in New York to pick a standard-bearer, and the deadlock between the hosts of McAdoo and the hosts of Al Smith lasted day after day after day, and millions of Americans heard through loudspeakers the lusty cry of 'Alabama, twenty-four votes for Underwoo—ood'—and discovered that a political convention could be a grand show to listen to and that a seat by the radio was as good as a ticket to the Garden."[2] (The nomination eventually went to none of these, but to the conservative lawyer

John W. Davis.) The year 1924 was one of mild recession in the general progress of the economy through that decade, but sales of radios rose by more than 250 percent, the greatest gain ever, because everybody was talking about the broadcasts from the convention. (At least, that's what Allen says; one should probably remember also that 1924 was the year of the introduction of Armstrong's superheterodyne radio, a better mousetrap.) The first really giant audience—the broadcasters claimed forty million listeners—was for a blow-by-blow account of the Dempsey-Tunney rematch in Chicago in 1927; five people died from heart attacks, we are told, when the referee gave the prostrate Tunney a thirteen-second long count and let him rise to fight again, and win.

Broadcasting in those days created "news" events: a first broadcast from a train in motion, from a parachute jumper leaving an aircraft, from Antarctica, from the floor of the U.S. Senate (from which radio remained okay, but television was barred until June 1986). Things became events simply because they were broadcast; people were eager to hear the voices of the famous in their own living rooms, and broadcasters competed to be the first to present some banal statement actually spoken by the King of England, the Pope, Mussolini (in heavily accented English) or Mahatma Gandhi. This was checkbook journalism: the broadcasters paid for the speech, as a lyceum might pay for a lecture. In 1932, Cesar Saerchinger, representing the Columbia Broadcasting System in Europe, arranged a fifteen-minute talk by the rising German politico Adolf Hitler, to cost CBS $1,500; but New York cabled back: "Unwant Hitler at any price." In 1933, CBS paid Mrs. Wiley Post for the right to be beside her with an open mike at the airport when her husband came down from his round-the-world flight.

It was important that these things were live, and came mostly by shortwave radio, the crackle of the atmosphere in the loudspeaker. They had to be live: well into the 1930s, the Federal Radio Commission had a rule (it seems very strange today) against playing recordings over the air "except in smaller towns and farming communities." "The public in large cities," the Commission wrote, "can easily purchase and use phonograph records of the ordinary commercial type."[3] The first network broadcast of a recording presenting a news event was NBC's use of Herbert A. Morrison's famous description ("Oh, the humanity . . . Oh, this is horrible . . .") of the burning of the dirigible *Hindenburg* on its arrival at Lakehurst.

Shortwave was especially important because federal rules prohibited the use of ordinary telephone lines for broadcast purposes: the networks could lease exclusive lines in advance for scheduled events or for the purpose of linking their studios and transmitters with those of their affiliates, but they could not broadcast phone calls. A telephone interview on an all-news radio station is still called "a beeper," from the requirement imposed by the Federal Communications Commission, after the old prohibition lapsed, that any phone conversation being recorded or broadcast must carry a periodic signal to alert those on the line. Recording telephone conversations without informing your interlocutor that you are doing so is still in theory prohibited unless you have a court order (in fact the widespread use of telephone answering machines, which will also record conversations at the push of a button, has made the prohibition nugatory), but the law no longer imposes a mechanical signaling device.

The fact that people were used to getting their broadcast news in the form of live events ultimately encouraged a great deal of fakery. Starting with *The March of Time* in 1931, all the networks offered dramatizations of news stories, using actors' voices to speak words put in the mouths of real persons who had participated in a real incident. (The modern "docudramas" on TV are by no means the novelty both their proponents and their critics seem to believe.) After *The March of Time* moved to NBC, CBS produced its own version, called *Report to the Nation;* and during the war CBS supplemented the work of its large staff of broadcast reporters with dramatized scenes from the fighting under the title *Dateline.*

The popularity and credibility of this sort of program were horrifyingly demonstrated when John Houseman and Orson Welles used the technique in 1938 for a radio play based on H. G. Wells's *The War of the Worlds,* and roused through the country the panicked belief that the Martians had invaded New Jersey. Davidson Taylor, a lanky, serious-minded upper-class mountaineer who had been hired away from the Louisville *Courier-Journal* and its station WHAS to read news bulletins on CBS, had advanced to the job of program producer and was in charge of this show. (Years later he would serve, briefly, as vice president for CBS News and public affairs, and become the first though not the last person in that sort of job to quit because a management reorganization took away his access to top management and made him just someone else who reported to the man responsible for entertainment.) The radio play had worried him a little, for all its obvious fantasy, and he had ordered the elimination of real scientific institutes and cities in New Jersey, a frail reed that collapsed entirely when actor Kenneth Delmar (later Fred Allen's Senator Claghorn) read the script's despairing call for calm in a voice admittedly a little like Franklin Roosevelt's.

Such incidents always have consequences, but the times determine what the consequences will be. Today the felt need would be to make sure that the purity of news was insulated from the contamination of entertainment, and all news dramatizations would be forbidden (except, of course, for the historical "docudrama," which is not news, and which sells tickets). Then the felt need was to insulate entertainment from the frightfulness of reality, and the prohibition imposed was against the use in entertainment shows of any format that might be mistaken for news. A residue remains: the horizontal trailer of text running at the bottom of a picture is still reserved for news announcements, and use of it for any other purpose would be violently opposed at all the networks. The sales department can sell just about anything at a network an advertiser might wish to buy, but not a text crawling on the bottom of the screen.

3

To speak of radio news in the years between 1929 and the war is to speak of CBS. For David Sarnoff, president of RCA and guru of what were then the two NBC networks, radio was a "Music Box" and a didactic tool when the music stopped. A Russian immigrant as a boy, and one of the great beneficiaries of the public's hunger for news—he got his start as the hero who stayed seventy-two hours at his earphones atop the John Wanamaker building to catch from the air the feeble telegraphic signals that told of the fate of the *Titanic* and its passengers—Sarnoff was self-taught, reverent of education, worshipful of science. NBC would eventually have newsmen as president, which no other network has ever done (first it was Robert Kintner, formerly a partner in column writing with Joseph Alsop, then Julian Goodman, a soft-spoken, thoughtful veteran of the network's own news service), but it was cultural affairs that really excited Sarnoff. During his lifetime, while CBS made the reputation of its television news with Ed Murrow's *See It Now*, NBC produced programs about Vincent van Gogh, Michelangelo, the treasures of the Louvre, etc. In the late 1920s and early 1930s, as CBS built an independent news service, Sarnoff plumped for good music (live, remember, not on records: NBC after the mid-1930s had its own symphony, with Arturo Toscanini as its conductor), and on the news front made do with whatever his program director, A. A. Schechter, came up with. In the time when the wire services would not serve broadcasters and newspapers refused the networks the right to quote from their stories, Schechter in NBC's new offices in Radio City clipped and had announcers read stories from London newspapers, and checked domestic events by telephone calls from "the office of Lowell Thomas at the National Broadcasting Company."

Broadcast news, as distinguished from the presentation of a live event, can probably be said to begin with election night of 1928, when Ted Husing posted himself in the newsroom of the old New York *World* and between musical selections from a live election night concert reported to listeners of CBS stations on the progress of the ballot count as communicated by the wire services. Adding up the totals himself with pencil and paper, he called Hoover's victory long before a newspaper went on sale with the story.

This was probably Husing's idea: he was among the century's most successful devotees of the faith that if you have enough brass you don't need much gold. Paley, acquiring the year-old Columbia Broadcasting System in 1928, found as president Major J. Andrew White, whose introduction to broadcasting had come in 1921, when with David Sarnoff at his side he had spoken for an audience assembled in theaters in the New York metropolitan area a blow-by-blow account of the Dempsey-Charpentier fight in Boyle's Thirty Acres in Jersey City.[4] This had made White, previously a magazine editor, a professional sportscaster. When Arthur Judson, a concert manager of classical conductors, pianists and violinists, started a radio network as a means of employment for his artists, he took White with him to diversify the product. White had hired Husing to be his office manager. "He had no idea how to manage an office," Paley wrote in his memoirs. "He drove me crazy, giving me wrong answers to everything." Then White called in sick on a day when he was to broadcast a football game, and Paley sent Husing, who claimed to have done some local sports broadcasting at some point in his history, to call the game. "I lost an impossible office manager and gained the best and most famous sportscaster in the country."[5] There was at that point no news staff; the election was a month or so after Husing's debut as a sportscaster; one suspects that Husing inserted himself into the news picture for election night. Clearly, it wasn't Paley's idea, for his memoirs don't mention it.[6]

By 1932, technology had made radio a ponderable force in the organization of American politics. CBS used page boys with lapel mikes to pick up speeches and balloting on the floor of the Chicago conventions of that year, to such effect that the organizers of the Democratic convention piped the broadcasts back into the hall through the public-address system. For election night that year, CBS canceled all normal network programming to permit continuous reporting of results from wire service bulletins, which were ripped from the machines and read by announcers usually employed to introduce musical performances. (But the news that drew the largest audiences that year was something very different and very awful: the deathwatch at the Lindbergh house after the kidnapping of the Lindbergh baby. CBS emptied its New York studios to send announcers to the great zoo of a journalistic encampment around Lindbergh's house, to talk with police and state troopers and neighbors in New Brunswick and Trenton and Hopewell, and keep the story on the air. NBC at first refused to broadcast a word of it; Sarnoff, to his credit or otherwise as the reader may judge, wished to respect the Lindberghs' privacy and rigorously avoid interfering with the efforts to get the baby back.) Roosevelt's inauguration the next March was covered by no fewer than fifteen CBS announcers; Husing boasted that somebody with a CBS mike in his hand had kept Roosevelt in sight that day from the moment he woke up until after the end of the Inaugural Ball. H. V. Kaltenborn rode in the inaugural parade in a car equipped with a shortwave radio set. The network presented nothing else all day.

Many years later, critics of broadcast news would make the point that it offered only a "headline service," and Richard Salant while president of CBS News would have the script of a Cronkite half-hour news show set in

New York *Times*-style type to show that it occupied less than two-thirds of the front page alone. But the wordage of the CBS coverage of Roosevelt's first inaugural (and of the six-hour coronation ceremonies of King George VI of England in 1938, and of the Apollo moon landing thirty-one years later) was substantially greater than all the stories printed on that subject in any one newspaper, including the *Times*. When its masters wish it to do so, broadcasting can provide a more extensive as well as a more rapid service than the press. The nation could more easily have done without newspapers than without television in the aftermath of the Kennedy assassination. Most of the time, of course, broadcasting has no desire to provide such a service, because the minute-by-minute material is of inherently limited interest, and audiences are discouraged by the slow time scale on which the real world plays. And while a story only 5 percent of the audience wishes to read can be a valid—indeed, vital—part of the newspaper coverage of an important event, and may enhance the value of the paper, a broadcast episode that turns off 95 percent of the audience is a catastrophe.

People who write about these matters are expected to chastise the broadcasters for their unwillingness to expose viewers to sufficient reality. Toward the end of the Eisenhower era, which history records as an island of relative calm in this agitated century, Edward Murrow in a speech to the Radio and Television News Directors Association said that the future would look upon the television of the 1950s as "evidence of decadence, escapism and insulation from the realities of the world in which we live. . . . Here you will find only fleeting and spasmodic reference to the fact that this nation is in mortal danger."[7] Murrow chaired an annual New Year's Day roundup by CBS senior correspondents on the preceding year's news, under the unvarying program title *Year of Crisis;* it is an occupational deformity of the news business. But people do not live in worldwide crises; they live, as Thoreau pointed out, in quiet desperation from which worldwide crises can be only an occasional distraction. They place a rather low ceiling on how much time they wish to devote to televised reality. In 1967, when something really was happening at the Security Council debate on how to stop the Arab-Israeli war, the three television networks together, all on the air live from the Council chamber, had a lower share of audience in New York (where lots of people care deeply about what happens in an Arab-Israeli war) than reruns of Alfred Hitchcock thrillers on an independent station. In the immortal words of the late Sol Hurok: "If people don't want to come, nothing can stop them."

A more interesting question is whether or not the owners of the stations that broadcast CBS's full day of Roosevelt coverage wanted to turn over all their time to the inauguration. The fact is that nobody asked them; as broadcasting had developed in the United States, they had no choice. Networks were not program services from which individually owned "affili-ated" stations bought material; they were purchasers of time from the stations, with the aim of reselling that time to national advertisers at a markup. Usually, the advertiser bought the network time itself and then produced his own program to be broadcast at that time by all the local stations that were members of the network. Sometimes, however (especially on a relatively weak radio network like the early CBS), the network sold the advertiser a package of the time and the program to fill it. If the network could sell a program to an advertiser in those days, whether it was a news program, an event, a concert or a comic, the network could commandeer from its affiliates ("option" was the term of art) the time and the facilities to broadcast it. Today, largely as the result of government intervention—an intervention widely if imprudently supported by liberals seeking to reduce the baleful influence of the networks—the stations have much greater power to reject network sales and put on their own programs, which greatly limits what network news divisions will try to do.

Howard K. Smith, who worked at CBS from 1940 to 1961, when he left in anger, once said that CBS "came out so far ahead of everybody else in news . . . by accident." This is (was intended to be) a little unfair, for without Paley's willingness to commit resources and his pride in being the boss of men like Elmer Davis and Ed Murrow, the leadership CBS achieved in broadcast news could not have been accomplished. But the man who did the work and set the pattern was Edward Klauber, who signed on to be Paley's assistant in 1929 and a year later was executive vice president of the company, and his presence at CBS was indeed an accident. A dour and rather stiff man who wore a pince-nez, Klauber was a veteran of the New York *Times* who had risen through its ranks to become night city editor. Gene Fowler commented wickedly on him in his memoir of the 1920s, remembering the parade to welcome the return of General Pershing to New York, a hot march of four miles on Fifth Avenue from 100th Street to Madison Square, which most of the city's reporters abandoned (despite their place of honor not far behind the general's horse) in favor of an illegal beer somewhere along the route. Klauber, however, "lasted out the long march. Ed was not an athlete. In fact he liked sedentary assignments, such as a night at the opera or at the horse show. But he was a *Times* man. As such he dared not reveal signs of weakness, moral or otherwise, while on duty."[8]

Klauber came to CBS because Paley almost immediately after he acquired his radio network signed up Edward L. Bernays, the pioneer public relations counsel, to give him good advice. Half a dozen years before, while still a college student, Paley had read Bernays' book *Crystallizing Public Opinion,* and had become intrigued with the idea of a public relations man. "I thought, My God, to be important enough to have a public relations man! Somebody who could tell you what to do and what not to do!" And Klauber arrived through Bernays.

In his memoirs, Bernays recalled that Klauber had married "a girl much younger than himself. His wife complained about his *Times* job because he was kept at the office until 2:00 A.M. She begged him to give up his abnormal hours. I got him a good job as a public relations man with an advertising firm, Lennen & Mitchell, but Klauber tired of agency activity after a year. He was a competent journalist, able in thought and action, but had a difficult personality. He was a misanthrope and moody, hardly suited for public relations. Despite my misgivings, I asked him to join us. . . . We did not have enough people to absorb Klauber's personality. But in a large organization, where personal contacts were less important and the big executive job was the thing, I thought Klauber would function. . . . I told Paley the truth about Klauber, stressing his exceptional executive ability. . . . At first Paley was reluctant. . . . But he took him on at my urging."

The undertone of nastiness in Bernays' narrative has an explanation, for a year later his agency was canned, and he blamed Klauber: "Shortly before my contract was to be renewed, Klauber invited me to lunch at the Berkshire. He told me Columbia's budget could not carry two public relations advisers—himself and myself. . . . Our contract was not renewed. . . . Some years later Frederick Birchall, acting managing editor of the New York *Times,* shed some light on Klauber's character in terms of his own experiences. 'Why didn't you call me before you hired him?' he said. 'I could have told you about him. Klauber used to send men on the *Times* to cover a fire on Staten Island when he knew they were just about to go on their honeymoon.' "9 What is so odd about this excerpt from a book by a highly sophisticated observer is that Paley got away with shunting the blame for Bernays' dismissal from himself to his employee, an art he was to practice successfully over and over again in the succeeding decades. (Not that Paley gets off scot-free with Bernays: "I felt that native shrewdness made up for [Paley's] lack of intellectual grasp of the realities he was dealing with."10 Paley makes no mention of Bernays in *his* memoirs, which were written ten years after the publication of Bernays' memoirs.)

After Bernays was removed, Klauber hired Paul White, a tall, heavy, tough journalist still in his twenties—but with a background as byline reporter and editor for United Press—to be "Director of Public Affairs and Special Events." This meant that White was available to start a real news division when the wire services, under severe pressure from their newspaper clients, cut off service to all networks and broadcasting stations (except those owned by newspapers) in April 1933. From early on, White had a drinking problem, and those who worked for CBS News inevitably saw beyond and above him the more impressive figure of Klauber, a Prussian in a pince-nez who sat at the right hand of Bill Paley and gave orders. (It should be noted that if Klauber was frightening, he was also fair: Davidson Taylor remembered with gratitude years later the morning after the stink over *The War of the Worlds.* Klauber summoned him for what Taylor assumed would be a firing session if not a firing squad, but what he said was: "I've read the script. Not knowing what we now know, I'd have cleared it, too. Welles has scheduled a press conference. . . . I want you to go and represent CBS.") But what evidence survives argues that White was the designer of much that became standard in broadcast news.

It was White, for example, who established for the news service correspondents a "broadcast" style, at once looser, more conversational than printed prose and yet more purposive and even orotund in its rhetoric: White's star was H. V. Kaltenborn, who when asked to speak for seven minutes and fifteen seconds would speak for exactly seven minutes and fifteen seconds, without notes or a stopwatch. When Murrow, who had no newspaper experience at all, began reporting from Europe, even on a schedule that gave him hours of preparation time, he rarely wrote a text in advance (and when he did work from a text, he vastly preferred to dictate it rather than write it). Hiring Charles Collingwood virtually fresh out of his Oxford Rhodes scholarship to be a scriptwriter for CBS in wartime London, Murrow brushed aside his concern about his limited experience with the comment that he wanted "people who haven't been too greatly contaminated by print."

Robert Trout, a self-educated North Carolinian newspaperman with the look of a British Army major, another of White's early hires, was perhaps the most accomplished of the ad-libbers; there is a story that Franklin Roosevelt, arriving in Portland, Oregon, from Honolulu, mischievously remained on his cruiser, listening on the radio as Trout, waiting to welcome his return to the mainland in a one-hour program, extemporized first on Hawaii, then on the nature of the differences among the ships in Roosevelt's flotilla, then on the history of the United States Navy and its heroes and battles, finally, still smoothly, on the beauties, recreational delights and civic virtues of the Pacific Northwest. As the scheduled hour neared its close, Roosevelt gave the order to disembark, and flashed Trout a big smile at the foot of the gangplank. "Won't you say a few words, Mr. President?" Trout asked. "Hello, Bob," said Roosevelt. "Yes, it's good to be home." "This," said Trout, "is Robert Trout, returning you to CBS in New York"; and Roosevelt roared. Roosevelt had reason to be fond of Trout, who in 1936 had done him the courtesy of smoothly describing the President's fictitious progress to the podium to make his acceptance speech at the Democratic convention, when in fact Roosevelt had slipped and sickeningly fallen in the soft mud behind the platform. Trout spoke for seven hours in the CBS studios in New York on D-Day, and ad-libbed a very moving half-hour obituary of Roosevelt that began a few minutes after the President's death.

Walter Cronkite and David Brinkley, one suspects, are the last of the great ad-libbers, and Cronkite once he had reached the top demanded endless work by his staff to prepare the giant loose-leaf notebooks from which he took much of his commentary on election nights, moon landings, funerals and such; the next time there is a moon walk, one fears that NASA will have to get the networks a script. The difference between the old-timers chosen in the Paul White days and today's script readers was frighteningly visible in the comparison between the networks' capacity to fill time meaningfully in the hours after the Kennedy assassination and the disastrous stumbling coverage of the attempted assassination of Reagan in spring 1981.

White made the key decision that except when emergencies suggested a "roundup" of stories from the men on the scene, a single person should speak the news, to avoid confusing the listener. But what made White a great news editor (as later it made Don Hewitt a great TV news producer) was an old-fashioned, inexplicable sixth sense, about who was going to make news where, that often gave CBS a leg up on its competition without anybody knowing why. The most spectacular example of this intuition was December 7, 1941, a Sunday when most of the news world was off duty (Murrow was playing golf at Burning Tree). White sensed something in the air; he came into the office in the early morning and sent out cables around the world asking CBS correspondents to stay in touch with their office that day, so CBS was ready when the word came that the Japanese had struck at Pearl Harbor. When Davidson Taylor, who had been producing the New York Philharmonic broadcast at Carnegie Hall, came galloping into the office to see what he could do, White had his assignment ready: call all the advertisers and tell them we've pulled all commercials.

But the policy and financial parameters of the service White would create were drawn by Klauber. Two or three months after hiring White, Klauber set out his view of what was needed in an undated memo to Paley that established the seriousness of purpose and clarity of view that was to distinguish CBS News well into the television era. It makes rather melancholy reading today:

. . .

3. There is to be consistent training of all permanent and temporary personnel of the department, by the head of the department, so that air news broadcasts shall attain a definite Columbia standard of excellence with a certain tone and tempo characterizing them just as each publication seeks, without the destruction of individual enterprise or initiative, to maintain a character of its own.

4. Columbia is to proceed on the principle that the primary purpose of a news broadcast is to convey information and that the time has gone by when excited, fevered, hysterical outbursts of words are an adequate technique. . . . Bear in mind that the audience is primarily interested in what is happening and not in the personal feelings of the announcer or his difficulties. . . .

5. In furtherance of the foregoing idea and to give more of a sense of impersonal dignity and responsibility, colloquialism generally and familiarity in particular are to be discontinued, along with thanks, backscratching and praise by one participant in a broadcast for another. . . .

7. We are to build up a staff of news reporters whom we can develop and whom we can call on for various types of work. These men are to be engaged

on a fee basis, and tried out on lesser events or even, where possible, in "auditions" as discussed. Persons to be considered in this connection are Elmer Davis, Alexander Woollcott, Bob Rhode, an aviation man or two. . . . The search is to be centered principally on former newspapermen now free-lancing or otherwise engaged, because the active working reporter is usually not available when we need him.

8. In addition to editorial control, training of men and upbuilding of staff, we are to devote greater attention than ever before to advance preparation of material for a broadcast. . . .

Then something happened that moved CBS away from Klauber's event orientation and toward a daily service, presenting news over the air whether anything much happened that day or not. The something was the arrival of an advertiser. In August 1933, General Mills came to CBS with an offer: if the total cost ran less than $3,000 a week, the company would pick up half the bills for the operation of a Columbia News Service. Paul White was put in charge, and moved quickly to establish an organization.

Its foundation stones were the Dow Jones ticker and the Exchange Telegraph news service in London, neither of them part of the AP–UP–INS cartel that had banned the broadcasters. CBS had long had a Washington bureau, mostly to arrange talks by senators and such; White added bureaus in Chicago and Los Angeles. "The managers of these bureaus," he wrote, "soon lined up correspondents in every city in the United States of more than 20,000 population. We paid these correspondents higher space rates than those commonly paid by newspapers, and thus we had a willing group of 'stringers' . . . Then, too, we won a major victory when Postal Telegraph and affiliated companies gave us a press rate on telegram and cables. Western Union and others soon fell into line. We were in business."[11]

CBS opened three program slots for the Columbia News Service: five minutes every weekday at noon and at four-thirty, and fifteen minutes every night at eleven. White recorded some triumphs—an interview with heiress Doris Duke on the eve of her twenty-first birthday, which was reprinted verbatim on the front page of the New York *Journal* with credit to the "Columbia News Service"; a clean beat on the news of a strike at the Ford plant in Camden, New Jersey, and of a forest fire in the Pacific Northwest. "New York newspapers generally ignored this fire," White wrote. ". . . We played it night after night. Within a few days the fire was front-page news in the newspapers."[12]

The newspapers struck back. Many dropped their listings of radio programs; some dropped listings of CBS programs only. Advertising salesmen who worked for the network found that newspaper representatives had been around to their customers, pointing out the folly of paying for commercials in shows that would not be listed in the papers. NBC, essentially a bystander, felt itself injured and aggrieved by both sides, and only three months after the first scheduled broadcasts by the Columbia News Service,

NBC vice president Frank Mason organized a peace conference at the Biltmore Hotel in New York. It lasted three days; at the end of it CBS was out of the news-gathering business and a new Press-Radio Bureau had been formed to serve information to all broadcasters. The Press-Radio Bureau supplied both NBC and CBS with a bulletin service drawn from the reports of all three press associations and specially edited for broadcast use. No story could run longer than thirty words. No network could broadcast more than two five-minute newscasts, one at or after nine-thirty in the morning (to make sure that the radio news would not substitute for the morning paper), one at or after nine in the evening (eliminating competition with afternoon papers). The newscasts could not be sponsored.

The authors of the agreement that set up the Press-Radio Bureau explained their purposes: "The public is entitled to be advised promptly of the news of the day. . . . there are thousands of radio listeners, invalids, shut-ins, and the blind, who are unable to read the newspapers. . . . large groups of listeners in remote places . . . get their newspapers long after the time of publication. . . . The service has a special value during vacation months when thousands of people are miles away from a newspaper, but still have access to radio."[13] (Six years later, telling America about the British declaration of war on September 3, 1939, Murrow would report that the anxious crowds waiting outside the Prime Minister's residence "heard that news through a radio in a car parked near Downing Street.") What the "compromise" said was that people who could buy newspapers on the news-stands should buy newspapers on the newsstands; radio would be for the others.

These arrangements began to come apart almost immediately. Non-signers of the agreement hired away some key Columbia News Service people and started a rival Transradio News Service, which sold to the stations individually, and to a Yankee Network that provided regional inter-connections in New England. One clause of the "peace treaty" had permitted the bureau to supply running copy on stories of "transcendent importance," a category quickly expanded in their own interest by the newspeople who worked there. Within a year, UP and INS had decided that the income available from radio would exceed any losses from cancellations by angry newspapers; they abandoned the bureau and began to offer continuous teletype service to broadcasters. AP remained unavailable in broadcast newsrooms until 1945, when an antitrust case opened its membership rolls. ("The First Amendment," Justice Hugo Black wrote for the Court, "far from providing an argument against application of the Sherman Act, here provides powerful reasons to the contrary. . . . Freedom to publish means freedom for all and not for some."[14])

Most important, however, looking at both the immediate and the long-term development of broadcast news, was the reclassification of the announcers forced by the terms of the "compromise." News programs could not be sponsored—but talk programs could be. The four most important announcers, Boake Carter and H. V. Kaltenborn on CBS, Walter Winchell and Lowell Thomas on NBC, were labeled "commentators," and their programs were taken out of the "news" category so that they could be sponsored. This gave them a quite extraordinary freedom. Sponsors could not control what they said, because that would be interference with free expression. Networks could not control what they said, because on-air talent, even though formally employed by the network, actually worked, in the traditions of radio, for the sponsors. Often enough the commentators spoke without scripts; when they did write it out in advance, as many did, the scripts were not subject to prior approval. To this day, though sponsors have essentially disappeared from the scene (they buy thirty-second commercial slots in programs rather than the programs themselves), the producers of the network nightly news shows know only the subject their commentators will discuss in the two minutes and eleven seconds allotted in the "lineup"; they find out exactly what John Chancellor or Bill Moyers or George Will has to say about his subject only as the comments go out on the air.

4

A few days before the start of World War II, Murrow noted in his broadcast from London that others were expecting further concessions to Hitler. "I have had my say concerning appeasement," he said in conclusion. "I reported that I have seen no evidence of it for some time. I have also given you such facts as are available in London tonight. I have an old-fashioned belief that Americans like to make up their own minds on the basis of all available information. The conclusions you draw are your own affair. I have no desire to influence them, and shall leave such efforts to those who have more confidence in their own judgment than I have in mine."[15] This was company policy: Paley, who had been badly burned first by what the proto-fascist Father Coughlin said over his network and then by the fuss over Coughlin's removal from CBS, liked to talk of "fairness and balance." As early as 1935 he had told a stockholders' meeting that "we must never try to further either side of any debatable question."

In 1943, after forcing the resignation of a CBS commentator who had said that "any reasonably accurate observer of the American scene at this moment knows that a good deal of enthusiasm for this war is evaporating into thin air," Paul White sent a memo to "CBS news analysts" which the company published as a full-page ad in the New York newspapers. "Each of you," he wrote, "has been chosen by us because of your background and knowledge, insight, clarity of thought, and special ability to make yourselves understood by vast audiences. We feel we have faced and met a considerable responsibility in your selection. We now feel that you must meet and face much the same responsibility in writing your analyses. For we have said to ourselves, 'We will not choose men who will tell the public what they themselves think and what the public should think.' And we ask that you say to yourselves, 'We are not privileged to crusade, to harangue the people, or to attempt to sway public opinion.'

". . . Actually, freedom of speech on the radio *would* be menaced if a small group of men, some thirty or forty news analysts who have nation-wide audiences and regular broadcasting periods in which to build loyal listeners, take advantage of their 'preferred position' and become pulpiteers. . . ."16

Ignoring the fact that nobody ever got in trouble for saying that the American people were gung ho for a war or indeed for their government's policies, White's message was also, more or less, maybe, the law. The Communications Act of 1935 established the Federal Communications Commission as the exclusive licensing agency for channels in the radio-frequency spectrum, instructed it to make sure these channels were operated in the public interest, convenience and necessity (a phrase copied from the act establishing the Interstate Commerce Commission, where the words applied to railroad lines), and ordered it not to interfere with broadcasters' programming decisions. The Act is not one of the glories of the legislative drafter's art. In the 1930s, broadcasters could cite it in proclaiming a policy of refusing to sell time to people who wished to use it to present their views on controversial issues (the one exception was candidates in the months just before an election). In the 1960s, activists could cite it when demanding that stations not only sell but give away time to those who wished to promote alternative lifestyles. In 1941, unquestionably guided to a degree by Franklin Roosevelt's dislike of the newspaper owners who owned most of the stations and always endorsed his opponents, the Federal Communications Commission ruled that "a truly free radio cannot be used to advocate the causes of the licensee. It cannot be used to support the candidacy of his friends. It cannot be devoted to the support of principles he happens to regard most favorably. In brief, the broadcaster cannot be an advocate."17

Eight years later, the Commission apparently reversed itself. With two commissioners signing the new rule, two abstaining, two opposing and one agreeing to be counted in favor of the rule if not the reasoning, the FCC in its clumsy way urged editorializing. "The Commission is not persuaded," the argument ran (perhaps stumbled would be a better word), "that a station's willingness to stand up and be counted on these particular issues upon which the licensee has a definite position may not actually be helpful in providing and maintaining a climate of fairness and equal opportunity for the expression of contrary views."18 In other words, *do* editorialize, and give the fellow on the other side airtime for a reply. (This assumes, of course, that there are only two sides.) Over a course of time, this metamorphosed into a "Fairness Doctrine," which seems to have been written into the Constitution by a unanimous Supreme Court in the *Red Lion* case in 1969.

Red Lion is a superb but unfortunately not unique illustration of what goes wrong when political decisions are left to courts. It is not so much that the Supreme Court gets things "wrong" (a logical impossibility: as Chief Justice Charles Evans Hughes once said, the Constitution is nothing more nor less than what the Supreme Court says it is) as that its rulings so often go to or over the edge of meaninglessness, a situation particularly worrisome when the author of the opinion is Justice Byron White, who writes the clearest prose on today's bench. *Red Lion* was a pathetic case for the broadcasting industry to support. Radio station WGGB in Red Lion, Pennsylvania (pop. 5,594), was an outlet for the evangelizing of Billy James Hargis, who used one of his radio sermons for an attack on Fred J. Cook, a New York reporter who had written a book critical of Hargis' hero Barry Goldwater. Hargis told listeners that Cook had been fired from the New York *World-Telegram* for fabricating charges against city officials and had then worked for a "Communist-dominated" magazine *(The Nation)*. Cook requested time to reply and was refused. The FCC ordered the Red Lion Broadcasting Company to give Cook time; the station went to court to appeal the order; and the National Association of Broadcasters supported the station, "as though," said NBC general counsel Corydon B. Dunham, rather bitterly, "this stuff was *broadcasting.*"

Given this easy case, Justice White grew expansive. There was, he wrote, an obvious difference between print and broadcast: anyone could start a newspaper, but only someone with a government-issued license could start a broadcasting station. In these circumstances, "it is idle to posit an unabridgeable First Amendment right to broadcast comparable to the right of every individual to speak, write or publish. . . . The licensee . . . has no constitutional right to monopolize a radio frequency to the exclusion of his fellow citizens." The FCC was not only permitted to demand that broadcasters present all sides of controversial issues, it was *required* to do so: "The right of the public to receive suitable access to social, political, esthetic, moral, and other ideas and experiences . . . may not constitutionally be abridged either by Congress or by the FCC."[19] Legal scholars have said for generations that there can be no right without a remedy, which has led citizens' groups and others to hunt through the Commission and the courts looking for the remedy Justice White must have foreseen, but it is still hiding, and the suspicion has grown that it does not exist. This has left broadcasters aggrieved that they do not have First Amendment rights, but comforted by the likelihood that nobody can make them express or communicate an opinion if they don't want to do so.

It should be noted that the Fairness Doctrine and the FCC's "personal attack" rule have been helpful to broadcasters in avoiding the plague of libel suits that has struck the newspapers and magazines. Print media cannot be forced to carry corrections or replies except through the instrument of a libel suit; broadcasters can, via a demand on the FCC. Thus there is some tendency for courts to require that those aggrieved by what has been said about them on the air exhaust their "administrative remedies" before seeking damages. CBS made General William Westmoreland say "uncle" mostly because a stream of witnesses from the cadre of his former colleagues were willing to testify that they had believed at the time that Westy was cooking the books on intelligence estimates of Vietcong strength, the allegation Westmoreland called libelous—but the chances of his winning had been reduced from the start by the network's offer to give him time to reply. These rules are by no means absolute—nobody gives white racists, anti-Semites or Shiite terrorists a right of reply (though sodomites, black racists and IRA terrorists will probably get a turn at the wheel). Fred Friendly reports that Murrow once asked disgustedly, "Would you give equal time to Judas Iscariot or Simon Legree?"

There was, in short, a "chilling effect" on the expression of opinion by network employees, from early on. "We were warned over and over again," Eric Sevareid wrote, recalling Klauber's and White's reactions to his comments from Paris in the years before the United States entered World War II, "to speak calmly, dispassionately; we must not display a tenth of the emotion that a broadcaster does when describing a prize fight. America was neutral; our company at least was determined that it would never be guilty of propagandizing Americans into war. This was right, it was the only legitimate way to perform our function—but it was very hard."[20] What got Sevareid in his worst trouble in those years, however, was an oddity. Returned to Washington after the fall of France, he found himself at odds with a superior who was "neutral in his mind." Reacting to his distaste for those who lacked his commitment against Nazism, Sevareid "wondered how much time and space one should give to their remarks. During one morning broadcast I wondered out loud about this problem into the microphone, for I could not forget the stifling role played by the press in France when it was a distinct force for defeat. I was denounced by some isolationists, my superior was shocked, and I received a letter of expostulation from New York. I was given to understand that the opposition was entitled to equal time and equal space, and that I had no business even raising the question."[21] Sevareid wrote those words in 1945, when it did not seem as strange as it does today, after our bitter experiences with the Marcusean crookedness of the 1960s, that someone should claim his own First Amendment rights to advocate the exclusion of others'.

With all that, the broadcast commentators who started in the radio days were much more opinionated than what the American public hears today. Murrow, for example, expressed his views on Eisenhower's decision to install Admiral Darlan as the American surrogate in North Africa: "Let us look at the man's record [in the Vichy government]. On February 10, 1941, he became vice president of the council, secretary of state for foreign affairs, the Interior and the Navy. One of his first acts was to turn over political refugees to the Germans. He began at once to adopt Gestapo methods. His government was responsible for the sending of foreigners, mostly Spanish Republicans, from internment camps in France to slave-gang labor on the Trans-Sahara Railway. He intensified anti-Semitic measures. . . . And now this man is given political dominion over North Africa, with American support. . . . One wonders whether or not we may stand dishonored in the eyes of the conquered peoples on the Continent. This is a matter of high principle in which we carry a great moral burden which we cannot escape. . . . There is nothing in the strategic position of the allies to indicate that we are either so strong or so weak that we can afford to ignore the principles for which this war is being fought."[22]

A quarter of a century later, Walter Cronkite narrated a special report on Vietnam after the Tet offensive, and concluded: "To say that we are closer to victory today is to believe, in the face of the evidence, the optimists who have been wrong in the past. . . . It is increasingly clear to this reporter that the only rational way out then will be to negotiate, not as victors, but as an honorable people who lived up to their pledge to defend democracy, and did the best they could." A frisson ran through the political community; Lyndon Johnson is reported to have said that if he had lost Cronkite he had lost his consensus.[23] Johnson's memoirs, it should be noted, make a rather different comment: "There was a great deal of emotional and exaggerated reporting of the Tet offensive in our press and on television. The media seemed to be in competition as to who could provide the most lurid and depressing account . . ."[24] But in any event, Cronkite's supposed blockbuster is quite a lot calmer than Murrow's utterance on Darlan.

As late as 1977, Howard K. Smith spoke out on ABC about the automobile companies and emission controls: "The auto makers were given several years to meet certain emission levels by the coming model year. Foreign producers, like Volvo, have had no trouble doing it. But that great repository of American skill, Detroit, says it can't. Unless our elected representatives amend the law, they will simply not produce, throw half a million out of work, do great damage to our not fully recovered economy. It is not too harsh to call that blackmail. Government, naturally, is caving in. But it should accompany surrender with saying firmly, Never Again. It fouls the whole principle of democracy."[25]

In spring 1985, Congress took up the not dissimilar matter of a request from General Motors and Ford for a waiver on the fuel economy standards imposed in 1975 for the model year 1986. It would, I think, have been quite beyond anyone's imagination that one of the commentators on the network news shows of 1985 should take after the automobile companies so impolitely. Today's commentators are not radio people; and today's network news shows are ultimately controlled, as never before, by corporate officers rather than by their producers, which is a recipe for timidity. But it is also true and significant, as Stephen White pointed out in his *Report on the Chatham Seminar on Television and Society,* that people who appear regularly on television are celebrities who, uniquely in the history of celebrity, live amongst us; that their views therefore have a different resonance in our homes; and that in the case of the journalists "it is no longer what they say that matters, but that they said it."[26] And it is therefore not only possible but necessary to hold the anchors accountable for the stories they tell and introduce.

5

When Smith said CBS had lucked into its dominance of broadcast news, what he meant was the extraordinary good fortune that moved Edward (né Egbert) R. Murrow out of his role as an arranger of talks and "roundtable discussions" and behind a microphone as a reporter and analyst of events. It was, moreover, luck that carried over into the early days of television. ("The important thing," producer Don Hewitt said, "was that Edward R. Murrow *looked* like Edward R. Murrow. If you were making a movie of the life of Ed Murrow and you had a casting call for fifty actors and one of them was Murrow, you'd immediately take Murrow.") But if what we are talking about is 1938, the coverage of the Anschluss and then the Munich conference that gave CBS its admired standing in the world of news gatherers, the lion's share of the credit should go to Paley himself. He not only paid for the work, he dictated the procedures and the format.

Murrow had gone abroad in 1937 to replace Cesar Saerchinger as the man who organized talks and bits for programs like *American School of the Air.* He was based in London, where most of the English-speaking foreign talent was to be found. He felt he needed an assistant in Central Europe, to find programs there and act as correspondent keeping CBS informed of the increasingly inflamed international situation. William Shirer was in Berlin, where he had served as the German correspondent of the Universal Service news agency, which suddenly collapsed in the summer of 1937. Shirer had made one CBS broadcast a few months before, reporting on German reaction to the *Hindenburg* disaster, and though he had a squeaky voice his command of both the situation and the language made up for it. Murrow was in Salzburg soliciting broadcasts from its festival on the day Universal News went under, and he put in a hurry call: could Shirer meet him the next day at the Hotel Adlon in Berlin? Presently Shirer had joined Murrow on the CBS European staff, and had moved to Vienna, which offered a less constricted and censored atmosphere than the capital of the Third Reich.

A few months later, the Reich absorbed a mostly enthusiastic Austria. It happened on a Friday. Murrow was in Warsaw buying a Polish children's program for *School of the Air;* Shirer was in Yugoslavia to arrange a similar transmission of a miners' children's chorus. Shirer hustled back to Vienna, observed the rapid takeover of government installations by the local Nazis in anticipation of Hitler's arrival, and went to the Austrian radio for access to the shortwave transmitters that would enable him to broadcast to New York. He was told they had broken down; communication would have to go via Berlin; and all the lines to Berlin were completely taken up by military messages.

News bulletins were arriving in New York through NBC, which had official arrangements with both the German and Austrian state broadcasting companies, and employed German and Austrian nationals rather than Americans in those countries. Paley was home with the flu; told that his people in Europe were unable to get their reports out, he put through a call to the head of the Austrian state company, whom he had met at international gatherings, and for a wonder got through. The Austrian, in tears, said he could do nothing: "The Germans are here." Paley suggested to Paul White that he put together a collection of comments from American newsmen abroad that could be broadcast live, from multiple pickup points, on CBS. He refused to believe it couldn't be done—and on consideration, White joined his refusal. The engineers got to work; telephone calls and cables crisscrossed the Atlantic and flowed through Europe.

Both White and Shirer reached Murrow in Warsaw, and among them they arranged that Shirer would go to London to make his eyewitness report from a place where the German censorship did not reach; and Murrow would proceed to Vienna in hopes that the shortwave transmitter would open again. By the time the engineers had cleared the feasibility of Paley's idea, Shirer was in the CBS London office. It was Saturday afternoon. White called, and asked Shirer to set up live shortwave pickups from Paris, Berlin and Rome for Sunday, 8 P.M. New York time, which would be Monday, 1 A.M. European time. In a frenzied thirty hours (broken by Shirer's report on what he had seen in Vienna, which aired in New York at 6:30 Saturday evening), the two men set up the round robin, with Edgar Ansel Mowrer in Paris, Frank Gervasi in Rome and Pierre Huss in Berlin, none of them employees of CBS. Arrangements were made with the local authorities to time their broadcasts—plus one from London and one from Murrow in Vienna, where the transmitter *had* been opened, at least for relay through Berlin—on the schedule cabled by White. Meanwhile, White arranged for comment from Washington by Senator Lewis Schwellenbach; CBS did not at that time have a staff reporter in Washington.

At 8 P.M. on Sunday, March 13, 1938, Robert Trout in New York announced calmly that "the program *St. Louis Blues* will not be heard to-night." He fudged a little on what would be in its place, promising only "pickups direct from London, Paris and such other European capitals as at this late hour abroad have communications channels available." (One notes in passing the Latinity of Trout's speech, the placement of "at this late hour" and of the verb.) In fact, everyone got through but Gervasi in Rome, and the show ran precisely half an hour. It was Murrow's first broadcast as a CBS correspondent. Reprinted in *In Search of Light,* the book of excerpts from his commentaries selected by Edward Bliss, Jr., the talk is entirely professional, informative and personal ("This is Edward Murrow speaking from Vienna. It's now roughly 2:30 in the morning and Herr Hitler has not yet arrived . . . a tremendous reception is being prepared . . ."[27] He did not say that his own arrival had been by a chartered twenty-seven-passenger Lufthansa airliner on which he had been the only passenger, at a cost of $1,000 of Paley's money). The next night they did it again—this time with Kenneth Downs of the International News Service (Hearst) from Paris and Albion Ross of the New York *Times* from Berlin. What had been a miracle was en route to becoming routine.

Thus CBS was ready to move again that September when Hitler at the end of his Nuremberg rally announced that he could no longer bear the sight of the Sudeten Germans ground under the heel of democracy in Czechoslovakia. The American networks carried the speech live, Kaltenborn performing feats of simultaneous translation on CBS and delivering a nine-minute analysis of the menaces in the speech at its conclusion. That evening CBS reactivated the roundup, and during the eighteen days before the crisis ended with the surrender of the democracies at Munich there were fourteen such broadcasts, plus innumerable individual commentaries. On September 22 the American audience for the first time heard what became Murrow's trademark opening. "This . . . is London . . ." In these round-ups the hero was the veteran Kaltenborn, with his upper-class Prussian manner and his mellifluous Anglican accent. He literally lived in Studio 9 on the seventeenth floor of the CBS building, sleeping on a cot between broadcasts. He made eighty-five extemporaneous talks, one of them lasting two hours, and commercial programming was routinely interrupted for news broadcasts. Paley sacrificed the income gladly: this was exciting, and Paley all his long, rich, silver-spoon to Picasso-collection life—it is the cement in that implausible story—was a sucker for excitement. It was also the most remarkable accomplishment of broadcast journalism to that date, and perhaps the most remarkable ever.

A British newsmagazine recommended shortwave broadcasts from America as the best guide to developments in the crisis: "Vivid on-the-spot relays from European capitals, plus expert commentaries by students of foreign affairs, have kept Americans abreast of events. Fortunate are those Britons who have receivers which bring in the Columbia broadcasts." James Rorty of *The Nation* described Kaltenborn's talks as "poised, accurate and brilliantly timed, many of them brilliantly illuminating. . . . A new dimension has been added to politics and diplomacy. For the first time, history has been made in the hearing of its pawns."[28]

When it was over, Murrow made a quick trip to New York to consult with Klauber and White, and to urge the case that with war on the horizon CBS should no longer rely on his and Shirer's ability to round up stringers for crisis coverage: the news department needed a European staff of size and quality. He got his budget, and before the end of 1939 CBS had its own men not only in London but in Paris (a two-man bureau, with Thomas Grandin and Eric Sevareid, whom Murrow had casually stolen away from the Paris *Herald* and the United Press on the strength of his writing—he was for years hopelessly nervous before the mike), Berlin (Shirer, still squeaky), Helsinki (William L. White), Rome (Cecil Brown) and Bucharest. Presently Murrow would add Charles Collingwood and Howard K. Smith, both recently down from Oxford (Smith after a year at Heidelberg: a Louisianan who had benefited from one of Hitler's scholarships to get a European education, he had become a Rhodes scholar and the president of the Labour Club at Oxford). This was an extraordinary crew, with intellectual attainments beyond what could be found in almost any city room, but broadcasting was still not respectable journalism: Murrow was turned down on his first application for membership in the Anglo-American press club. No matter: from Munich on, Americans relied on broadcasting first of all when they needed to know (as distinct from merely wanted to know) the news. There was an oddball symbol of it when Roosevelt at a press conference awarded an Iron Cross to a New York *Daily News* columnist who had written something the President thought damaging; the Iron Cross had been given to Roosevelt as a souvenir by Larry LeSueur of CBS. Arthur Hays Sulzberger told Meyer Berger that several of the changes he made at the New York *Times* in the late 1930s and early 1940s were done because "I saw the effect that radio commentators were having."[29]

Murrow's intense and evocative descriptions of London under the Blitz had made him a national figure. And shared experiences in London, where Paley in 1943 joined Eisenhower's staff as a colonel advising on broadcast psychological warfare, made Murrow a power in the councils of CBS. Paley, half a dozen years older than Murrow, was still in his mid-forties, very much looking for friends, for people who did not (this he thought was the real problem) envy him. It would not have occurred to Murrow to envy Paley. Except for the (false) statement that he had not invited his mother to his wedding, nothing in David Halberstam's book about Big Media so offended Paley as the implication that Murrow had felt Paley let him down; in his memoirs, Paley prints a faintly embarrassing and probably solicited letter from Janet Murrow, specifically in reply to Halberstam's effusions. With Paley elsewhere, incidentally, Paul White had a terrible time with the corporate controllers of the network. On D-Day, the two NBC networks and Mutual canceled all programming, but CBS cut back to soap operas at 10 A.M., and it was not until noon that White could pry Paley's surrogates away from their commercials.

After the war, Paley asked Murrow to become a corporate officer, vice president for news and public affairs, and then a member of the CBS board. Klauber had retired, and his successor, Paul Kesten, was about to go; Frank Stanton, an academic psychologist Kesten had recruited to head CBS's research department, was about to succeed Kesten, and Stanton was never someone with whom Paley socialized. (Those who were perplexed by the war that broke out between Stanton and Murrow in 1959 had forgotten the 1946–47 period when Stanton must have regarded Murrow as a potential threat; after all, Klauber had been a newsman.) Murrow found himself inevitably conducting a holding action: with the war over, people were much less interested in news; with radio swimming in advertising money, and Paley raiding talent from NBC with the original idea of incorporating comedians and letting them sell their companies for a lump sum (taxed at capital-gains rates when personal-income rates ran up to 92 percent), news was losing status on the network totem pole. Murrow did have the clout to expand the network's bureau system inside the United States, and to add a domestic news roundup with pickups from these bureaus to the now well-established *World News Roundup* with its live pickups abroad. But he got into a painful fight with Shirer, the only commentator on the air to criticize Truman's new doctrine and the resulting support for the Greek and Turkish governments in their fight against Communist guerrillas. Shirer's sponsor, who had the right to decide what commentator he wanted to put in his time, asked for a replacement. Shirer lost his time slot, and with the loss of sponsorship the bulk of his income, and he quit CBS in fury. Then Murrow had to fire Paul White, whose arthritis and drinking habits were feeding on each other. Shirer wrote a novel in which the villain was a war correspondent who became a vicious and dictatorial executive; White wrote a book of reminiscences in which Murrow was not just a star but a friend.

In 1947, Campbell's Soup, which was not getting the ratings it had hoped for from Robert Trout in the 7:45–8 P.M. period that was then the radio news hole, came to Paley with an offer he couldn't refuse: $3 million for Murrow at 7:45 in the evening and Lowell Thomas, who would move over from NBC, at 10:45. In fall 1947 Murrow returned to radio in a five-nights-a-week show that usually included just over ten minutes of hard news (including remote pickups) and just under three minutes of what he liked to call a "think piece"—roughly the formula television would follow in later years. His salary, incidentally, was $130,000 a year, plus $20,000 in expenses, in purchasing power roughly the equal of the "fabulous" salaries paid today's anchormen for what is in truth a much more time-consuming job. At about the same time Murrow resumed his career as a broadcaster, far below his notice, the cherubic Douglas Edwards took over what had become a two-nights-a-week news show on the tiny CBS Television Network.

8
With Pictures

Our brethren in television are light-years behind. They are dealing in a still vastly more complicated medium and they're dealing in time frames that I don't think they've even begun to master. They have turned loose an incredible number of people, some of whom I liked very much, to stand around on lawns and mountaintops with microphones thrust in front of them, with no responsible editors between them and what they're uttering into the microphones. Nor do they have behind them, as yet, a sense of how much of those advertising revenues that they have stolen from the print press really ought to be devoted to the business of information-gathering as opposed to the 75 percent of the day which is devoted to their other business, that of mounting entertainment programs. They're still struggling, in TV news, to assert themselves as a serious information medium, and the literacy level, the expertise level, even the sense of what is news in relation to the camera, all this is still very raw. . . .

> –Max Frankel,
> editorial page editor,
> New York *Times,* 1984

. . . a double standard . . . is turning the American public against broadcast journalists, and I think that, in their zeal to get us, the print people are getting stung with the same thing. . . . I think the publishers are fanning the flames because television is cutting into advertising revenues . . . they're stung by the fact that when their guy goes out to write a story, the reader has seen it better and closer on television the night before than the reporter saw it.

> –Don Hewitt, producer,
> *60 Minutes,* at
> the same meeting[1]

For the unorganized taxpayers, workers and producers of the nation to get and keep their tax cut, the White House had to become the dragon slayer of the organized spenders. . . .

But . . . that . . . would have meant a bad time at reality
time—every night at 7:00 P.M. . . .

[There was] a recurrent, symbolic incident at the LSG
[for Legislative Strategy Group] meetings in his [James Bak-
er's White House] office. They were often held late in the
afternoon. There was always a hand calculator next to my
place at the table and a TV remote control switch next to his.
From a distance they're hard to tell apart—electronic marvels
both.

But at 6:30 P.M. the early edition of the network news
came on. At that point, the remote control switch always won.
The meeting shifted from the policy problem in the numbers
to the political problem on the screen.

–David Stockman, 1986[2]

1

A couple of weekends after the American attack on Libya in spring
1986, John J. O'Connor of the New York *Times* wrote a Sunday column in
which he singled out the moment when Dan Rather, live on the air on the
seven o'clock news, asked the CBS correspondent in Tripoli to hold his
microphone out of his hotel window so the audience could hear the bombs
blasting. That moment, he said, was something new in the history of communications. But it was, of course, merely a copy, and a rather pale copy at
that, of what Ed Murrow did during the German firebombing of London in
1940, when he went onto the roof with his microphone and broadcast
descriptions of where the bombs were falling and how the antiaircraft bul-
lets were tracing the sky. Murrow could see more because he was on a roof
rather than in a room, could tell more because he could see more and
because he had more time, and could set the scene more effectively because
he had never become accustomed to using pictures as a crutch. But Rather's
April 14 program was, I guess, the first time that a television news
anchorman in a studio spoke on the telephone with a fellow journalist
whose still picture was framed beside his head about something that was
happening in the audio that neither of them could see.

Elihu Katz of the Communications Institute at Hebrew University in
Jerusalem some years ago wrote a report to the BBC on "Social Research on
Broadcasting," in which he suggested that research-based policymaking at
an early stage in the development of television services might have made a
considerable difference in what happened to this monster of modern times.
"A policy research group," he noted, "might have considered leaving the
news bulletins off television altogether, and perhaps not weaning people
away from radio news. Radio could then do the main bulletins; television
could specialize in public affairs."[3]

Radio unquestionably has great advantages over television as a device for delivering news. The role of the mediating intelligence is far greater; the decision to report this story rather than that story draws much more directly and powerfully on the editors' view of the relative importance of the different items; and the rather more personal involvement of the speaker tends to add dignity. "You had to be able to write and describe," Eric Sevareid remembered a little wistfully, "and make the thing come alive with words. And you had five minutes for a commentary, time for a beginning, a middle and an end, for some of the graces of language." On Murrow's and Elmer Davis' evening news shows, as on Sevareid's late-night commentaries, there was a commercial at the beginning and a commercial at the end, and between them nothing but the web of news as seamless as its creators could make it. Singing commercials were forbidden—indeed, all music was prohibited. In the early 1970s, Richard Salant as president of CBS News again prohibited music on all news and documentary shows, even killing the splendid Aaron Copland orchestration of "The Gift to Be Simple" that had always led *CBS Reports.* Today, of course, television documentaries have more music than a Hollywood movie; but, then, they tend to deal with softer, more "social relations" subjects, and with wooden celebrities, like Hollywood movies.

On radio, moreover, the story can be told straight, without worrying about the distractions invariably introduced by the excess richness of information in the pictures. This apparent richness has become in itself a source of poverty—poverty of background, imagination, significance—that increasingly afflicts television news. Thus on the night that Reagan was to introduce his new tax plan, the *CBS Evening News* (always "with Dan Rather," even when Rather is absent) showed pictures of a machine tool factory to illustrate the proposed loss of the investment tax credit, pictures of kids moving between hamburger bin and customers in a fast-food restaurant to illustrate the benefits service industries would receive, pictures of the floor of the New York Stock Exchange at the close of day, the bell ringing madly in the background, to express the fact that Reagan's plan would reduce the capital-gains tax. None of these bits of film was in any way informative with relation to the story reporter Ray Brady was competently telling in voice-over. They were not very distracting, mostly because they were not very good; there was no way they were going to be helpful, except to the extent that they would relieve the people who ran CBS News of their terror of losing viewers asked to concentrate on the substance of a narrative.

The argument that we have been luckier than we knew was pressed by Bill Leonard—an avuncular, overweight, earnest authority figure who did everything for CBS News from being on-mike and on-camera talent in a splendid local show called *Eye on New York,* to directing, to producing, to running the first "election unit," to serving as president of the organization (and defending, with an embarrassment that can scarcely be imagined, the network's decision to pay H. R. Haldeman to let Mike Wallace interview him). "Radio had got infused by journalistic standards thanks to a few, a very few people," Leonard said; "the one I knew was Ed Klauber. And the second lucky accident was that we took over the visual end ourselves. It was one of the most important things that happened in this country, that broadcasters rather than the motion-picture business took over the news function. Just think of those newsreels!"

In a world where Katz's policymakers had restricted television to special events and public affairs, Leonard's nightmare would probably have been realized, for the public at some point would have liked the idea of seeing as well as hearing the news, and the only organizations equipped to show them what they wanted would have been the newsreelers. "Out of the nettle danger," the critic Gilbert Seldes wrote in 1950, "the newsreel companies may yet pluck a golden rose. . . . The late Fred Ullman, when he was head of Pathé News, had foreseen this and planned a major change in the character of his service; he intended to eliminate entirely the tediously recurrent clips of motorcyclists climbing hills, slow-motion reversed film shots of shapely young women leaping from pool to diving board, parades, and the like; the newsreel was to become a brief documented report on important subjects, with a strong editorial stand. . . . Action must follow as soon as the feature-movie audience begins to fret at seeing the older kind of newsclips which no longer have any news value. Television will carry fashion shots, on film or with live models, and will pick up important news events on the spot when the coaxial cable is completed."[4]

At the beginning, Fox-Movietone, which was a newsreel maker, supplied the film NBC used on news shows; Telenews, a supplier to newsreel makers, served CBS. For the Murrow-Friendly *See It Now,* a weekly half-hour newsmagazine of the 1950s that might cover several stories or concentrate on a single topic (this was the show on which Murrow made his careful but devastating presentation of the work of Joe McCarthy), film was supplied through the first four years by Hearst's News of the Day, and the link with Hearst was broken for entirely extraneous reasons—because Hearst columnist Jack O'Brian had repeatedly excoriated CBS newsman Don Hollenbeck as a left-winger who ought not to be on the air, and Hollenbeck had committed suicide, and Murrow had gone to Paley to say that CBS should not continue any relationship that yielded profits to Hearst.

At the start, however, *force majeure,* television news was little more than radio news with the announcer on screen and a map behind him: the newsreel film was silent and added little to the announcer's presentations, it was half a day or more behind the news, and it had to be run through "telecine" chains that yielded gray and jerky television pictures. The first popular news program was *Camel News Caravan* in spring 1948. (Quite apart from the cigarette question, it rather takes one's breath away these days to think of a network news show named for its single sponsor.) This ran on NBC from 7:30 to 7:45 five nights a week, a straight newsreel from Fox-Movietone,

with an unseen and anonymous voice-over, the package supplied by an
advertising agency without any editorial control by the network. In early
1949 someone at NBC, quite possibly Sarnoff himself, decided that this
approach to television news was too unprincipled, and a rather flamboyant
Kansas City newsman named John Cameron Swayze, who had been relatively unsuccessful on the network as a radio announcer, was made the
leader of the Caravan. Swayze heartily welcomed his audience and in his
carnival-barker way told them what the wire services had told him: "Let's
go hopscotching the world for headlines . . ."

The more sedately named *CBS TV News* achieved its nightly time slot
in August 1948, soon after the nominating conventions that were television's debut as a serious news medium (and also, as Seldes harshly pointed
out soon thereafter, its debut as a bearer of false witness: his example was
the piling up of delegates' badges on a table before the TV cameras as the
Southerners at the Democratic convention protested the passage of a civil
rights plank Mayor Hubert Humphrey of Minneapolis had hallooed onto
the platform; later, having made their point for the tens of thousands of
viewers television commanded in 1948, they reclaimed their badges and
returned to the floor).

The on-camera talent at CBS was Douglas Edwards, whose show this
would be for fourteen years (after the first two of them it bore his name:
Douglas Edwards with the News). The behind-the-camera talent after the first
few weeks was Don Hewitt, a brash New Yorker then twenty-five years old,
a college dropout with six years' experience of trying to break into the
newspaper business. Edwards was a more convincing presence than Swayze,
and Hewitt was more imaginative than God. The title "producer" in television was invented to describe what Hewitt did, because he took responsibility for so much more than the traditional "director" who had run the radio
shows and filmed the movies. Necessarily: a television news show, which
requires the coordination of filmed and live material, is an order of magnitude more complicated than a radio news show, and because it is live it is
horrendously more tense than even the trickiest takes for a film. Russ Ben-
gli, who did it, described directing a TV news show as "like running down a
railroad track ahead of a freight train."

Interestingly, Hewitt dropped the "single system" camera that Murrow
had fought for and paid for in Korea: he wanted the chance to dub new
sound and comment over the original film, and to cut back and forth between the scene and the correspondent reporting it, and to add sound effects and even music. Thirty years later, Roone Arledge, president of ABC
News, got into an argument with Hewitt, who had moved on to be the
founding genius and executive producer of *60 Minutes* (and thus perhaps
more important than a mere division president), about the best way to
handle a 1980s interview with the extinct but still interestingly ghastly volcano of Richard Nixon: "I wanted to do it *live*," Arledge recalls. "I said,

'There's an electricity and a realness to a live interview that an edited interview just doesn't have.' Hewitt maintained the opposite. He didn't want Nixon on live, he wanted to edit it." *60 Minutes* has of course had its moments of making news (Hewitt could make news with *Love Boat*), but it is fundamentally a scripted show: Hewitt was once indiscreet enough to say, "There are shows on TV about doctors, cowboys, cops. This is a show about four journalists. But instead of four actors playing these four guys, they are themselves."[5]

Hewitt, who is compact and noisy and theatrical, has always had a classic, 1920s view of news, a mix of Chicago school and early Hearst (his father was a Hearst executive). Fred Friendly, who would tangle with Hewitt on various occasions (and dismiss him as producer of the *Evening News* in 1964), liked to say with distaste that "Don thinks news is an elephant on water skis being towed at those gardens in Florida." That's fair enough, once it is admitted that if you got an elephant up on water skis and towed him around Cypress Gardens it would be news, the first time. ("The only way I got *60 Minutes* on the air," Bill Leonard recalled, thinking back to the time when he was executive vice president of the division, "was by telling Dick Salant that Fred Friendly had been against it.") But Av Westin, who worked with Hewitt when he was a beginner and later ran ABC's *The World Tonight* and then that network's *20/20*, remembers gratefully that "Hewitt was the guy who invented the wheel in this business."[6] It was, perhaps inevitably, a more theatrical, less explanatory wheel than the radio wheel.

What helped was the fact that television was growing in recesses of the radio broadcasting operation. "I had absolute freedom," Bill Leonard recalls of his own *Eye on New York* show. "Now I perceive that as a measure of my lack of importance." Years later, when Leonard produced a show about hunting and gun control called *The Guns of Autumn*, the network got 30,000 abusive letters, 5,000 of them with copies to the FCC, and he could not avoid knowing that a lot of people in the corporation didn't like it.

Walter Cronkite got his start on television doing the local news on WTOP in Washington, then owned and operated by the network. (Ted Koop, a former AP editor who had become CBS bureau chief in Washington, was asked by WTOP management to release somebody from his nine-man staff to read the news on television; he looked around the room and said, "Try Cronkite there. He's the newest man.") The studios were a long cab ride from the bureau office, and it was believed that Cronkite memorized his script in the cab, giving him a unique capacity (this was before the days of the TelePrompTer) to mesmerize his audience by staring at the camera rather than reading. Cronkite was surprised to hear it. "I never had a script," he said; "I don't think a good newsman needs a script. If you go to a cocktail party and someone says, 'What happened today?' you should be able to tick it off just the same way you would on the screen." By the time he got to the national news, of course, such initiative was forbidden, and the best Cronkite could do to maintain what he considered a valuable spontaneity was a fast rewrite of what had been prepared for him, done in the last fifteen minutes before he went on the air. Covering moon shots or the funerals of great men or elections, however, Cronkite regained his power to improvise, and was marvelous at it, blending the events of the moment with the remembered contents of the giant black loose-leaf notebooks (typed in a large, TelePrompTer-style typeface in case Cronkite wished to read it on the air instead of reabsorbing it during commercial breaks).

When the Korean War began, Hewitt first stocked the Edwards show studio with detailed maps, and then ordered and bought a permanent relief map made of clay, on which little figures in uniform and tanks could be moved, while Edwards indicated the battle lines with a pointer. The active film library of the show was stuff Hewitt had squirreled away in his desk drawers. ("You'd have a story about Eskimos," Edwards recalled, "and Hewitt somehow would have some film. He'd put it on and I'd say, 'Eskimos like these.'") The most famous of Hewitt's contrivances for the Edwards news show was the "visual" to accompany the story of the first Sputnik. Hewitt sent the office boy out to buy a globe, a small electric motor, a Ping-Pong ball, string and some toothpicks. He stuck the toothpicks into the Ping-Pong ball and rigged it onto a wire clothes hanger attached to the electric motor, so that it could be swung around the globe. As Edwards read the story of the Soviet achievement, the camera followed the toothpicked Ping-Pong ball endlessly circling the earth. Gary Gates in his fine history of CBS News reports that this device "greatly helped [Edwards] explain . . . what Sputnik was, and what it was doing Up There."[7] Both Edwards and Hewitt have more cynically said that they thought most of their audience believed they were actually watching the Russian satellite in action.

Still, the fact was that Swayze's medicine-show flamboyance was more popular than Edwards' earnestness for the first six years of their competition. NBC had many more affiliates—indeed, more owned stations, for CBS had been slow to apply for channels—and from December 1948 to April 1952 new channel allocations were frozen by the FCC, initially with fairly open recognition that the government had goofed in its initial original technical specifications for channel separation, later as a pious expression of austerity in the Korean War period. Still significantly outgunned in radio news, and interested in promoting the sale of RCA television sets even if the price was an unprofitable broadcasting network, NBC was ready to make greater investments in television. Thanks to *Today,* a morning newsmagazine show invented by Sylvester (Pat) Weaver, a jug-eared Dartmouth-educated idealistic advertising man who became president of the broadcasting network in 1950, NBC had a much larger appetite for nonfiction television film than CBS did, and began hiring newsreel cameramen away from their former employers as early as 1949, when CBS was still entirely dependent on Telenews.

Interest in news and dependence on broadcasting for it steadily declined in the years after the war, a trend perceived quite early on (of course) by Bill Paley, with his born showman's antennae for public attitudes. Having detached Murrow from executive office in the news division, Paley now commanded that the news operation report to Hubbell Robinson, another adman, somewhat less intellectual than Weaver, who had produced shows for Young & Rubicam in the radio days and had moved on to be CBS program director. Davidson Taylor resigned as news v.p. in protest (Weaver then hired him into NBC, where Taylor hired his successor, Reuven Frank, a transplanted Canadian newspaperman, and John Chancellor, and Chet Huntley; and somewhat reluctantly went along with Frank's recommendation to give prominent airtime to David Brinkley, like Taylor a fundamentally shy, very bright, serious-minded, self-educated mountaineer). Paley asked Taylor to choose his own successor, and of course Taylor did so. This was Sig Mickelson, a paunchy, matter-of-fact, soft-spoken Scandinavian-American, formerly a journalism school professor, who was at CBS affiliate WCCO in Minneapolis, running a local news operation that had an astonishing lock on its own market and probably made more money than any other news division in the country. The CBS News that became nationally dominant was in large part Mickelson's creation, and he did it without the direct relations with Paley that his predecessors and his successors (especially Richard Salant and Fred Friendly) enjoyed.

"When I came," Mickelson recalled, "the total manpower pool for television news was thirteen people—four producers, two graphic artists, four technicians, two producer-directors, and Edwards. We had one corner of a floor at 485 Madison Avenue, and we were forever running from there to the studios at Liederkranz Hall [about eight blocks away]. Telenews gave us inferior dog and pony shows and monkey acts, and occasional presidential speeches. We had no way of coordinating oral reports with film. The first job I had was to build a film organization, and I had to do it at long distance, I had no time with Paley, I had to make the sale to Jack Van Volkenburg [then president of the network]. I needed two million dollars, a ridiculous figure, and eventually I got it."

Mickelson actually hired Fred Friendly, though he had of course talked it over with Murrow (who had gone off to Korea to do some firsthand reporting of the early months of the war). Friendly had worked with Murrow on a free-lance basis to make phonograph records, but he was employed by NBC. Even then, it was understood that to hire Friendly was to hire trouble—he was big, a moose of a man, to use the image then current, aggressive, excitable and very, very confident: "a lot of courage and zip and zeal and oh, boy!" Paley said some years later, "but a difficult guy." Still, Mickelson wanted a sort of *Time* magazine of the air; Murrow would be much more likely to do it with Friendly at the controls, and it was clear that only Murrow could get the necessary clearances. (When they brought the idea to Paley, indeed, *Hear It Now* was to be a half-hour weekly radio show, and Paley said, "Why don't you take an hour?"; on television, *See It Now*, sponsored by Alcoa, was a weekly half hour.) Once the program was launched, however, Mickelson was out of the loop: the budget for *See It Now* was roughly double that of the rest of the television news department put together, and it was approved directly by Paley without submission to Mickelson.

It was Mickelson, too, who picked Cronkite to "anchor" (he seems to have invented the word) the CBS coverage of the 1952 conventions, hired reporters Charles Kuralt and Harry Reasoner and producers Ernest Leiser and Les Midgley, and really established the rule, which held until the early 1980s, that in television as on radio, CBS news would not be entertainment or personality features. (Interviews, those quintessential pseudo-events, were absolutely forbidden on a CBS network news show.) If Mickelson gave Hewitt his head—and he did—it was on the understanding that Hewitt *wanted* to run a headline service. What did him in, oddly enough, was the increasing importance of the news service in the aftermath of the quiz-show scandals.

CBS president Frank Stanton had not taken a major interest in news before (his entry into broadcasting, after all, had been as a psychological researcher who developed, with Paul Lazarsfeld of Columbia University, the "Stanton-Lazarsfeld Program Analyzer," still in use and still bearing their names, standardized tests of approval or disapproval of the elements of an entertainment program by a more or less random audience gathered on street corners and shepherded into studios). When congressional committees jumped on the bandwagon of the quiz-show scandals to garner ink and TV attention for their members, the industry needed a spokesman, and Stanton, suave and smart, blond, square and horn-rimmed, a fully credentialed "Dr." and a man of considerable real accomplishment, fit the bill precisely.

Early on in the scandals, the Eisenhower administration seems to have decided to use them for public benefit—i.e., to force a higher standard of programming behavior on the networks. On instructions—possibly from as high up as the President himself—John Doerfer, then head of the Federal Communications Commission, a political appointee generally regarded as a friend of the industry, summoned the presidents of the three broadcasting companies to Washington for a meeting. They came: Kintner, the growling, crew-cut, overweight newsman who had taken over for Pat Weaver at NBC; Leonard Goldenson, the handsomely tailored oh-so-smooth bankruptcy lawyer who had parlayed his control of Paramount Theatres into control of a broadcasting empire; and Stanton. Doerfer said that the Administration was prepared to preserve the industry from some of the more rugged new regulatory restrictions being discussed in Congress, provided there was a pledge by the networks to expand their coverage of public affairs, which had shrunk to virtually nothing beyond the fifteen-minute nightly news shows and the news component of the breakfast shows.

To give the public full benefit, Doerfer added, the networks should come to an agreement that they would schedule these new programs in prime time, and in different slots on the three networks, so that people would have access to all such shows. The broadcasters had been tipped that something of this sort was in the wind, and one of them said to Doerfer with the air of a sympathetic parent explaining something to a child that of course this was an excellent idea, but the antitrust laws forbade their meeting together for such an allocation of time. Doerfer heard him out, and pulled from his desk drawer a letter from Attorney General Herbert Brownell to the effect that the procedure outlined would not violate the law.

The result was a sizable expansion of the news staffs at NBC and CBS (the frugal Goldenson arranged with an outside supplier, Drew Associates, to provide *cinéma-vérité* for ABC's use; this generated, in a program called *Primary* about the Kennedy-Humphrey contest in West Virginia in 1960, with the candidates and their supporters closely miked and no announcer at all, an astonishingly original and revealing piece of reporting). At CBS, a weekly half hour was committed to Les Midgley, a veteran of the Paris *Herald Trib* and *Look* (and a laid-back long-headed Mormon from Salt Lake City, who gave orders by crooking a finger rather than, as had been the tradition, by screaming). Midgley created the equivalent of a newsmagazine lead story, occupying a half hour every Friday night. By temperament and early training, Midgley had a preference for the late-breaking story (as did Cronkite, his most frequent anchor, establishing the credentials that led to his takeover of the Edwards job two years later); he pioneered the use of electronic news gathering (ENG) resources, particularly the newfangled videotape cameras. NBC's equivalent show tended to be on Saturday night (the NBC system created "instant specials," but the instancy might be influenced by the price of the time in which the show was to run), and helped promote the careers of John Chancellor, Edwin Newman and Frank McGee.

As part of this expansion, Kintner gave hands-on attention to his news division (with varying degrees of pain, people remember being called at four in the morning because the boss, who didn't sleep, had an idea for a story). On Eisenhower's departure from office Goldenson hired his press secretary, the hugely competent James Hagerty, to be ABC corporate director of public affairs. Hagerty was too amused by the world to fight for airtime, but he brought over from CBS the experienced producer Elmer Lower to run the news division and the irritated Howard K. Smith to anchor ABC's nightly news show. Mickelson's job at CBS was upgraded when a separate news division was formed and he was made its president, reporting, for the first time, directly to the president of the parent corporation (Stanton) rather than to the president of the network (then James Aubrey, a Hollywood type who was both elegant and intelligent, but much too tough not only in his attitude toward news—which he openly considered a waste of what would otherwise be profitable broadcast time—but also in regard to the perks of his office, which he abused to his own as well as the network's damage).

Only Kintner in this group really believed in news as a service to the community, and kept his finger always poised above the button that cut away from entertainment programming to news. Fred Friendly wrote sourly of an occasion in 1964 when "Bill McAndrew, head of NBC News, and I were returning to New York from Washington by plane. Over Philadelphia, word was flashed to us that Nikita Khrushchev had fallen from power. As soon as we landed we each called our offices, I to plead with Aubrey, and then Stanton, to get a half-hour for a special report that night, and McAndrew to hear that Kintner had already ordered a one-hour program."[8]

The operation was now too large for Mickelson's span of control, and the people he hired to help him were utterly unable to handle Hewitt or Friendly, or to make sense of Midgley's budget for the weekly *Eyewitness* show. Moreover, Huntley and Brinkley were beating up the Edwards show in the ratings (and absolutely destroyed Cronkite & Co. in the coverage of the political conventions in summer 1960: in one measured time period, the NBC convention coverage had an unheard-of 4–1 edge over CBS). Early in 1961, Mickelson was fired, and Richard Salant, a lean and argumentative lawyer from one of New York's biggest and most political firms, who had signed on as CBS vice president and general counsel nine years earlier on Stanton's promise that he would get more to do than just law, was installed as Mickelson's successor. It is probably fair to note that Salant was well connected in the Kennedy camp, and that temperamentally Mickelson was part of the Eisenhower era.

The early 1960s saw a great reduction of the heat on the networks to make time available for public affairs programs and documentaries; despite Newton Minow's rhetoric about the "vast wasteland" of television programming, the Kennedy administration was far more tender than Eisenhower had been about leaning on broadcasters. Midgley's *Eyewitness* show retained its Friday-night slot, Friday being a low-audience night anyway (parents of high-school-age children go to basketball games: it is understood that commercial networks will not schedule athletic events on television on Friday nights). "The show got a stable audience," Midgley recalled, "a 25 share [i.e., 25 percent of the homes watching television, perhaps 15 percent of all U.S. households, watched *Eyewitness*]. It didn't matter if we put on Marilyn Monroe's death or a show on the balance of payments, we got a 25 share." The importance of the program, Midgley argued, was that "it opened people's eyes to the fact that you *could* do a half-hour news show."

This was something Salant wanted on principle, and also because he felt it would be an accomplishment that would help his relations with a news division suspicious of a new boss who was not a newsman by training or profession. (Hewitt, interestingly, "did not think a half-hour show was such a great idea. I thought we had a good product, people were watching, people didn't want a half hour of local news and then another half hour of national. It was easier to do a half-hour show, of course—wasn't it Lord Chesterfield who apologized to someone for writing a long letter because he didn't have time to write a short one?") When *Eyewitness* lost its slot, which inevitably would happen, there would be plenty of staff to send out on stories for a longer news show; meanwhile, Salant, who had access to budget, added news bureaus in Los Angeles, Atlanta and Dallas to the established operations in New York, Washington and Chicago. On Labor Day 1963, the *CBS Evening News* became a half-hour show with a broadcast that in a way—though nobody could have known it at the time—made history.

It is an instructive lesson in the way the world really works. Hewitt was getting married, and the bride was a friend of Jack Kennedy's. The President invited Don and Frankie to the White House for a celebratory drink, and asked the prospective Mrs. Hewitt what she would like for a wedding present. With some courage, she noted that her husband's news program was about to go to half an hour, and that it would be very useful if for that first show, the Labor Day Monday, when audiences might otherwise be light, they had something immensely promotable—like a live interview with the President in his summer retreat at Hyannis Port. Kennedy punched the intercom and asked his press secretary, Pierre Salinger, whether he could see any objection. Salinger said no, and the deed was done. And it was during this interview that Kennedy said, more or less in passing, that while the United States was committed to preventing an armed takeover of South Vietnam by its northern neighbor, it was not pledged to any particular non-Communist government in Saigon. The generals, who had grown tired of Ngo Dinh Diem (and of his sister-in-law, with her publicized scorn for self-immolating Buddhist monks), took this comment as the signal for which they were waiting, and presently Diem and his brother were dead, and the United States, like it or not, had a different kind of commitment in South Vietnam. At the moment of its execution, Cronkite's exclusive Kennedy interview was a perfect pseudo-event, staged to make the show look important; in retrospect it was proof that even pseudo-events can make history. One can speculate idly whether the course of events would have been different if American views on the Diem government had been otherwise communicated.

2

One event changed relations between television news and the American public: the assassination of John F. Kennedy. Virtually everyone who was sentient that Friday afternoon remembers what he was doing when he heard the news (I was lunching with Paul DeWitt, executive secretary of the City Association of the Bar in New York, arranging among other things my use of their library while working on my book *The Lawyers*). People who worked for broadcasting network news divisions also remember what they did next: they went to the office to attach themselves to the ganglia of their communication centers, and many of them did not go home again for eighty-odd hours. They called it, later, "the four dark days," because for four days the entertainment divisions were, in theatrical lingo, "dark," and the news divisions filled all the time, twenty-four hours a day, without commercial interruption.

As communications professor Wilbur Schramm at Stanford wrote a year later, "television journalism grew up in Dallas, for never before had it faced such a story with so much of the responsibility for telling it."[9] Gary Gates leads his history of CBS News with the tale of the four days, stressing that they established Walter Cronkite with the American audience, in part by his tears when announcing the President's death and in part by his calm communicativeness as the most frequent anchor (Harry Reasoner spelled him) in the days ahead. But the crucial difference was in the relations between the consuming public and television news as an institution. Before 1963, the Roper Poll question "Where do you usually get most of your news about what's going on in the world today?" always showed newspapers ahead of television; after 1963, television took a clear and steadily widening lead. Ben Bagdikian has shrewdly pointed out that the words "going on in the world" bias the answers, because people rely on newspapers for their local news, which except at moments of emergency (if then) nobody expects to get from the sex-and-violence, service-and-sports, people-as-entertainment stuff on the local channels.[10] Still, at those less than frequent but more than scarce moments when nonlocal news commands popular attention, people since the four days of Kennedy do turn to television, as they had not in the years before.

CBS's man on the scene was Dan Rather, just starting out as the reporter in the network's Dallas bureau. More or less by inadvertence, he got a beat on the news of the death: he was talking from an office with someone at the hospital, trying to confirm an anonymous doctor's previous "my understanding" statement, and not realizing he was also on an open line to the CBS Radio editor in New York. NBC got even on Sunday when New York went live to Tom Pettit at Dallas police headquarters (where there had been a lot to look at: the murder weapon, carried through throngs in the hallway before the cameras, the coffee can with paraffin wax that had been used to test the prisoner's hands for gunpowder, etc.) just as Lee Harvey Oswald was brought down to meet his fate at the hands of Jack Ruby. (Fortunately, videotape had arrived, and only a few minutes later CBS was able to show *its* viewers the murder on the tape, almost as good as live.)

Robert MacNeil (later of MacNeil-Lehrer) handled the nonpolice material from Dallas for NBC; Sandor Vanocur, quickly recalled from vacation, covered the White House angles. Roger Mudd, also a newcomer, did the commentary for CBS from the Capitol Rotunda, where the body lay in state. ABC, still lightly staffed (its regular nightly news show would run only fifteen minutes for another four years, and it was still farming out its documentary productions), relied heavily on Howard K. Smith and Edward P. Morgan at anchor desks. At CBS, Don Hewitt produced the daytime hours, which were heavy on news and traditional political commentary, while Les Midgley took charge of the evening hours, including a two-hour obit of the President narrated and partly written by Harry Reasoner, a symphonic concert on Sunday night and a two-hour roundup of the four dark days, the work of Charles Collingwood, on Monday night. The film librarians and editors performed heroic labors, going through a vast mass of Kennedy material for the obituaries; the assistants and secretaries manned the phones perpetually, recruiting political personages, academics, old acquaintances of the late President to come to the studios for roundtable discussions; the foreign bureaus gathered official and man-in-the-street reaction to be fed into the great maw of the clock.

According to Nielsen, 96 percent of the nation's household television sets were tuned to stations covering the assassination and its postludes, and people watched on the average thirty-two of the eighty-two hours between the assassination and midnight on Monday night. For much of this time everybody was watching the same thing, for the networks pooled most of their coverage of the scenes in the Rotunda, the cortege, the funeral, Johnson's swearing-in, etc. There can be no question that the instrument of television tied the country together in ways unlike anything that had ever been known before. William A. Mindak and Gerald D. Hursh of the University of Minnesota did long interviews with "48 adult residents of Minneapolis during the week after the assassination," and came to several strong and definite conclusions: "In the uncertainty caused by the assassination crisis, television was an important source of information that alleviated some of the anxiety to test reality beyond the living room. It structured and clarified the extent of personal threat by providing believable standards of judgment. It was a catalyst for people's emotions, since it induced a deep sense of personal participation in the flow of events. It gave timely reassurance by showing the existence and continuity of cherished institutions and values. It reinforced social prescriptions of correct behavior by showing the exemplary conduct of the nation's leaders. It encouraged almost immediate faith in the new President by rapidly emphasizing his experience and capabilities. And it helped to narcotize behavior that might have been dangerous by exhausting the need for action."[11]

In 1979, I gave the equivalent of a keynote speech to a weeklong Seminar on Television and Society sponsored by the Sloan Foundation and held at the Chatham Bars Inn on Cape Cod, with a mixed bag of American, English and Israeli social scientists and print and broadcast journalists as participants. (Though none of us knew it at the time, this was the very inn where Roone Arledge worked as a waiter while a Columbia undergraduate, and by special courtesies to a stranger who drove up beyond the usual dinner hour won a later opportunity in television when the stranger turned out to be the vice president in charge of programming for the DuMont network. . . . They make history on Cape Cod.) I took the coverage of the Kennedy assassination as my centerpiece. Les Midgley was one of the planners as well as one of the participants in the seminar, and he brought along videotape to illustrate my points. Stephen White of the Foundation some weeks later wrote a report of the seminar that has never been published, and was indeed intended mostly for the use of the participants, whom White hoped to keep thinking about these matters. He described the discussion after the keynote as follows:

> . . . Several of the participants referred to the fashion in which the coverage repeatedly broke away from the Kennedy family and the ritual of the funeral to the business-like manner in which the new administration and President Johnson were carrying on the affairs of government. It was proposed that this was the calculated response of television to the uncertainty and indeed the terror that had swept the country with news of the assassination. The question that directly followed concerned the origins of that response. Was it dictated by the powers-that-be who govern the three networks from Sixth Avenue—possibly after consultation among themselves? Was it consciously devised by the journalists of the several news departments to meet some kind of social need they had perceived, analyzed and quickly met? Or was it perhaps a consequence of the fact that the journalists themselves shared the general anxiety and were relieving it for their own sakes the best ways they knew how?
>
> . . . It was pointed out that the seminar included the gentleman [Midgley] who had exercised much of the responsibility for the coverage. . . . The question might reasonably be posed to him. What, then, were the circumstances under which he made the long series of journalistic decisions he was called upon to make? What principles, journalistic or otherwise, governed those decisions? His response was immediate and brief: "I was doing my job." (He was quoted subsequently as having said, "I was *only* doing my job" or *"just* doing my job," neither of which is quite the same thing.)
>
> That remark, simple enough as it was, sent a perceptible shock wave through the seminar. In general, the seminar was marked by courtesy and amiability, but the discussions that followed indicated that those five short words were being construed in at least three different fashions, none of them at all complimentary to the man who uttered them. These were, in no particular order: 1) that he was being defensive, not being proud of what he had done; 2) that he was being evasive, not being willing to disclose why he had done it; or 3) that he was just plain stupid.
>
> Yet those journalists present who worked within television . . . found the answer not only satisfactory but something a good deal more: it was shorthand,

to be sure, but still the only straightforward answer that can be supplied such a question. Journalism is a craft; the superior journalist is the superior craftsman. He acts in response to the dictates of his judgment as it is brought into play by the nature of the material with which he is confronted. That is his job. To the extent that the activity in which he is engaged is collaborative—and in television it is extremely collaborative—his judgment at any instant may be affected by the judgments of his colleagues, who are craftsmen in his own mold. But it is part of the tradition of his craft that those collective judgments are not to be affected by any but fellow craftsmen—not by the people who sell advertising; not by those who provide capital for the enterprise or who represent those who have provided the capital; not by the accountants down the hall; certainly not by the government; and oddly enough not even very much by the people for whom his product is finally intended.[12]

Richard Salant remembers that when he was new on the job as president of the news division, he would drop down on the Cronkite show in the morning, carrying with him the lineup of the previous night. "I'd say, 'Why'd you play this story here?' and they'd say, 'Matter of news judgment.' Three years later, when I came down and asked the question, Cronkite said, 'If you don't understand it now, you never will.' " But after all the joking is done, this *is* the central question. When publisher Cathleen Black of *USA Today* says that her paper is not supposed to appeal to reporters and editors ("It's the first paper written for readers"[13]), she is saying that there's not really much reason why the First Amendment should protect it. When Van Gordon Sauter, while president of CBS News, related his show to "the proper use of the medium," he denied the relevance of the only judgment the people who work for him cared about, and ultimately stimulated Don Hewitt and Dan Rather in their quixotic attempt to buy the network news division and run it themselves. More than thirty years ago, I wrote in *Harper's Magazine* that, called upon to defend themselves, television programmers would say, "There's nobody here but us capons and we give the public what they want." This was not the attitude of the people in broadcast news: they considered themselves roosters. Now, one sometimes feels, they know better. . . .

To be fair, it is also possible for serious-minded people to take a more cynical view. David Adams, who was for years executive vice president of NBC, an owlish lawyer from Buffalo who was kept impartial by a personal combination of deeply conservative beliefs with Democratic politics, once recalled an episode with Lester Crystal, then president of NBC News (and later producer of the MacNeil-Lehrer show on PBS). Adams had been receiving complaints from Republican politicos that *Today* and *Meet the Press* had been neglecting the Republican side of the political coin and that the time had come to invite some Republicans. Crystal brushed Adams aside, and Adams, who had verified the Republican statistics but had not wished to make a major issue of the matter, asked him why. "News judgment," Crystal replied briskly. Two hours later, Crystal was on the phone to Adams: he had reconsidered his position, and the NBC shows had just booked two Republicans. Adams was unable to refrain from asking why the news judgment had changed, and Crystal, whose transparent honesty was and is among his major qualifications, replied, "I've just learned that CBS is doing it."

What remains to be added is that such questions could not conceivably have been debated about television news prior to the 1960s: among the points illustrated by the coverage of the Kennedy assassination was the fact that the medium had escaped the trap of available film. Also that this was not, for at least some of the participants, the moment of most unbearable tension. That came four and a half years later, with the murder of Martin Luther King, Jr. Robert Wussler, later to be executive vice president of Ted Turner's Broadcasting Co., was then in charge of special events (space shots, riots, assassinations, etc.) at CBS News. "I was in my office, at a planning meeting on the coverage of the '68 conventions, and we were totally bare. Bill Leonard was out of town. Gordon Manning (then v.p. for hard news) was in his car on the West Side Highway. Cronkite was in Washington, but Dan Rather was in New York because Johnson had been meeting with some Democratic fund-raisers. Stanton called and said, 'Whatever you do, please —please—stay on the air.' We did an eleven o'clock all-points roundup, preempting local news and running until one A.M. Then all morning we ran five-minute interrupts every twenty minutes. We brought in black leaders, and had a roundtable with Rather moderating. I have vivid memories of the confusion, the potential riots all over the country. In neither of the Kennedy things did there seem to be any danger of nationwide panic, but the King story was *very* dangerous."

3

There is also a date for the moment when the television news organizations were compelled to realize that they and not the newspapers or the wire services were the senior partners in the distribution of news to the American public. That date is June 4, 1964, and the event was the California Republican primary pitting Nelson Rockefeller against Barry Goldwater. Most of the polls closed at 10 P.M. eastern time, though those in San Francisco would be open until eleven. The results were going to be close. There was some question whether the traditional way of reporting election results, which was by the compilation of the figures AP and UPI gathered at the county centers, would give a result before the eastern time zone went to bed. And all three news divisions saw considerable prestige value, and probably some audience value, for the network that first called the outcome, especially if the call was correct. (Though calling elections wrong does not do as much damage as you might think: WCBS in New York called the 1981 governor's race in New Jersey on the basis of exit polls that showed Democrat James Florio defeating Republican Thomas Kean; Kean won, and today nobody except maybe Kean and Florio and a few people at the station remembers.)

"We realized," said Robert Chandler, who managed the CBS election coverage in 1964, "that the votes were available at the election precincts, and you didn't have to wait for them to be trucked to the county centers for tabulation. That was easy in New Hampshire, where there were only 302 election precincts. California was different—Los Angeles had something like 16,000 precincts. NBC and CBS each hired about 25,000 people, housewives, high school students, cabdrivers, to take down the results at each precinct; ABC hired about 15,000. We rented the Biltmore Bowl, had banks and banks of telephones. By eleven o'clock California time we were reporting ninety percent of the vote, and we showed Goldwater leading by a considerable margin. AP and UPI were reporting only about forty percent of the vote, and one of their big holes was Los Angeles, where the Goldwater voters were. The early papers in New York reported that Rockefeller was ahead, and that the networks had made a great boo-boo in calling the election. The later editions said, 'Goldwater has taken the lead.' The newspapers saw the election as a horse race of ballot counting, not of voting."

The importance of this event was missed in public commentary, because attention was focused on another aspect of the CBS election coverage, the prediction of results based on sample precincts through what pollster Lou Harris called "Vote Profile Analysis." Thanks to this computerized statistical system, CBS called the primary results as early as 7:23 P.M., when some of the polls in the northern part of the state were still open, and when the tabulation at the Biltmore Bowl was still well below 10 percent of the total vote. "Today," Chandler said a few years ago, "the public pretty much takes for granted the accuracy of projections. At that time, it was all new— and you had the emotional element of the computer making the statement for us." What dominated discussion of June 4 in the weeks immediately thereafter, then, was the propriety—even morality—of calling elections while some polls were still open. This issue, of course, is still very much alive, now that exit polls allow statisticians to know election results within a fairly narrow range of probable error long before the polls have closed. Exit polls were pioneered by CBS in 1967 to give the analysts something more or less real to talk about in the interstices of the real news (winners and losers) of election night, but they were not used to call an election until NBC accurately proclaimed senatorial and gubernatorial winners in 1978 (and then called Reagan over Carter at 8:15 P.M. eastern time in 1980, more than an hour and a half before ABC gave this datum its imprimatur, and more than two and a quarter hours before CBS was willing to move, though both had the same information NBC had).

Within the news business, however, the imbroglio of the 1964 California primary was a thunderclap. The wire services on that Wednesday afternoon tipped their flags and put in calls to the managements of the television networks, which were themselves somewhat distressed at the immense costs of the operation they had mounted. By the time of the political conventions, the networks and the wire services had agreed, with the consent of the Justice Department, to combine their narrow tally-gathering activities in a single News Election Service that would feed identical data to newspapers and radio and television news services. The relative financial shares of the broadcasters and the wire services in this effort have never been made public, and might not be meaningful anyway, because the wire services can directly contribute personnel from their stables of stringers, but there is no question that the networks are the senior partners. Since spring of 1964, people on both sides of the divide between print and broadcast have had to live with the fact that on sporting-events stories like elections, Washington stories, foreign stories and life/death stories like wars, famines, storms and earthquakes—all areas where the weight of temporarily purchased resources counts heavily in the immediacy and accuracy of the coverage—the television networks are likely to outperform the newspapers. Discreetly high on the pillars in the newsrooms of the New York *Times* and the Washington *Post,* and facing the producer and the writers of the Group W round-the-clock radio news shows in their studios across the country, are the television screens, usually blank, live when there is news in the air.

It has been almost as hard for the TV news divisions to live with this truth as it has been for the newspapers. Even today, as Stephen Hess of the Brookings Institution reports, "television and radio correspondents tend to take their cues as to what is news from their print counterparts, particularly from those who report for prestigious newspapers."[14] Evelyn Konrad, who covered business news for *Today* in 1980, remembers a piece she did on the dangers to the U.S. steel industry from mounting imports, complete with footage of ships and mills and interviews with chief executives of steel companies. It was a clear beat: nobody else had yet told that story. That afternoon she received a call from Richard Wald, then the number-two man at NBC News. "I don't remember seeing that story in the *Times,"* Wald said. "No," said Ms. Konrad proudly. "It was all mine." Wald said, "Let's not do things like that anymore, Evelyn. Remember, only two percent of our audience sees the New York *Times.* If we just follow the *Times* on stories like that, it will still be news for us." Roone Arledge, president of ABC News (and Wald's present boss), refuses to believe that such a statement could be made in this day and age, but the fact is that the front pages of the first editions of the New York *Times* and Washington *Post* are thermofaxed to ABC's London bureau at about one in the morning (six in the morning, London time) so that its chief can be plugged in to what will be on New York's mind before he gives the day's final assignments to his staff.

In general, the TV news shows give the story the evening before the morning papers have it—but they make their assignment sheets and first schedules for the show in the morning, with the *Times* and the *Post* on their minds. And these shows are very much controlled from New York: at the NBC bureaus, the New York producers are called "the grown-ups." Jack Reynolds of NBC, who has roamed the world for that network, says, "There are two kinds of producers. One says, 'Hey, what's going on out there?' and when you come up with a story that's news, he doesn't say, 'How come I haven't seen this in the *Times?*' That kind is in short supply. The other kind calls and says, 'At the morning meeting today'—and you know you're in trouble."

"When I read statistics that show sixty percent of Americans get all or most of their news from television," Av Westin said while executive producer of ABC's *World News Tonight* some years ago, "I shudder. I know what we have to leave out."[15] The problem is systemic. Gilbert Millstein, ex-New York *Times,* gray-haired, stumpy, crew-cut, gravel-voiced and almost seventy, a wonderful prose stylist and for twenty years the words editor for *NBC Nightly News,* says flatly that "the concept of news on television is often as not completely different from what it is in print. The picture determines whether it's news on television." As ABC's Arledge says, very sensibly and not at all defensively, "If we have a picture of a building collapsing or the MGM Grand fire, it is going to become a much bigger story on television because of the spectacular pictures." There is also a case to be made for Jack Reynolds' belief that you can compress the text more easily than the visual; as Reynolds puts it, "You have to let the film breathe." Thus the running antagonism of the print and broadcast reporters. The newspapermen resent the TV correspondents' money; the broadcast journalists envy the print reporters their relative freedom to work on their own, go where they wish when they wish, put together their story from multiple sources, write it to much greater length—and see it played with the prominence sophisticated news judgment would give it.

The resources available to television news are truly incredible by the measurements of twenty years ago. As late as the early 1960s, very high, almost uncomfortable light levels were needed for a TV camera to take pictures, and feeding pictures to the home office could be done only through coaxial cable from a studio: TV news coverage was almost all on film, which would have to be physically transported and developed before it could be used. Fred Friendly compared television reporting to writing a news story with a two-ton pencil. Political campaigning concentrated on the noon hour, when you could get the crowds and still have time to put the meeting on the evening news. The visual side of European or Asian news pretty much had to be flown across the ocean (BBC and NBC had a very slow facsimile arrangement that permitted about one minute of film per day to be moved through the telephone cable). When videotape came into use,

European and American news services could not interchange, because the 625-line, 25-frames-per-second European picture was incompatible with the 525-line, 30-frames-per-second American picture. There was one machine in London—just one—that could convert one kind of tape to the other: it completely filled a studio and had to be booked in advance. Editing video-tape domestically took an extremely skilled hand, because sound and picture were geographically separated on the tape. When the synchronous satellite came in the late 1960s, its use by news divisions was strictly curtailed for budgetary reasons, because the FCC had set a rate schedule that required the booking of at least ten minutes at a time from point to point, with a price of more than $2,000 for the transmission. (In Canada, where prices for satellite circuits were uncontrolled, the cost was $50 a minute for a TV-capable transponder.)

Now all that has changed. There are lightweight cameras that can use available light, and portable videotape machines and heavy but movable editing machines and trucks with dishes that can make contact with the satellite from anywhere; and the cost of a minute on the satellite is trivial. In 1984, NBC switched its transmitting network from AT&T cable to a Ku-band satellite system operating very high up on the radio-frequency spectrum that can work with dishes only three feet in diameter. Ku-band dishes made possible "uplinks" from relatively small trucks that could go to any story, trucks that were in fact put in service by KSTP-TV of Minneapolis and its allies in Conus Communications even before NBC was ready to use the technology for news (sports came first, by a large margin); we shall examine the details of the story in Chapter 15.

Even without this wonderful new technology, however, television's capacity to get to a story, display it, and even give the background (if anybody cares) has become a miracle of the age. Speaking of his network's plans to cover live from Ho Chi Minh City the Vietnamese government's parade in honor of the tenth anniversary of the fall of Saigon ("It might well happen during *Nightline,* and Ted Koppel will be over there"), Roone Arledge noted that "we can always interrupt. We can cut away. We can be live for two minutes and on tape for ten or we can be live for ten and on tape for two—the whole thing is in our control. We can split the picture. We can point the cameras wherever we want to point. We can do anything we want to do."

The difference between twenty years ago and now may be even more striking in terms of the financial resources of the news divisions. In 1966, explaining CBS's decision to stay with a fifth rerun of *I Love Lucy* rather than cover George Kennan's testimony on Vietnam before the Senate Foreign Relations Committee, Frank Stanton said, "The specific cost incurred by the CBS Television Network in covering . . . the Vietnam hearings, for exam-ple, amounted to just over one million dollars. . . . Obviously, since CBS News cannot be self-supporting, we must pay some attention to the economics of broadcasting in making decisions involving such costs."[16] As late as 1975, Fred Friendly was saying that the networks put money into news because it gave them "identification: ask people what network a comedian is on, and nobody knows. But ask them what network Cronkite is on, and they'll tell you."

By the 1980s, the news divisions were profit centers. In early 1985, a thirty-second spot on the *CBS Evening News* cost $55,500; on *NBC Nightly News*, $47,300; on *ABC World News Tonight*, $46,500.[17] Local stations are paid for carrying news programs by a minute a night of dead air within the show that they can sell for their own account, so the network keeps the money—probably something like $80 million for CBS, $70 million or a little less for the other two. Let us add in the revenues from *Today* and the *CBS Morning News,* and from the twenty minutes a day of *Good Morning America* for which ABC Entertainment pays ABC News, from *Nightline, 60 Minutes, 20/20,* whatever magazine show NBC attempts, occasional documentaries, weekend news, talk shows and bits and pieces (the one-minute bits and pieces in prime time are very lucrative, bringing as much as $200,000 for a thirty-second spot; but of course the spot could be sold for that price without the newsbrief). The gross revenues for commercials on news shows may touch $300 million on CBS, and probably approach $250 million on the other two networks. In short, today's revenues from the news divisions alone roughly equal the total revenues of the television networks twenty years ago.

The result is a lavishness of personnel and expenditure that has to be seen to be believed. Among them, the three networks have Washington bureaus totaling just under 2,000 employees, and London bureaus totaling more than 600. But the lavishness is deceptive, for the expenditures are concentrated on a few places and a few people. The agents for the on-camera talent and the unions for the rest eat up an amazing amount of money (by contract, the lowliest grip or driver in a network news camera team must be flown first-class whenever the team travels). Moreover, as we shall have occasion to consider in the next chapter, being a profit center is not entirely a luxury, because the proprietors of profit centers are expected to show better profits every year, while the operators of cost centers often find their budgets accepted with weary resignation. But it continues to be true, as Arledge puts it, that "there is a correlation between how much news you can cover and how much money you've got to spend." And that the wire services, the newsmagazines, the New York *Times,* the Los Angeles *Times,* the Washington *Post, The Wall Street Journal* and the Knight-Ridder's KNT news service all have more offices around the world than any of the networks. ("A newspaper," Arledge grumbles, "can afford to have a correspondent and an office with a secretary. For us to have a bureau in Santiago, we would have to have nine or ten people.") Of course, the KNT service transmits about as many words every twenty-four hours as a network news service will carry in a year.

9

The Feelies

(1) Pseudo-events are more dramatic. A television debate between candidates can be planned to be more suspenseful
. . . than a casual encounter or consecutive formal
speeches. . . .

(2) Pseudo-events, being planned for dissemination, are easier to disseminate and make vivid. . . .

(3) Pseudo-events can be repeated at will, and thus their impression can be re-enforced.

(4) Pseudo-events cost money to create; hence somebody has
an interest in disseminating, magnifying, advertising and
extolling them as events worth watching or worth believ-
ing. . . .

(5) Pseudo-events, being planned for intelligibility, are more
intelligible and hence more reassuring. Even if we cannot
discuss intelligently the qualifications of the candidates or
the complicated issues, we can at least judge the effectiveness of a television performance. How comforting to have
some political matter we can grasp!

(6) Pseudo-events are more sociable, more conversable, and
more convenient to witness. Their occurrence is planned
for our convenience. . . .

(7) Knowledge of pseudo-events—of what has been reported,
or what has been staged, and how—becomes the test of
being "informed." . . .

—Daniel Boorstin, 1962[1]

America [is] the home of the right to know. Lip service is
still paid to this ideal. Network presidents are combatively
eloquent about it. There are serious differences between their
principles and their practice.

. . . Items of important news are used as anchors for
commercials. "There has been a grave development in Saigon;
we shall have that after this message." . . . Less important
news is often given before more important news, merely to
ensure that the audience continues to be held. . . .

The constant urge to parade faces before the camera,
strings of people, some hardy regulars, others with little or no
relevance, each uttering one or two sentences of hardly any

value, is another example of the subordination of news to entertainment. . . . Brightness is all.

> –Sir William Haley, former
> editor of the London *Times* and
> director-general of the BBC,
> after sixteen months of watching
> television in Chicago, 1969[2]

"My Achilles' heel has always been that I'd rather do
something of quality than make money."
> –Roone Arledge, 1983[3]

1

The congruence of the three nightly news shows has been an article of
faith in commentary about television. Edith Efron wrote from the right of
"the rule of network conformity on major issues," and with considerable
pleasure cited a comparable comment from the left by former FCC commissioner Nicholas Johnson.[4] Cautious scholars like Edward Epstein and Herbert Gans could write books supposedly about the national TV news establishment at large based almost entirely on work done at NBC (Epstein) and
CBS (Gans) because it was generally assumed that the three networks were
essentially indistinguishable. Visiting perhaps half a dozen times at each of
the three while working on my book *About Television* in 1969–71, I found no
differences significant enough to highlight. And presumably the similarities
should be even stronger now, with CBS's Mudd at NBC and NBC's Brinkley at ABC and ABC's Ann Gorrels at NBC. Executives—Richard Salant,
William Small, Richard Wald, Paul Greenberg—have been moving about
all but interchangeably from one network to another for more than a decade. And all the big-time talent is represented and advised by the same big-
time agents.

The formats and the technical procedures are of course very similar. At
one time or another ABC has used triple anchors (Washington, Chicago,
London) and NBC for many years had a double anchor (Washington and
New York). Today everybody has a single man at a desk where no one in
fact works, though the newsrooms behind that desk are now real enough,
thanks to major construction expenditure by CBS and ABC. And the approach of having someone at a desk introducing reports from the field (or
reading stories too remote or too brief for direct exposure) has been common to the genre from early on. For good reasons and bad, it was inevitable
that the same person would be at that desk every night, and that the show
would become identified with the anchor. Cronkite's distaste for being considered an entertainer led him to demand the title of "managing editor"

and final authority if he chose to exercise it over which stories would be staffed and which correspondents would get airtime. (For many years this was more important than ego gratification or bylines, for by contract network employees were paid extra when they appeared on the screen.) Cronkite's status meant that CBS did more science stories, because Cronkite was fascinated by science (especially space, which the sailor in Cronkite saw as analogous to the great days of oceanic exploration), and fairly heavy emphasis on Washington, because Cronkite was idealistic about the importance of government and politics. This was to a degree generational. Not long before his death, Frank Reynolds told Barbara Matusow that he felt much better about anchoring from Washington: "Things don't really *happen* in New York, apart from the United Nations. . . . Washington is different. I mean I can talk to the [correspondent] on the Hill, and I can talk to *people.* I mean real people."[5]

Les Brown of *Variety* found a reason for the similarities among the network news shows: "an adoration of the New York *Times.* . . . It is the model, the textbook newspaper, from which the network news shops derive their standards for news judgments; it is secondly the supreme evaluator of their performance. Its favorable recognition of a network news effort is a source of elation within the company and held up as proof of distinguished achievement, its criticism a cause of anguish. . . . Once, to NBC's Reuven Frank, I made the observation that all three network newscasts were much alike and that with all the news stories available on any single day in a large world it was surprising that the networks seemed to cover the same ones and in roughly the same order. 'Why is that surprising?' Frank snapped. 'Look at the New York *Times.* They give the same importance to the same stories that we do.' As if to say the *Times*'s news judgment proved the validity of their own."[6]

That the minor differences in style among the three networks were indicative of major differences in substance was not apparent to me—or, I think, to anyone else who wrote for the general public about these subjects —prior to 1985 and the publication of *Nightly Horrors: Crisis Coverage in Television Network News* by Dan Nimmo and James E. Combs of the University of Tennessee. This is an intensive study of how the network newscasts dealt with five large and nasty stories in the late 1970s and early 1980s: the mass suicide at the People's Temple in Guyana, the Three Mile Island nuclear accident, the crash of an American Airlines DC-10 right after takeoff at the start of a Memorial Day weekend, the Mount St. Helens eruptions and the Iranian hostage seizure. Both by specific quotation and by clever categorization of the pieces of coverage put together by each of the news shows, the authors demonstrate clearly that each network news division maintains cultural traditions that lead to the selection of different *kinds* of information as the building blocks of a story and determine the attitudes toward that information. As the book was ignored not only in the general review media but also in the professional journals (I found out about it because the University of Tennessee Press sends me its catalogues), I consider it both an obligation and a pleasure to put some of the Nimmo and Combs material before what should be at least a somewhat larger public.

Perhaps the clearest indication of the differences is the titles the three networks chose for their special programs on Three Mile Island, which were done by the staffs and anchors of the nightly news shows. CBS had "Danger at Three Mile Island," NBC used "Crisis at Three Mile Island," and ABC trumpeted "Three Mile Island: Nuclear Nightmare."[7] This was not a question of degree of sensationalism. The three titles reflected differences in attitudes toward such a story, differences that played through all five of the examples Nimmo and Combs have pinned to the wall. CBS took the basic position that something terrible has happened, but we understand what it's about and the experts can handle it; NBC offered down-home explanations and analogies, and told viewers that things were terrible but somehow we'll muddle through because we always do; ABC warned that at the end of the day there was *nobody* in charge and real prospects that things will get worse, much worse, undefinably worse.

When CBS panicked—on March 30, after radioactivity vented from the plant and the hydrogen bubble was announced—the natural reaction was to run down some numbers: radiation would continue to leak for five days, pregnant women had been advised to leave homes within a five-mile radius of the plant, all the area's twenty-three schools had been closed, 20,000 residents within ten miles were to stay indoors, and care centers were being set up fifteen miles from Harrisburg. A report from New York's Mount Sinai Hospital explained that "the average American absorbs 100 millirems of radiation per year; a normal chest X-ray adds ten more; 5,000 millirems per year is 'considered allowable by the Government'; and 200 yards from TMI radiation was measured at 30 millirems, equivalent to three chest X-rays." On Monday, Cronkite informed the world that "the $600 million structure is 365 feet high and contains two steam generators, four pumps, and a pressurizer . . . the troublesome bubble is inside this eight-inch-thick, carbon-steeled pressure cooker," but the bubble had been reduced from 1,800 cubic feet to an estimated 47 cubic feet. . . . As Nimmo and Combs put it: "Fallout there was, but a fallout of numbers from the lips of CBS correspondents."

NBC's approach, Nimmo and Combs continue, was one of "demystification." They quote a Chancellor piece from the second evening: "A nuclear power plant is really just a big tea kettle . . ." and his introduction to the events of "Black Friday," when the existence of the hydrogen bubble was recognized: "There was serious trouble today at the Three Mile Island nuclear plant in Pennsylvania, trouble serious enough to cause the evacuation of small children and pregnant women from a five-mile area around the endangered plant. The problem is that it is more difficult than had been thought to cool the radioactive fuel inside the power plant, and until it is cooled, it is very dangerous . . ." Steve Delaney was on the scene, interviewing residents: "The people here in Goldsboro don't seem to know whether the nuclear power plant is more beneficial or dangerous; some are scared, some are not." NBC under Reuven Frank had also acquired a taste for the brief episode in which people are talking to each other rather than responding to an interviewer, and caught one here between a local fire chief and a civil defense director. The point of it all, Nimmo and Combs write, was that things "seem less critical once their sources are revealed, once it is clear, as the Wizard of Oz said to Dorothy, 'I'm not a bad man, just a bad wizard.' "

ABC, on the other hand, offered what Nimmo and Combs call "a tradition of fear. . . . The thrust of the verbal, visual and sound imagery conveyed the basic elements familiar to fans of nightmare melodramas: a Gothic setting, a populist leaning which stressed sentimental values, and unrelenting threat." The ABC correspondents "did stand-up reports with the plant's massive cooling towers, enveloped in mist, looming in the background. Frequently the network's films cut from such a plant setting to panoramic views of farms, cattle grazing on fields, and school buses departing the area. While ABC correspondents narrated accounts of school closings, evacuations, worried farmers and housewives, lead-ins and summations took place before the turret-like cooling towers, the icons of a Frankensteinian castle. . . . On April 3 as a correspondent hinted at 'new problems,' a camera panned back from a close-up of the towers, across the river to houses, abandoned bikes and an abandoned little red wagon. Radioactive iodine was showing up in milk, said the reporter (actually it did not). The camera, with the cooling towers still visible in the background, focused upon grazing cows. Off camera came the cry of a baby and the crackling of a Geiger counter."[8]

In all the cases Nimmo and Combs examine, the pattern is similar. Dealing with Mount St. Helens, ABC "was distinctive for its focus upon melodramatic features: the death of victims, the search for survivors, the spirit of heroes, and the plight of fools. 'The Mount St. Helens volcano continues to darken the skies for hundreds of miles and slash a path of death and destruction across the ground,' said anchor Frank Reynolds in the first ABC report on the disaster." Later, there was "still the threat that the mountain might erupt again . . ." and there was an earthen dam "that might give way . . ." On balance, however, ABC remained relatively cool by its usual standards, interviewing, for example, an eleven-year-old girl who said, "Daddy's okay and our house is okay and puppy's okay and I'm not very worried . . ."

In the Mount St. Helens story, incidentally, *everybody*, print and broadcast alike, missed the political side of the story, which was that the state had classified its volcanic hazard zone (the area from which the public was barred) not by geological structure but by the ownership of the land, seeing to it that Weyerhaeuser Co. timber property (on which thirty-six died) remained in the zone of free access. Reporters John Snell, Leslie L. Zaitz and Alan K. Ota of the Portland *Oregonian* figured this out by comparing the state hazard-zone maps with U.S. Forest Service access-road maps while working on their forty-page "special report" that appeared five months after the eruption.[9]

Again, on the airplane crash, Nimmo and Combs report that the other networks were mostly reassuring, whereas more than half the ABC material was "alarming"—the FAA had found "grave and potentially dangerous deficiencies in many of the pylon mountings" of other DC-10s. "The ABC narrative . . . was a tale of a cause more obvious to ABC than to officials, of bureaucratic mismanagement, and of human disruptions." The network found an FAA official to say, "We still don't know what caused this; that's what scares me." The theme, again, was that no one was in charge. Perhaps the central reason for the great success of what ABC News did with the Iranian hostage situation (apart from the fact that only ABC had a camera crew in Tehran on the day the balloon went up) was the congruence of its attitude with the realities, for unless you count Harold Saunders, assistant secretary for Near Eastern affairs at the State Department and not very countable, it was true in the Iranian hostage "crisis" that no one was in charge. On either side.

It is in this context that one should consider Frank Reynolds' Monday-night comment in the Tylenol story, noted with amusement in the Tylenol section, that "the massive nationwide campaign to keep people from taking Extra-Strength Tylenol seems to be working. There have been no further reported deaths." In their discussion of what the networks did with the Tylenol story, Nimmo and Combs miss this comment—as, indeed, they miss the entire large trend of the coverage on all networks away from essentially reassuring ("only in Chicago") the first nights to essentially panicky (Louisville and Philadelphia and Oroville) to keep the story front-and-center after the FDA was satisfied that the cyanide-in-Tylenol problem was restricted to a few shelves in a few drugstores in and around Chicago. What they do note about the ABC Tylenol coverage (which I had not) is its harping on the theme of Halloween, mentioned on the first night's *World News Tonight* on September 30, which permitted the producers to keep tying the story to other, unrelated news through the entire month.

Nimmo and Combs note that despite large changes in anchor, producing and executive personnel at all the networks in the twenty months between the Iranian story and the Tylenol scare—Cronkite to the far more dramatic Rather, Van Sauter in the boss's chair at CBS, wiggling his spyglass around the world in search of moments; Reynolds to the more suave and better-educated Jennings at ABC; the folksy, foxy Brokaw *vice* plain blunt John Chancellor—the essential styles of the three networks were unchanged. Cultural phenomena lie deeper than the conscious decisions of corporate officers or even on-camera talent. But the era in which those cultures were created and made dominant is passing, and where the networks go next is far from obvious.

2

The beginning of the end of the glory days of network news can be seen in a basement under a low-rise colonnaded mock-mansion red-brick office building off the expressway a few miles from downtown Atlanta. The building is the headquarters for Ted Turner's broadcasting operations, and the basement houses the studios and office space for Cable News Network and CNN Headlines (in fairness, one wall on this level, not visible from the newsrooms, has windows on a sloping greensward). Most of the day's forty-eight hours of news and public affairs talk (twenty-four per channel; Headlines has a separate studio in the rear) originates in one large, low-ceilinged room, with its hum of computers and low conversation as a background for the CNN anchor at his or her desk. The text on the TelePrompTer under the camera is even narrower than usual, no more than a word or two per line, to guarantee against eye movements by not very experienced anchors. Over the course of a 168-hour week there are thirteen pairs of anchors.

Physically, the feel of the place is entirely different from the feel of a network news operation, where a small newsroom with perhaps a dozen desks is surrounded by a warren of private offices, and the producer and anchor are remote presences behind closed doors. Though everyone makes a pretense of broadcasting from the actual newsroom, the people who count don't work there, and still must make a mad dash to get in place before the first feed at 6:30 P.M. EST. This runs live—in the Midwest at 5:30—and is also taped, and what the viewer in New York or Washington sees at 7 P.M. is almost always a tape rather than a live show, though the news staffs stick around in case something happens and a new bit must be patched in). At CBS, with a floor space of more than 50,000 square feet on one floor in the old dairy, an area was carved out for use as studio while broadcasting and newsroom while preparing, and since 1986 the nightly news has originated from a lavish center with high ceilings (a huge glass-walled office like a VIP box in a sports arena overlooking that office was built for the now departed Van Gordon Sauter). But Rather and his producers like the camera tight on him, so there's not much use of the artful background that used to appear over Cronkite's left shoulder.

At CNN, the ambience is more egalitarian but also more zoo-like, complete with a platform by the elevators where a visitor can stand and without getting in anyone's hair watch the animals at work. One does indeed see everyone. Directly behind the anchors is a sort of conversation pit where the five people immediately responsible for the show, producer, directors and technicians, work at their screens and consoles. Behind them are writers, editors, producers for the next hour, designers and executors of the graphics, various production assistants and gofers and clerks, glass-doored rooms to tape-editing facilities, solid doors to the Headlines area and the little radio newsroom which make the operation feasible by permitting several sales of each piece of material. About a hundred people work in the room at any one time.

Some programs originate at studios in New York, Washington and Los Angeles, there are correspondents in nine bureaus in America and ten abroad (including one shared with Canadian TV in Peking), and in addition to the 35 million or so homes to which cable carries its service CNN has arrangements with no fewer than 140 U.S. stations which receive its feed through satellite dishes. The same dishes also serve as uplinks when CNN wants to pick up from these stations their coverage of stories in their own area. "They have almost unlimited access to CNN product," says senior vice president Ed Turner, a black-haired bespectacled bulldog of a man who produced the *CBS Morning News* with Hughes Rudd in the mid-1970s and was in charge of news for the Metromedia stations when Ted Turner recruited him to launch CNN. "We have unlimited use of their news product. They buy the dish, and we make the arrangements. There's very little cash: we do a lot of helping each other. For them it's a hell of a deal, day in and day out. For us it's a hell of a deal when a local story breaks. We call them 'correspondent stations.' I set it up in 1980, had to rely on my friends— people didn't think we'd survive, and philosophically they didn't think they should do business with a cable outfit."

Turner has made similar arrangements for CNN with Globo TV of Brazil and Mexican TV, the various participants in Eurovision (including both BBC and Independent Television News—the networks also have these contacts, but they very rarely use the material). When Solidarity was striking, Ed Turner made a deal with Polish television that enabled him to offer Americans the view of that story being given to the Poles themselves. During the British royal wedding, CNN took a BBC feed to give its audience the flavor of the British description; during the Falklands War, CNN carried both British and Argentinian news shows (so did NBC's 1:30 A.M. *Overnight* show, but not anything in normal hours). It should be noted in passing that maximum reliance on people already at the scene is the correct approach to news coverage both in theory and in practice. The most detailed and often the most informative news service available to Americans (something like two million people hear some part of one of the shows every day) comes through *Morning Edition* and *All Things Considered* on National Public Radio. While some of these stories are the doing of highly skilled NPR employees like Cokey Roberts and Nina Totenberg in Washington, and Mike Schuster in New York, most of them arrive over the telephone from NPR member stations and stringers—plus various national broadcasting systems, especially the BBC (NPR has a three-man office in their building in London, and the Beeb allows NPR people to construct shows by interviewing its correspondents). These three- and four-minute pieces (they usually come in at twelve and fifteen minutes and have to be edited down) are paid for at a rate of $100 to $225. The member station is entitled to 20 percent of that sum off the top before the reporter sees any of it (some stations, feeling that their audience has more faith in the competence of their own news people if they are on a national show, waive their share as an inducement to staffers to call NPR with ideas).

At CNN, Ed Turner has complete flexibility. He has made something of a specialty of live courtroom coverage, doing the lawsuit brought by the Creationists to force their view into the biology classes of California, the Carol Burnett libel suit against the *National Enquirer* and the suit against *60 Minutes* with the hilarious footage of Dan Rather chasing the wrong man in hopes of provoking a confrontation, the gang-rape trial from Fall River, Massachusetts, and the von Bülow trial. He has also carried full senatorial confirmation hearings, notably of Sandra Day O'Connor and George Shultz, and most of the hearings by the Rogers Commission investigating the *Challenger* disaster.

Because of all the stringers and bureaus, and the decision to make CNN a less repetitive service than the radio news shows, the daily assignment sheet goes on and on, literally hundreds of items every day from which Turner's morning meeting can choose the less than firm lineups from which the producers make their hourly choices. CNN also does some of its own enterprise. Turner has a ten-man staff of sportscasters, five weather casters, three "medical reporters" and five "economics correspondents." And there is a twenty-five-man unit based in Washington "at a cost of $2 million a year" to do investigative work, mostly on the government and on its relations with private industry. "I call it the 'Holy Shit' unit," Ed Turner says. "Ted doesn't like the term."

CNN started in 1980 with a maximum audience of about 1.5 million homes hooked into cable systems that carried the service and a budget for programs of about $24 million. In 1986, there were more than 35 million homes on line that *could* tune in on the service. The summer 1985 weekend of the TWA hostage release, which its cameras covered more intensively than those of the networks, CNN had as many as 2.5 million viewing households during times when the nets were carrying entertainment. Since fall 1985, CNN service has been available via satellite to European broadcasting companies, governments, hotels and multinational companies. In 1986, spending on programs probably crossed the $100 million mark, and CNN was profitable, probably (these are Wall Street estimates: no figures are published) in the area of $15–$20 million.

The cable services pay a per-subscriber fee, which rose to $2.50 a head per year at the start of 1987 (and is guaranteed not to rise again before 1989). Revenues from commercials probably run about $75 million a year; when you have 100,000 thirty-second spots to sell, an average price of $750 gives you that. Direct-sales commercials (buy it from the air: call such and such a number, write such and such a postal box) have been quite successful, and the number of national advertisers, especially travel and hardware and brokerage services, has been rising steadily. There has always been a certain amount of barter in the news business: we carry a commercial for your hotel chain, you pay us with a due bill for use by our traveling correspondents. CNN is a nonunion shop, with lots of kids breaking in as "video journalists" for little more than the minimum wage; but by the time the kids have been in Ed Turner's pressure cooker for a year or two, they're pretty professional. A lot of them then go out and get better jobs, but by no means all. There has been enough money around to buy high-quality younger talent from the networks themselves, for example, ABC's John Donvan.

"If you like to do newsie's news," Turner says, "it's here. My gimmick is that if a reporter standing before a building has a good story, we use it. I don't care if she's not pretty, so long as she's believable and there's some enthusiasm for her work. For me, this place is a joy every day. I get here at six in the morning, every day, we have our assignments meeting at eight; once I told Ted that when he said he was going to do twenty-four-hour news I didn't realize he meant we were all supposed to work twenty-four hours. But Ted helps. He's either a loose cannon or a free spirit, depending on how you feel, but never once, even when advertising is soft or the war with ABC [which set up a competitive satellite/cable news service, then sold out] cost $75 million, have I heard so much as a rumor of 'cut back.' He's not going to jeopardize the news coverage." No doubt the people who were terribly upset at Turner's ludicrously underfunded grab for a hostile take-over of CBS had reason to be concerned about his apparently unformed political opinions and the linkage between him and the right-wing groups that have declared anathema on the television network. But the fact is that the news service as Ed Turner was allowed to build it, with Tom Braden as well as Patrick Buchanan commenting, Dan Schorr and Charles Bierbauer as well as Evans and Novak, has been quite decently balanced—and what with Wussler in the front office and Turner in the basement, CNN could lay at least as strong a claim to the spirit of old CBS News as Van Gordon Sauter and Ed Joyce could in the CBS building itself.

CNN symbolized the beginning of the end for network news as we have known it, but not because it was a better service. It rarely though not never is a better service: the networks' greater resources and experience usually overwhelm the cable news operation, except on the occasions when the networks send in a celebrity "correspondent" to do on-camera narration —"big footing" the reporter who knows the story—and CNN then has the more interesting coverage because its kids are reporting what they have learned themselves. It is also true, moreover, that through long stretches of the day and night the quickest way to find out what is happening on a major world story is to turn the TV to CNN. The all-news radio stations bump a Mexican election fraud or an Afghan/Soviet air attack inside Pakistan or the Senate vote on confirming a judge to make room for allegations that traffic tickets have been fixed for the mayor's brother's wife, while CNN stays with the big stories. But what gave CNN its status in the revolution was that it was the first service to offer local stations a choice. Prior to CNN, a television station that wished to include national and international stories on its own news shows, and most do, was stuck with whatever its network news division chose to feed out from the reject pile of the network's own nightly show. "When we first began to make that feed," Richard Salant recalls, "I made a speech to the affiliates and said, 'This will be our overset matter, our outtakes, not our best stuff.' "

There was some pressure on the news divisions to be forthcoming with the best stuff, because network relations with affiliates are important and tender, and because public acceptance of the local news show is crucial to the success of the national. (People tune in to Rather or Brokaw or Jennings, of course, but the fact is that where local news precedes national, as it usually does, there is an 80 percent correlation between leadership in the local time slot and leadership in the subsequent network time slot; "giving them material to enrich their show," Larry Grossman said soon after he became president of NBC News, "benefits us.") But the politics of the situation was such that the network show held on to everything it might conceivably want, and the affiliates took what they could get. On the weekends the affiliates would get even: they wouldn't clear the network show, but they would tape it and then use what they liked on their own news programs; "when we caught them," Salant remembers, "they'd say, 'We just got this new executive producer, he didn't know the rules.' "

Now comes CNN, with its offer to swap worldwide coverage for occasional local help (lancing another boil at the better local stations, which are forever offended that the network insists on parachuting in its own people to cover their stories). Then Westinghouse started its Newsfeed Network, which quickly acquired eighty clients, partly by offering to tailor Washington stories for their individual needs. Soon there was the Chicago *Tribune*'s Independent Network News, with its New York base in the Tribune Corp.'s Channel 11; and then Conus Communications, organized by KSTP-TV in Minneapolis, with its own Ku-band satellite and mobile uplinks on trucks ("one person can have this unit set up and broadcasting in fifteen to twenty minutes' time from almost any location anywhere in the United States"). Conus was advertised as "a national interconnected TV service in which the major television stations involved will participate in ownership," a service which "will enable a local television station to strengthen its news programming by allowing live, interactive and participatory presentations from anywhere in the United States." Now Washington crawls with recently established broadcast news bureaus that offer local stations a chance to get stories about executive branch and congressional actions and court decisions that especially affect their areas; one of these bureaus, indeed, is official, and operates out of a White House basement, and maybe if you're very good your anchorman can have his own remote on-camera five-minute interview with the President. . . . If the network refuses to make good stuff available to the local stations, and the alternative services don't have it, NBC's Grossman comments sourly, "they'll steal it from the satellite."

In 1969, William Haley of the London *Times* and the BBC worried that the local and national news shows in Chicago, where he was a visiting professor, were "appreciably repetitive. The viewer who settles down to give an hour's serious attention to the news hears much of it twice over."[10] Like Haley's concern over commercialization and entertainment, expressed in the epigraph to this chapter, the worry was premature: the local stations devoted relatively little of their time to national and foreign news. Now all those concerns are real: led by Arledge, who came out of the sports department, where one hand washes the other all the time, the networks began to use their news shows, including the local shows on their owned-and-operated stations, to promote other products from the same division. Classically, on ABC, *World News Tonight* makes room for a segment on, say, sexual abuse of children (always a favorite), ending with a note that this nastiness will get fifteen minutes from Barbara Walters later that night on *20/20* with a full half-hour follow-up from Ted Koppel on *Nightline.* Larry Grossman, who came out of promotion and public relations to be president of the Public Broadcasting Service and then of NBC News, sees nothing wrong: "Reuven's feeling [the reference is to Grossman's predecessor, Reuven Frank] was that every program stands on its own feet; my feeling is that there has to be an integrated institution."

News presidents like Arledge and Grossman now get involved in a hands-on way to a degree that their predecessors would not have ventured. (Grossman goes to the *Today* show control room most mornings, and noted recently that he had personally made the decision to keep on the home screen the narration of Jeremy Levin, the newsman who had just escaped from—or been released by—Shiite terrorists in Beirut: "I said, 'Let it run.' Fascinating voice—something like Liberace.") These are able, and mostly serious-minded men—Arledge and Grossman are friends from their days on the student newspaper at Columbia University (where their colleagues included Max Frankel, later editorial page editor of the New York *Times*). But since those student days, none of the network news presidents ever reported, edited, laid out or produced a news story. If their "news judgment" governs, the world is different.

Grossman argues that it has to be, and indeed it should have been from the beginning, because television news must deliver narration and exposition through a medium that "conveys experience"—and because the local stations' capacity to obtain the first cut at the national/international story from sources other than the network has changed the nature of the national news service. The local news shows, after all, have a larger audience than the national, in market after market; most people who watch the national have already seen the local. "What do you do with a headline service," Grossman asks, just a little plaintively, "when people already know the headlines?"

Welcome, say the newspaper editors, to the club.

3

But in fact the television networks have gone to another club. The end result of pressure from broadcast news above and neighborhood/suburban papers below has been a significant improvement in both the reach and the grasp of the urban newspaper. There are fewer big-city papers, but almost without exception the survivors have cast their net more widely. They are more capacious, more thorough in their coverage of their catchment areas, more analytical and more serious-minded. The improvement extends to organizations one would have thought incorrigible, like Gannett and Newhouse. The Portland *Oregonian,* for example, which now generates a forty-page supplement that breaks ground as well as examines what has already been plowed around Mount St. Helens, was best known in the trade in earlier years as the place where old Sam Newhouse broke the print and editorial unions, starting a pattern of which we have not seen the end. I have before me a copy of Gannett's Binghamton (N.Y.) *Sun-Bulletin,* acquired on a trip to that city to speak to an IBM group, and you couldn't ask for a better front page, interestingly laid out in five columns, seventeen stories either presented or "reefered" with headlines and a page reference (in the Gannett style, nothing jumps to an inside page). Of the seven stories written out, three are local, one is arms control, one is MIAs, one is the flight of a NASA engineer back to his native Germany because he was threatened with war-crimes trials in the United States, one is lightweight. At the top of the page is a headline about oil prices, followed by a headline on the prevalence of tax-exempt property in New York State. The judgment on what interests people and news judgment seem to me intricately and well balanced.

By contrast, the reaction of the network news departments to the growing national emphasis in the local news shows has been a steady loss of intellectual and moral fiber, an accelerating descent into entertainment and a discreditable drive to making news rather than reporting it. The effort to make news *looks* like an improvement, because it appears as a longer piece, or a one-week miniseries on some place or "theme" or "problem," but on examination the thing is hype. Americans believe that there are about two thousand times as many missing children as there really are because some clowns at the FBI thought this would be a good way to boost the agency's image and audience researchers at the television networks urged the news-people to inflate such a "popular" story. NBC gives us a week of Sunday supplement feature material on the Soviet Union, CBS offers a weeklong look at the year 2000, ABC gets a week's kicks from drugs—all planned in advance, all assuming that what the network puts on the news show is "news."

Reality, of course, rebukes. My favorite news shows of 1986 were in the February week Marcos fell, with Dan Rather actually, physically down on the farm to tell America about the crisis in agriculture (CBS gave nine minutes to Rather in the cornfields and only one and a half minutes late in the show to the populace on the Manila streets and the military in their fort and the President demoralized in his palace on the Monday that was the big news day), and Peter Jennings in Moscow trying to drum up interest in the first Party Congress since Gorbachev's accession. Pierre Salinger, chief of ABC's Paris bureau, who has kept up contacts in the Kremlin he made while Kennedy's press secretary, had been given reason to believe something would happen at this Congress, and indeed the personnel turnovers an-nounced and approved were matters of considerable substance in the Soviet Union—but not in the United States, especially by comparison with what was happening in Manila. And of course, though Jennings is extremely intelligent and has specialized in European political affairs, ABC's regular bureau in Moscow could have covered this story more knowledgeably than an imported anchorman.

It was for this viewer a source of special delight to see these monsters of the midway, one amidst the accouterments of family farming, the other sniffling on the street on a Moscow February day, reaching out for the ganglia of communications that would put them in touch with the only story the world was interested in that day, and falling on their faces. The ines-capable analogy was to Molière's hilarious *Fourberies de Scapin,* which builds its plot line on an effort by the scoundrel Scapin to extort money from an old miser as a ransom for his son, supposedly held by the Turks after the capture of the son's ship in the Mediterranean. The miser keeps muttering (ten times in the course of the play), *"Que diable allait-il faire dans cette galère?* [What the devil was he doing on that ship?]" Later, NBC's Larry Grossman sent his *Today* team on a cruise ship the week everybody wanted to know about Chernobyl. The idea of establishing a cruise ship as background for a news crew—even the *Today* news crew—would have been stomped to death at NBC even in the days when the cast of regulars included a chimpanzee.

The man who led the networks down the garden path, I suspect, was Reuven Frank, though he passed his baton to Larry Grossman just as the brambles closed in. A small, agile, kindly Canadian who came out of the Newark *News* to edit John Cameron Swayze's *Camel News Caravan,* Frank may have a more interesting and penetrating mind than anyone else who has been permitted to produce television news, and he has been the least self-protective man in the business. Edward Epstein hung him on an old memo in his book *News from Nowhere,* Frank still resents it, and I don't want him to resent me. Reuven Frank wrong is more interesting to hear and watch than almost anyone else right. And despite his theories that television news must be an entirely visual medium and seek as a serious matter to tell only those stories that can be told with pictures, Frank kept before the cameras, against some discomfort elsewhere in his organization, wordsmiths like David Brinkley and John Chancellor; and he hired Gilbert Millstein from the *Times* to give his reporters and anchormen a verbal polish higher than that they could otherwise achieve. It is a measure of what has gone wrong at NBC News—and a source of bile and fury for the survivors—that Larry Grossman, confronted with a nonnegotiable demand from upstairs that despite the profitability of the network the news budget had to be greatly cut, decided in December 1986 that the producer most conveniently eliminated was Reuven Frank.

We let the most articulate of those who have sat at Reuven's feet express and interpret Frank's position:

"The idea that television had to be more than radio with pictures was unfamiliar to me until I met Reuven Frank," Linda Ellerbee writes, "but that's understandable. At the time, I'd been a television reporter for only *six years.* Pictures, I was coming to learn, were different from words; as different, Reuven pointed out, as smells are from sounds. Words, he said, go mostly to the intelligence; pictures go more to the feelings and responses. . . . Reuven once used the example of a plane crash to explain. What are the best pictures from a plane crash? . . . According to Reuven: a stocking hanging from a tree, a doll with a broken face—these, in their way, tell you more than words do, more even than pictures of body bags being carried down the hill."[11]

This is useful as a corrective to McLuhan, for whom words were hot and pictures were cool, but like many correctives it falls down on the opposite side. Sound, which includes but is not limited to words, has at least as much emotional force as image. It wasn't Hitler's appearance or his stagings that got all those storm troopers on their feet in front of their radios at home; it was a supreme combination of voice and words. Some of us can be deeply moved with our eyes closed when we hear a Shakespeare speech (not to mention a Verdi aria), and the generation that grew up with the Beatles and Woodstock and such should understand without argument the strength of Noël Coward's insistence on the emotional power of cheap music. The studies done by psychologist Ed Palmer for Children's Television Workshop indicate that sound grabs attention *and holds attention* better than pictures. Sound gives continuity to motion pictures, binding the wounds of incessant cutting. It's the comedies, not the tragedies, that survive from the days of silent film.

Moreover, while pictures may have great power, they tend not to be news. If an airplane crash were a unique event, then perhaps there would be news in a torn stocking or a doll, but there are at least a dozen of these incidents around the world every year, and no small part of the news of a crash relates to the fact that it happened to different people, for different reasons, in different places. The doll, in short, is a genre piece. The fallacy is not, of course, exclusively Frank's or NBC's. Shortly after the DC-10 crash on Memorial Day weekend in 1979, ABC sent correspondent Julie Eckert and the usual panoply of director, cameraman, sound man, etc., to the former home of a nuclear family of four who had been killed in the accident, and here the audience met "a collie named Charlie" who barked and barked around the deserted swing-and-slide set. Frank's doll and stocking and ABC's collie are part of the definition of what CBS's Van Gordon Sauter meant when he spoke of "moments."

As noted earlier in criticism of Sauter and his ilk, there's no reason why what is being shown should be a doll or a stocking from this airplane—any doll or stocking would do. There would be no violence to tradition by showing the viewer any old doll or stocking, saving the money it would cost to find the real doll or stocking. For years the news shows on all the networks filled in sound effects from a catalogue—hubbub in congressional hearings, Arab crowd noises, bombing raids. CBS—under Dick Salant, too —even used a photograph of a baby dying from a disease, with a voice-over leaving the clear implication that the child had starved to death, as the leading episode of its documentary *Hunger in America*. The error was innocent, but not the defense, which was that at that hospital at that time babies were dying of malnutrition. There *were* children on that plane, and doubtless they had dolls like this one. . . .

For years, radio and television news programs have ended with a "closer," something that leaves 'em smiling out there in the good old U.S. of A. Now that the producers of the evening news shows know that most viewers already have the headlines from the local news show (or the radio while driving home, or CNN), they are free to move the closers earlier in the show and use lots of them; and they do. We get more and more attention to stories that are guaranteed to appeal to everyone, like weather phenomena, abused children, celebrities (Boorstin supplies the definition: "A celebrity is a person who is well-known for his well-knownness"), heart transplants, terrorist activity (especially if Americans or Israelis or Irish are involved).

One should not, I suppose, be too censorious. The categories of things that interest people and the categories of things that don't interest people have scarcely changed in recorded history. Organizing the United Press for

E. W. Scripps before World War I, Roy Howard insisted that "people are more interesting than the things they are doing. Dramatize them." Meyer Berger in his *Story of The New York Times* reproduces the front page of the paper for October 18, 1907, the day the *Times* received the first wireless (i.e., radio) transmission across the Atlantic. That took about a third of the page. There were also thirteen other stories: a report that a New York bank was okay despite the failure of a correspondent in Montana and a client on Wall Street; a story of the swindling of the superintendent at the Metropolitan Opera by a phony stockbroker who was the brother of the general manager; a story about an American hotel to be opened in Berlin; an automobile accident involving an old lady who got a broken back; a speech by Rudyard Kipling to the effect that the way to protect the West Coast from the yellow menace was to recruit lots and lots of Northern European immigrants; the decision by the governor of Mississippi to pardon a man convicted of murdering someone accused of sexually molesting his sixteen-year-old sister; testimony by a man accused of murdering his first wife so he could marry his second; a heroic consulting engineer who stopped a team of horses that was about to trample some children on the streets of the borough of Queens and a heroic U.S. senator who did more or less the same in Mexico City; two stories, one from Madrid and one from Newport, about Miss Gladys Vanderbilt's concerns that she might not be received at the Spanish court after marrying Count Széchenyi; Frank Carnegie and Harry Payne Whitney had been accused by a Colorado game warden of wanton destruction of deer; Rockefeller's caretaker on his Cleveland estate had quit because John D. didn't give him enough money to pay for garden equipment; a German passenger ship arriving in town had run aground near its pier. At their most accommodating, the network news shows are nothing like as bad as the old Hearst and Pulitzer papers, or the modern Murdoch's.

Moreover, there is a case to be made that the network news divisions in the Elmer Davis and Ed Murrow and even Walter Cronkite and David Brinkley days had misconstrued their social function in the society. Broadcast news, say the advocates on that side, is first of all for the others, especially for the illiterate and marginally literate, who are not necessarily without interest in public affairs. I have been booed in public only once, at a CBS-sponsored forum on public affairs programs, when I pointed out to an outraged audience in New York's Lincoln Center the fact that the average viewer of TV news and public affairs shows is considerably older than and educationally and economically downscale from the average viewer of entertainment shows. The differences among the media are very substantial: the audiences for the CBS and NBC evening news shows are well over fifty, and Roone Arledge of ABC argues that their programs outdraw his because "older people watch every single night. They have nothing else to do. If our average viewer watches three nights a week and we raised that to four, we would be ahead of CBS." But even the younger audience for ABC's evening news is ten and more years older than the average reader of *Time* or *Newsweek*.

The lessons to be drawn from the demographic data are not entirely self-evident. William Belson of the London School of Economics, originally a BBC researcher, did a study in 1951–52 of the "comprehensibility" of a BBC radio feature called *Topics for Tonight,* a show on the Light Programme following the ten o'clock news and attempting to give the background on the day's lead story. The show had an 11 rating, but over the course of the week a third of the population heard one or more broadcasts. That third was predominantly working-class, and persistent, for the show was not really written for them. "Even when people listened carefully," Belson reported, "they took in (on average) less than a third of the ideas and information presented. . . . Even major or central points were no better understood than were minor points and small details. The main reasons for the comparative failure of these talks to communicate their messages to listeners," Belson concluded grimly, "appears to have been (i) that broadcasters wrongly assumed that the listener had the background knowledge necessary for grasping what was being said; (ii) that the talks were deficient in logical structure and that main points were not highlighted or emphasised; (iii) that broadcasters frequently used language which was not familiar to listeners."[12] But news and public affairs shows are almost never criticized from below their intellectual level; instead, critics above their level complain that they are sensational, tawdry, overpersonalized, stupid, etc. So, sometimes, they are; and, maybe, up to a point, they should be, too.

When this argument was an attack on a proud and dedicated service, it was fun, an important corrective to self-importance. Insistence that nothing counts but the opinion of fellow professionals can create a hermeticism that denies the fundamental populism of a news enterprise. But in television today the profession is losing control, thanks largely and strangely to the unexpected emergence of news services as a profit center for broadcasters. When he wrote *Due to Circumstances Beyond Our Control* in 1966, Fred Friendly could tell a story of Paley saying to Stanton, "I suppose the mistake we made was in ever going public." This had put everyone under pressure to show better earnings results every year. "If profits had stayed at $1.27 a share," Friendly wrote, "where they were in 1958 when Stanton said that CBS would have to work hard to stay at that level, all the public service we could have conceived in our wildest dreams would have been within our means. But . . . by the end of 1965, the 'proper' balance between revenues and public service had permitted the net income, like the company's growth, nearly to double, to $2.47 a share. Too many unscheduled news programs could drive those figures down."[13]

Friendly as the head of news had not been expected to make money, and the pressure he resented was from people who wanted him to ignore big events to make sure he didn't lose more than expected. Ten years earlier, profitability had been so far from Sig Mickelson's mind that he said, "We function as the conscience of the network. The big problem in this business is to strike a balance between showmanship and the objectives of public enlightenment. . . . We think of our programs in terms of good will, proof of the public-spiritedness of the officials of the network."[14]

Life was thus a lot easier for Mickelson and Friendly and Lower and Frank than it is for their successors. A man who runs a cost center is not really expected to come to the end of the year with fewer losses than his budget envisioned; management is happy if he doesn't lose even more than planned. You sit below the salt, and your status as the conscience of the network means people don't like you, but the pressures are fairly easily bearable. Once the division becomes a profit center, however, the corporate managers begin to expect a better profit every year, and both the kudos and the substantive rewards for doing better become very attractive. Well, one rating point 260 nights a year in fringe time with an aging, downscale audience is worth, say, $12 million a year. We've got here the results of seventeen focus group sessions with people who think stories about births in the zoo are the big cats' pajamas, and we can make it pretty cute on the sex life of the animals and still keep it tasteful, can't we, Paul? And once you pay him the Danegeld, as Rudyard Kipling put it, you never get rid of the Dane.

With varying degrees of willingness, all three news divisions have simply rolled over. Ed Murrow had worried from the beginning about television news. His biographer Alexander Kendrick noted that Murrow felt television news posed problems of editorial control and "impinged on the issue of the invasion of privacy. Moreover, 'most news is made up of what happens in men's minds, as reflected in what comes out of their mouths. And how do you put that in pictures?' he wondered. The man who read the news in front of a television camera was not the man who had written the news, much less gathered it himself, and he was certainly not the man who decided what the news was."[15] Cronkite's historic accomplishment was to change that situation: he used the muscle of his ratings appeal to make himself "managing editor," the man responsible for the contents of the lineup.

By their contracts and their importance to the operation, today's anchors could at least retard the spoilage, but they don't. They are all men of obvious ability and good repute, but I fear it's bad for people to make all that money. Dan Rather introduces a ninety-second feature on people who look like celebrities (on the *CBS Evening News!*), and then signs off as "the real Dan Rather"; Peter Jennings looks seriously into the camera and promises those who tune in tomorrow night that they will learn the identity of ABC's Man of the Week, and by God if you do tune in tomorrow night he kills three of the twenty-two minutes available for news by telling you about ABC's Man of the Week (this may be a compromise: Arledge wanted to put sports on Friday's *World News Tonight,* presumably to promo what will be featured on the weekend's *Wide World of Sports);* Tom Brokaw flies to Beirut, where he has never worked and has no contacts and no expertise, to pretend to be reporting on the TWA hostage case.

And then, of course, it doesn't help. After we roll over and do all those other undignified things, GE acquires NBC and Cap Cities acquires ABC and CBS loads itself up with interest payments in nine figures on debt incurred fighting off Ted Turner and then invites to leadership the fierce skinflint Larry Tisch—and they all turn to the news divisions with angry and jaundiced eye and say, "Cut those budgets." And those of us on the outside who would once have been sympathetic, and whose sympathy in the crazy politics of this business might have meant something, watch it all with dry eyes. The network news divisions would have done better to stand and fight while they still had a defensible product to fight for.

Part Four

ITEM:
THE 1984 PRESIDENTIAL
ELECTION

10

Controllables

The hallmark of the American journalist is a direct and coarse attack, without any subtleties, on the passions of his readers; he disregards principles to seize on people, following them into their private lives and laying bare their weaknesses and their vices. That is a deplorable abuse of the powers of thought. . . . The result is that the personal views expressed by journalists carry, so to speak, no weight with the readers. What they look for in a newspaper is knowledge of facts, and it is only by altering or distorting those facts that the journalist can gain some influence for his views.

–Tocqueville, 1883[1]

We are collectively becoming the arbiters of more and more important things in this society. We are very important arbiters in the political process, and I think that as our political parties have declined as legitimizers of candidacies, the press and television have, in fact, assumed more and more of that burden.

–Max Frankel, in a "panel discussion" on "the status, credibility, and responsibility of the news media," published by the *Columbia Journalism Review* in 1983 under the title "Why Do People Hate the Press?"[2]

William Bradford of the *New-York Gazette* declared in 1776, "I once thought a little *Politics* now and then thrown out among our Readers, might whet their Appetites," but on "second thoughts," he added, "we had as good let that alone."

–Leonard W. Levy, 1985[3]

Mr. O'Neill said that in the private meeting with House members Mr. Mondale had responded to suggestions that he

was not hitting Mr. Reagan hard enough on the issues. The
Speaker quoted Mr. Mondale as saying, "Tip, I think I'm out
there slugging. The question is, is the press showing it?"

—New York *Times,*
September 7, 1984, p. A15

1

No one is interested in the 1984 presidential election as an individual,
freestanding event; it seems likely that no one ever was. "The landslides of
the recent past," Paul West of the Dallas *Times Herald* wrote at the beginning of October, "—Johnson in 1964 and Nixon in 1972—at least had
colorful, controversial personalities or a galvanizing issue to relieve the
tedium. At mid-point, this year's matchup seemed to offer neither."[4] Jack
Germond and Jules Witcover wrote a book about the campaign and gave it
the title *Wake Us When It's Over.* On Tuesday, September 4, after the traditional Labor Day "kickoff," the Miami *Herald* had nothing about the election above the fold on the front page; the Washington *Post* had a headline
above the right half of the paper, "Candidates Launch Races"; the Philadelphia *Inquirer* presented a staid "Campaign Is Officially Under Way"; the Los
Angeles *Times* offered the marginally livelier "Race for President Begins in
Earnest." Everyone dutifully noted that the Mondale campaign had started
with a disaster in New York, a walk alone with Ms. Ferraro and local Democratic officeholders up a deserted Fifth Avenue at an hour on Labor Day
when no workingman would be out of bed. What made it a disaster, of
course, was not the lonely stroll itself but the fact that tens of millions of
Americans would see those empty streets on their news programs that night.

Eight months before, during the run-up to the early New England
primaries, Mark Shields of the Washington *Post* had done a reporter's horse-
back survey of bumper stickers in Massachusetts. "The campaigning here,"
he wrote, "has been intense. But all the presidential candidates together are
trailing radio stations by a margin of four to one. I don't know what future
anthropologists will tell us it meant that Americans in 1984 identified more
passionately and publicly with radio stations that promised 'More rock—less
talk' or 'Country Cool' than with presidential candidates who pledged a
nuclear freeze or a balanced budget."[5]

One does not need future anthropologists: a lack of interest in an election in the United States means that everybody knows who's going to win.
Looking back on the Nixon-McGovern election, Av Westin of ABC remembered his experiment of stationing a producer and correspondent in a town
near Columbus, Ohio, through the entire two months preceding the election, to make a report every Friday that would tell the national audience
how the Nixon and McGovern campaigns were playing in the heartland. "It

turned out," Westin said a dozen years later, "that people in Columbus were more interested in the university marching band. We thought our idea had failed, but really those stories told us the truth—which was that Richard Nixon had been reelected when he was renominated in Miami. People were not interested in the election because they had made up their minds."

Similarly, Ronald Reagan had been reelected when he was renominated in Dallas: no Democratic nominee was going to beat a well-liked incumbent at a time when the economy was on the upswing. Moreover, to appropriate Haynes Johnson's quote from an anonymous liberal Democrat, "Reagan is the people's candidate. Mondale is the government's candidate. That's the way it is perceived."[6] But it was not in anyone's interest to admit that: the Reagan camp lived in fear that it would lose its fighting edge (which quite apart from the reelection of the President was going to provide "a historic realignment" between the parties), the Democrats lived on hope—and for the news-gathering and news-distributing organizations, elections are heart's blood. There is symmetry as well as symbiosis here: the candidates' committees and the parties spend about $160 million on the election, and the newspapers and wire services, television networks and stations, spend about the same amount to cover the campaigns.

For all their complaining about the Holiday Inns and the food and the various indignities of the life, moreover, the camp followers, Joe McGinniss' "boys on the bus," truly admire their job. "The dullest campaign is more fun than the daily routine," says Walter Mears, executive editor of the Associated Press and a longtime political correspondent. "You take a guy and you give him an Air Travel Card and walking-around money, say, 'Write about these guys who want to be President . . .' It's exciting." Moreover, the opportunities are dazzling, especially for the television reporters, because the conventions and to a lesser extent the campaign are perceived by network management, Ernest Leiser of CBS told Jeff Greenfield, as "a chance to show your people off." The Huntley-Brinkley team, which would dominate network news for a decade, was first put together by Reuven Frank as an anchormen combo on NBC for the 1956 conventions. Everyone involved in the process has a strong trope toward anything that makes people think the news of the election is something that mustn't be missed. In general, says Hale Champion, "executive dean" of Harvard's Kennedy School, a round-shouldered politico with thinned hair who worked for the governors Brown in California and was perhaps the first liberal political commentator to say where it mattered (in the Washington *Post*) that Ronald Reagan was likely to win not only the 1980 Republican nomination but the presidency, "People who pay a lot of attention to these things don't stop to think of how little attention most people pay."

Thus the issue of the *National Journal* that appeared fifty-three weeks before election day (and included a Germond and Witcover column with the already tired lead: "The straw votes on 1984 Democratic presidential preferences have finally, mercifully, run their course") led with an article summarized on the contents page as: "portends a hotly contested, issue-oriented and probably very close election."[7] Throughout the election period, despite the hammering insistence of the public opinion polls (played somewhat less prominently in 1984 than in some other years, mostly because they lost their news value early), the papers and the television talk shows were full of punditry about new registrants and gender gaps, and the disaffection of the blue-collar workers who had supported Reagan in 1980 and watched industrial jobs vanish ever since. In August, Peter Jennings of ABC made a small bet with his election coverage co-star David Brinkley that the blacks and the Hispanics and the women and the industrial labor unions, the groups that had been "outraged" by "a very polarizing President," would come through for the Democrats and Mondale would in the end squeak it out.

Let it be noted in passing that the networks—now in partnership, CBS with the New York *Times,* ABC with the Washington *Post* and NBC with Dow Jones—commission the most expensive and the best polls, up to and including daily local tracking polls before primary dates, which enabled ABC to forecast the Gary Hart phenomenon in New Hampshire in 1984 on the same morning that the *Times* and CBS were featuring the figures from a somewhat dated national poll that said Mondale was a shoo-in. The results have been greatly counterproductive for the networks in terms of public attentiveness. Audiences and readership are down for everything that pertains to an election campaign, which means that advertisers are far less likely to pay premium prices for time or space adjacent to such material. The use of exit polls to predict election results, which congressmen have been attacking at least since 1980 as a demonstration of the venality and commercialism of the television networks, is an astonishing example of self-denial in the name of news. Election night was a showcase for advertisers until 1984, and the commercial "minutes" sold at enhanced rates into the early hours of the morning on the East Coast. Now most viewers drop the election coverage by nine or at most ten at night in the Atlantic time zone—six or seven in the evening on the West Coast—because they know the results and nobody wants to listen to these mostly self-anointed experts chat each other up for hours. The Nielsen ratings for election night 1984 gave the three networks combined a 51 percent share of audience from 7 P.M. to 11 P.M.; their usual Tuesday share in that period would be 80 to 85 percent.

Among them, the three networks probably sacrifice $6 million of revenue—and this is revenue that would drop right down to the bottom line—by calling the elections early on the basis of exit polls. And they are looking forward to worse yet: "My own vision of the ultimate election night," said Russ Bensley, who ran the 1980 election coverage for CBS, "is one in which every voting machine in the country is wired directly into a central computer some place, and there is a common across-the-country poll-closing time. So, at nine o'clock, you push a button and all the results will print out instantly or display themselves on your screen. You go on the air, do a half-hour broadcast; you go off the air, and that's your election."[8] It is by no means atypical of attitudes in network news divisions, mostly for the good, of course, that Bensley never stops to consider how any of this (or, indeed, how his own work) is to be paid for.

Elections are profitable to broadcasting stations, because state and local as well as national candidates purchase time for commercials. Though the time itself must by law be sold for the lowest prices the stations charge anyone, the candidates by absorbing the "availabilities" in the fall of even-numbered years push up the prices that must be paid by advertisers. For the networks, presidential election years promise disrupted schedules (especially with the growing popularity of the five-minute spot, which requires advance planning of entertainment programs—for the media buyers of course want to wedge into the hour of the most popular shows—and costs audience for the next show because people turn the dial and don't come back). Direct sales of commercial minutes or half minutes are not as great as viewers think, because the campaigns tailor a lot of their advertising buys to specific geographical areas. Nobody wants to waste too much money on the states a candidate is certain to carry (or certain to lose), and when you buy a network you buy a lot of those. But in the early years of television, it was possible to recoup by selling time at a premium both during the conventions and on election night to advertisers who wanted the audience and the identification with matters of national concern. Now the audience is down, and the identification is probably less valuable.

Of course, it is also possible that audiences on election night have diminished simply because more people are less interested in who wins elections, whatever hour they are determined. That would not be an exclusively American problem. In spring 1981 I went to a Dublin pub on election night to find out how the Irish reacted to their news, which comes in a slow buildup and cannot be projected, thanks to the proportional representation system that lets people who voted for hopeless candidates decide among the hopeful by the casting of their third- or fourth-preference votes. It was exciting for a visitor but not, apparently, for the natives. In my pub, I found that nobody was paying the slightest attention: Kraft cheese, Jacobs' coffee, Madison ginger ale, Ryvita Krisp, Renault cars, Coca-Cola, Zirconian antiperspirant and Stag beer were just wasting their money, so far as the crowd at the bar with me was concerned.

In August 1984, I asked Robert Strauss to predict the coverage of the election in the last weeks of the campaign. Strauss, white-haired, chunky, amusing, Texas-nasty, was a former Democratic National Committee chairman, chairman also of the only successful Democratic presidential campaign in the two decades since 1964 (Carter's in 1976) and head of an alleged advisory committee to Walter Mondale, which in fact never met and never made any input to Mondale. "In October," Strauss said, "they'll run horse-race stories saying it's closing up. The last week the press will say that the polls have it too close to call. I made a hundred-dollar bet that Gallup will have them dead even in October. The press always has its own dog in the race—the underdog. That saved Mondale's ass in the primaries, and they haven't had a good word to say for him since. But none of this," Strauss added rather sourly, "is incompatible with a landslide for Reagan on election day."

Strauss was not entirely wrong. *Time* magazine for October 22 (on the newsstands a week earlier) appeared under a cover of the four presidential and vice presidential candidates mounted on horses with winged television cameras for heads (Reagan had a small lead, but Ferraro was a little ahead of Bush), with the cover line "A Real Race?" Tom Wicker of the New York *Times* was finding comfort for Mondale in registration figures in Texas as late as the last week, when the candidate himself had despaired. In a *New Yorker* piece dated October 21, Elizabeth Drew began with the rather wistful comment that "the first three weeks of October will go down as the period when the Presidential campaign either did or did not turn around . . . the answer is not in just yet . . ."9 But it was ritual; nobody's heart was in it; and the public knew for sure.

The coverage of the 1984 presidential election was dreadful in a peculiarly American way ("the scramble of celebrity interviewers," Garry Wills wrote in a report on the televising of the Democrats' convention, "to be the first to ask celebrity politicians, in their moment of most demand, what they were about to say on the podium or what they had just said at the podium"10). One compares again, sadly, with the Irish election, and television commentator Joe Bermingham, a bald man with bushy gray eyebrows, who cheerfully greeted the announcement that an incumbent had been deemed to have met the quota in his district (proportional representation has a language all its own) with the comment that "Brian Cluskey gave a highly creditable performance in the Dail [the Eire Parliament] and in the campaign, and besides, he's a friend of mine." But to think seriously about these subjects one must first disabuse oneself of the common elementary school sententiousness about the failure of "the media" (especially television) to pay enough attention to "the issues" or to force the candidates to tell the public what they will do in the world if they win.

2

"Let's be a little bit realistic," George Reedy of the University of Minnesota, once Lyndon Johnson's press secretary, told a meeting at the Kennedy School after the 1980 election. "Number one, these men don't know what they are going to do after they get elected. For the love of God, we do not give them the authority to do anything. . . . Number two is I do not believe that the political campaign is any place for a deep discussion of issues. I think we get it after the election. I think we get it when the issues become real, when they are presented to Congress where they can be analyzed the way issues should be analyzed."[11]

A great deal of what does and should happen in a great industrial democracy, moreover, does not benefit from attention in the context of an election—or, indeed, from publicity at any time. There are many and varied reasons, most of them good reasons, why the Founding Fathers set out a scheme for representative government, where the public would rely on elected representatives to show good judgment in situations where crowds might be pressing round them. Even in the eighteenth century, it was a matter of some importance that governmental decisions be made by people who had opportunity and reason to think about them—or regular contact with people who had reason to think about them—rather than by people whose minds were fully occupied by other things. The voters chose someone they trusted to cast their joined vote on "issues" in the legislature, and if they grew to dislike him or his votes, they chose someone else. A presidential election has a more plebiscitarian character, but even here the "issues" are clearly subsidiary to the choice of a person, and a good thing, too. For it remains true, as Thomas Jefferson put it in his first inaugural address, that "every difference of opinion is not a difference of principle."[12]

"Consider civil rights," the elegant MIT political scientist Ithiel de Sola Pool wrote in 1973. ". . . It was a widely recognized conclusion of social scientists working on civil rights in the 1950s that the way to integrate places of work, restaurants, parks, or swimming pools was just to do it without discussing it at all. If not discussed, the physical presence of blacks tended to be taken for granted as natural, but once the issue was raised, polarization, dispute, and deadlock followed."[13] Most of what the complainers about American politics want aired in the backyard and beaten like a rug is the kind of thing that destroys civility, the willingness to lose and try again, without which democracy fails. The tail that pins neatly on the bias of television and big-time newspaper and newsmagazine coverage is that environmentalists' campaigns to eliminate the "dirty dozen" who are poisoning the air you breathe and the water you drink are regarded as innovative and public-spirited, while anti-abortionists waving pictures of dead fetuses are considered bigots and kooks. From the point of view of someone concerned about American institutions, they are in reality two faces of the same coin.

"What is really important," Reedy said, "is the character and the philosophy of the people who are running." That and what Harvard political scientist Gary Orren calls " 'valence' issues," which "do not reflect a 'left' or 'right' position, but involve identifying a party with some 'value'—peace, corruption, or whatever—or an assessment of its performance in office. Which party, for instance, does the public see as the party of 'prosperity,' or which party do people think has done or is likely to do a better job handling unemployment? Unfortunately," Orren adds, ". . . political scientists . . . have invariably emphasized position issues and ignored, trivialized, and denigrated valence issues. The media suffer from the same myopia. Overlooking the role of valence issues in a campaign, they complain about 'issueless' elections . . ."[14]

In the context of television's influence on "visuals," of course, serious attention to "issues," desirable or not, is very difficult (and one notes quickly that the word "issues" is neither very precise nor very useful). This is a general truth, not just an election question. Christopher Matthews, Tip O'Neill's press secretary when O'Neill was Speaker of the House, remembered a "battle of the visuals," the day "they had the Republicans out here with fifty shopping carts showing how much you'd save because of the Reagan tax cut and [social justice advocate] Mitch Snyder shows up with fifty shopping carts showing how much food [Reagan's] cutting from social programs." Nothing ran that night on the networks because, Matthews said, "they couldn't figure out what was going on with all those shopping carts."[15] Senator Alan Simpson expresses more bitterly the contempt virtually everyone in Congress feels for the typical television coverage of that institution: "They run up to you with a mike, stick it under your nose, grab the camera and the sound man and say, 'Simpson, you've failed, haven't you? . . . your bill is dead.' "[16]

As Thomas Patterson and Robert McClure put it in their study of the 1972 election, presumably our most ideological, "the candidates' positions on issues generally were reported in ways that ensured they would not stand out in the viewers' minds. For instance, news film pictured the candidate wading through a crowd, while his comment on the issues was relegated to the audio. And even when the candidates' statements on issues were on film, they were sandwiched between pictures of a rally. Policy statements were lost in a reel of exciting pictures." (Of course, in fairness, what were the networks to do? Find pictures to illustrate a candidate's points, thus giving him a helping hand—or accept illustrative film material from the candidate's campaign, turning their news coverage into an open part of his advertising?)

Patterson and McClure isolated eighteen "candidate positions" in 1972, noted that most of them were mentioned only two or three times on the weeknight television news in the last six weeks of the campaign, and that "more than 50 percent of the discussion of issues by candidates took place in news segments of 20 seconds or less, and most of these occurred in 10 seconds or less." A content analysis of what people not greatly interested in politics knew of the candidates' positions on these eighteen issues showed that on six of them regular viewers of television news were more likely than occasional viewers to *misstate* what the candidates had been saying.[17]

As the game played in 1984, the choice of "issues" to be presented on the evening news and discussed in the newspapers was overwhelmingly in the hands of the candidates and their staffs—and that is exactly where it should be, says Jim Lake, a conventionally handsome, clean-cut, soft-spoken almost-young man with candid blue eyes and thinning brown hair, who ran the publicity end of the Reagan campaign. "The press forgets what its job is sometimes," Lake said amiably shortly after the election, when he had moved on to the chore of planning the publicity for the inauguration. "Their job is to report what's going on. What was going on in the election was what we did. It's our responsibility to set the agenda and meet it; it's the press's responsibility to report what we're doing." The summer before the election he had put the matter more operationally: "The first job of the press representative," he said then, "is to give television the news hook for each evening. If you don't give the networks a news hook, they go off on their own and get in trouble."

Not everyone in the news business would disagree. "I don't think it's my job or my newspaper's job," says Albert Hunt, Washington bureau chief of *The Wall Street Journal,* "to say what the issues should be in an election." Henry Grunwald, of *Time* says that "it certainly *is* the function of the news media to define the issues, but it's tough. If we decide the campaign should address Third World debt, we can press it, but we can't force it on the public." In point of fact, interestingly, *The Wall Street Journal* did grumble, much more than most papers, about the candidates' failures to debate the nation's problems, giving the stories their own running head, "Absent Agenda," every week or ten days through the fall: "Candidates Avoid Medicare Cure"; "Candidates Duck Arms Cut Issue"; "Candidates Skirt Hard Farm Issues." But all these were on the back page, which managing editor Norman Pearlstine has made into a kind of ghetto for political news in a business news paper (prior to Pearlstine, of course, politics didn't even have a ghetto).

Writing in 1982, Thomas Patterson had argued that the lengthening of the campaign meant that the candidates had lost "control over their news coverage. . . . The shorter campaigns of the past worked to maintain the candidates' control of the agenda—what they had to say was less likely to be old news. There are, however, 300 days in current presidential campaigns, each one of which is reported by the news organizations. . . . The lengthening of the campaign has created new opportunities for reporters to base news selections on their own interests." Moreover, Patterson argued, the familiarity of the candidates' positions biases news gatherers toward the detailed reporting (suspicious reporting, too) of any variations. His example is an October 1980 *CBS Evening News* show in which Bill Plante "enumerated positions that Ronald Reagan had either altered or, more typically, ignored since his nomination. As Plante talked, X's were drawn across Reagan's face to dramatize his apostasy. Plante suggested that Reagan had moved to the political center in order to gain election.

"Had Reagan actually changed his policies? The answer is no, apparent from a reading of Reagan's standard campaign speeches in the fall of 1980. He spoke then mainly of big government, high taxes, and inadequate defense, the same things he had been attacking for over fifteen years. His positions were those of a conservative Republican, not those of the centrist that Plante portrayed. The reason he looked so different in Plante's report was that Plante, like other journalists on the campaign trail, focused on what was new in the candidate's statements, however slight these changes might have been."[18] One notes in passing the mode chosen in this case to make "issues" visual for television. One notes also that Plante seems to have changed his approach. Scoring the network journalists for whether their "candidate stories" were positive or negative in 1984, Maura Clancey and Michael J. Robinson showed Bill Plante with a whopping +18 (the next most positive was at +8, Sam Donaldson was only at −11, and John Severson of NBC the negative champ at −36).[19]

In fact, of course, it turned out that Reagan in 1984 had all but absolute control over "the agenda." Nit-picking by an oversophisticated press was reduced in effectiveness by the avoidance of specifics and reliance on weekly "themes" within which the President set a tone rather than made a case (man of peace, devotee of education, friend of religion, deregulator, etc.). The modus operandi was the stump speech exactly as before, with a single insert for the newspeople to pick up. "If you know what you're doing," Jim Lake says, "and if you're the incumbent or the front-runner, you can keep control. You don't go out there and debate your opponent's stuff: it's a failure of discipline if you're answering his questions."

This was not easy to do with Reagan, who resents attacks: "He doesn't," Bill Kovach, chief of the New York *Times* Washington bureau, said in the early days of the campaign, "take criticism well, and the longer he's in office, the less well he takes it. He could lose his temper and hurt himself badly in the area where he can't afford it, war and peace matters or the fairness issue." But Ed Rollins and Jim Lake (who had worked for Reagan in California) were able to convince the President that victory was the best revenge, and he avoided the exercise of his right of reply to keep attention focused where he wished it focused. When he absolutely had to get even, there was always the one-liner, often a very good one-liner, like the comment that for Republicans it was always the Fourth of July while for Democrats it was always Halloween. Though I voted (I think this declaration is required) for Mondale, I see nothing illegitimate about what the Reagan campaign did. The great "issue" of a presidential election *is* "leadership." A President running for reelection has a record that can be combed, and this record is infinitely more important than the contents of his speeches. If his "themes" contradict what he has done, presumably he will be vulnerable to attack. If they are consonant with what he has done, he is, like Franklin Roosevelt asking voters to give him a second term to meet their "rendezvous with destiny," honestly exploiting the practicalities of campaigning. There is a great fall from "rendezvous with destiny" to "you ain't seen nothin' yet" (which is, as Germond and Witcover point out, a line Reagan borrowed from Al Jolson[20]), but the genus is the same.

Reagan's advantages of incumbency and of money are easy to over-state, though they were real enough. Writing a few months before Jimmy Carter beat Gerald Ford, and four and a half years before Ronald Reagan beat Jimmy Carter, Newton W. Minow (a former head of the Federal Com-munications Commission) and his law partner Lee M. Mitchell stressed that "since television became a major factor in American communications in the 1950s, no incumbent president who sought reelection has been defeated." Like so many people whose lives are saturated by Washington politics, Mi-now and Mitchell tend to see news gatherers as the real surrogates for the public, and find it somehow a little sinister that "[John] Kennedy's aide Theodore Sorensen acknowledged that the televised press conferences were intended 'to inform and impress the public more than the press.' "[21] Simi-larly, Sam Donaldson of ABC News is reported to have said, "They're trying to go over our heads," when he learned that the White House had set up a special studio and satellite transmission facility to permit President Reagan to do live remote interviews with local TV anchormen (even what he admittedly said—"They're trying to go round our end"—is bad enough). And incumbency does give a candidate an immense advantage in gaining attention from the press.

But the very fact that this attention is assured provokes negative com-ment. News gatherers feel that because they *must* report what a President does and says, whether or not they regard it as worth their time, they have become whores for the incumbent. This is especially true on television, where decisions are made by the producers in New York (the "grown-ups") rather than by the "correspondents," a preposterous word in this medium. "Jim Lake," says *The Wall Street Journal*'s Al Hunt, "understood the insecuri-ties of network television, the shallowness of it. He understood that they were video nymphomaniacs, they couldn't resist the visual story. Network coverage of Washington is abysmal, because they're not willing to say, 'The President of the United States didn't make news today.' " Lake himself looked at it just a little differently: "It's easy," he said in August, "for Dave Broder to buy an airline ticket and go to Chicago. But TV has to go where the candidates go. There's a minimum four-man crew, and it's a very costly business."

The reporters themselves try to fight back a little. William Greider, formerly assistant managing editor of the Washington *Post* (who moved on after selling his Stockman interview material to *The Atlantic Monthly* rather than to his employer), described the technique to Jane Mayer of *The Wall Street Journal:* "tag lines dripping with irony saying 'this is a manipulated image.' The message is that 'this smart reporter hasn't been fooled by this bilge.' But the truth of the matter . . . is that they put the bilge on the air anyway."[22]

Still, challengers in the actual election months have most of the advantages of incumbents, if only because they, too, benefit from "the body watch," the feeling at the network news divisions that if a candidate, like a President, gets shot, they must have their cameras on the event. The economics of the business dictate that if a team is assigned to someone, he must get airtime—correspondents are no longer paid extra for every minute their face or voice is on the air, but the controller still wants figures on how many minutes on which shows the news divisions got from each crew. After all, it takes a lot of the controller's time to process that expense account, just as it takes a lot of the crew's time to put it together convincingly. And because the reporters have had less time to get sick of nonincumbents, they may receive fewer nasty tag lines. "Television," Michael J. Robinson and Margaret A. Sheehan wrote in their book about the coverage of the 1980 elections, "particularly needs a theme in its campaign reporting and one perennial theme is the manipulative incumbent."[23]

Campaign money multiplies the value of incumbency. "The Reagan administration," Hale Champion noted, the winter sun pouring in over the Charles River and over his shoulder in his Harvard office, "did in a large way what other administrations tried but never carried through. That grew out of the tremendous influx of money into this business. The Republicans have built a structure that works all the time: the full-fledged apparatus of the political consultant sits in the White House now." But Robert Strauss doubts that Reagan got any real advantage from the superfluity of cash: "It's like sugar in your tea," he said; "after the third spoonful you can't taste it anymore." Mondale had three teaspoons, too, but he couldn't make the tea sweet.

Mondale "knew intellectually" that the Reagan approach was correct, says his levelheaded, wavy-haired late-thirties press secretary, Maxine Isaacs, who, after the election was over, solaced her misery (and his) by marrying Mondale's campaign manager, James Johnson. The August before the election, David Broder of the Washington *Post,* courteous, lean, more or less bald, by no means a cynic, the political commentator most often cited by broadcasters, had snorted over a visitor's comment that it would be hard for Mondale to get a *news* story about, say, the "danger" that Reagan in a second term might have the chance to appoint a majority on the Supreme Court. "He spends the morning flying to Denver," Broder explained, "to give a luncheon talk to the Denver Bar Association. At that lunch, all he talks about is, 'Who will pick the next Supreme Court?' Then he gets on a plane to fly to Spokane. He has to get the time on TV: they have no choice. There's nothing esoteric about this—they all know how to do it now. And that's the criterion on which they operate: 'What do we want on the news tonight?' "

There were various reasons why Mondale could not do that. "Other issues kept cropping up," said Robert Boyd, chief of the Knight-Ridder Washington bureau. "Lance and Ferraro, the special interest thing, what Jesse Jackson was doing. Tip O'Neill." After the networks gave O'Neill the political lead story on the evening of the day the candidate had made a largely unnoticed major speech on the religion issue at a B'nai B'rith lunch, Mondale said publicly that this sort of thing would have to stop, because "I get forty-five seconds on the networks each night and Reagan gets forty-five seconds. What happened was Tip stepped on my message, and I can't have that from my friends."[24]

Horace Busby told James Perry of *The Wall Street Journal* in January that "the Democratic Party is a franchise operation. McDonald's, or whatever. It's the kind of thing I grew up with in Texas, in which every candidate built his own political party with his own money, his own workers, and his own managers."[25] This turned out to be true, and was a stone around Mondale's neck even after the field had narrowed down to one and presumably all the fiefdoms were fighting under the same banner. Finally, there were the polls: Isaacs remembered bitterly that when she would get a reporter an interview with Mondale it would begin with the reporter pulling the most recent poll out of his pocket and asking Mondale why he thought he was losing.

Right after the election, Mondale felt that a mismatch between himself and television was part of what had gone wrong: "I think you know I've never really warmed up to television," he said at his final press conference, "and in fairness to television, it's never really warmed up to me. . . . The thing that scares me . . . is that I think more than we should American politics is losing its substance. It's losing the debate on merit. . . . More and more it's the twenty-second snip, the angle, the shtick, whatever it is, and we need—I hope we don't lose in America—the demand that those of us who want serious office must be serious people of substance and depth." Isaacs said that after a few months' consideration, Mondale "learned better," and came to understand that many of his problems with television had been matters of technique. "We didn't want to limit access to the candidate," she says, "so we'd do two, three news conferences a day, which meant that every time Reagan threw a dart someone would bring it up and we would react. Reagan was always alone, or with one or two people; Mondale was always surrounded, you had to pick him out of a crowd. It gave Reagan an image of strong leadership, he was controlling his setting, he was in charge, while we looked confused. And we had no benefit from it."

One can argue that the impact of this confusion was quite serious. In his book about his vision of the 1972 election, *Rolling Stone*'s Hunter Thompson insists that what did McGovern in as a plausible candidate was the loss of belief in his competence that followed the Eagleton fiasco. (Those who worry about the damage done by the cynicism of conventional reporters might consider for a minute the vicious irresponsibility of "committed" writers like Thompson, who was willing to protect his fallen hero by putting in print an alleged diagnosis of Eagleton's condition as "severe manic-depressive psychosis with suicidal tendencies," and his own description of the senator, who served another fourteen years in the Senate with considerable distinction, as "an opportunistic liar."[26]) A combination of things deprived Mondale of the belief in his competence that his public record would seem to have earned him—the Bert Lance flap, the realization that no serious examination of John Zaccaro's business had been undertaken before his wife (and business partner) was offered the vice presidential nomination, the decision to stress the need for a tax increase without enlisting a single follower in the cause, the Labor Day parade. But the visual image of confusion may be the reason for the depth of that disaster. John Chancellor reports that in a talk he gave at George Washington University not long after the election, he made reference to the Mondale anti-Hart commercial in the primary campaign, with the red telephone ringing and the message that at that moment "the man whose hand you would want near that telephone is Walter Mondale." Chancellor shook his head. "There were two thousand people in the room, and they roared with laughter," he recalled. "That's what the campaign did to Mondale." Not the coverage: the campaign.

11

Uncontrollables

In the supreme forensic effort of his campaign for reelection, President Roosevelt tonight failed to give a specific answer to the challenge of Governor Alf M. Landon that he declare his future objectives. . . . He maintained silence . . . concerning the methods he will pursue to carry out his purposes.

–editorial, Chicago *Tribune,*
October 31, 1936[1]

Today's sentimental journey through California ended the highly staged, low-risk campaign of a big front-runner . . . a campaign long on glitz and short on substance . . . a cynical campaign. Protecting a big lead, the President offered pomp and platitudes, but never told us what he planned to do the next four years.

–Chris Wallace on NBC,
election eve, 1984[2]

1

In 1984 as in 1980, those who follow such things found that the heavier the attention to the election campaign on the network nightly news, the more likely the show was to suffer in the ratings. The kind of campaign the news gatherers had to present, *faute de mieux,* did, I think, contribute to driving the public away, but the loss of public interest in the 1984 American election was also, clearly, the sort of thing that happens these days in all the news-saturated democracies when landslides impend. I spent two weeks of June 1983 in London to watch how the British covered their campaign, and subsequently wrote in *TV Guide* that the involvement of television with the election was both more interesting and more valid in Britain than in the United States, especially in the honest use of real voters in studio panels and on the telephone to ask unrehearsed questions of real politicians, up to and including the Prime Minister (not infrequently addressed as "Margaret" or even "Maggie" by the anonymous potential voter) and the Leader of the Opposition (in 1983 Michael Foot, almost always addressed by the voters, though not by the TV correspondents, as "Michael": so much for British deference as against American irreverence).

The phoned-in questions show is *Election Call*, a 10 A.M. program that runs half an hour every weekday for the three weeks of a British campaign. As a BBC radio program it goes back to the early 1970s, and in 1983, the first year when cameras were added to the mix, the radio transmission outdrew the television transmission by five to one (roughly 2 million to 400,000). Its host is Sir Robin Day, who got his knighthood for interviewing people on television, and as critic Richard Last of the *Daily Telegraph* put it, he "revels in his task of holding the ring between the powerful and the normally powerless and putting them briefly on level terms." Producer Alastair Osborne said that turning on the cameras made a considerable difference: "It's been quite an education, watching some of them desperately trying to appear sincere all the way through. When it was just on radio, they could grimace, they could scratch, they could loosen their ties. Now they have to go on pretending to look interested."[3] These programs help maintain interest in even the most hopelessly boring election, simply by giving the governed a moment to relate in their own way to their governors. And they do, of course, allow individual members of the public rather than the candidates or the press or the poll takers to influence the saliency of issues at any given moment.

I was also enchanted in Britain by an hour before the returns began arriving at the studios, when teams of comics made fun of the election just ending. In 1970, the BBC had used the actor who played Alf Garnett, the truly nasty original copied in America in the form of the half-lovable Archie Bunker, as one of the commentators on the returns: "It would do a lot to brighten our election night," I wrote, "if one of the networks . . . would put on the *Saturday Night Live* crew with Johnny Carson as moderator, to let the politicians have it at the end of the campaign."[4] I have also from this visit an irresistible there'll-always-be-an-England note. Because the British elect a Parliament, not a President, there are 650 separate constituencies on which television must report, with about 550 decided between eleven at night and four in the morning, when the reporters pack it in for a few hours' sleep. In 1983, ITN, the private sector's television news service, published a special edition of its staff paper, *The Lens,* to describe how the show would run, and did a back-page feature on Diana Edward-Jones, who had directed the coverage at the studio the previous two elections and was about to do so again. One quotes: " 'I spent hours swotting it all up and everyone's yelling staccato intelligence like "David Steel's home." The whole thing is bloody difficult. What do I like most about it? The drink afterwards.'

"Di is glued to her seat without a break for anything for six to seven hours. 'There's one thing I have to do before I have a drink,' she flushed."[5]

But the most remarkable aspect of the British election coverage for me was the fact that during the last week of the campaign (and there were only three weeks, by British law), London's solitary afternoon newspaper, the tabloid *Evening Standard,* headlined an election story on its front page only once. Nobody, its editors figured, was going to buy a newspaper to read about that thoroughly predicted bore. And in England, of course, the percentage of the population that votes is more than half again as high as it is in the United States: people care about their vote, even though a campaign bores them.

It must also be said that the British press is even less effective than the American as a surrogate for the public. In the United States the government communicates with the governed to a large extent by leak, a relatively ad hoc contact between someone in government with a desire to get out some information or disinformation or opinion and someone gathering news "inside the Beltway" who makes a living mostly by presenting stories others don't have. In Britain the ability of dissidents within the government to call attention to their views by leaking is greatly constrained by the Official Secrets Act, which the Thatcher administration especially has used to shut up both the recalcitrants in the civil services and the press. And leaking by the government is systematized in Britain, with rules of the game that are not broken, through the institution of "the lobby," a club of journalists accredited to Parliament and through similar clubs accredited to major departments of government.

The members of these clubs, which have had official recognition since 1884, are formally briefed every day on a not-for-attribution basis, by both government and opposition leaders, permitting them to write that "sources close to the Prime Minister" or "Foreign Office authorities" or "the shadow cabinet" believe such and such. The result, write Michael Cockerell, Peter Hennessy and David Walker, alumni of BBC News and *The Times, The Observer* and *The Economist,* is that "newspaper and television news cannot on the whole be trusted, tainted as they are by official information."[6] As David Leigh of *The Observer* wrote bitterly: "From the point of view of a bureaucrat or a politician, the ideal journalist is the one who will accept misleading statements and disguise their source."[7]

Christopher Underwood of the BBC gives a delightful example of how this game plays. A "Home Affairs Correspondent," he was asked to cover the Foreign Office (the British equivalent of the State Department) for two weeks as a sub for the BBC's "Diplomatic Correspondent." He wound up, it turned out, in the wrong room: "I went along to the afternoon briefing and received certain background information which I used for a story that figured prominently in the six o'clock radio news. What I didn't realize was that I had been at the wrong briefing; that British journalists were being briefed in another office; that I had been shown inadvertently to a briefing intended for journalists from Europe. After the six o'clock broadcast, all hell broke loose because two different versions of this story were available—one for British journalists, another for Continental journalists. Quite by accident, I had stumbled on the accurate version and not the one intended for the home market."[8]

What happens is that British journalism splits into two camps that parody each other: an "establishment" group (the term is of course English originally, referring to the established Church), who belong to the lobbies and cherish their contacts and acquaintance with the high and mighty; and a rapscallion group who can be left or right in political orientation (*Private Eye* to one side, Rupert Murdoch's various unclassy enterprises to the other), who do not have membership in the lobbies and who consider all politicians fair game. In fall 1986, a new paper, *The Independent,* attracted scores of Britain's best-regarded journalists, in part by announcing that its reporters would never join the lobby, and the Manchester *Guardian* resigned from it. The Parliamentary correspondents then met in solemn conclave and voted to continue the traditional system. But the vote was close.

The community of supposed insiders has a great tradition in Britain: John Delane of *The Times* in the 1850s and 1860s dined every night with political figures and royals ("swelling," he called it), with splendid results; Lord John Russell wrote to Queen Victoria in 1854 that "the degree of information possessed by *The Times* is mortifying, humiliating and incomprehensible."[9] In 1936, the physician attending the dying King George V gave him an injection to hasten his death, so that it would be reported in the next morning's *Times,* rather than in the afternoon papers. But there is no question that people whose information derives from their social acceptability eventually go soft, because they cannot afford to offend their contacts. In the savage but accurate words of Edward Epstein: "When journalists are presented with secret information about issues of great import, they become, in a very real sense, agents for the surreptitious source."[10] Meanwhile, the other kind of British journalism is as offensive as it can possibly be, concentrating on salacious material where available, digging out or inventing disreputable nicknames, always asking, to quote Chesterton, a Conservative outsider, "whether the Health Ministry are in it for their health."

Much the same dichotomy has begun to appear in the United States, where the stories that the government wants the public to believe without wanting its name on them are handed out to a favored cadre of Washington correspondents (favored entirely because of their access to the ink that gets read in Washington or to the televised minutes that go to the entire country: David Schoenbrun in his memoirs noted with interest that when he resigned from CBS he lost not only his invitations to press conferences but also his invitations to parties). These journalists—I would not myself call them reporters—write the columns, and get quoted on television, and when they give their parties the leaders of the world attend.

Such luminaries, and indeed some lesser lights, had been cultivated by the Reagan White House as never before. Robert Strauss as the campaigns got started predicted that the President would have the best press any incumbent had ever enjoyed, because the White House staff had given all the reporters a stake in his victory. "This administration," he said, "has co-opted the press more than any other. They have taken the press into their confidence, let the press get a peek under the kimono. People in the press take good care of their sources in the stories they write. It's good for the President's publicity, bad for the conduct of the government." What Strauss feared did not in fact happen: in their analysis of the nightly news shows, Clancey and Robinson found that three-fifths of the time given to the Reagan campaign had no "spin" added by the presentation, but in the remaining 40 percent, 7,230 broadcast seconds were "bad press" and only 730 seconds were "good press."

The close relations between the reporters and their White House sources did, I think, help to bury the most surprising and perhaps most revealing story of the election season, that of the dog that didn't bark. For the staff whose cultivation of the press had drawn Strauss's scorn was nowhere to be found once the year passed Labor Day. Rollins and Lake of the campaign committee had sat them down and, with Reagan's approval, read them a riot act on the need to be absolutely sure that nothing they said or did could possibly interfere with the maximum attention in the press and on television to whatever theme the President was supposed to be presenting that day. "Rollins," Lake recalled affectionately, "made me the absolute spokesman. Nobody else spoke to the press, except Rollins, and I sat in on every interview he gave. My assistant John Buckley took two hundred, three hundred calls a day, and told them all the same story." Lake paused. "It's not quite that simple," he added. "The guy who runs the Northeast, knows who killed John and how we're going to handle it, he can talk to the press, I have no objection, provided I know about it. But not at the White House. Anybody at the White House can talk only about the business of government, not about the campaign. People were told it was no part of their function to become a spokesman for this campaign, on or off the record. And people would have been fired if they had breached the rules."

A great deal of this was possible because the people around Reagan, in the White House and in the campaign, had no great affection or respect for reporters. John Chancellor cites a motto from old-timer Andy Glass, that "government has to feed the press and the bears; well-fed bears are happy bears." Maxine Isaacs argues that Mondale couldn't play that game. In fall 1983 she mourned that "what I would like to see happen will never happen: that some of the journalists I really respect and revere would take a fresh look at Mondale. . . . I don't think Jack Germond will stand back and say, 'Holy Cow, look at this guy.' It just will never happen. They know Mondale already, and they're always going to assume that the readers are as familiar with him as they are. And the readers aren't."[11] After the election, she said,

"Mondale has excellent relations wth the press, he's friends with reporters, likes to bullshit with them. Every candidate needs someone to believe he is going to deliver on his promises. Reporters like Broder and Hunt know him too well, he's their next-door neighbor, they've seen him in the Safeway, played ball with him. They can't give him that aura a man needs when he's running for President."

This is a little disingenuous. The fact is that nobody in public life likes "the press" much, though most successful politicians have pets. Hugh Carey, then a congressman, later governor of New York State, rented the house next to mine on Shelter Island one summer, and I saw a little of him in Washington when I was on the President's Panel on Educational Research and Development in the Kennedy and Johnson administrations and he was Cardinal Spellman's man on the Hill, with powers plenipotentiary to negotiate Catholic support for aid to education in return for some concessions by an administration very sensitive about favors to Catholics. I became (and remain) an admirer, but there were aspects of his handling of the New York City debt crisis that I thought unwise, especially the decision to empty the city's coffers entirely to repay the notes that came due in November 1975, and I said so in print. I ran into him at the golf club that Thanksgiving weekend, and he chewed me out with some violence before a lot of people, ending with the bitter line: "And I thought you were a friend of mine!" To which all I could do was shrug and say, "Then we can't be friends." A couple of days later, an associate called to explain he's been under heavy pressure, and I said he shouldn't worry about it, but the fact is that I haven't seen much of Hugh since, and that's probably correct. Even sophisticated politicians can't avoid a feeling of betrayal when a reporter with whom they have some personal relation emphasizes something they would rather see ignored.

And apart from questions of loyalty, which is life's blood to politicians and corruption to reporters, people with public responsibilities cannot understand the mind-set of people whose business is to let the chips fall where they may. Michael Deaver, Reagan's deputy chief of staff in the first administration (who then capitalized on the relationship—the word "capitalized" is exact—in the second administration) recalled the week when U.S. intelligence thought it had reason to believe Libyan hit teams were in the country. Among the precautions taken by the White House was the construction of a dummy presidential limousine and the suiting of the President in a bulletproof vest. Deaver called the networks and asked them not to publicize these precautions—"what they would do was invite an assassin to shoot for the head"—but the stories ran. The other side of this coin, of course, is that there weren't any Libyan hit teams.

Mondale, who had been through these mills both as senator and as Vice President, may not have had the attitudes Isaacs imputes to him (and he imputes to himself). Early on, during the run-up to the New Hampshire primary, Mondale appeared at the home of a Nashua, New Hampshire, alderman, and spoke to assembled supporters about other visits to New Hampshire when he'd come alone, without the gaggle of media that helped crowd the alderman's living room. "The people standing next to you," he said, "aren't real people. They're reporters."[12] Isaacs says uncomfortably that Mondale "has a flip sense of humor—he meant that as a joke." Maybe. Mondale was open with the press because strategically he had to make news (Jim Lake remembered that in 1976, when Reagan was running for the Republican nomination against an incumbent President, "we tried to make real news every day"). If reporters are more his kind than Ronald Reagan's (or more Joan's kind than Nancy's), that was a plus, but scarcely a determinant.

2

The searchlight of news picks out, and wanders off. The man who basked most usefully in its beams in the politics of 1984 was Jesse Jackson, but in the end the surrender value of his celebrity was small. Roone Arledge of ABC says, probably correctly, that the great issue to be decided in the Democratic National Convention was whether or not Jackson would get prime time for his speech. He won that, at the price of trading away everything else, but it's doubtful that he could have had anything else anyway. With a single exception, *news* decisions related to this election were relatively unimportant. Abe Rosenthal of the New York *Times* had become fascinated in 1983 with what looked to him like a drift at the Supreme Court toward some reconciliation of judicial precedent and the growth of national good feeling about religion and religious values. As a result, Linda Greenhouse, part of the *Times*'s unusual cadre of legally trained reporters, was assigned to a religion-and-the-law beat, and was thus right in place when Reagan and the evangelical Christians launched their mutual admiration society. Because a *Times* reporter was au courant and in place, Reagan's prayer breakfast speeches received somewhat more attention than they might otherwise have been given, with considerable impact on a Jewish vote that was teetering on the edge of neoconservatism.

Three times the press picked up and flaunted pieces of verbiage that were not supposed to be public knowledge. Once it was Jackson's reference to New York as "hymietown." Once it was when Reagan warmed up the mike for his Saturday broadcast with the line: "My fellow Americans, I'm pleased to tell you today that I've signed legislation that will outlaw Russia forever. We begin bombing in five minutes." And once it was George Bush telling a longshoreman that he had "kicked a little ass" in his televised debate with Geraldine Ferraro. All three hurt, Bush's least—except with the press itself (asked what was surprising about the campaign, Knight-Ridder's

Bob Boyd said, "The ineffectiveness of George Bush as a campaigner"). The most controversial aspect of the press coverage was the investigation into the finances of the Zaccaro family and the business practices of John Zaccaro. The waves of publicity on these subjects washed the glow of excitement from the announcement that a woman would be the Democratic nominee for Vice President, but that glow had never looked likely to survive the full length of a campaign (though in fact Ferraro as a celebrity drew excellent crowds from start to finish). More worrisome was the possible parallel with the Eagleton phenomenon, the doubt cast on Mondale's competence by the failure to do a respectable investigation of whether his running mate could (in a fine phrase attributed to Mark Shields of the Washington *Post)* "stand the frisk."

The first and possibly most damaging story about Zaccaro's business ethics was in the New York *Times,* where Jeff Gerth detailed the candidate's husband's use of the funds of a widow for whom he was conservator under New York's very political surrogate court system. He had taken her money to make the down payment on a shaky real estate deal from which he hoped to quintuple his own money, while paying her about 1 percent monthly interest, within a few weeks. This looked and was bad—it was something for which Ferraro as a lawyer would have been disbarred—and in the end it turned out to be worse than it looked, for this deal is the one in which Zaccaro was linked to an ex-con and had filed false information with Prudential Insurance to get a mortgage, an action that later cost him the suspension of his license as a real estate broker. The national flap was over Zaccaro's refusal to reveal his, as distinguished from her, income tax return, after she had made a statement that he would do so. "If you're married to an Italian man," she said, "you know what it's like." One notes that in the 764 pages of her play-by-play account of the 1984 campaigns, Elizabeth Drew cannot bring herself to include this sentence (though she did find space for Ferraro's comment on the misapplication of the widow's funds, that when her husband had told her it was legal she replied, "Sure it was, but it doesn't look so hot."[13] In fact, as the New York courts presently ruled, and Ferraro knew all along, it was not legal, which Drew also fails to mention).

In the end, the press let Ferraro off easy. When a reporter from *The Wall Street Journal* asked her at a press conference whether Zaccaro would release the tax returns of his real estate partnerships (which was where, if anywhere, the hanky-panky would be), she replied, "Have a heart," and no further request for those returns was made. As Democratic politico Anne Wexler put it, "The networks pronounced her innocent."[14] One of the early bits on the Zaccaro problem was the fact that a building he owned, right next to his office in fact, was home to a Mafia-related producer and distributor of pornographic publications—and he was allowed to get away with the claim that he hadn't known what business was being conducted there, although, as Jeff Greenfield of ABC pointed out (but not on the air), nobody who visited Mulberry Street, let alone kept his office there, could have the slightest doubt of the use of those two floors. There were two stories that cut close to the bone, one in *The Wall Street Journal* (but it was run on the editorial page, not on a news page) by Jonathan Kwitny, the paper's rough-stuff investigator, asking about certain contacts the Ferraro and Zaccaro families had with known Mafia capos and their deputies, the other in Rupert Murdoch's New York *Post* about Ferraro's parents' arrest on a gambling charge shortly before her father died, when she was eight years old. Ferraro had never known about this, and its revelation (a source of deep embarrass-ment to her mother) was the only moment in the campaign when her sur-face cracked.

By far the most extensive job of reporting on the Zaccaro/Ferraro situation was done by the Philadelphia *Inquirer* for itself and for the Knight-Ridder chain (and other subscribers to the KNT news service, though they were not, like the chain's own papers, alerted to news breaks coming down the pipe). At one time or another, Eugene Roberts, editor of the *Inquirer,* had as many as forty people working on the business, social and funny-business contacts of the two families. Roberts had put in some time as ethnic affairs reporter (a North Carolinian, he specialized in black civil rights ques-tions, but these things are not so far apart as you might think), then as Saigon bureau chief and national news editor for the New York *Times* be-fore coming to Philadelphia, which has its own mob interests. He knew something of the Mulberry Street scene. "Zaccaro's company," Roberts said some months after the election, "acted as a real estate broker for known organized crime figures in New York. Everyone who knows anything about New York knows that there are mob ties to properties in the Mulberry Street area. The amazing thing to me was how she dealt with the question of contributors to her campaign. We thought when we printed the name of a gangster who had contributed, she would go, Oops, we never intended to accept that, we're sending the money back. That's what happens in Philadel-phia. She, interestingly, said, 'I'm not going to kick a guy when he's down. I know him as an upstanding businessman.' Her performance was one of the most impressive I have ever seen by any politician, better than Nixon's Checkers speech because he just had to give a set presentation.

"Contrary to the heat we took during the campaign," Roberts added, "we showed a great deal of restraint. We reported more than any other paper, but we knew more. That kind of story is hard to do during an election, because everything you do becomes a story in itself. The really interesting thing is the upward mobility of these families, and especially of Ferraro's mother, a great lady. We haven't finished yet, we're going to do it all as a magazine piece someday."

In the end, I think it is fair to say, Ferraro got off easily because she was a woman and the press as well as the public admired her fighting loyalties to her husband and to the grandparents of their children. There are many worse reasons for underplaying a story. Mondale had already paid the price. Between the effort to make Bert Lance chairman of the Democratic National Committee and the nomination of a Mafia-related real estate broker's wife for the vice presidency, he had lost the chance to hammer Reagan for the fundamental sleaziness and crookedness of so many of his appointments. There had never been any way to say that Geraldine Ferraro was the second most qualified person in the country to be President (something Carter and Kennedy and Johnson could have claimed for their running mates); she was an able representative of no special distinction, and was on the ticket for reasons of gender. Under those circumstances, it had been all the more necessary to make sure that nothing in her background would be an embarrassment. Maxine Isaacs says bravely that Mondale wanted to treat her just as he would have treated a male running mate, and nobody did big explorations of the private business lives of politicians' wives, but this was the summer that Senator Mark Hatfield's wife got into all the trouble on finder's fees for apartments for promoters looking to tap the Treasury to subsidize their trans-Saharan pipeline.

Sidney Blumenthal, reviewing Ferraro's post-campaign campaign biography, puts the matter, I think, in its correct if ungenerous frame: "The aspiration to legitimate power is an old story. . . . The die for Ferraro was cast when she married her husband. . . . She could never reject her past without rejecting her husband—and most of her life. Because of the opportunities suddenly opened to her, she attempted to become completely legitimate in a telescoped period of time. . . . [Like Joseph Kennedy, Sr., Ferraro] was too close to the primitive accumulation of the family fortune."[15]

The Ferraro story and its echoes were important to the election because they raised the McGovern questions of competence. What the newspapers did with the material was highly controversial in the trade (which meant that the television networks, cautiously, did virtually nothing with it). In December 1984, David Shaw of the Los Angeles *Times* wrote two long articles on the press and Ferraro, and wound up rather like the traveler who had come many miles to watch the rabbi famous for settling difficult disputes. (The rabbi heard one side and said, "You're right." Then he heard the other side and said, "You're right." And the traveler interposed himself. "Wait a minute," he said. "They can't *both* be right." And the rabbi said, "You're right.")

Unable to trace Zaccaro's partnership interests, which were not listed in his name or that of his company in the tax books, the reporters who worked on the story found much more smoke than fire. Abe Rosenthal of the New York *Times* told Shaw that he thought the *Inquirer* material had been "blown out of proportion. . . . Never in a million years would we have emulated what the *Inquirer* did." But, of course, both Roberts and his managing editor, James Naughton, were men who had quit the *Times*, which Rosenthal never forgives or forgets (something Shaw probably should have mentioned but did not). Ben Bradlee of the Washington *Post,* clearly uncomfortable with the whole business (for he was a friend of Kennedy's, remember, and Jack Kennedy's—and his father's—mob connections were much closer than Geraldine Ferraro's), told Shaw that he had avoided using the material the *Inquirer* dug up because his friend Nicholas Pileggi, who has written knowledgeably about the Mafia, had thought it unfair to run stories implying that Zaccaro was "mobbed up." But Pileggi himself told Shaw that "organized crime guys go to guys they trust. . . . They were using him. . . . If the Zaccaro firm is going to let itself be used in such a manner by organized crime figures, you should certainly write about it."[16] The *Inquirer* team found and headlined a particularly damning episode in which Zaccaro had urged a client in trouble to sell property to "Joseph (Joe the Cat) LaForte, a major figure in the Gambino crime family." Shaw notes dryly that "even many of the *Inquirer*'s critics agree with Roberts" on the saliency of that story.

In the end, all the attention to Ferraro's background and husband was not something the press *did:* "that's the kind of story," Hale Champion said with a touch of scorn, "that the press will always do without fear or favor. I can't imagine *any* paper not doing it." One suspects that if it had been the *Times* or the Washington *Post* carrying twenty-take pieces about the families, the broadcasters might not have let Ferraro's press conference performance put a halt to their "enterprise" in these matters. In any event, the real damage was done at the very beginning, by what Ferraro said herself, more than by the coverage.

3

One story one morning in one newspaper did make a major difference in the campaign, and perhaps in the results: a story that ran in *The Wall Street Journal* on October 9, under the headline "Fitness Issue / New Question in Race: Is Oldest U.S. President Now Showing His Age?" It was by Rich Jarislowsky and James M. Perry. The lead read: "When he was born, the flag that flew over the post office in his home town had 46 stars. William Howard Taft was president. And windshields had just been introduced as standard equipment on automobiles.

"At the age of 73, Ronald Reagan is the oldest president the nation has ever had."

The genesis of this piece was a couple of hours of thinking about the future that Al Hunt of the Washington bureau gave himself the summer before the election. "I asked the reporters to give me memos," he said, "not about what John did yesterday, but about the broad issues we should cover. One of them was the age issue. Every doctor I talked to said it was something that scared him. In early September I asked Rich and Jim to do it, and they gave me a piece in late September. I said, 'Yeah.' They redid it, and I still thought, well, it was very balanced, but who cared? Then came the debate, and it was what everybody was talking about on Monday. Jim called me and reminded me we had that piece. I called New York about noon, and said, 'I think we ought to run it tomorrow.' " Glyn Mapes, the *Journal*'s page-one editor, remembered that "I'd had it in the drawer, hadn't liked it, it seemed a little forced. Reagan had seemed on top of things, in good shape. I'd forgotten we had it. The minute I spoke to Hunt, I knew that now was the time. That happens a lot with our front-page pieces, it's the advantage of having a backlog of stories. We usually have to scramble to update it, but in this case it only took a couple of paragraphs."

Everything written about the election says that Reagan's performance in the debate revived the age issue, which had in fact lain dormant. But it was not the debate, nor the Monday stories in the newspapers or the broadcast news, that brought the age issue to the front. Jim Lake of Reagan-Bush recalls that the "three most sophisticated political writers—David Broder, Jack Germond and Walter Mears—wrote that Reagan wasn't as good as he usually was, Walter Mondale was better, but it wasn't enough. They usually move the press. But on Monday, Tony Coelho [representative from California and chairman of the House Democratic Campaign Committee] was up and down Mondale's press plane, pushing the age issue, and the networks were insisting Reagan was awful." In fact, there was nothing on Monday. Bob Schieffer on CBS said that the Mondale staff was "tap-dancing down the aisles" of the plane, and noted in passing that Coelho was talking about age. So far as can be learned, only one television commentator related Reagan's bumbling performance in the debate to his age, and that was Johnny Carson. "The good news," he said in his opening patter on Monday night, "is that Reagan gets to debate Mondale again. The bad news is that he'll be two weeks older." Broder's column, written on Monday for Tuesday, suggested that Reagan's debate performance would "let the age issue emerge as it had not done in any of his previous campaigns." But that was all, until after the *Journal* struck.

Before the campaign began, there had been general agreement that the list of things that could hurt Reagan was very short. Unemployment or interest rates could rise in the fall, casting doubt on the reality or the durability of the recovery from the recession (interestingly, once the recession had ended, it had become impossible to get anyone to blame Reagan for it —and the news gatherers, who had been tigers in 1982, became pussycats in 1984, permitting the President to compare current economic performance not against 1979 or even 1980 but against the trough of the recession that had, after all, occurred on his watch). The Middle East could blow up (though once we got past the spring with nothing worse than civil wars in Lebanon, Reagan was probably proof against foreign disaster, because—

as Edward Kennedy learned the hard way in 1980—the country will rally round a President in the first months after foreigners do nasty things: "If the Iranians had seized the hostages in June 1980 rather than in November 1979," Robert Strauss said in summer 1984, "Jimmy Carter would still be President"). Reagan could "lose the debates" (indeed, the cant line was that all Mondale had to do was hold the President level to "win," because he would make himself the incumbent's equal). Or something could happen that would remind people that this remarkably vital old man was nevertheless an old man. My own shorthand for it was that he would have a nosebleed, and that night each network news would have its own pet doctor on camera discoursing learnedly on the significance of a nosebleed in a man of seventy-three.

"Can't happen," said Michael Deaver in the White House. "Reagan is in better health today than he was when he came here. He works out every day, which he didn't do before the assassination attempt. We've had to buy him new shirts with larger collars." This was before the negotiators had reached agreement on the debates between the candidates, but Deaver had no doubt there would be a deal. "Sure there are bear traps," he said, "but Reagan has always done well in debates. And remember that this time you have the benefit of a man who is much better informed on the issues, because he's been briefed on them every day for four years."

Watching from his aerie at the Kennedy School in Cambridge, Hale Champion was less certain. "When he was governor of California," Champion said, "he would take a briefing from Stuart Spencer and he would do a good job in a press conference. It was not just the ability to respond, but the ability to pick up the spin and turn it to his own use. That ability has gone down, greatly deteriorated in the four years of his presidency." Haynes Johnson of the Washington *Post* agreed: "I think the White House people are terrified of letting Reagan get out there. He could destroy himself in thirty seconds in a debate, not with the people watching, but with the people who write the stories afterward, who tell the viewers what *did* happen." Lake didn't much disagree with that, either, though before the debate he certainly seemed to be and probably was entirely confident of how his tiger would perform. "The television people will find out who won the debates," he said about two months before the first of them, "by reading the New York *Times* and the Washington *Post.*" And the public at large, of course, would find out by watching television and listening to radio, and to a somewhat lesser degree by reading the newspapers: if there is one subject on which all commentators have reached agreement, it is that public opinion of the victor in a debate is overwhelmingly influenced by "the media."

USA Today, ABC and the Republican Party all ran instant polls during and immediately after the first debate. The Republicans claimed, not honestly, that theirs showed a victory for Reagan by a 49–31 margin. ABC showed Reagan slightly ahead by 40–37. *USA Today* had Mondale the winner by 39–34. The man-in-the-street stuff on television and in the newspapers awarded the palm to the President: "In Bar," ran the headline in *Newsday,* the dominant paper in the great suburban belt stretching east from New York City on Long Island, "Round Goes to Reagan." This is not just a matter of sophistication: Haynes Johnson reports that more than a third of the Washington *Post* newsroom, watching the Roger Mudd interview with Teddy Kennedy in fall 1979, thought the senator had come out of it well, but within a week everyone at the *Post* believed that Kennedy had made himself seem unsuitable for the presidency. Until the press highlighted it the next morning, few Americans had seen anything especially wrong with Gerald Ford's answer to Max Frankel of the New York *Times* to the effect that Poland was not a Soviet satellite. Similarly, in the first Mondale-Reagan debate opinion was mixed at first sampling, but by the end of the week after the debate all the polls showed more than 85 percent of the country quite certain that Mondale had "won."

Jeff Gralnick, who planned the election coverage for ABC (starting about eighteen months before election day), had originally thought that Reagan could not hope to escape the age issue. "Every time somebody who is over seventy and of some prominence dies," he said in summer 1984, "it will come up, all depending on how Mondale decides to handle it. You've already heard the age shot fired twice this spring, once with Reagan's polyp, and then with a statement by a group of doctors that these things lead to cancer." (Smart fellows, those doctors.) But the question of the President's age really did lie dormant until October 9. "I think what happened," says John Chancellor, "was that their careful programming of the President made us *forget* the age issue. I hadn't even thought about it for weeks. I did a little commentary after he stumbled in the first debate. I said, 'He was terrible.' I didn't mention age—he had looked vigorous enough until he began to stumble at the end. Tuesday we all did it, and I think every one of us mentioned the *Wall Street Journal* story, we sheltered in the lee of their journalism."

Some of what was done was very rough. On ABC, executive producer Bill Lord demonstrated that the problem of inconsequence had been with the President for a while by putting together three brief pieces of film, one showing him nodding off while listening to Pope John Paul II, one at Camp David in a photo opportunity interrupted by questions, smiling idiotically and not responding until his wife gave him the answer in a stage whisper, and the third in his rambling final statement of the previous Sunday night's debate. The portrait was of a man who had gone absolutely gaga. The Reagan campaign reacted as best it could, taking the limousines off the tarmac and having the candidate stride through crowds instead of waving and plopping into the car on arrival at his campaign appearances, releasing full medical reports, shouting "Foul!" in loud voices at the Democrats and the press. But the week after the first debate was one of rapid reduction in the President's lead in the polls, from 18 percent on Sunday to 12 percent on Friday. Then the situation stabilized; there being no news, the age story died down. The Republicans still had to worry that the President would stumble again in the second and final debate—Sam Donaldson the morning of the second debate spoke of "the senility factor," and said that people would be watching that night "to see whether the President stands up, makes sentences that make sense from the standpoint of not stammering and stuttering, and doesn't drool" (Jimmy Carter on leaving the White House told a friend there were two people whose acquaintance he was delighted to leave to his successor: Menachem Begin and Sam Donaldson). Barring that, they were home free.

Now the President benefited from the format the League of Women Voters had established for the debate. A head-to-head classical debate would have left the age issue unmentioned, for it would have been bad form for Mondale to bring it up, but with questions posed by reporters a direct challenge was inevitable. Reagan, without telling his staff (who asked, and received the answer that "I can handle that"), found the two-liner he wanted. "I want you to know," he said when the question was asked, "that . . . I will not make age an issue of this campaign. I am not going to exploit for political purposes my opponent's youth and inexperience." Jim Lake relished the memory of that moment: "You could hear the sound of television sets being turned off, all over the country." Maxine Isaacs didn't think it was that great a line (understandably), she thought Mondale had easily won the debate (correctly), and she thought Reagan really was no more convincing in this appearance than in the previous one (again, correctly). But that line was the one thing that every television news show and radio news broadcast picked up, and aired over and over again through the next morning and indeed the next evening's nightly news. It was the one "sound bite" from the debate that was universally used; and that was the end of the age issue and of the election.

As Robert Strauss had so scornfully said, the press has its own dog in every race, the underdog. The coverage of the age issue in the aftermath of the first debate had made Reagan not a shoo-in winner who was pushing our White House correspondents around but a victim of unfair presentation. The Pope's speeches, after all, might put anyone to sleep. The President's confusion at the Camp David helipad was easily attributable to his hearing difficulties, which he and his entourage had freely admitted since 1981, when he had begun to wear a quite visible hearing aid in public. The stumbling in the peroration of the debate came in a section of his statement where he had already used the phrases in his notes in answer to one of the questions, and what he had been doing was looking for new words to express something he had previously said, an activity that can daunt even an experienced wordsmith. It was possible to argue that Ronald Reagan's intellectual primitivism, limited curiosity and ideological rigidity poorly equipped him for the presidency (also to argue on the other side—at least until the Iranian-arms-Contra-money fiasco opened an abyss beneath his feet —that he was the first President since Eisenhower to understand that "presiding" over a government does not require a mastery of the details of the decisions brought to the desk in the Oval Office), but there was no real evidence for the case that his capacity to do what he could do had been diminished by the passage of four years. The age stories of the week of October 8 had been legitimate but a bum rap. So the authority figures of the television tube, who had been very cautious in their views of the results of the first debate, all opened their comments on the second one with expressions of admiration for how well the President had laid the ghosts of sickness and death, and the President's margin in the polls returned to 18 percent.

But Haynes Johnson of the Washington *Post* believes that Reagan's performance in the first debate and the coverage it occasioned did in fact make a major difference in the results of the election. "Before that," Johnson says, "the Republicans *were* headed for a realigning election. The Democrats were about to cut and run from their ticket. There was going to be a swing of forty, fifty, sixty seats in the House. All my interview material plays back that way. Then, the week after the debate, people decided to hedge their bets." What can be said for sure is that in 1980 Republican candidates for the House outpolled Democratic candidates, nationwide (the Democrats controlled the House anyway because state legislatures have been Democratic for decades and gerrymander the districts), while in 1984, with a very much heavier vote for the Republican President, the Democrats kept a narrow edge in the vote for congressmen. One notes admiringly that this result was in effect encouraged, and perhaps made possible, by a newspaper on which the editor, Robert Bartley, really believed that Tip O'Neill had horns and a tail. Right on.

Part Five

IN PRINT

12

The Big Business of Newspapers

THIS IS A PRINTING OFFICE
CROSSROADS OF CIVILIZATION
REFUGE OF ALL THE ARTS
AGAINST THE RAVAGES OF TIME
ARMOURY OF FEARLESS TRUTH
AGAINST WHISPERING RUMOR
INCESSANT TRUMPET OF TRADE
FROM THIS PLACE WORDS MAY FLY ABROAD
NOT TO PERISH ON WAVES OF SOUND
NOT TO VARY WITH THE WRITER'S HAND
BUT FIXED IN TIME,
HAVING BEEN VERIFIED IN PROOF
FRIEND YOU STAND ON SACRED GROUND
THIS IS A PRINTING OFFICE

—sign in the anteroom
of the old London
Times building on
Printinghouse Square

Now that the provider of the newspaper capital hires the editor instead of the editor hiring the newspaper capital, the paper is likelier to be run as a money-maker pure and simple— a factory where ink and brains are so applied to white paper as to turn out the largest possible marketable product.

—Edward Ross, pioneer
sociologist, 1903[1]

Newspaper wages are a disgrace, especially in editorial offices . . . the average starting salary for journalism graduates last year was below $12,000. . . . The brightest and most ambitious young people will not be attracted to newspapers at that salary level.

—John Morton, ex-newspaper reporter, analyst
with Lynch, Jones & Ryan, members, New York Stock
Exchange, January 1986[2]

My colleague, reporter Susan Ager, cannot believe "anyone who is sincere would shy away from journalism because salaries are too low. . . . The sort of person who is attracted to journalism is not attracted to engineering."

> –David Lawrence, publisher and chairman
> of the Detroit *Free Press*,
> and chairman of the "credibility"
> committee of the American Newspaper
> Publishers Association,
> January 1986[3]

1

TV Guide announces that the revenues of the three network news divisions, "reportedly $830 million in 1984, total more than the gross national product of some Third World Nations."[4] Another comparison might be to the Los Angeles *Times*. In 1985, according to Otis Chandler, who was still chairman and editor of the *Times* when he said it, that one newspaper, all by itself, was expecting revenues of more than a billion dollars, and that was something like one-thirtieth of the revenues of all U.S. daily newspapers. Readers and advertisers between them spent about $30 billion for papers and advertising space therein in calendar 1985. Newspaper classified advertising alone took in more than nine times as much as advertisers spent for time on the network news shows in 1984. At a generous estimate, including technicians, executives and the dedicated ad sales staff, the network news divisions employ maybe 7,500 people; newspapers directly employ more than 425,000. As a business, television news is very small potatoes next to the newspapers.

Newspapers have been a big business for a very long time. Pulitzer owned a yacht bigger than Morgan's. Edward W. Scripps endowed a university and an oceanographic institute. The Whitelaw Reid mansion on Madison Avenue, where the proprietor of the New York *Tribune* lived, was home to the Archdiocese of New York and Bennett Cerf's Random House (both of them at once) after Reid's death, and when Harry Helmsley bought the land for his Palace Hotel the Landmarks Commission wouldn't let him tear down the old pile, forcing him to incorporate it as part of the most expensive large hotel in the city. In 1983, four years after the old man's death, the IRS filed suit against the estate of Samuel Newhouse, last of the giant private proprietors, for $609,519,855 in back taxes (plus $304,759,927 in fraud penalties), the largest such action on record. Every year *Forbes* publishes a list guessing the identities and fortunes of the 400 richest Americans. More people on that list got their money from real estate than from any other source, but the second most common avenue to great wealth is publishing.

Until fairly recently, this was a reward for genius (talent is a separate issue) in the publishing arts themselves. Very few men went into newspaper publishing strictly as a business venture. Even James Gordon Bennett and Horace Greeley, who separated the daily press from political sponsorship, had strong views that they promoted in their columns, and Henry Raymond, who founded the New York *Times* and moved beyond Greeley and Bennett by separating news and editorial matter, served as a Republican congressman during the Civil War while continuing as editor and publisher of his paper. Pulitzer also served in Congress, as a Democrat, in 1885, but resigned after four months because the work interfered with his duties at the New York *World.*

Scripps, one of the earliest chain owners, called himself a "people's champion" and a "damned old crank," and ordered his papers to operate on the principle that "whatever is, is wrong."⁵ But Scripps's mean-minded successor, Roy Howard, was a little man with a Napoleon complex, who liked to associate with the rich and famous and whose vanity made him the real begetter of the Newspaper Guild. Hugh Baillie, who ran the United Press for Howard through the 1940s, remembered that the union originated in 1932 in Cleveland (not, as official histories have it, at Heywood Broun's penthouse in New York in 1933) when Howard came to visit the newsroom of the Cleveland *Press,* and, playing one of the boys, as always— he had started life as a sportswriter, like Al Neuharth of Gannett—sat himself down on a table in the newsroom, swinging his leg, to discuss the depressed world with the working stiffs. One of them inquired why the people in the newsroom had to take a pay cut while the people in the composing room didn't, and Howard replied, "Well, *they* have a union." As if by magic, the meeting immediately adjourned to the speakeasy next door, and suddenly the Cleveland reporters had a union, too. Tough as he was on his employees, and resistant as he was to unionism, Howard was an ardent supporter of the New Deal until he broke with Roosevelt in the late 1930s (mostly over what he considered Roosevelt's attacks on him), at which point all forty Scripps-Howard papers became strongly Republican.

Until recently, it was considered rather disreputable for a newspaper proprietor to have no interest but money. When Frank Munsey died, after buying and demoralizing (and sometimes liquidating for the real estate value of the properties) a chain of papers that included Charles Dana's New York *Sun,* William Allen White, Franklin Roosevelt's Republican friend at the Emporia (Kan.) *Gazette,* signaled the event with an obituary:

> Frank Munsey, the great publisher, is dead.
> Frank Munsey contributed to the journalism of his day the talent of a meatpacker, the morals of a money changer, and the manners of an undertaker.

He and his kind have about succeeded in transforming a once-noble profession into an eight percent security.

May he rest in trust.[6]

It was an exquisite revenge: nobody today remembers Frank Munsey, but the obit is cited a lot.

A few years later, A. J. Liebling had occasion to write to Arthur Hays Sulzberger about the willingness of the New York *Times* to accept advertising from a clearly fake "union" of "tool owners," supposedly representing 7,500,000 small businessmen, advocating legislation to restrict the activities of labor unions. He thought the *Times* should establish a committee of its reporters to vet political advertising "for obvious flapdoodle," with a copyreader "to edit this stuff for factual basis." A newspaper, Liebling felt, had to take responsibility of a sort for everything that appeared under its logo. Failing that, he wrote, "I can imagine a new paper in New York to be called the *Daily Pontius P.,* with a basin and ewer at the masthead, and *no* content for which it is responsible—just syndicated columnists and controversial ads. It is a humiliating conception, for the publisher, who becomes merely the proprietor of a *maison de passe,* rents the rooms and doesn't care what happens in them."[7]

In our time, it is more or less expected that newspaper publishers will be businessmen like other businessmen, and the behavior that turned White's stomach and roused Liebling to such glorious protest has become routine. The Gannett chain with ninety-three wholly owned daily papers in its stable (as of mid-1986) boasts that it does not seek to violate the editorial independence of the newspapers it acquires. By common agreement, that's tricky and unrewarding work: "Newspapers are a lot like old shoes," says David Laventhol of the Los Angeles Times-Mirror Corp., reflecting on his experiences after his company acquired the Hartford *Courant.* "Some people would rather wear old shoes than the shiny new ones you offer them."[8] The Newhouse chain has refused to take responsibility even for egregious behavior by its editors, including those of the Birmingham *News,* who were entirely on the side of Bull Connor and his dogs and cattle prods when the civil rights marchers came. Newhouse, *News* publisher Clarence Hanson swore in an affidavit in 1973, "has taken no steps to interfere with or influence the editorial policy or local management of the *News,* and he has not suggested any editorial position on a local, state, or national matter."[9]

The fact that most American central cities are now served by only one or two newspapers does not mean that there are fewer papers or fewer newspeople. At the end of World War II, there were about 1,750 daily papers in the United States; in 1985, there were about 1,675. When the Washington *Star* folded in 1981, it became an opportunity for five formerly weekly or biweekly papers in the Washington suburbs to convert to daily status. Daily paper circulation was up from about 51 million to almost 64

million from 1946 to 1985, with a switch from 60 percent evening paper to
55 percent morning paper in the distribution. Advertising revenue was up
from a little more than $1 billion to about $24 billion. These last figures
more than make up for the rather disappointing growth in circulation (up
less than 25 percent in a period when the number of households grew by
about 90 percent), for the drop in center-city circulation means the loss of
an audience advertisers don't much want anyway. A newspaper lives or dies
on its advertising revenue, which normally adds up to three-quarters of its
total revenue and is by no means entirely a function of circulation numbers.
By dint of enormous effort, including lots of prize contests for heavy
money, the New York *Post* at one point in the 1980s pulled its daily circulation ahead of that of the *Times,* and the ad sales executives went calling on
the department stores that didn't advertise in the *Post.* One of them was
Bloomingdale's, where the advertising manager explained, "Their readers
are our customers; your readers are our shoplifters."

Despite the revolution in newspaper production machinery, total employment over the forty years was up from less than 250,000 to almost
450,000. As the recent sales prices for newspapers indicate—twenty and
more times the cash flow, forget about the profit, of the paper being acquired—a big metropolitan paper without direct identical-geography, identical time-frame competition gives its owner the same sort of license to steal
that was, Lord Thomson of Fleet once said, the nature of a television channel. In 1984–86, the Gannett chain spent more than a billion dollars to buy
three newspapers: the Des Moines *Register,* the Detroit *News* and the Louisville *Courier-Journal.* Thanks to the changing production processes, the
newspaper publishers, Roy Howard's successors to a man, have been able to
clobber the unions that had kept the newspaper business labor-intensive and
high-cost. The clobbering continues, and not merely of the craft unions
whose crafts have become obsolete: in 1985–86, in as strongly unionized
and strong-arm a town as Chicago, the *Tribune* was able to claim victory
over as potent a union as the teamsters who trucked the paper around town.

Strikes by reporters have been especially unproductive. Typically, the
publishers replace the reporters, and a year later, when the law permits,
have the National Labor Relations Board hold a decertification election in
which the strikers are not permitted to vote. In Wilkes-Barre, Pennsylvania,
when the union set up a rival community paper as its only possible counter-
attack, the owners of the struck *Times-Leader* (Capital Cities Communications, which later bought ABC) brought an NLRB proceeding to punish the
strikers for violating their former contract, which prohibited them from
working for competing papers. The old definition of the Yiddish term
"chutzpah" was the man who murdered his father and mother and claimed
clemency because he was an orphan; now we have a new one.

The strongest case is that newspapers have been too profitable. In recent years, newspaper stocks have been sold at a multiple of earnings higher

than the stocks of almost any other industrial group. Return on equity for most of the newspaper chains listed on an exchange runs consistently over 25 percent. Stock in the Washington *Post* sold in early 1986 for roughly six times what it had cost a decade earlier, and the reason is classic Marxist surplus value: the *Post*'s profits had been under $8,000 per employee in the latter 1970s, and were over $20,000 per employee by 1986. Some part of this comes from the fact that the journeyman *Post* reporter makes almost $15,000 a year less than his equally experienced colleague on the New York *Times*.

Not that the *Post* reporter, with a Newspaper Guild minimum salary of $35,000 a year going into negotiations in mid-1986, had anything to complain about by comparison with the run-of-the-mine newspaperman. Osborn Elliott said in 1985, as he completed his penultimate year as dean of the Columbia School of Journalism, that his graduates typically got jobs at $12,000–14,000 a year—and these were people with college degrees, a couple of years of experience and a master's degree from the most highly regarded school in their profession. A 1985 study by Jean Gaddy Wilson of the University of Missouri, with responses from 648 newspapers, showed an average salary of just under $19,000 for the longest-term general news reporter and only $25,921 for the average city editor. For the same year, the National Education Association claimed an average teacher salary of $25,725 (for about 200 days of work as against 240 for the newspaper people), and bitched bitterly.

Much of the extraordinary profits of the newspapers since the early 1970s has been invested in machinery. Members of the American Newspaper Publishers Association (about a third of all papers) owned 10,230 "hot-metal linecasters" (Linotype machines) in 1970 and only 23 video display terminals. By 1982, they owned only 194 Linotypes and 46,217 VDTs. Meanwhile, there are computers that paginate, computers that take direct insertion of employment ads for the classified section from the employment agencies' own PCs, etc. The rising cost of such machinery, which means the rising price of entry into the business for newcomers, is perhaps the prime source of the monopoly that yields the monopoly rents to the present proprietors.

But the fact that people can be got to work at newspapers for cheap has encouraged publishers to gun the size of their news staffs, too. When I first began looking around, in the 1950s, newsrooms were typically empty until an hour or two before the first deadline, because people were out on stories. Only the New York *Times* had a bunch of people sitting around what was then a giant bullpen with a tile floor, reading the paper and waiting for something important to happen that would command their attention. (The *Times* no longer has a bullpen; instead there are private offices with windows along the periphery of the news area, and a tasteful collection of carpeted smallish rooms, each a shared area for eight to twelve reporters, in the core.) With improvements in telephone service, more reporters stayed in the office all day, but even after allowing for this not entirely fortunate sea change, the staffs are now typically a little larger than needed for every day. Richard Harwood of the Washington *Post* gave a veteran editor's perspective on the problems of managing a modern newsroom: "We have 550 people, and there's not enough news to go round."

Harwood was speaking the week of the New Hampshire primaries in 1984, when the *Post* had fifteen people covering what was a media event, a distraction from the real world (though for a while there seemed reason to believe maybe it was more). Only a couple of weeks before, seventeen *Post* reporters had gone to Tampa for the Super Bowl. (In sum, the "media" asked for 3,000 accreditations to the 1985 Super Bowl, and got 1,500. At both 1984 political conventions, the press outnumbered the delegates.) In the case of the New York *Times* there is an element of vanity in the expansion of the staffs, a belief that *Times* people will always do a better job: "The national editor is all het up about agricultural news," said assistant managing editor James Greenfield (also in 1984, before everybody got het up about agricultural news). "So we've built up an agricultural staff, even though we're an urban paper and you can get the news on AP and UP." But it is also true that lavishness in staffing has vastly improved the capacity of the papers to dig out stories, either because they have an able man on the spot or because they can blanket the possible sources.

Perhaps the most spectacular example of the values of individual initiative during the years of process on this book came in 1984, when Dusko Doder of the Washington *Post* noted a shift from the previously announced jazz concert to classical music on Moscow television, drifted around town and noted that "lights were on in numerous offices in the headquarters of the KGB, the Soviet secret police, as well as in the buildings housing the Soviet general staff . . ."[10] He deduced the death of Andropov, and the *Post* played it on the front page. But not only were the *Post*'s editors unable to get any confirmation from the State Department or the CIA; they got a statement from high up at State that the report was "bullshit" and a scornful query about what their Moscow man had been smoking. (Rumor has it that the reason for the official scorn was the fact that the *other* Moscow television channel was broadcasting a hockey game and did not interrupt it, and those Americans who were on duty were watching the hockey game.) After the first two of five editions, the *Post,* cowed, moved the story off the front page. But Doder was right.

The Doder story also illustrates that while team journalism and beat expertise have become increasingly important, thanks in part to the complexity of the stories to be covered, newspaper work of prime importance can still be done by the skilled snoop, the alert observer with, as they say, the nose for news. One of the most startling stories of 1983—Michael Robinson of George Washington University described it as the most important story about a media subject that year—was the man in Jacksonville, Alabama, who doused himself with gasoline and set himself afire for the television cameras, while the local station news crews filmed the story, waiting until he was well and truly alight and the picture was on the tape before they moved to rescue him. This broke in the New York *Times* almost a week after it had happened. Judith Miller of the *Times* was on temporary assignment to that paper's Atlanta bureau between her tour in Washington and her assignment to Cairo. She heard about this incident in Atlanta, scurried to Jacksonville, and raised as uncomfortable a set of questions as the news business had to confront in the first half of this decade. Of the other newspapers, television network news shows and newsmagazines that picked up this story, incidentally, only one—*Newsweek*—thought it important to credit Miller.

But it is the group resources of the modern paper that are most striking to the visitor. I will argue in the last chapter that the truth about what had happened to the *Challenger* would have been buried by the Rogers Commission (who had been appointed for the purpose of saving NASA) if the beat reporters who knew the agency had not been available to spark their contacts until a motor started. Certainly the truth about the Bhopal catastrophe would have remained mysterious—because neither Union Carbide nor the Indian government nor the vultures from the personal-injury bar had any stake in getting the story straight—without the twenty-man team the New York *Times* deployed in India, West Virginia, Connecticut and Washington.

2

The product of the newsroom is by no means all there is to the making of a newspaper. Sam McKeel, the long-headed, white-haired Southerner who has been publisher of the Philadelphia *Inquirer* since 1972, remembers that he started as a reporter on the Charlotte *Observer* and got into the business side of newspapers only after the Knight family acquired the paper and put in a new CEO, who suggested he move over. "Like everybody else offered that sort of move," McKeel says, "I got him to promise that if I didn't like it, I could return to the newsroom, but I never did. I found I had a proclivity. It's still newspapering, but it's more complex and interesting. Reporters live in a protected world and tend to be arrogant, think they are all of what's important to the paper, and nothing could be further from the truth." One starts with the interesting fact that for most papers the expenditure for paper is greater than the expenditure for news. A "special report" in the official journal of the American Newspaper Publishers Association puts the matter infelicitously but not incorrectly: "Despite their uniqueness, all newspapers function similarly. . . . Their work flows the same way:

advertising and editorial matter in one end and the product out the other."[11]

And quite a lot of the contents of the news hole is as much purchased goods as the newsprint is. Except for the handful of providers who sell their stuff to others, most modern papers fill most of their columns with "syndicated" material—the comic strips, the crossword and bridge puzzles, the TV listings (the supplier sells the stations or the networks or the program producers the boldface or asterisked items, splitting the proceeds with the paper, which appears to be recommending the shows), the columnists and of course the national and international news, which is printed as it comes off the wire from AP or UPI, or Dow Jones or Reuters, or one of the national services offering the stories that will be featured tomorrow in the big-city papers. Syndicated news and features are quite cheap: of the $30 billion of revenue received by the daily papers, only a little more than 1 percent goes to the wire services and syndicates combined (and much of that pays for stock market tables and other statistical business news). As Jonathan Fenby writes in his book on AP, UP, Reuters and Agence France-Presse, "an agency service offering an around-the-clock reporting of the world may cost a newspaper less than a single journalist's salary."[12] Except at AP, which is a cooperative financed by "assessments," the prices reflect relative bargaining strength and the negotiating abilities of the seller and the buyer rather than objective elements. Even at AP, until the 1980s, prices were set under a strange formula which rewarded the established and successful papers (the only members of the co-op before the Supreme Court intervened in 1945) by assessing on the basis of potential readers, the population of the marketing area, rather than actual circulation.

Nearly all the syndicates cover the waterfront of material, from humor to punditry. In summer 1985, Rupert Murdoch's News America Syndicate led its advertising with a picture of Pope John Paul II ("The Holy Father is a prolific author whose constant theme is the dignity of humanity"), because it was offering a column to be called "Observations by Pope John Paul II," which it later turned out the Pope had not authorized. "We have enjoyed major successes," the ad proudly proclaimed, "with the syndication of Richard Nixon's *No More Vietnams* and Greg Evans' new comic strip *Luann* . . ." Later, incidentally, News America trumpeted that the papal column, now called "Selected Observations of Pope John Paul II" and admittedly a culling from what the Pope had already published elsewhere, was being "read by 60 million." The ad, which ran in *Editor & Publisher*, was illustrated by a picture of syndicate president Richard S. Newcombe in a crowd of tourists, with the caption: "Archbishop Foley arranged for Newcombe to be present at a papal audience in St. Peter's Square." Other tourists presumably had their arrangements made by the concierge at their hotel.

Syndicated columnists give newspapers their big names; astrology columns and advice on social problems make for habitual readers, which are certainly the best kind. The comic strips are of course central. You can tell one paper is really going after another when it arranges with the syndicator to steal its competitor's comics: when Time Inc. was trying to make the Washington *Star* a real rival to the *Post,* it swiped "Doonesbury"; and Rupert Murdoch's secret in bringing up the circulation of the Boston *Herald* by more than 50 percent was less the prize games—for the demographics of the paper improved, too, and prizes won't do that for you—than the switch of comic strips: the *Globe* sued, and lost.

A lot of the syndicated material is glitzy or worse, and emphasizing it has been the desperation doomed response of many papers on their way down. An article in the final issue of the Minneapolis *Star* expressed the working newsman's contempt for these procedures: "Suddenly, or so it seemed, the newspaper's most basic ingredients—City Council meetings, news conferences, speeches—were gone. In their place was an unpredictable front-page mixture of blazing illustrations, Hollywood features and all sorts of things that had once been tucked away inside the paper." On the other hand, virtually all the international and most of the national coverage in all but the dozen or so largest papers *must* come from some sort of syndicated service. Much of the improvement in the quality of metropolitan newspapers outside the five biggest cities comes from the availability of reports and commentary from the New York *Times* or the Washington *Post*–L.A. *Times* joint venture, or the KNT service (Knight-Ridder, New York *Daily News,* Chicago *Tribune).* For this is, after all, what the broadcast news doesn't have—and, meanwhile, the broadcast news has created an appetite for reading about subjects that once seemed so remote it was impossible to care but are now part of the view from this special window in the living room.

Increasingly, the advertising content of newspapers is also syndicated. This is not new in kind—for decades, the most profitable period in the newspaper business was the end of the second and the start of the third quarter, when the automobile companies announced their new models by dousing the nation with advertising, identical full-page "stereotypes" shipped to every paper for publication the same day, paid for at higher, "national" rates. But today an increasing share of retail advertising, the life's blood of the newspapers, is also placed by national decision: Leo Bogart, a serious-minded sociologist who runs the Newspaper Advertising Bureau, points out that the top one hundred national advertisers place about 45 percent of all advertising outlays in all media, and the top ten advertising agencies, after the recent rash of consolidations, will place a third of all advertising. They are looking for efficiency, they dislike "duplication," and they want not just numbers of people but quantities of disposable income: "In Philadelphia, the *Bulletin,* with over 400,000 circulation, strangled on a deficit of $21 million in a market where advertisers spent $1.8 billion on all media in 1981. In that same year, the *Press* had 43 per cent of the daily circulation in Cleveland, but only 28 per cent of the advertising."[13]

Advertising has arrived at the papers increasingly in the form of preprinted inserts that will use the news sections as a wrapper. The "manager of field media services" for Sears, Roebuck explained the economics to a conference of newspaper financial executives in mid-1986: "If you take the cost of a Sears 16-page preprint, the costs of creation, printing, paper and shipping plus insertion, and divide it by 16, it would take the pro-rate cost of four of those pages to pay for one full page of ROP [run-of-paper, the term of art for a standard newspaper display ad]. . . . In reality, however, the comparison is more dramatic. When faced with a choice of adding pages to a preprint, and using the incremental cost as a measurement, it would take more than eight preprint pages to pay for one full page of ROP."[14]

The prime beneficiaries of this development have been the local "shoppers," giveaway (or "controlled circulation") papers that get into the hands of all the households of an area, but established newspapers, if they organize themselves for the purpose, can put these color brochures into their subscribing households at a cost less than postage charges even for third-class mail (which the publishers say the post office has been unduly subsidizing). If the distribution operation has been sufficiently computerized, the newspaper can according to the preference of the advertiser either restrict the circulation of the insert to a certain geographical or demographic group, or supplement its normal distribution with mailings or carrier drops to nonsubscribers to give an advertiser universal coverage. This has in fact been moving along, under the rubric of TMC, for "total market coverage"; most newspapers now offer it, except in the very largest cities. Revenues from national display advertising in newspapers have been stable or slowly growing in the 1980s, but revenues from inserted preprints have been rising at a 20 to 25 percent annual clip, and probably approached $4 billion in 1986.

The costs of gearing up for this sort of activity are substantial—the Philadelphia *Inquirer* budgeted $20 million for its new "mail room," and then had to take a strike to get the benefits of its efficiency—and they come at the same time that money has to be found for newsroom and pressroom automation. In 1985, Otis Chandler of the Los Angeles *Times* reported that his board had approved expenditures of $150 million for new presses in Hartford, Denver and Dallas (presumably the Dallas expenditures were recouped when the *Times* sold the paper in mid-1986). Together with inheritance taxes, the capital demands of modern newspapering have been a strong force in the growth of the chains.

3

There are chains and chains. One cannot imagine a statement about itself by the McClatchey company that did not mention its flagship paper, the Sacramento *Bee,* but Harte-Hanks, shortly before it bought up its own stock and became a private rather than a publicly held corporation, described itself in an ad in *Barron's* as a company that "owns and operates 28 daily newspapers and 75 non-daily publications" and "six marketing services companies and 18 direct mail systems, which can offer advertisers direct mail programs reaching 96% of American households." The names of the papers didn't matter. Michael Hoyt and Mary Ellen Schoonmaker note sourly in the *Columbia Journalism Review* that the Newhouse family chain (Cleveland *Plain Dealer,* Portland *Oregonian,* New Orleans *Times-Picayune,* Newark *Star-Ledger,* etc.) is "a system where excellence may be applauded, but it is not demanded, where no one at the top cares as deeply about the words as they do about the money."[15] The Donrey Media Group, named for its proprietor, Donald Reynolds, owns 54 dailies in fifteen states, with a total circulation of only 728,000; the man who was general manager of the largest of them told *Forbes* that "Reynolds couldn't care less what's in his 54 dailies. . . . But it's his low commitment to editorial quality and personnel that has enabled him to operate so profitably."[16]

Still, the fact is that all but a handful of the nation's better newspapers are in one way or another part of a group. Even apparently separate operations like the St. Petersburg *Times* and the San Francisco *Chronicle* also own, respectively, *Congressional Quarterly* and KRON radio and TV. The New York *Times* owns a string of papers, mostly in North Carolina and Florida (the largest of them is the Sarasota *Herald-Tribune,* with more than 100,000 circulation; in 1985 the *Times* spent $23 million to build a new printing plant there, and the designers gloried in its technical sophistication by installing white carpet in the wholly computerized composition area—"I thought it was a little excessive myself," said corporate chairman and publisher Arthur Ochs Sulzberger). The Los Angeles *Times* owns *Newsday* in the Long Island suburbs of New York, the nation's largest suburban paper (with urban ambitions: a New York City edition was launched in 1985, and by 1986 had its own newsroom with no fewer than 160 reporters); plus the Denver *Post,* the Baltimore *Sun,* the Allentown (Pa.) *Call* and the Hartford *Courant,* among others. *The Wall Street Journal* owns the Ottaway chain, mostly in the Midwest; the Washington *Post* owns *Newsweek* and a little paper in Everett, Washington, and several television and radio stations; the Chicago *Tribune* owns one of those superstations that go on cable TV all over the country, and the New York *Daily News,* and papers in Florida, and until it sold out to sports promoter Jack Kent Cooke in late 1985 a Los Angeles

Daily News (started as a shopper only a dozen years before) that was out-
selling the L.A. *Times* in the San Fernando Valley.

What the commentators on the multi-paper corporation phenomenon
usually mean, however, is the chain where the corporate entity is more
important than any of the individual papers—the Hearst or Scripps-Howard
sort of operation (to take examples that have faded out a bit, though by no
means disappeared, in the postwar era), San Diego-based Copley and At-
lanta-based Cox, and giants like Gannett, Knight-Ridder and Newhouse,
plus oddities like Rupert Murdoch, who acquired papers in New York, San
Antonio, Boston and Chicago (to add to his collection of papers in Britain
and Australia) before deciding that openly fictional entertainment on film
and TV tape was more fun and possibly more profitable, too.

As of 1984, the largest of the chains in newspaper revenue was Knight-
Ridder, with about $2.5 billion in gross income (the next year's figures
were warped by a long strike at the Philadelphia *Inquirer;* and in 1986
Gannett's billion-dollar acquisition program put that much less interesting
chain clearly in the lead). The Knight-Ridder group, to use the preferred
term, was stitched together in 1974 by the merger of two established chains.
Knight, with headquarters in Miami (which became headquarters for the
chain), was based essentially there and in Detroit, Akron and Charlotte.
Ridder was an outgrowth of the German press of St. Paul, Minnesota, that
had expanded its New York beachhead from the *Staats-Zeitung* to the *Journal
of Commerce,* and had made the wise strategic decision to collect California
dailies, most notably in San Jose, Long Beach and Pasadena. Considering
the very different styles involved—the Ridder papers had been run by their
publishers, to whom the editorial side reported, while the Knight papers
gave their editors a separate channel of communications and authority running through corporate headquarters—the mix has been smooth. The group
is run by newspapermen rather than moneymen.

Albert Hunt, a Philadelphian now chief of the huge *Wall Street Journal*
Washington bureau, says that in every instance where he knew the before-
and-after story, Knight-Ridder has improved the newspapers it has acquired. For 1985, Columbia University awarded eleven Pulitzers for news-
related stories and photos: Knight-Ridder won seven of them. The papers
rewarded were the Lexington *Times-Herald,* the Miami *Herald,* the Philadelphia *Inquirer,* the St. Paul *Pioneer Press* and the San Jose *Mercury-News.*

It is also fair to say that nobody keeps everyone happy all the time. "An
industry granted great constitutional privilege on the premise of diversity is
fast becoming the domain of a handful of vast oligopolies," writes Hodding
Carter, whose own family paper in Mississippi was rather messily sold to a
chain with political positions far different from those of the family. "An
oligopoly in the field of news, no matter how professional the product, is a
mortal threat to press freedom in the long run and adequate press performance in the short run. . . . I am unimpressed by the assertion that bigger,

more 'professional' newspapers are an adequate substitute for real diversity."[17] As we shall see in Chapter 13, the sort of papers the Founding Fathers had in mind—the local and neighborhood sheets, not infrequently quite opinionated—are still arising and growing all the time, and newspapers devoted to occupations, also typically possessed of a point of view, are a commercial and political feature of our time. A small city with eight radio stations, four television stations, five suburban weeklies and two neighborhood broadsheets is not necessarily without diversity of opinion even though the metropolitan paper is a monopoly owned by a distant chain. Still, there's no doubt Carter has a point. So does the Philadelphia *Inquirer*'s Sam McKeel, who argues that "you have many more good papers than you used to have. But the chance that there will be more *great* papers may have disappeared."

His own paper is perhaps the strongest piece of evidence on the other side. As one of the most famous advertising campaigns of the postwar period had it, in Philadelphia nearly everybody read the *Bulletin,* and when the Knights acquired the *Inquirer* from the Annenberg family in 1969 it was neither a good paper nor a moneymaker. To run the news operation, Knight brought Gene Roberts from the New York *Times* and gave him an increased budget and his head. As late as 1977, when the *Inquirer* suffered a twenty-three-day strike that the *Bulletin* avoided, the odds looked long. People do not easily break newspaper-reading habits. The only known persuaders, Derek Jameson, editor of Rupert Murdoch's *News of the World,* said recently, are "war and bingo."[18]

Neither Roberts nor Knight-Ridder was interested in bingo, but Roberts was fascinated by the moral equivalents of war. His theory was that the number-two paper could make it in a city like Philadelphia if it became the indispensable source of full-scale coverage on really big stories. People would switch and stay. This was an unconventional approach, and required major new resources when, for example, the cooling system failed in the reactor at Three Mile Island. Knight-Ridder gave Roberts the resources (the *Inquirer* under its new management won Pulitzers for one thing or another six straight years), and eventually put the *Bulletin* under in January 1982. Most remarkably, for 1982 was not a year when the newspaper or any other business was full of loose money, this event became an occasion for a vast expansion of the budget for the *Inquirer*—the news staff rose by 30 percent, the news hole was increased, new bureaus were opened domestically and abroad—to grab and hold former readers of the *Bulletin.*

By 1985, the *Inquirer* was solidly profitable, but Knight-Ridder's Detroit *Free Press* was playing scorpion-in-the-bottle with the Detroit *News* (and not winning—Detroit is one of very few cities in the United States where the afternoon paper seems still to have a lifestyle advantage over the morning paper), and the home office came looking for more ("Philadelphia's doing very well and God bless you," said chief financial officer Robert

Singleton, "but we need you to do it again this year"). "They've got a lot of chips," said McKeel early that year, "and now they're calling them. If I were the owner of this newspaper I would be more willing than they are right now to build for its future, I wouldn't feel the need to compound the increase in our earnings, I would not trigger circulation price increases to improve our earnings, I'd accept flat earnings to trigger some other developments. But without Miami's involvement in the early seventies, we would never have got where we are now." Then McKeel needed Miami again, to fight the strike by mail-room operatives unwilling to take what was in fact a quite generous "no layoff but we assign you where we need you" clause associated with the automation of the insertion and distribution systems, and Miami was there. Presumably, the pressure from the Detroit paper will be relieved if the Justice Department approves the joint operating agreement worked out with Gannett when that chain acquired the Detroit *News* in early 1986. The Department shouldn't approve it—the law that allows supposedly competing newspapers to join their business operations applies only when one of the papers is "failing," and neither Gannett nor Knight-Ridder would permit its Detroit paper to fail. Moreover, it is now admitted that before purchasing the *News* Gannett reached at least tentative terms with Knight-Ridder on a J.O.A., which is a pretty obvious no-no. But this is the Reagan administration.

Unlike Gannett, Knight-Ridder is a union shop, dealing with almost a hundred locals representing 23,000 workers, of whom about 3,000 work in the newsrooms. Corporate headquarters runs very lean, with fewer than a hundred people all told occupying a fraction of the top floor in the Miami *Herald*'s green building where the Venetian Causeway goes over the lagoon from Miami to Miami Beach (newsprint can be delivered to the plant by barge, which saves a lot of money). Not much authority is centralized. Negotiations with newsprint suppliers are conducted for the group as a whole, to maximize leverage (with annual consumption of more than 700,000 tons of newsprint—at a cost of almost a quarter of a *billion* dollars, half again as much as the total editorial payroll—Knight-Ridder is that industry's largest customer), but then each paper orders separately from one of the suppliers. Different papers buy from different vendors of computer systems and terminals, make their own decisions about presses (Miami likes the new flexographic printing presses, most of the papers don't), mail-room equipment, etc. Profit targets are negotiated out between the local publishers or managers and Miami, capital expenditures of more than $2 million must be approved by the head office, and local leadership must be able to make a case that its budget will come out where Miami wants—but in general each paper can establish its own mix of economies, advertising rate increases or cover price changes.

Knight-Ridder papers can make their own arrangements to sell national ads, using an outside sales rep rather than K-R's own if they wish. When the

Wichita *Eagle & Beacon* decided to give national advertisers the same rate card they used for local advertisers as a way to stem the industry-wide erosion of nationally booked run-of-paper newspaper advertising, it did so on its own motion, with Miami taking an entirely noncommittal view. "The operating manager at each paper," said senior vice president William Ott, who was headquarters man on operations until early 1986, when he went to California to be publisher of the San Jose *Mercury-News,* "brings in a blueprint every year—circulation, advertising, costs, a very substantial document. We ask him to consider, are the ad rates high enough in this section, should we be going for a circulation price increase? Should we be serving the public better? There are things we usually give lip service to that we really have to take seriously sometimes because they affect our long-term security. Once we have a plan to work with, corporate backs away. We get monthly reports, all the stats, plus a narrative as to why, we're interested in significant deviations from budget."

"Each property," Singleton says, "is a stand-alone operating unit. They gather and disburse their own money." One of the few tasks headquarters does assume is the calculation and payment of income taxes. Though each paper has its own bookkeeping system and its own computer systems, Knight-Ridder sends auditors at regular intervals to keep the books comparable. Ernst & Whinney does the corporate books, and on its own motion may go off to any of the individual papers and put them through a pretty thorough examination; but the results, of course, go only to Knight-Ridder headquarters. Numbers are taken very seriously in Miami. "We had down years in '74 and '75," says Jim Batten, K-R's president, another Southerner, handsome, prematurely gray, pulled in to corporate administration from a career that included time as a reporter in the Washington bureau and in Detroit and as editor in Charlotte. "We were beat up for them by the stock analysts and by the market. We have to be sure here that our earnings are growing in a consistent and relatively predictable way." It was extremely difficult for Miami to accept McKeel's decision to tough out the strike in Philadelphia in fall 1985 rather than lose the productivity gains planned for the giant new Swiss-made Ferag inserting machines in the mail rooms, because the strike meant that for the first time in a decade Knight-Ridder would have to show a fiscal quarter with a decline in profits.

Knight-Ridder supports a twenty-six-man Washington bureau, nine of whom work for the chain and seventeen for the individual papers. The seventeen are chosen jointly by the local editors and bureau chief Bob Boyd, who has been in Washington for Knight since 1960 and became chief in 1967. Most of the papers credit all Washington stories as coming from their own bureau; the Charlotte *Observer,* with great purity, credits stories from its own reporter to itself, stories from the others to the Knight-Ridder bureau. The Washington jobs are plum assignments within the company, and the bureau recruits exclusively from the staffs of the papers.

Allocating the personnel of the Washington bureau takes diplomacy, because everyone has a first loyalty to his own paper. "But it's rare," Boyd says, "that anyone gets an assignment we think is dumb." Wichita wants heavy Agriculture Department coverage; Gary, Indiana, wants anything on steel, plus Richard Hatcher and Jesse Jackson and national black politics in general. For each paper, there is the mayor coming to Washington to fight for a grant, or the spelling-bee contestant, or some high school beauty queen seeing the President. Some of the correspondents shared among the smaller papers can be torn by varied obligations: "The interests of our papers," Boyd says, "as I am constantly and sometimes painfully reminded, are very different. Tallahassee, Bradenton and Boca Raton share a reporter. Tallahassee has one of the youngest average ages in the country, twenty-six; Bradenton, one of the oldest, fifty-six; and Boca Raton is all rich retirees and high tech. Detroit's interests and Wichita's and Miami's are all different, and we have to serve everybody." In fact, the bureau serves more than just the Knight-Ridder papers, because much of its output feeds onto the KNT wire, which is in fact physically housed (i.e., the computers are situated) in Washington. When the bureau has a real exclusive, the preliminary message to alert recipients goes out only on an internal wire to the Knight-Ridder papers, but the text itself moves to all subscribers at the same time. If the bureau is busting its buttons with pride, which happens perhaps half a dozen times a year, the story may be copyrighted to make sure the subscribers to the wire give credit.

One of the two reporters in Washington on the Miami *Herald* payroll has a Latin American beat, covering the State Department's Bureau of American Republic Affairs and the Organization of American States. Other Latin matters are covered in the British manner, by a staff resident in Miami who go out for the story. As recently as the mid-1970s, that was all the foreign coverage Knight-Ridder attempted, but now there are eighteen overseas bureaus, each reporting to one of four papers (Miami, Philadelphia, Detroit and San Jose) and carried on its budget. These are one-man, take-care-of-yourself bureaus, but they can do distinguished work: Lewis M. Simons, the one-man Tokyo bureau for the San Jose *Mercury-News* (and thus for the chain), put together a team that nailed the U.S. investments of Ferdinand Marcos and his buddies well before the Aquino election/revolution unseated him, uncovering so much previously unknown stuff that Abe Rosenthal's New York *Times,* which hates the very idea of crediting another news organization, quoted the articles. (This was San Jose's Pulitzer in the list of Knight-Ridder's seven.) Everything from the bureaus abroad feeds onto the KNT wire, and thus through Washington, but there is no overall director of foreign news: the foreign editor of the *Inquirer* coordinates, more or less. "It's a question whether this is the best way to organize a foreign news service," says Knight-Ridder chairman Alvah Chapman, a courteous Georgian, son of a publisher, president of the American Newspaper Publishers Association in 1986–87. "There's at least one other opinion —I'm not sure it's a good idea—but since foreign was nonexistent when I took over as CEO in 1976, I'm not in a position to complain."

The most unusual person in the Knight-Ridder system is an academic psychologist, Dr. Byron Harless, who until his alleged retirement in 1984 was a member of the executive committee and the corporate board of directors as well as the company's specialist in management selection and training. Before World War II, Harless had been a professor at the University of Florida, running a clinical department. "It was," he recalls, "pretty dull, and after four years in service I decided I didn't want to go back to that. I thought Tampa was a city with a good potential for a consulting practice, and I set up there in January of 19 and 46. We had a one-stop service station —industrial, research and clinical psychology. Then I became associated with a psychiatrist and we started a hospital in Tarpon Springs. Byron Harless Associates; the place still exists. In 1950, Nelson Poynter of the St. Petersburg *Times* put me in the newspaper business. He'd heard about some things we were doing in executive selection and thought we could do them for him. I spent two years with him, just learning the newspaper business, seven days a week—I got fascinated. One of the people I found for Poynter was Alvah Chapman, who'd been in Columbus, Georgia."

Harless had continued his consulting practice while working with Poynter, but when Chapman went to Miami he lured Harless to join him on an exclusive basis. "The most significant thing I've done for this company," Harless says, "is the personnel management audit. We identify people in this organization who are performing well, and we determine their training needs. From that we decide what programs we offer in the Knight-Ridder Institute of Training, which now gives forty courses, each a week long, here in Miami, you can get college credit for them. [Formal classes are in a windowless conference room on the K-R headquarters floor in Miami, but a lot of work is done via group visits to different aspects of the *Herald* operation.] And I've worked out ways to identify individuals not in one of these programs who are capable of moving on a fast track. I'm a strong believer that the people who know the problems and the solutions are the people who work in a company, not the outsiders."

Harless in St. Petersburg was one of the first to develop what are now called Quality Circles, and he brought that philosophy to the Knight-Ridder papers, which have had labor troubles. "In 1979," he recalls, "we completed a fifty-million-dollar production plant in Detroit, among the very best in the country. Now, Detroit's a labor union market, and newspapers are a labor-intensive business, and we'd had our share of problems with unions in Detroit. When we put up the plant we found we had not done an adequate job of preparing employees to move to the new location, the quality of the building, the aesthetics of the building. . . . In 1979 the economy was in bad shape, Detroit was in worse shape, the three-year contract was up. The new presses didn't operate properly, we had problems getting the paper out." In other words, the workers sabotaged the new machinery.

"Don Becker was then the president of the *Free Press* [this was one of the Knight papers that didn't have a "publisher"], and asked Chapman for someone from Miami to help. I was there almost nine months, using techniques to focus trust on management, get people to identify the problems themselves, make suggestions about what to do about them. Consistency is the key. . . . Participants in Quality Circles get trained for them, learn statistical techniques. When you get started"—Harless paused, then leaned forward with a big old man's grin—"you've got all these people raised in typical union-management situations, where you don't talk to management. Union said, we don't believe in our people meeting with management one-on-one. But one pressman's union man said, 'Hell, we don't have anything to lose. Put me first on the list.' I came into the meetings, introduced myself as a vice president and executive committee member, and listened. First it's 'We need more shower stalls,' and 'It's too far to walk to the cafeteria,' and 'When we break at eleven, we should have a different kind of meal,' but then it matures to 'One of the ways we can reduce accidents is this and this and this,' and then they do the study themselves, how much is it going to cost, and they gain confidence in their skills. They come back and they say, 'We need another press line,' the company provides the resources; they want an expert, the company provides him. It takes constant monitoring by the CEO of the company responsible, the *Free Press* was the first newspaper ever to do this throughout, it's not a panacea by a long shot, but it can be a good method."

In other words, there is a lot more to this business than Hildy Johnson digging through the wastebaskets in the jury room. But it still starts with Hildy Johnson.

4

Chain ownership by corporations with directors who also serve other corporations, reliance on syndicated services, apparent monopoly status in a city—all these contribute to concern that the public will receive a warped version of the news (however defined). The worries are, I think, misplaced. The larger publishing operations have been more or less neutered, for reasons well put by Patrick Brogan of the New York *Daily News*, who wrote the sad, short history of the National News Council for the Twentieth Century Fund, which had sponsored it. Papers like the Washington *Post* and the Los Angeles *Times*, he wrote, "have become practically invulnerable. . . . There is no commercial power in the country to menace their stranglehold over local advertising. As monopolies, they cannot be repudiated by their readers and advertisers, any more than utility companies can be repudiated by incensed customers."[19] Under these circumstances, newspapers *do* become like public utilities, subject to requirements that they present a variety of viewpoints, print letters from the aggrieved, sell space to those with ideas to peddle, etc. "When there is only one game left in town," writes John Hulteng of Stanford, "it must be an honest one."[20]

The Florida Supreme Court in 1972 upheld a state law (fifty years old, but never before invoked, presumably because it had not been needed) that required the Miami *Herald* to print a letter of reply from a union official running for the state legislature who had been attacked in a *Herald* editorial. The *Herald* appealed to the U.S. Supreme Court, which unanimously held the law unconstitutional.[21] But the argument is a much closer call than the newspapers like to believe, especially before a Court which in the *Red Lion* case gave aggrieved victims a *constitutional* right of reply on the broadcast facilities from which someone had maligned them, even though there are more than five times as many broadcasting stations as there are daily newspapers.[22] No doubt the Court was wrong in *Red Lion*—confronted with a hard case, it made bad law—but that doesn't matter when it's the Supreme Court. Interestingly, Gallup's survey of public attitudes toward the press in autumn 1985, on commission from the Times-Mirror Corporation, found general agreement with the Court's position: 61 percent of those questioned thought "freedom of the press" meant that "the public has a right to hear all points of view," and only 21 percent thought it meant that "the press can cover and report what it chooses."[23]

Ithiel de Sola Pool pointed out that the Court was prepared to continue the newspapers' "full autonomy of editorial decision" at least in part because the papers, "as they moved into the status of monopolies, had the wisdom to diffuse hostility by acting in many respects like a common carrier. . . . Unlike their nineteenth century ancestors, they see themselves as providing a forum for the whole community. They not only run columnists of opposite tendency and open their local news pages willingly to community groups, but also encourage letters to the editor. Most important of all, they accept advertising for pay from anyone. Only rarely does a newspaper refuse an ad on grounds of disagreement. If newspapers were as opinionated as they used to be in the days when they were competitive, public opinion would have long since acted against their unregulated monopoly."[24]

Today, certainly, the Miami *Herald* would think long and hard before denying its letter columns to a criticized candidate. "This institution is so strong and influential," says Richard Capen, the handsome, casual, gracious publisher of the *Herald,* who came to Miami from the Copley chain in San Diego about seven years after this lawsuit, "and the political process here is so weak, that we are the only institution that cuts across to all communities. That implies certain responsibilities." Capen says his paper is the only general-circulation daily in the country with two blacks on its editorial board. That editorial board, incidentally, voted to endorse Walter Mondale. Capen

overruled it, and the paper somewhat tepidly called for the reelection of
Ronald Reagan. But the editorial board was given a column in which to
express its dissent. Michael J. Robinson of George Washington University
points out that there was only one major change in public attitude toward
the papers revealed by the 1985 Gallup study (as compared with other
studies going back to the early 1930s): "During the last five decades the
number of Americans who believe editorial endorsements should not be
permitted has jumped from 34 to 48 per cent—a remarkable finding
whether one looks at the responses from 1938 or 1985."[25]

In other words, Liebling's case against the newspaper as a *maison de
passe* has been turned on its head. He thought that newspapers, especially as
they were liberated from the pressures of competition, had to be especially
careful to assure the bona fides of those to whom they opened either ad
pages or news pages. But it turns out that monopoly and near-monopoly
papers are virtually required to open their pages to columnists, advertisers
and letter writers attempting nonlibelous, arguably rational communication.
(Newspapers remain responsible for libel in letters and ads—the case of
New York Times v. *Sullivan,* which established the requirement that public
figures prove "conscious malice," grew out of an advertisement placed in
the paper by the National Association for the Advancement of Colored
People.)

In October 1985, a company that produces job fairs sued the Los Angeles *Times* for refusing to distribute a preprinted insert advertising its next
"Career Expo," charging a violation of the antitrust laws by a newspaper
that carries almost three-quarters of all the employment classified advertising in Los Angeles. The odds seem to be with the paper, which after rejecting the preprinted insert did carry the company's material as a display ad
on its own pages, but if the *Times* had simply refused the insert without
offering an alternative there would have been a real possibility of a Great
Case. Because the Supreme Court always has the option of shifting the First
Amendment right from the publisher to the reader—one can easily imagine
an opinion that takes off from *Red Lion,* cites Liebling's sarcastic dictum that
"freedom of the press belongs to the man who owns one," and imposes
access obligations on newspapers—there is a real danger to print journalism
in the broadcasters' contention that they should have all the rights the papers have. Accepting that argument, the Court could react by restricting the
press rather than by entitling the broadcasters. A small step was taken in that
direction at the end of the 1986 term, when the Court in *Posadas de Puerto
Rico Associates* v. *Tourism Company of Puerto Rico,* approved a Puerto Rican law
prohibiting the advertising of gambling casinos in any medium. The New
York *Times* was editorially shocked at this decision, though it had not been
upset when the Court upheld the law that banned cigarette commercials
from broadcasting.

Beyond the cultural and legal restraints on aggressive unfairness by "monopoly" newspapers and chains, there is a strong institutional structure that limits the willfulness of those who decide which national and international stories merit their readers' attention. (Local is another question.) Competition among news wires, syndicated services, broadcast news divisions and individual papers with their own bureaus assures that even stories both sources and management dislike will pour into the office from Washington (especially) and from the major world capitals. A large "public" inside the newspaper sees this material as it arrives, and if there's anything interesting the whole newsroom knows almost at once.

The first cut at the day's "news budget"—the summary sheet of stories various members of the staff are working on plus the advance menu from the wires—is made at a fairly low level and is designed to be inclusive, as an agenda for the committee meetings that will first forecast tomorrow's front page (between noon and two-thirty or so at most morning papers) and then argue about what should be on it (sometime between four-thirty and six-thirty, depending on press schedules). The first of these meetings usually involves a large fraction of the people who assign reporters or editors to stories, and unless they run into a consensus against their claims, which for the usual reasons deep in the laws of human behavior in committees is pretty unlikely, they will do in their own fiefs what they came to the meeting planning to do. The second is smaller, but the people at it represent their juniors and will have to explain any disappointments to them. The proceedings are essentially public to members of the organization. At the Washington *Post*, decisions are made in the open at a meeting with more than twenty people in it, and can be discussed and hooted at by the aggrieved; at the New York *Times* under Rosenthal, a large meeting discussed and decisions were then taken at a small meeting of four or five people (and the fifth, photo editor Carolyn Lee, spoke when spoken to).

I have before me the fourteen legal-size sheets prepared for the early meeting at the Washington *Post* on March 14, 1984, and graciously given me so I could make sense of what I was hearing. There were twenty-seven people at the meeting, summoned by the sweet yet penetrating sound of a tinkling triangle to a long, narrow conference room along the row of editors' offices facing into the posh Madison Hotel across Fifteenth Street. The day sheet for the sports page has twenty-six items, each with the reporter's name and a three- to eight-word description ("COLTS: Checking news of possible move. ATTNER"), with a note that the piece has already been written or that it's a "day story," will be coming in later. The "Style" section is much the same, but enigmatic for those of us not in the know ("MENS-WEAR: Hemlines are dropping for men. N. HYDE"). The "financial budget" (i.e., business stories, not the *Post*'s strength) is half from the wires, and the term of art for what is being written is not "day story" but "dev" for "developing."

"National" and "Metro," however, are mostly in full paragraphs, sometimes with opinion ("CIVILIANS: New weapons, other equipment so complicated Pentagon can't do maintenance on its own. So contractors have 6000 civilian 'tech reps' on ships and at other installations around the world, keeping their products running. Problem is, what do these people do when shooting starts? HIATT." This one got checked for the front page). "Foreign" for some reason has the dignity of double spacing. There are twenty-eight possible items on the foreign budget, just from the places where the *Post* has staff or stringers. Relatively little of this is today's hard news, because the wire services can't provide internationally the sort of agenda they offer for local and national events (Eurovision does it for the television networks, but all they need is film, for which they can do their own voice-over). Instead, it tends to be prospective ("BALLYPOREEN: OS- NOS visits the south Tipperary village whose Gaelic name means 'town of the small potatoes' where Ronald Reagan will pay homage to his roots in June") or analytical ("CRONIES: 'Crony capitalism' in the Philippines, which has enriched many friends and relatives of the Marcos family, is under siege as never before; bankers and businessmen say the system bears much of the blame for the country's current economic crisis. BRANIGAN"). Two-plus years later, the selection of stories to be following looks very good.

In part, news selections are predictable because they are repetitive. Change may be the only constant, but not in the news business. The easy accessibility of foreign news has added a tad of unpredictability, but the added emphasis on why the stock market went up or down (especially in the imitators of *USA Today)* has made for still greater repetition. The daily conferences to choose the front page and guide the editors of the sections are fun to visit (executive editor Ben Bradlee himself, though he no longer chairs them, attends religiously at the Washington *Post* because "I'm a news junkie"), but the key decisions are of course the allocation of resources that get your people where the news is going to be happening.

Most readers with the slightest interest in these things have in effect been to these meetings. A little cleaned up in language and without the fairly pervasive unconscious cruelty that news gatherers share with doctors, lawyers, cops and undertakers, they have been accurately portrayed not only in movies but (for a wonder) on television, in the *Lou Grant* show, which was immensely and deservedly popular with newspaper people. Visually, the television show is a little misleading, for these are functionally middle-management people, and while they may work in shirt sleeves they are rarely without their ties.

These committees do not vote, and one individual, who may have any of a number of titles, makes the decisions, but apart from questions of self-interest—local, national and foreign (in the papers where there is a foreign editor), all want to be sure one of their staff gets a piece of the front page— the discussions usually generate a fair degree of consensus, and the makeup of the front page will almost always reflect that consensus. (Bradlee remembers an editor who was forever trying to scare him: "You're going to go into the history books, Benjy, like that editor who didn't play the atomic bomb on page one.") Inside the paper decisions may be a little more arbitrary, for they are made by individual editors, given 85 columns between the ads this day—that's total, local and national and foreign, everything but style and sports, business and editorial page—and deciding how to allocate them. On March 14, assistant managing editor Richard Crocker had to cut the rest of national affairs down to 15 columns because the New Hampshire primary was commanding 15 all by itself.

But the bias is always toward running as many items as possible. Eighty-five columns adds up to less than half a typewritten page per reporter at the *Post,* and reporters whose stories don't run are disaffected reporters. No editor likes that. Moreover, the stories that disappear will usually be items that are fascinating and important to their subjects if not to the outside world. Paul Steiger of *The Wall Street Journal* reports that on an average day in 1986 his paper discarded fifteen to twenty columns of "our bread and butter," the news about smaller companies and their appointments, earnings, product developments. Within the paper, the trope is very strongly toward printing the pieces that the professional judgment of a fairly large group of middle management believes to be "today's stories." Chain ownership does not change that, because the publisher or editor who runs a rebellious newsroom damages his chances of promotion within the chain. National advertising decisions reinforce it, because preprints are distributed through newspapers rather than through direct mail for reasons that will not be influenced in the least by the stories the paper does or does not carry. Having said all that, and praised Knight-Ridder, let it be noted that early in 1986 the Kiplinger syndicate distributed a not very unusual consumer service piece about watching your step with used-car salesmen, which annoyed automobile dealers. One paper, Knight-Ridder's Wichita *Eagle & Beacon,* responded to the threats of the local auto dealers by publicly apologizing for the piece as "inadequately researched," which may indeed have saved some advertising revenues—at a very high cost.

One story that would have been of great interest to newspaper readers was entirely buried in 1985: a finding by the Occupational Safety and Health Administration that the unrefined oils used in newspaper inks were carcinogenic, and that the barrels in which these inks were transported would have to carry a legend warning of the dangers. The labeling rule took effect November 1. *Editor & Publisher* had an occasional queasy reference to this matter in terms of the workmen's compensation or even asbestosis-type cases that might be brought by diseased pressmen or their widows, and noted possible p.r. concerns ("Many newspapers have chosen to pay higher prices rather than use inks requiring warnings as possible cancer causes"[26]) but not even John Oakes, former editor of the New York *Times* and the doughtiest of environmental warriors, who writes frequent op-ed pieces on how inadequately the public is protected from industrial hazards, felt that this matter deserved his attention. By the end of the year, many papers (but not the *Times*) had switched to offset presses that use more expensive water-based inks or to inks made from more refined oils, which have the additional advantage that they don't rub off as easily. Donald Graham, incoming publisher of the Washington *Post,* noted that the only real applause he ever received when he represented the paper in public came in response to his announcement that the *Post* was upgrading its inks and readers would no longer have to wash their hands (not to mention clean their clothing) every time they picked up the paper. (In summer 1986, however, Gannett backslid: the new "low-rub" inks had a tendency to dry on the rollers of the presses, and, after all, the hazards of the old inks were statistically minor.) The changeover was done very quietly, with nothing about it in the papers and no criticism of the papers by the broadcasters, in accordance with Michael Robinson's findings in 1983—that there is a pecking order in the news business, with the "establishment press" doling out the pecks, the broadcasting media and magazines receiving them.[27]

13

Nationally

The assumption that the *[Wall Street] Journal* is a "second buy"—every reader also reads something else—has proved liberating. At the *Journal,* news is not whatever happened yesterday, but whatever requires explanation. Investigation isn't the uncovering of scandal, but the reporting and untangling of complex stories. Anecdote and color are generously employed, not just as leavening devices, but to demystify institutions and issues. The analytical feature piece, deprecated as a Sunday "thumb-sucker" in so many other newsrooms, is prized at the *Journal.*

–Robert Kuttner, 1984[1]

Thanks for publishing what is likely the finest newspaper of the century, USA TODAY.

–"Mr. and Mrs. LaFermes, Virginia"
(the first item in the *Newsline*
feature on "Reader Reaction
to USA TODAY" in the throwaway distributed
in New York in 1983)

1

On St. Valentine's Day 1985, the three lead pieces on the front page of *The Wall Street Journal* were bylined John Valentine, Damon Buss and David Darling. This was noted by someone at *USA Today,* who called to inquire whether those were real reporters and real stories, or whether the *Journal* was running a hoax. Front-page editor Glyn Mapes assured the caller that they were real reporters and real stories, as indeed they were, and life went on.

Among all the world's newspapers, *The Wall Street Journal* is unique in its freedom to decide what merits attention on the front page. The fact that there's a great photo of something doesn't matter, because the *Journal* doesn't run photos, just pen-and-ink sketches (reproduced with deliberately visible ink dots) drawn from photos by a staff that has been as large as ten artists. Big news can be played anywhere in the paper, or just ignored if the editors are not amused: the *Journal* is a "second buy," and most people presumably take their straight news from elsewhere. Still, two of each day's six columns, linked under the invariable heading "What's News," offer a neat summary of what happened yesterday in business and the markets, and in national and international political, military and scientific life (even sports and entertainment events get an occasional sentence). These are, incidentally, the most heavily read things in the paper, in all surveys: the *Journal* may not be a second buy for everyone. One column goes to a subject keyed to the day of the week (an essay in economics on Mondays, and on the other days groups of news bits and sometimes gossip from the worlds of labor, taxes, smaller business and Washington). The column-four story, which runs under a boxed graph of data revealing the course of some economic phenomenon, is called an "A-head," for reasons related to the appearance of the headline in past layouts, and deals with some preferably humorous oddity, from walking fish to astrologers to the foofaraw of presidential travel; and columns one and six are almost absolutely ad-lib, "the left-hand column more featury," says Charles Stabler, whose job is to be the final reader of the front pages of the paper's two sections, "the right-hand column more weighty." As newspaper stories go, these are long—1,500 words is standard.

Once or twice a week a front-page piece deals with the same subject you find on the front pages of other newspapers that day. Between them, managing editor Norman Pearlstine and associate publisher Peter Kann, who won a Pulitzer Prize for the *Journal* for his reporting from the India-Pakistan war in 1972, run the paper day to day. Both are former foreign correspondents and bureau chiefs still in their mid-forties, sharing what Kann calls "hard-news attitudes." (Kann was the *Journal*'s correspondent in Vietnam, and he had a front-page feature in the paper on the morning after the day the Tet offensive began. The story was an A-head about the farmers who grew a special kind of watermelon eaten during the Tet holidays, and how Vietcong and government soldier alike expected to wake up to a feast of watermelon. It was very embarrassing.) "The fact that more front-page pieces now write off the news," Kann says, "reflects the coming of age of the newspaper. We do it when we feel we can go out front with something that's not precisely what's on the network news, where we can compete with our kind of reporting talent and expertise."

Twice in 1985, the *Journal* found itself stuck with hard news it would much rather not have seen, and both times the editors nailed their colors to the mast and sailed into the storm. Once it was the revelation that the chief of enforcement for the Securities and Exchange Commission was a wife beater ("I never thought when I took this job," Norm Pearlstine said with remembered misery, "that I'd lose a week of my life worrying about whether to print a court deposition that a prominent man beat his wife"). And once it was a horror story in the *Journal*'s own family, when R. Foster Winans, a reporter who worked on the "Heard on the Street" column that accompanies the stock tables, was caught tipping off buddies in brokerage houses to what the column would contain. This was an ugly story, involving homosexual lovers, and the *Journal* gave it voluminous, nervous, constant, dog-with-a-bone attention. But even the *Journal* didn't make room for a wicked little survey done by a division of the advertising agency J. Walter Thompson, which queried a hundred corporate executives and a hundred business writers and editors about the implications of the case and found that 70 percent of the executives (31 of 44 who responded) thought "reporters should be legally required to disclose to their readers their financial interests in the companies or securities about which they write," while less than 25 percent of the editors and reporters (4 of a measly 18 who replied) agreed.

The *Journal*'s independence of conventional judgment can also go the other way—some things get deliberately short shrift in the *Journal*. "When Andropov dies," Kann said, "somebody at the *Times* says, 'That's worth four pages—pull in everybody who knows anything about Russia.' We say, we don't have anything unique to contribute. On the *Journal*, the administrative agency beats will get you into the paper more often than the White House beat will."

Kann is probably most proud of the front-page stories in areas where most people would not expect the *Journal* to be fully competitive, like the shrewd (and anti-Reagan) analysis of why the American forces had to be withdrawn from Lebanon. Business stories, however, are more common, for obvious reasons. In March 1985, for example, deputy managing editor Paul Steiger looked at the coverage of the failure of Home State Savings & Loan in Ohio, the swindle at ESM Securities of Fort Lauderdale that had caused it, the damage to the dollar in European markets, the loss of money by municipalities like Beaumont, Texas, that had done repurchase agreements with ESM—and decided that nobody had got anywhere near the bottom of it. (Steiger had started his career with the *Journal* in the 1960s, gone on to be business editor of the Los Angeles *Times*, then returned: "I'd worked with him," Pearlstine says, "and I'd competed against him, and I decided I'd rather work with him.") He called front-page editor Mapes at home on Thursday night; Mapes agreed. Steiger put through messages to the *Journal*'s Cleveland, Miami, Washington and Houston bureaus, which mobilized a score of reporters (seven from Cleveland alone, where the entire bureau was assigned to the story). Mapes told Henry Meyer, the page-one editor/ writer best plugged into financial questions, not to come in at all on Friday but to be prepared for a long, long day on Sunday.

About 30,000 words came in from the field between Friday afternoon and Sunday afternoon; Meyer, "who can write," Steiger says, "as fast as I can type," digested them into "seventeen or eighteen takes" (i.e., double-spaced pages), twelve of which were ready for the early edition. "We did updates all day," says Mapes; "it was like a real newspaper." This was an important story, though its full significance could not be explored in a daily paper, because it demonstrated how bank regulatory and supervisory procedures have fallen short of current needs. Prior to the *Wall Street Journal* monster story, emphasis had been placed on the inadequacies of the Ohio state S&L insurance fund by comparison with the two federal deposit insurance funds, with a dollop of scandal-cum-human interest in the relations between the governor of Ohio and his chief political fund-raiser, Marvin Warner, who owned 96 percent of the failed S&L and had close personal and investment relations with the crooks at ESM. By the time the *Journal's* reporters and Meyer were through, it was clear to the knowledgeable reader that there were more serious problems in the failure of the Ohio supervisory authorities to police their wards, the absence of any regulatory control in the government securities market, the reluctance of the Federal Reserve Bank of Cleveland and its lady president (the first such) to take the slightest risk of losses to their institution however great the threat to the financial system, and the incomprehension at the Federal Reserve Board in Washington of the size of the avalanche that could be begun by the fall of such a pebble.

The *Wall Street Journal* is the last of the newspapers operating the old-fashioned way, with reporters expected to send in fairly rough-hewn logs, from which editors will make handsome structures. With ten full-time editors (plus Stabler as final reader) for three daily stories, page one especially resembles the paper where reporters called stories to the rewrite man a great deal more than it resembles, say, today's New York *Times,* where everybody carries some kind of personal computer and puts his or her piece onto the modem to print out in the newsroom. The strength of the editor at the *Journal,* however, is not the "rewrite man's" mastery of the techniques needed to meet the deadline but an ability to convey the importance of a story that is not usually the top of the news elsewhere and may not be regarded as news at all. "This started," says president Warren Phillips, "with Barney Kilgore [who ran the paper from 1941, when he became managing editor of a stock-market publication with less than 100,000 circulation, to 1966, when he retired as president of a company publishing a paper with more than a million circulation]. His innovation—people think of it today as second nature—was that news didn't have to be what happened yesterday. If a company or a society or a government's strategies are changing, *that's* news." Under such circumstances, front-page stories can be polished and inventoried. "Everybody accepts that today," Phillips adds, "but not then."

Until *USA Today* reached nationwide distribution in 1984, *The Wall Street Journal* was the only national paper of anything like general interest.

(A number of specialized businesses—fashion, with *Women's Wear Daily;* broadcasting, with *Radio & Television Daily,* etc.—had generated newspapers, but they were strictly for insiders.) But long before the newspaper became national with the publication of a San Francisco edition in the 1940s, the Dow Jones Co., founder and proprietor of *The Wall Street Journal,* had been in the national news business. The company had started distributing stock prices electrically in the 1870s, when Edison perfected the ticker tape, and had offered a "broad tape," carrying news summaries as well as statistics, as early as 1897. Emerging from a press conference or covering a story, the Dow Jones reporter put in his phone call to the editors who ran the broad tape before he called his desk at the *Journal.* In the 1930s, there were years when the revenues from the broad tape carried the newspaper.

Partly because of the importance of the ticker, Dow Jones in 1935 launched a research lab working mostly on the improvement of techniques for replicating copy at long distances, headed by a former ten-dollar-a-week male stenographer named Joseph Ackell, who had turned out to have a genius for electromechanical invention. In 1962, the *Journal* began facsimile printing in the southern part of California to bring the San Francisco edition to Los Angeles, using microwave transmissions. By 1975, it had become possible to feed what have since become seventeen printing plants through a single satellite transponder in synchronous orbit above the equator. Advertising may be different in different regions (though it must fit into the same dummy), and every so often the West Coast paper is remade to include stories occurring after the close of shop (essentially 7 P.M.) in New York, but basically *The Wall Street Journal* printed in seventeen plants around the country is set in "type" on the computer in New York, and the plants merely convert the radio signals to plates and print them.

Because front-page stories are stockpiled, their editors usually are not working on deadline, and can thus maintain a more civilized relationship with reporters than was true on the traditional newspaper. Steiger remembered a war at the Los Angeles *Times* when the computers first came. Among the demands of the reporters was that they have access on their screens to what the rim and the slot had done to their story (which, as a normal matter, they would be signing). In the old days, after all, those who cared enough could always go down to the composing room and grab the proofs from the Linotype operators before the page was locked up. Among the demands of the editors was the chance to put something through as they wanted, without argument or delay, to make sure the paper made its deadlines.

While sympathetic with the editors (one of the reasons to go to newsroom automation, from the news staff's point of view, was that you could use later deadlines), Steiger in his business news department, and most of the other department chiefs at the L.A. *Times,* finally decided that there were too many advantages in a last check by the man who did, after all, know what the story was about, and reporters were given access through the computer to what the editors had done with their pieces. ("Better," Steiger said, "you should not have a libel suit the next morning than you should have a relaxed evening.") At *The Wall Street Journal,* the rule has always been that where humanly possible the reporter must sign off on the editor's changes. "The reporters are responsible," Steiger says rather sternly, "for seeing to it that errors do not creep into the story." And there are technicalities which an editor simply may not understand. The Ohio S&L story, Steiger recalls, saw "ferocious wrestling over the definitions."

Mapes, a matter-of-fact, round-faced, round-shouldered editor who picks all but a handful of the front-page stories, was a *Journal* reporter (for two years in San Francisco), then a bureau chief, and came to New York to take his present job in 1975, when he was thirty-five years old. "He has genius instincts," Steiger says. It was Mapes, for example, who decided to devote both column one and column six to space stories the morning after the shuttle blew up, the first time the same subject had been featured on both sides of the *Journal*'s front page. Neither he nor the other editors (nor the bureau chiefs) are normally the initiators of the story. Front-page pieces are supposed to rise spontaneously from the three hundred or so reporters outside New York, and most of the time they do. The procedure is that the reporter sells the idea to his bureau chief, who authorizes a couple of days of work on it and passes on a one-page (300-word) suggestion paper. Mapes personally then says yes or no, "based on all sorts of criteria. We may find we already have the same story in work at another bureau—I can't keep these things absolutely straight, we're trying to computerize it. Or the *Times* has just done a big story on it, and unless it's really our story and we have to swallow our pride, that will kill it. Sometimes I'll say no because I know the reporter and I don't think he can handle it, especially when it's an A-head and I know the guy doesn't have a sense of humor. I have to dream up a good way of declining, otherwise it comes in and it doesn't get used and we have morale problems."

Usually there are about three hundred pieces in the WIP (work in progress) file, anywhere from twelve to fifty in the ready-to-go drawer. There is always a shortage of A-heads, and one of the most common and least appreciated messages from New York to the bureaus is the one calling for quick resupply of light and airy and charming stuff for the front page. Sometimes a reporter drops an approved idea himself, which gets him good marks with Mapes, but usually a piece comes in whether it's suitable or not because the reporter hates the idea of wasting two or three weeks of interviewing and digging in some agency's files. Mapes reads it and assigns it to one of three categories, Rewrite, Fiddle or Markup, this last a survivor from the days when everything arrived all-caps in teletype and could not be sent to the printer without someone taking the time to underline the caps, etc. The decision about what to put on tomorrow's front page is made by Mapes before the noon meeting of twenty or so of the editors in New York (held until 1986 in a kind of closet, now in an immensely spacious boardroom at the new Dow Jones headquarters in what is grandly called the World Financial Center on the Hudson River), but sometimes managing editor Pearlstine or one of his two deputies, national news editor Nancy Cardwell or foreign news editor Karen Elliott House, or (by open phone line to the meeting) Washington editor Al Hunt, will have an alternative. "I suppose the most important thing at the noon meeting," says Cardwell, a lean woman with straight dark hair, "is what *doesn't* get said, and by whom."

Cardwell started at the *Journal* as a proofreader, and turned out to have remarkable talents ("I would pull sentences out of stories because I thought they shouldn't be there, and it would turn out they were wrong"), which led her to a year at the Columbia Journalism School and back to the paper as a copy editor, then as a reporter. "I loved reporting," she says a little sadly, "and I hated writing." After two years in Washington, she returned to New York to be what was called night editor for what was still in those days a 24-page paper. "I was the person who had to read all the stories before press time, decide what was important, what still had to be revised. Bill Kramer was then national editor, a man of prodigious memory and great ability, and I had nothing to do because Bill had done it all before he went home at seven. We abolished the job." Cardwell and her four assistants work Sunday through Thursday. Given a template of where the ads fall (sometimes damned awkward at the *Journal,* where space may be left for a headline, three inches in one column and two in the next), they lay out virtually all the paper except for the front page, the split page and the two foreign pages behind it, and the back page, where the Washington bureau has preemptive rights for one of the two stories and may not supply it until just before deadline. All told, each issue of the *Journal,* now usually 40 to 64 pages, carries about a hundred stories, with the most significant hard-news pieces displayed on pages two and three. In recent years, if a story seems to her to be developing the right way, Cardwell has been encouraged to call Mapes and suggest he take it for page one. They talk, and sometimes he does. Managing editor Norman Pearlstine will usually know about it, but if they agree they inform him rather than ask him. Which is fine with him: "This paper works best," he says, "when things bubble up."

The rule is, whatever the department, that an editor is a reader. "Editors do not call sources on a story someone else has written," says Cardwell. "It's *not done.*" If an editor wants to see another point covered, or has doubts about a quote, he (at the *Journal* it is she almost as often as he) will call the reporter and probe: "Do you know this because Ralph said it, or because you found out?" Normally, if a story involves contributions from more than one bureau, Cardwell tries to assign the writing to someone in the bureau most involved: "Otherwise you have the *Time* magazine problem of an editor putting together a story he knows nothing about." One of the things that made the Ohio S&L story so exceptional was the fact that it was initially written not by a reporter but by an editor. The failure of organization to date has been the inability of the U.S. paper to tap reporting by its Asian and European editions, a failure compounded by the arrival of the *Financial Times* of London in a transatlantic edition. *The Wall Street Journal* is much more deeply staffed than the *Financial Times,* and does big features that require teamwork much more effectively, but its daily coverage of both European and Asian business is inferior. "What happens," says deputy managing editor Paul Steiger in deep frustration, "is that there's a terrific file flowing past us like a river. It's full of fish, but we're not getting the right ones."

Prosperity changed *The Wall Street Journal* greatly. "We've moved," says associate publisher Peter Kann, "from a feudal empire to a nation-state. There used to be a duke of Los Angeles and a baron of Chicago and a king of Detroit. There was a very small staff in New York, a managing editor and a few assistants. We had little wars on the periphery: did West Virginia belong to Chicago or to Pittsburgh? The bureaus are still important. They provide the corporate coverage, and they allow us to hire very junior reporters and bring them up as part of *The Wall Street Journal.* But I think mine will be the last generation of leaders of this paper where it was more or less expected that you'd have spent time in the Detroit bureau—tough sources to deal with, an ongoing story and a place where the paper wasn't liked. Very good training. Now the bureau system doesn't work well to cover an auto industry that's become global or a computer industry that's scattered all over the world. Part of the answer is that the New York reporters have been given a bigger beat. They travel nationally and internationally, and maybe pick up a bureau reporter to help them. And New York has assistant managing editors and senior editors who cover three or four bureaus. Pearlstine sends out memos, I want this or that or this." In 1985 a little of the bloom came off the rose: circulation dipped briefly below two million, advertising diminished, and Pearlstine, who had been allowed to expand his news staff from 400 to 525 in his first eighteen months as managing editor, was pulled back by about 25 job slots. In 1986, however, the paper appeared to be returning to its expansive course.

How well the *Journal* system will mesh with a modern front-end newsroom is an interesting question that the editors as of spring 1986 still had not been forced to face. The move from the land side to the water side of the World Trade Center was presumably going to be marked by the end of the typewriter and the arrival of the terminal on the desks of the reporters and editors, but it turned out that the Digital Equipment processing units (or the programs written for them) were not well suited to the job of putting out the *Journal.* Among the embarrassments of the *Journal* planners in the years before the move was the fact that upstairs had decided that the old pneumatic tube system for delivering hard copy from the teletypes to the editors would be kept, though in an age of computer screens nobody knew what would be sent through them. So when the computer screens stayed dark, a very cheerful staff went about their business in the new brown decor with carpeting and views still using their typewriters and flimsies and canisters for the pneumatic tubes, just as they had in the old cream-colored decor with linoleum and nothing to look at.

2

One of the problems of *The Wall Street Journal,* Peter Kann said a little smugly early in 1985, was the absence of serious competition: *"Time* has its *Newsweek,* the New York *Times* has its Washington *Post,* CBS News has ABC. What do we have—the *Journal of Commerce?"* His sidekick Norman Pearlstine, curly-headed where Kann is nearly bald, brown-eyed where Kann is blue-eyed, is not quite so sure: *"Forbes, Fortune, Business Week* are our competition," he says. "When *Time* does a cover on Boone Pickens, that's my competition. *USA Today* is in competition for the same demographics. And you have to watch papers like the San Jose *Mercury-News.* They're not that strong on business, but in covering the semiconductor industry they're terrific." Since then the *Financial Times* of London has begun printing in the United States. It's a flyspeck, with less than 2 percent of the circulation of the *Journal,* but it is worrisome. As deputy managing editor Steiger put it: "We've noticed that there are offices especially in New York where it's fashionable to tell people you saw something in the *FT."* Especially, of course, when it isn't in the *Journal.*

News is a business where people are intensely competitive: the practitioner gets not only his salary but his kicks from the story he breaks. One school of thought says these are necessary kicks: Linda Rawlings, a therapist who is a fringe benefit for employees of the Los Angeles *Times,* says, "Most of the reporters I've seen manifest some degree of depression. For a lot of them, reporting keeps them going. If a good story comes along . . . they know they'll be all right—at least until that story's over."[2] The Washington *Post* is not really a national newspaper, and the New York *Times* is (the *Times* sells almost 200,000 copies a day of an abbreviated, two-section national edition rather light on advertising), but they define themselves as competitors. Their rivalry is incessant and frequently amusing. In 1985, the *Post* ran a three-part story about Abe Rosenthal's last years as executive editor of the *Times,* which were to end May 2, 1987—a date everyone on the *Times* knew —pursuant to what has been proclaimed an inflexible retirement-at-sixty-five policy. (In the event, the plug was pulled in October 1986, and Max Frankel took over as executive editor on November 1.) A report reached Washington that Rosenthal had noted these pieces, which were not kind to him, and commented that Bradlee's retirement would be worth one paragraph in the *Times.* Bradlee sent him a note: "Abe, here's the paragraph: 'Benjamin C. Bradlee retired today as executive editor of the Washington *Post* after 30 years in the job. He is 70.' "³

In theory, every daily paper is now somehow challenged by one of the three national papers—*USA Today,* the New York *Times* or *The Wall Street Journal*—but in fact these challenges do not materialize. The *Journal* remains, as noted, a "second buy," though many people seem to use its "What's News" column as a reliable summary on busy days. The *Times* by delivering its New York front page at a time when its coverage of New York City news is on the rise presents a parochial image when it goes afield (I was in Washington one weekend in November 1985, staying with a friend, when the outlying stretches of Northwest were sampled by the *Times,* plastic-wrapped newspapers thrown into every garden walk; what you read through the plastic as the paper folded was some story about trouble in the Brooklyn borough president's office). *USA Today,* which the Gannett chain launched in 1983 as the paper the sociology doctors ordered for the television age, claimed more than 1.4 million daily sales in spring 1986, but most of those represent what is taken from street-corner boxes or placed on racks at hotels or air terminals for free distribution (early in 1986, in an obvious and distasteful attempt to bully the Audit Bureau of Circulation, which had refused to give full value for these giveaways to the readers —the airlines and hotels pay some fraction of the cover price in a bulk purchase—Gannett pulled fourteen of its papers out of the organization; when ABC didn't cave, they all returned). So far as I could find out, no big-city paper in the United States considers *USA Today* to be competition.

Gannett has advertised *USA Today* as a "second buy," and that's probably right, though there is a bewilderment factor here, for the new paper claims the same demographics as *The Wall Street Journal,* which would seem to make it a "third buy," and not many people take three papers. Gannett chairman Al Neuharth has explained its purposes quite simply: "We felt if we could produce something journalistically that would appeal to a big enough audience, and sell it, then we'd also make some money."⁴ The paper's style book says the readers are "upscale" and "well-informed," which means that "stories may contain less background on events, more emphasis on what's new." Everyone admires the quality of the color reproduction, the thoroughness of the sports coverage (with its column after column after column of statistics: *USA Today,* notes a *Columbia Journalism Review* article on the phenomenon, "was the first daily paper to fully realize that quite a few so-called sports junkies are actually *statistics* junkies"⁵) and the imagination that has gone into finding graphs by which trivial information can be presented as though it had some significance. Indeed, staffers report that finding the graphs that appear in the bottom corners of the front pages of the four sections, and writing the text for them, is the first and major task of each morning. This graphics orientation, a reflection of the rise of computer-generated graphics in network television news, derives from the public opinion surveys by which Gannett decides what people want in a newspaper. The bulk of the paper, very obviously, is a digest of wire service copy with input from Gannett's own news service and its mostly small-town newspapers.

USA Today is somewhat different from others in its structure. The key meeting to design tomorrow's paper, for example, occurs not in the late afternoon but at nine-thirty in the morning ("The editors sit around in a glass booth," says one of the grunts in the trenches—management declined to cooperate in the preparation of this book—"and talk about the world as they know it"). The late-afternoon deadline, preset for each page of the paper (but sports has a separate, very late deadline), is a broadcast deadline, because the satellite on which the information for the paper travels to the printing plants is booked for other purposes later in the evening. Like *The Wall Street Journal*, but for entirely different reasons, *USA Today* regards itself as free to choose what it wishes to feature on the front page. Incessant consumer research, specializing in repeated focus group sessions, tells management what people want to have on the front page, most frequently some piece of economics or business news that may affect them, or sports, or entertainment. At a time when dailies as a group have greatly increased their international news coverage, *USA Today* offers from abroad little more than its name would predict. The prejudice at Gannett is for upbeat stories where possible. Within these parameters, the editors decide in the morning what will be under the picture in the center (a 12-inch story), what will be beside it stage right (in what is called "the silly little hole," a 4-inch story) and what will be in column six, an 18-inch story. The layout of the paper is invariable.

The other key decisions usually taken in the morning meeting involve the contents of the box in the top right-hand corner of each of the four sections—the "top-off," the salable contents of the section: "part of your job evaluation is whether you've provided top-offs." The lower left corner is for a snapshot, the lower right is the "hot corner" and must have graphics. Finding the material for those boxes is the most carefully considered work of the day. The copy desk is responsible essentially for pages three, four and five, plus the page of local reports and a briefs column of ten to twelve items. The rest comes out of the sausage factory. The editorial staff of 325 spend most of their time in the office, because management does not seek to gather news unavailable elsewhere.

The product is much admired in the trade, and not only the detailed and lucidly organized sports section and the colorful weather map. The internal clutter of two-paragraph items apparently does not make readers itchy, though my own observation is that the weather page is what absorbs the most attention from people on the Eastern shuttle, where you can get it for nothing and about 5 percent of the passengers do pick it up (leaving

huge stacks to be pulped at the end of each day, all considered "paid circulation" by Gannett, because the airline in some form "pays" for them). Television newsmen especially (perhaps predictably, considering how much of
USA Today is designed to be the printed equivalent of a television news
show) are impressed with the consistency *and utility* of the paper, and several producers and anchormen said more or less off the record that they
read it every day to get ideas for things to be done on that night's show.
("News"—that which producers find useful in a paper put together the
morning of the day before the night on which they will broadcast it.) In
fairness, one should also note that Gannett chairman Neuharth chewed out
the staff because the anniversary issue on September 14, 1984, did not have
a single item of hard news or even almost-hard news above the fold.

The paper is printed mostly on Gannett's own presses around the country (though one of the largest orders is contracted out to the Chicago *Tribune),* and the quality of the printing (which means also the quality of the
paper on which the printing is done) is closely monitored, sometimes by
Neuharth himself. Over the course of its first four years, USA Today has lost
roughly $400 million, but the losses diminish every year, and Gannett's
attitudes are of course wholly optimistic. The claimed continuing circulation
increase comes in the face of steady increases in the price of the paper, from
25¢ in 1982 to 50¢ in 1985. Originally, break-even was scheduled for
1985; as of early 1986, the accounts were to move into the black at the end
of 1987. That Gannett may have larger plans was suggested by an experiment in 1985, when the local Gannett paper in Cocoa Beach, Florida (site
of Neuharth's first managerial job with the chain), changed its name to
Florida Today, limited itself to state and local news exclusively, and offered
delivery with a cut-rate subscription to USA Today. Ben Bagdikian, interestingly, had predicted this gimmick from the start: "One could foresee," he
wrote, "the possibility that it would become a wraparound for other papers
which would then abandon their present function of providing both national and local news. We might then see the local press in the United States
become, for the first time, a provincial press on the European model."[6]

In the event, this project boomeranged: the local paper lost almost a
fifth of its readership to the nearby Orlando *Sentinel,* a more solid paper than
either of the *Todays,* though influenced—as indeed *The Wall Street Journal* by
Norm Pearlstine's admission has been influenced (note the boxed graph on
the split page)—by the graphics and layout of USA Today. One hopes the
reason for the failure of this first effort at substituting this paper for more
normative national coverage was that suggested by Bagdikian in early 1983:
"Since most metropolitan papers, and a lot of smaller local ones, do a better
job with important national news than USA Today, that possibility does not
seem to be in the near future."

The real target of USA Today may turn out to be the newsmagazines.
Much of the polling that determines the content and approach of USA Today

has been done by Lou Harris, who sold his firm to Gannett some years ago, and at one of the meetings to introduce the scheme, he is known to have told Gannett executives that "the newsweeklies are up for the taking." Twenty years ago, certainly, anyone writing about news in America would have had to reserve considerable space for the newsmagazines, which were more serious and wider-ranging than any but a handful of the best American papers. Today, the papers present a higher horizon and a wider focus, while the newsmagazines are more mired in Washington and more dominated by the cult of celebrity. Occasionally, newsmagazine "enterprise" breaks a significant story—for example, the mining of the Nicaraguan harbors by the CIA, which was uncovered by *Newsweek*. Occasionally, the newsmagazines are significantly suckered, as *Newsweek* was by the fake Hitler diaries. They are still, as *Time* demonstrated with Mikhail Gorbachev, a prized way for important foreign personages to get a message to America. As the authority of his presidency vanished in the slime of the Iranian arms deals, Ronald Reagan chose *Time* as the medium for his claim that when the American people knew the whole story they would agree with him that he'd done right. Most commonly, however, the newsweeklies seek to fill in, usually in a rather opinionated way, the background of stories already presented by broadcast media and newspapers.

This was rather more convincing when the pieces were unsigned and the magazines spoke as it were *ex cathedra,* but the Wizard of Oz aspect of the newsmagazines was disturbing to their own people in the field (whose insights were totally at the mercy of the writers in New York), and its elimination has been a cause for their rejoicing. I had a friend who had worked for *Time* in London during World War II and once marched despairingly into Churchill's office suite to ask the Prime Minister's secretary to put a spittoon in the Old Man's office. He'd had, he said regretfully, a cable from New York asking how many spittoons in Churchill's office. That meant someone in New York thought he had seen such a thing. If he cabled back that there was none, the authority figure in New York would probably order the writer to say, "Two." So he wanted to cable back, "One," and he humbly begged Churchill's secretary to permit one to be installed for a week or so, in order that his magazine be accurate.

"You read the *Times* and the Washington *Post* and *The Wall Street Journal* and *The Economist* and *The New Republic,*" said a friend at *Time*. "Of course you don't find anything in *Time* that you haven't already read. Suppose you lived in Cincinnati and you had to work for a living." That's fair. The newsmagazines began as a sort of intelligent clip-and-rewrite service, and slowly, slowly, they are returning to that function, which is by no means without its values. How much more than that they can do, in an age with great quantities of broadcast news and much-improved newspapers, is hard to say.

At one time or another I have had access to the voluminous "files" from which the *Time* editors work, and the material tended to be a combination of personality gossip and coarse-grained background drawn directly from self-interested sources (there is a terrible weakness for "inside stuff"), with little analysis other than that volunteered by the sources. The intended recipients, after all, are editors locked in an aerie, expressing at best their own, and not infrequently their superiors', prejudices. Osborn Elliott, who went from being editor of *Newsweek* to being dean of the Columbia School of Journalism, argues that the interaction of reporter, editor and researcher yields a higher level of accuracy, and it may be so, despite the bad vibes from the Ariel Sharon libel suit (in which the magazine's own witnesses demonstrated that *Time* had, as Steve Brill of *American Lawyer* wrote, "simply made up" a story that a secret section of the Israeli government report on the massacres in the Palestinian refugee camps near Beirut had accused Sharon of plotting with the Phalangist forces to take revenge on the refugees for the murder of Phalangist leader Bashir Gemayel[7]). But after eighteen months of earnestly reading all three of the newsweeklies, I found it impossible to work up much interest in how or why they produced the sort of impressionistic quasi-interpretative essay they now feature.

14
Loyalties

I worked as a copy boy on a little paper in Beverly, Massachusetts, and I didn't have many of these highfalutin ideas there. And you're much more part of the community in a town like that. You walk down Main Street and go into every store and pick up the little notes on who was visiting with whom and who was sick and things like that. And in a quite literal sense the owner of the paper did the same thing, and he wouldn't any more put in anything bad about any friend or . . .

Q.: Is that okay?

It's just different.

—Ben Bradlee of the Washington *Post*,
in an interview with Michael Gartner,
1982[1]

We have one advantage over WCBS. They're stuck with a national affiliation. Every morning at six-forty CBS goes to a canned report from Washington, and if something happens in New York they're locked out. We are never locked out.

—John Waugaman, general manager, WINS,
"all news, all the time," New York, 1985

1

In fall 1984, the Louisville Orchestra suffered a destructive strike by its musicians, apparently over salary, more realistically over management's desire that the orchestra be, as the press presented the story, "restructured." Louisville is a port town on a great river (in the nineteenth century it had a busy customs post, because the boats could make it all the way up the Mississippi and the Ohio to the falls at Louisville before they had to unload and transship), essentially a blue-collar community with a leaven of German and Jewish cultured families. The greatest Jewish educational family in American history went through the public schools here, Simon and Abraham Flexner, who founded, respectively, the Rockefeller Institute (now

Rockefeller University) in New York and the Institute for Advanced Study in Princeton. I was intrigued a generation ago, visiting Louisville for my book *The Schools,* to learn that at Male High School, of which they were the most illustrious graduates, neither administration nor faculty (let alone the now largely black student body) had ever heard of the name Flexner. But Louisville—together with every journalism school in the country—does remember the name of Marse Henry Watterson, who in the nineteenth century made the *Courier-Journal* one of the nation's great newspapers.

The city has a varied cultural history, the last fifty years of it built mostly around the orchestra, which was founded in 1937 and achieved national prominence in the 1950s with a Rockefeller-financed program of commissioning and recording contemporary (mostly American) symphonic pieces. The presence of this ambitious orchestra eased the task of Moritz Bomhart in founding the Kentucky Opera, also in the 1950s. Both the opera and the Louisville Ballet leased the services of the symphony for their seasons, making it possible for the orchestra to recruit more professional players. But these were shoestring operations, and they could not afford to pay for a full symphony orchestra in a pit. Instead, they paid for the players they used, usually no more than half the seventy-man permanent ensemble.

The early 1980s was not a good time for Louisville, which lost its General Electric assembly plant, the largest such in the nation, but the arts world gained support from the growth of Humana, the most venturesome of the new for-profit health-care companies, which has its headquarters in this city. Henry Werronen, president of Humana, became chairman of the orchestra, and was appalled to find that its members were being paid very differently, depending on whether they were or were not engaged for the opera and ballet seasons. In 1981, he gave the musicians' union what it most dearly wanted in Louisville, which was thirty-odd weeks of work guaranteed for everyone. Nobody seems to have realized that this in effect made the orchestra a subsidizer of the opera and the ballet. With the stately majesty of an ocean liner holed on the high seas, the orchestra began sinking. By fall 1984, despite a fund-raising effort that had just crossed the million-dollar mark for the first time, only the poop deck was still above water. On that deck, shouting, stood manager Karen Dobbs, a former trumpet player in Pittsburgh who had been brought to Louisville by orchestra president Don Sorensen, a GE executive and putative labor-relations expert. As the 1981 contract neared expiration, the orchestra offered its players a two-year renewal with a raise considerably below what they had expected. When the union turned it down, management withdrew the offer and began muttering about "restructuring" the orchestra, returning it to a pay-per-service basis.

The result was a truly awful strike (someone once said that faculty politics are the worst kind because the stakes are so small, and musical labor disputes have similar characteristics). It is of the nature of such disputes that public sympathy goes to the musicians, especially in a situation where their average annual income from the symphony ran about $13,000, the business-man/chairman of the orchestra has just received a rather well-publicized $17 million profit on his stock options, and the manager says, well, after all, they have time during the season to take pupils, and in the weeks they don't work for us they can collect unemployment insurance. "We called it her Marie Antoinette statement," said *Courier-Journal* publisher Paul Janensch, a dark-haired, serious young man. "I asked for an editorial on the strike. When it ran, I had a call from Don Sorensen at GE which began with the words 'I am incensed,' and ran on for forty minutes."

This was also the year when Louisville had opened its glorious new Kentucky Center for the Arts, a three-theater complex with lavish public spaces and a $5 million endowment over and above the cost of building it. "While attending the Louisville Orchestra's recent first concert of the season," *Courier-Journal* culture critic William Mootz wrote soon after the strike started, "I looked about the Kentucky Center for the Arts and imagined myself a member of the orchestra. I looked at the highly publicized artworks that adorn this handsome facility and knew that, for a fraction of what they cost, the Louisville Orchestra's deficit could be eliminated and management could offer me a living wage.

"And my heart turned bitter."

"The media told our side," union steward Jack Griffin said contentedly. "Of course, part of the reason for that was that management wouldn't talk to them for the first month." Mootz, a serious-minded professional critic, large, wearing earnest horn-rimmed glasses, put it slightly differently: "Union people around here," he said, "are very well trained in how to meet the press. The people on the board are not. They think they can handle an arts labor situation as they would handle other labor situations." As the strike dragged on (it lasted for seventy-one days), pieces about musicians and their children struggling to make ends meet on $13,000 a year ran in both the *Courier-Journal* and the Louisville *Times* (morning and afternoon, both owned in those days by the Bingham family but with separate newsrooms). "In the community," said Janensch, "we were perceived as being pro-players." Eventually, the manager quit or was fired by a 10–8 vote of the board, president Sorensen resigned, the union took a five-year contract with modest wage increases in the first two and accelerating gains thereafter, to be paid, however, only if new fund drives in which the musicians would participate were successful in raising the money. Performances resumed, at the opera as well as the orchestra. Even under the new contract, incidentally, the wages in Louisville are the lowest paid to any of the forty-eight orchestras where the musicians' union is affiliated with the International Conference of Symphony and Opera Musicians.

The opera, which had major financial problems of its own in 1984–85, reopened with Benjamin Britten's *Albert Herring,* a chamber work requiring thirteen musicians in the pit. I was there, as it happens, wearing my other hat as a music critic, and it was a lovely performance. It did not occur to me (or to the locals in the audience) that in addition to the thirteen players in the pit, another fifty-five were being paid for that night's performance by the management of the orchestra under the terms of the labor contract. I learned about it the next day when I had a talk with Bill Mootz, whom I knew through *our* union (the Music Critics Association). He explained about the "restructuring" the orchestra had hoped (and failed) to get from the strike. Mootz was deeply concerned that in the aftermath of the strike and the settlement the performing arts institutions of the city, which were linked in the nation's most successful annual Arts Fund drive and had always got along more or less well, would be at each other's throats as the orchestra tried to force the others to bear some of the costs of the contract. "And I don't know," he added, "if they can keep it quiet."

He didn't, of course, mean "they"; he meant "we." He had written in one of his Sunday columns during the strike that "I am anything but a disinterested commentator. I grew up listening to the Louisville Orchestra . . ." As an observer and as an employee of a paper owned by the most public-spirited and culturally supportive family in Louisville, he was fundamentally on the side of the musical institutions trying to avoid what would be harmful publicity. There was no pressure on him in this matter, though publisher Janensch sat in on our talk (which was an interruption in a longer interview I had arranged with Janensch). There was nothing to gain, so far as either Mootz or Janensch could see, in rocking this particular boat.

Now Gannett owns the Louisville papers, the Bingham family having split apart volcanically in 1985, and what will happen to loyalties, no one knows. Part of the classic criticism of the chain newspapers is that they are edited by people with no stake in their community, who will work here for three years and get promoted there, like the vice presidents of multinational banks or rising foreign service officers. From the public's point of view— though Gannett as veteran and savage cost cutters are not likely to run the same quality papers that the Binghams offered Louisville—it's possible that the news of their city will be more revelatory. If the reporter is the essential outsider, as I have written *supra,* it is by no means clear that the editor should be an insider. Most of the great editors and publishers came from far away—Ochs and Pulitzer were in every way immigrants to New York (Ochs from Germany via Chattanooga, Pulitzer from Hungary via St. Louis), Beaverbrook and Thomson were Canadians in London, and visitors to editors' aeries in northern newspapers have long found their questions answered in the ripest of southern accents.

The resident owner/publisher/editor is far more susceptible to pressure from the resident businessman/booster/advertiser. One need not— perhaps one should not—be "part of a community" to perform the services the community needs. Among the more courageous pieces of investigation in recent years was the revelation by reporters Jeffrey Marx and Michael

York of the Lexington (Ky.) *Herald-Leader,* a Knight-Ridder newspaper, that alumni boosters of the University of Kentucky basketball team (who were named) had for years been making illegal payments to star players on that team (also named). Basketball is to Kentucky what Catholicism is to Vatican City. At the *Courier-Journal* (which handled this story with kid gloves in the dying months of the Bingham ownership), one of the known elements of controllable expense was the $30,000 a year for facilities permitting the downstate editions to be held on the nights of UK basketball games so that the final report would be in every edition of the paper.

The *Herald-Leader* series brought 369 canceled subscriptions, threats to the persons of various people associated with the paper, denunciations from the local television stations (the station manager of the ABC affiliate said the series demonstrated the *Herald-Leader*'s "self-serving sensationalism"[2]), and the cancellation of most advertising from the city's automobile dealers, acting in concert. (It also won a Pulitzer Prize.) Eventually, of course, the ads were restored and the circulations resumed, but in the meantime Knight-Ridder lost some tens, perhaps hundreds of thousands of dollars. Neither of the reporters was a Kentuckian (though one was an alumnus of the university), and one was a total outsider, a twenty-three-year-old New Yorker recently graduated from the Northwestern University journalism school. Michael York, the senior of the two, had been assigned to Knight-Ridder's Washington bureau and was recalled to wield his shovel for the nine months the story required; he left a pregnant wife in their new Washington apartment, but that's the news business. York and Marx protected themselves by taping all the interviews, some without the knowledge of the person being interviewed (Kentucky has a permissive telephone recording law). A local proprietor, with family and friends who would never speak to him again and with bank loans and local stockholders, might not have had the stomach for the story.

2

Nationally, the competition to the newspapers has been broadcast competition, and the problem has been that steadily increasing numbers of Americans who would once have read the papers are satisfied with the national and international news they get from television, with radio to supplement in times of crisis. Despite the polls, it is probably true that more Americans get more of their news from the papers than from broadcasting, but the trend lines are disheartening. Half a century ago, there were more newspapers sold than there were households; now the ratio is below two-thirds. Researcher Ruth Clark, who devised media studies for Lou Harris and Daniel Yankelovich before going out on her own in 1983, sees "generations who have not developed the regular newspaper habit. I don't see any sign that they will ever read papers as regularly as their elders do." She notes also that "regularity is tied to home delivery. You've got to worry about the fact that the newspaper is virtually the last home-delivered product."[3]

The solution to the problem has been to become more interpretive, softer, more open to features, more receptive to specialist material, usually syndicated. Despite the pressure from the researchers to tighten up, most papers also carry more long and detailed stories, simply because that is what broadcasters cannot offer. And, for what it's worth, the newspapers are *much* better written than they used to be. Better writing and longer, more explanatory pieces do not, unfortunately, sell a lot of papers. (Anywhere in the world, incidentally: encountered in Stockholm, Christine Jütterström, editor-in-chief of *Dagens Nyheter,* Sweden's largest paper, noted that when she took over in the early 1980s "there was reporter power on this paper. We ran long articles. Circulation went down, because people wanted news in the morning paper and felt they weren't getting it.") What does sell papers regularly—and advertising, too, as the shopping moves out of downtown and into malls—is breadth and depth of *very* local, even "neighborhood" coverage.

"People look for local news," said Paul Tash, the young city editor of the St. Petersburg *Times,* which does five separate regional editions seven times a week. "They think they get the national and international news on TV." James Batten, president of Knight-Ridder, discussed the development of the Miami *Herald's* eleven "Neighbors" sections with the example of a story "about the plans to tear down a gas station on Dixie Highway and put up a Wendy's. That was a bigger story for me than Bert Lance or the Panama Canal. It meant that those two honest garage mechanics who know my wife's name were going to have to relocate. One of the sins of the newsrooms in middle-sized and larger cities has been that they had no interest in golden weddings and Eagle Scouts and chicken dinners. Nobody went to journalism school to write about some freckle-faced fourteen-year-old who's been made an Eagle Scout—but that's what built the newspapers. We're going back to our roots."

Growing emphasis on small-scale local coverage for zoned sections of metropolitan papers has attracted little attention from commentators on the business, partly because they tend not to notice those sections of the paper, partly because academic wisdom has pointed the other way. Indeed, the academics have insisted that when the chains take over a paper they reduce its presentation of good hard local news. Ben Bagdikian says it's so, and has offered to sell *USA Today* on the corner of Fourteenth Street and F Street in Washington, where the National Press Club is located, if he's wrong. (The New York *Times* put Bagdikian's expression of confidence onto another piece of land, printing that he had agreed to sell Gannett's toy flagship on the corner of Fourteenth and M, identified as the heart of the city's red-light district. The *Times* acknowledged its error the following day with a retraction that added greatly to the delight of everyone who did not work for that paper and some people who did.) But Bagdikian's offer is not proof, and does not square easily with his own residence in the Bay Area, where Knight-Ridder's San Jose *Mercury-News* has been steadily increasing its market share both on the Peninsula and in the East Bay at the expense of the independently owned San Francisco *Chronicle* and the Oakland *Tribune*, simply because it's a more interesting and more complete newspaper with better coverage of the area.

The most disliked of all the chains, indeed, probably devotes a higher proportion of its resources to local hard news than any group of independently owned metropolitan papers. For all their bosomy vulgarity and political one-sidedness, their old-fashioned (unsuccessful) kingmaking in New York politics, their willingness to tout, say, a claim by the *Ukrainian Weekly*, an anti-Russian (not just anti-Communist) sheet, that "up to 15,000" people had died in the Chernobyl explosion, Rupert Murdoch's papers do their job in New York, San Antonio and Boston (and did it in Chicago, before the chain sold the *Sun-Times*). Tom Goldstein, who went from the New York *Times* to be press secretary for Mayor Edward Koch, reports that "to a degree unimagined by most New Yorkers, [Murdoch's] *Post* set the agenda for the other papers. It carried more exclusive stories about city government than the others, and it played them more prominently, particularly in the very late editions of one day or the very early editions of the next morning. This meant that in the morning, radio reporters, eager for a fresh story for their noon newscasts, would frequently question the mayor about the latest disclosure in the *Post*. The other reporters would listen. Often the mayor embellished upon his original remarks. And a day later the *Times* and the *News* would carry stories on what the *Post* had run earlier."[4]

Others have argued that the chain papers have displaced the locally owned papers, and the morning papers have beat up the afternoon papers, because the afternoon and local papers gave readers more local stories than they really wanted, and the chains by playing down these less important bits of news were closer to the public mood. Peter Benjaminson, in his book on the troubles of the afternoon newspapers, reports on the competition between the Philadelphia *Inquirer* and the *Bulletin*: "The *Bulletin* devoted a sizable portion of its resources to covering local school board meetings and neighborhood controversies, trying without much flair to compete against Philadelphia's forty-nine suburban papers and one hundred weekly papers in exactly those reporting situations those papers handled best. . . . The *Bulletin*'s style of coverage made a lot of sense when most Philadelphians were blue-collar workers who lived within the city limits. These readers wanted to know, in detail and with great accuracy, what was going on in each of their neighborhoods. But during the 1960s and 70s, many of Philadelphia's residents moved to its suburbs, where the area's suburban papers provided them with all the local coverage they needed."[5]

Benjaminson's point is well made and well taken, but the argument here will be to the contrary—as, indeed, would be the argument of today's *Inquirer,* which, having made itself indispensable with its big-story coverage, is now devoting much larger resources to the neighborhoods and the suburbs than the *Bulletin* ever commanded. "We have fourteen suburban dailies and seven Sunday papers in our metropolitan area," says *Inquirer* publisher Sam McKeel. "We publish a New Jersey edition, a city edition and a Pennsylvania edition, every day, and we publish 'Neighbors' sections twice a week in Pennsylvania and once in New Jersey. They're very expensive in newsprint and in people. But we price them competitively with the local papers, and we're reaching advertisers we did not have in the *Inquirer* before." The strike in the mail room at the *Inquirer* was over the loss of jobs from the substitution of the Swiss-made Ferag folding and inserting machines for hand labor in the assembly of these zoned newspapers. (One notes in passing, in a different area of concern, that the Swiss publish relatively thin papers and have no need for machinery that can fold one 126-page section inside another one—but they make it for the American market and no American manufacturer does.)

Television diminished the newspapers' share of national display advertising, and in the 1970s began to cut into department store and supermarket, auto dealer and furniture store advertising, just a little. But the real pressure on the papers, for circulation and advertising both, has come from the ground rather than from the skies. The Los Angeles *Times* utterly dominates the one other paper with a Los Angeles residence—but sells to only about 30 percent of the households in its metropolitan area, and the total paid circulation of the papers in the small cities and towns of the area is greater than that of the *Times.* "The temptation these days," Otis Chandler said in 1985, "is to put *all* your resources into diversity. We say we have two papers, the core paper and then these horrendous huge six Thursday and Sunday zones. In our total market coverage we have two hundred grids, and advertisers can buy any one of them. We're staffed in these bureaus. We used to worry all the time about the little guys. The *Daily News,* the San Diego *Union,* the Knight-Ridder papers; I like to think that now they worry about us."

In theory, the metropolitan paper can do a better job with news from within the communities than the suburban paper can, if management puts its mind to it, because the knee bone is connected to the thigh bone. In practice, however, local coverage by the metropolitan paper is expensive, in manpower and in production capacity, because the way the big paper holds off competition from start-up suburban and neighborhood papers is by getting there first with the news. Especially when something big breaks, moreover, there is no substitute for expertise on local stories, too. Tash of the St.

Petersburg *Times,* for example, remembers being able to cover the catastrophic freeze in the orange groves in 1985 because he'd sent a team of
four reporters to talk with the growers, the university, the packers about the
mini-freeze and the citrus canker scare the previous year. "We had a story
every day for four weeks." When the temperatures collapsed the afternoon
of Super Bowl Sunday, Tash had a staff ready to go. "Larry King," Tash
said, speaking of one of the team, "went out to the groves at five in the
morning, the coldest time, and was back by noon to write the obituary of
the citrus industry in the northern part of the state."

With its series on the disasters in the citrus industry, the St. Petersburg
Times in effect created a kind of neighborhood, a community of people with
strong shared interests and a need to know each other's news. No small part
of the future of the newspaper business is here. Among the interesting
demonstrations are the "Business Monday" sections pioneered by business
editor Larry Birger of the Miami *Herald* and now pushed rather vigorously
at all their papers by the Knight-Ridder operation. Birger, a busy, fast-
talking Miamian who worked for years as the Florida end of *Business Week*
before coming to the *Herald,* insisted on an entirely local business publication to keep the area's businessmen in touch with each other. "The general
public," Birger says, "is interested in local business more than national
business, and there's been no place where they can get local business news."
He makes virtually no use of syndicated material, and a staff of eighteen
reporters spends the week on the various South Florida beats gathering
enough stories to fill the news hole of a tabloid insert that averages 76 pages
and often runs over 100 pages. This is about the best advertising medium
that ever was—anyone selling to business in the Miami area *must* be in
"Business Monday." The key is staffing and relentless emphasis on the local.
Note by contrast *The Arizona Republic*'s "Econ Monday," six lousy pages in
the issue I picked up (April 15, 1985), nine of the twelve stories from an
array of national syndicates (this is a rich paper that takes everything: AP,
UPI, Universal Press, New York *Times,* Washington *Post,* Knight-Ridder).
And no ads whatever from the business vendors of Phoenix.

One of the most remarkable accomplishments in the 1970s was the
creation of a number of synthetic small communities by the New York
Times. The dimensions of the crisis at the paper were not generally understood (certainly not by most of the people who worked in the newsroom),
but the fact was that the paper's circulation had dropped by 80,000 between
1969 and 1973, and profitability was down to 1.7 percent of sales. One Wall
Street analyst says that "the *Times* almost went under."[6] The strategies that
were effective in cities like Miami and Philadelphia worked only fair in
New York, because the geographical communities—Westchester, New
Jersey, Long Island—were too big to offer chances for penetration deep
enough to hold the mass-market advertisers. New York City business was
national business; most commuters were not much interested in what the

city's shoe manufacturers were doing (though it's probably true that the paper's coverage of strictly local business stories does not have to be as sporadic and incomplete as it is).

But the richest and best-educated 20 percent of the New York area households made one hell of a market for advertisers, and in terms of *interests* this enormous mass is "made up of tiny constituencies," as Jim Greenfield (who manages the editorial budget) put it. "Somebody is interested in cooking and foreign news, and that's all. Chess. We've got to have a bridge columnist and a do-it-yourself guy, books and arts. People open the magazine—I mean the newspaper—looking for what interests *them.*"

Segmenting the paper according to the interests of the readers was an assertion very bold in the context of its history—for the *Times* has never carried comics or astrology columns or advice to the lovelorn and prints color only in its Sunday magazine. The result was a four-section daily paper: national/international/comment; then local; finally business, with a section-three insert on a different subject every day: sports, science, food (called "Living," but it's food), household furnishings and entertainment. These brought the paper advertising it had never had before (especially the supermarkets on Wednesdays: prior to the "Living" section—incredibly, in retrospect—the *Times* had never seriously sought such undignified ads). Some of the staff were bitter at what they considered the downgrading of their profession, the invasion of the world's greatest newspaper by the ethos of *Family Circle* (a magazine owned by New York Times, Inc.), and sometimes the paper's catering to the phenomenon that later got the vulgar name "yuppie" could be indeed distasteful. But as a statement of what the newspaper *did* in the later years of the twentieth century, it was correct as well as clever. And management, after all, could atone by taking the *Times* national in a two-section version that would carry all the news but only a few selected highlights from the service material. Meanwhile, *everything,* including the food and arts and business stuff, could be sold to the rest of the country by the Times Syndicate.

There are, of course, striking differences between what the *Times* deals with as "local" and what a truly local medium looks at. The assignment sheet for New York's all-news WINS for April 3, 1985, for example, shows five available reporters, who start work at various times from 5 A.M.: "Paul Parker . . . at the Fulton Fish Market, where he filed on their reaction to Albany legislation regarding striped bass . . . then headed to the Union Square station in Manhattan where a woman was pushed to death this morning when she was shoved in front of an oncoming LL train . . . will then head to 45 Wall Street, 12th Floor, where the Life Saving Benevolent Association of New York presents awards to 13 New York Police Officers for heroic rescues they have performed in the waters around New York . . . Jim Asencio heads to the Sheraton Inn La Guardia where labor talks continue between executives of four Queens bus companies and the Transport

Workers Union Local 100 . . . Stan Brooks will work on the New York State Budget story . . . Doug Edelson [covers] a 10am hearing [at the City Council] on the proposed 'Consultant Control Act' . . ." Could be anywhere, but it's not easy to do. "You can teach somebody to write clean copy," said twenty-six-year-old overweight news director Scott Herman, who started with WINS when he was nineteen years old and a student at Brooklyn College, "but you can't train a newsman—it has to be there. We don't allow conversation between the anchor and the reporter, not even follow-up questions. When we turn our air over to a reporter, we expect him to tell the story."

3

One of the great myths of American history has Abraham Lincoln greeting Harriet Beecher Stowe on her visit to the White House with the words: "So this is the little lady who made the great war!" In the same spirit, one could envision an overweight, blond, lightly mustached middle-aged Irishman in shirt sleeves gawking around Washington one summer's day and being spotted by the chairman of the Nuclear Regulatory Commission. "So this," that eminence might say to David J. Willmott, founder and editor and publisher of the weekly *Suffolk Life*, "is the big salesman who killed atomic energy in the United States."

Suffolk Life, which Willmott began on his parents' kitchen table in 1961, is a weekly paper published in twenty-three geographically distinct editions in the eastern two-thirds of Suffolk County, which in turn makes up the eastern two-thirds of the 120-mile Long Island that runs out into the ocean from New York City. It has been one of the fastest-growing counties in the United States, and in the 1980s it has had the most rapidly growing per capita personal income of any county in the country. The territory includes the great South Shore resorts, Southampton and the like, the second most productive agricultural region in this highly agricultural state, aircraft factories, a growing high-tech center radiating out from the long-established Brookhaven National Laboratory and quite a lot of blue-collar workers who commute scores of miles a day. As late as 1980, builders were selling new homes near the Long Island Expressway for less than $25,000, and in some years more than 10 percent of them were offered with Farmers Home Administration mortgages subsidized by the government down to 5 percent or even less.

The various editions of *Suffolk Life* run between 46 and 120 pages a week, with a concentration in the 52- to 60-page run. The typical circulation is 12,000, though some editions go to as many as 50,000 households and two are sent to only 6,500. In the summer months, when the papers are heaviest, there will be 1,700 pages printed for the twenty-three editions, with a typical breakdown of 1,200 of advertising and 500 of news. In 1986, all the papers were distributed gratis through the post office (to which Willmott paid almost $2.5 million for postage) to some 322,000 householders. Once a year, Willmott includes with the paper an appeal to readers to subscribe at an annual price of $4.99 and help pay for it, and he claims that 56 percent of the recipients of the paper do indeed pony up their five bucks for something they receive free and will continue to receive whether they subscribe or not. (It should be noted that at $4.99 a subscription, the receipts from a 56 percent return pay less than 40 percent of the postage bill alone.) Willmott employs a national agency to solicit national advertising for his papers, in addition to the twenty-seven display ad salesmen and twelve classified salesmen who bring in the local advertising, and the agency warned him not to use that 56 percent figure in sales presentations, because if he did nobody would believe any of his other numbers either.

Before beginning *Suffolk Life* at age twenty Willmott had never been particularly interested in journalism (he'd always wanted to be a veterinarian, "but my grades weren't good enough to get into those schools"). He made a lot of money driving overtime for United Parcel Service on a summer job serving the resorts not far from his home in Riverhead, the county seat, and was planning to go to California with some fraternity brothers from his community college when the family's next-door neighbor, a cop, suggested that he fill in some time in the fall selling advertising space on public trash cans for another neighbor, who had such a business and was looking for help. Willmott turned out to have a great talent for selling ads on trash cans, and he began looking around for ways in which that rather special talent could be exploited.

"There had been five penny-savers in this market," he says reminiscently, "and they'd all failed. I decided you could make the penny-saver format work if you also printed a lot of pictures of people who never get their pictures in the paper, plus controversial editorials." His mother and then his wife were invaluable to him in the early years, because they could spell and knew about grammar, which is still not Willmott's strong suit. He did have some interest in community affairs and in politics, and, as he wrote in his twenty-fifth-anniversary edition, he wanted to "publish a meaningful newspaper that would be the voice of the average citizen, who so persistently had been ignored. The average person who earns 90% of the income in our community, pays 90% of the taxes, but has only 10% of the voice in how his life is run and regulated. We developed a means of communication for this person and provided an outlet for their voice, their emotions and their feelings."

The first issue of *Central Suffolk Life,* then advertised as a monthly, went in early May 1961 to all residents of what Willmott liked to call "the golden horseshoe"—the higher-income section of Riverhead itself and the agricultural/resort towns closest to Riverhead on the North and South Forks of what becomes at Riverhead a bifurcated island. Universality has been the essence of the penny-saver format from the beginning, for the warranty given to the advertiser is that all the families in the paper's catchment area would at least have the opportunity to see the ad. In later years, when the inserted chain store or mail-order "preprint" became so important a form of newspaper advertising, universality would be the means of exalting the "controlled circulation" paper in its battle with papers for which readers paid. *Newsday*, Long Island's premier daily, reaches 46 percent of Suffolk County households (but only 13 percent of the households in the East End, where Willmott is strongest). If the marketing plan of a supermarket or a hardware chain or a warehouse store calls for reaching everyone, stuffing Willmott's paper is cheaper than supplementing *Newsday* with direct mailings, and very possibly more efficacious. "Our guys back there," said Otis Chandler, whose Los Angeles Times-Mirror Corp. owns *Newsday*, "have been jumping up and down about the way their basic market is suffering in Suffolk County because of competition. I can't feel too sorry for them. We've learned to compete; they can learn, too."

This advantage is by no means exclusive to Suffolk County. In mid-1986, Ralph Ingersoll II, proprietor of a chain of free-distribution suburban weeklies and semiweeklies in the St. Louis suburbs, announced that he considered his group "in an end-game struggle" with the St. Louis *Post-Dispatch*, "but we are winning." He thought the *Post-Dispatch* might later "prosper as a sort of boutique operation, one that will serve the understandable need for a local daily newspaper." Ingersoll claims a circulation of 900,000 households, and K-Mart buys 810,000 of them every week for a stuffer. Ad sales run $60 million a year. These free suburban papers, Ingersoll argued, citing a Simmons readership study, were better read than most of the daily papers people bought.[7] Ingersoll's grandfather, of course, was the progenitor of *PM*, a New York newspaper from the late New Deal and early World War II days that proclaimed but did not demonstrate the possibility of living entirely on newsstand sales and paid subscriptions, without any advertising at all. *Sic transit*.

Willmott's first editorial said that the paper would be "delivered free to over 9,625 families. . . . As time goes on, we will extend our coverage so that it embraces the entire North and South Forks." Willmott did almost everything himself, reporting the stories, taking the pictures, selling the ads, laying out the paper and driving the truck from his parents' kitchen to the post office. His mother typed most of the stories and helped paste up the pages to make them camera-ready. By February 1962 circulation was up 23,000, and Willmott was on his way. Sometime in 1987, he expects to add the two westernmost towns in the county and bring his circulation almost to the half-million mark.

Suffolk Life also owes a great deal to Willmott's love for electronic toys and his sense of distribution, which one likes to think was honed by his adolescent job as a driver for UPS. An IBM System 36 keeps the circulation list and the invoices, and an associated laser printer turns out 326,000 labels a week, plus the bills. The mainframe for the production unit is a 9766 Control Data. A Seaboard Energy Systems computer regulates heat and air conditioning through the enormous (110,000-square-foot) abandoned Great Eastern single-level department store Willmott bravely acquired for $1.5 million in 1985. An Executone telephone system can handle up to 1,600 phones, about sixteen times more than *Suffolk Life* now requires, but you've got to be prepared. The system, moreover, records all calls coming into and going out of the office, channeling long-distance calls into the least expensive service and enabling Willmott to police the use of his paper's telephones for personal matters.

The front-end units for the reporters and classified sales staff were made by Unitek, a Litton Industries subsidiary which Willmott had hoped would be the first to develop a truly viable computer pagination system but which then greatly disappointed him by going out of business instead. The ad pages are prepared on what Willmott says were the first Comp-U-Graphic units installed in New York State. Two News Key presses (black-and-white only: the influence of the New York *Times* reaches out to Suffolk) can turn out 64-page papers at a rate of 32,000 an hour. The presses are also used for about a million dollars' worth of job printing a year, "but I won't do it," Willmott says, "if it's a pain in the ass." What with changing plates, the press run takes not much less than thirty-six hours, from three in the afternoon on Monday till sometime in the early morning on Wednesday. But all the papers get to their recipients by Wednesday afternoon at the latest.

From 1969 to 1980, Willmott distributed the papers through his own organization. "The post office," he says, "was giving mailers a hard time, refusing to treat business mail as a business. We had papers not delivered, papers delivered days late, and it was too expensive. I decided to go into competition, started a business called Certified Audit and Control of Circulation, with an office in Jersey, and developed the best hand-delivery system in the country. Studies showed we had 97.8 percent regular receivership, 88.8 percent regular readership. But you can do it faster and better through the mails. I got a representative from the Postmaster General's office, the Northeast regional rep, and presented figures to him showing that if they did it our way, at the price we wanted to pay them, they'd have at least a $100,000 net profit a year. Last year, I think they made $625,000."

Willmott already had maps of his distribution area, with every house spotted. His labeling and packaging system was organized so that the papers came off the back of the truck in the order in which they would be delivered. "I showed them at the post office what their normal pattern of handling material would be, and how we could eliminate duplicate, triple, quadruple handling that they did. Now we are a substation of the post office.

They dedicate a fleet of trucks to us on Tuesday and Wednesday. The papers load from our dock directly onto their trucks, they've eliminated wasteful handling patterns, we've missed the Wednesday delivery we guarantee to our advertisers only once in the last six years."

Except for Willmott's editorials, some stories about county matters (nothing beyond the county is covered at all, saving only an occasional piece from the state capital in Albany), the twenty-three editions are quite different, one from the other, both in advertising and in the lesser news stories— but the front-page pieces are often the same. My "North Fork Edition" for June 18, 1986, for example, features two extended stories that jump to inside pages. The lead sets up a forthcoming public hearing by the county legislature on the relevance of the Russian experience at Chernobyl to the prospects for operating the Long Island Lighting Company's still unlicensed nuclear plant at Shoreham, on Long Island Sound about fifteen miles from Riverhead. On the left side of the tabloid, beneath a photo of six toothsome young ladies in white dresses with bouquets of roses signaling their status as finalists in the twenty-third annual Mattituck Lions' contest for Strawberry Queen, the story is about a push by the supervisors of five of the six eastern towns to persuade the state legislature to permit a special tax on real estate sales for more than $100,000 to fund a program of land purchases to save open space. In the bottom right-hand corner there is a picture of three vocational students from the town of Southold, one the Most Improved Student, Small Engines Course, one a third-place winner in Cosmetology in the New York State Vocational Olympics competition and one of an "alternate officer" in a vocational club "whose team placed first in New York competition and will compete for national honors in Phoenix, Arizona, this summer."

Willmott's years building his newspaper were years when Suffolk had plenty of issues on which to editorialize. The "board of supervisors" system of government, by which the executives of the county's ten towns formed the county legislature, fell before the Supreme Court legislative reapportionment decisions. The failure of the postwar developers to install sewage systems for their tract houses (often enough as densely sited as four to an acre) left the county with a need to spend literally billions of dollars to lay sewage pipe and build treatment plants, in a political culture that was rife with petty larceny waiting hopefully to become grand larceny. Storms created beach erosion and demands for the government to take care of the families who had built or bought their houses in places where houses should never have been. Ecologists worried about the great "pine barrens" beneath which lay the aquifer that provided the county's drinking water. A local legislator ran for governor. About all such matters and many others, Willmott had views, and printed them. He also endorsed candidates; speaking with clearly mixed emotions, county councilman Joseph Townsend, Jr., told a reporter for *Suffolk Life*'s anniversary edition that "the paper seems to have its finger on the pulse of the people, because usually when a candidate is endorsed, the candidate has become a winner in the elections." The severe editorialist of Max Beerbohm's *Seven Men* ended all his leaders with the words *"Quod deus vult . . ."* Willmott, less pretentious, ended all of his with the phrase "And why not?" The editorial column soon acquired the name "Willmotts and Why Nots?"

But whatever else Willmott wrote about, he kept returning to the nuclear plant at Shoreham. Before Willmott got to work, this must have looked to the students of these matters like the plant least likely to run into political problems. It was located in the town of Brookhaven, home of one of the nation's earliest and largest national atomic laboratories: the scientists lived there, had great influence locally, and were of course all but entirely committed to nuclear energy. It drew its water from and returned its waste to Long Island Sound, which meant its presence would present no threat to ground waters, and the sound is such a large sea (quite apart from being a branch of the Atlantic Ocean) that its effluent would scarcely affect the temperature of the water. Not many people lived in the immediate neighborhood—a small resort community at Rocky Point, farmers and the residents of what had been the declining town of Shoreham, where the biggest business had been the antenna farm maintained by RCA Communications, which used it as the U.S. end of its transatlantic shortwave facility. The satellite killed that.

"Like so many people who grew up with atomic energy," Willmott says earnestly, "I was fearful of it, awed of it. I heard in school about the atom bomb, but they told us there was nothing to fear from peaceful uses. Then they held hearings in Riverhead for the first plans to build the plant in Lloyd Harbor, and I covered them. I kept asking, 'Could it blow up?' And they kept saying, 'No.' Then I asked, 'What if a plane fell right on top of it,' and they said, 'Anything's possible.' I felt I'd been lied to.

"I'm a boater. I keep a boat in Hampton Bays. Back in 1976, there was a fellow named Mike who also kept his boat in the same marina, he was an engineer on nuclear projects. He'd floated from job to job, and he said the Shoreham plant would be his last. He loved it on Long Island. He was a happy-go-lucky guy. He bought a cottage near the water for himself and his wife and their six kids, to bring them up here. Then one day in 1977 he was glum, he told me he was putting the house up for sale. 'The way they're building that thing at Shoreham,' he said, 'it's a time bomb, and I don't want my kids living anywhere near it.' About that time Grumman [a Long Island aircraft manufacturer] and MIT announced a scheme for a new power plant to use the tides in the ocean, they said it would meet Long Island's energy needs to the year 2030. I went to find out about it, and they knocked down their own announcement. I became suspicious, I became an opponent.

"Then, about six years ago, my daughter was in elementary school and the class did a study on nuclear energy. She came to me for help, and I told her what I thought. She said, 'If it's so dangerous, Daddy, why aren't you doing something about it?' Since then, we've devoted about ten percent of our news hole to Shoreham." At about the time Willmott decided to take on the Shoreham crusade he persuaded Lou Grasso that he wanted to transform *Suffolk Life* into a "serious newspaper." A rumpled professional who had worked for Newhouse's now-defunct Long Island *Press* and had competed more or less disgustedly with Willmott at a gaggle of much smaller paid-circulation weeklies around the county, Grasso supervised the coverage of the Shoreham controversy. "We had a young lad named Peter Scully on the staff," Grasso recalls, "and we sent him to a seminar in Boston to learn all about the Nuclear Regulatory Commission, and he made sure we got our hands on everything we could get about nuclear power, the NRC and regulation. When Peter left to become involved in the town of Brookhaven, we had another young reporter, Dan Aug; and when he was promoted to more general assignments we hired a young man named Jeff Sievers. I play the story big. Readers sometimes complain we do too many Shoreham stories, but there's something happening every day. You'll get a week when *Newsday* does six stories; we're a weekly, so we do six at once."

While Willmott's editorials grew increasingly strident (among Willmott's favorite conceits is that the radius of danger from a Shoreham "explosion" should really be seen as ninety miles, which brings in both Boston and New York, "with a loss of life in the millions and a loss of property in the trillions") the news stories were sober. "The credo in my newsroom" Grasso says, "is that every story has to be fair, has to be balanced, has to be accurate." (Headlines are not always held to that rule: "Chernobyl vs. Shoreham" just over the picture of the six pretty candidates for Mattituck's Strawberry Queen would seem to prejudge the contest.) Fairness, of course, becomes a bit of a problem when the people you are writing about won't talk to you. "Lilco [Long Island Lighting Company] decided that because we were editorializing we were hostile, and they never gave us anything but a No Comment to any question we asked. The NRC wasn't much better. We got wind of the fact early this year that there had been a year-end report inside NRC on Shoreham, but when we called and asked to see it they said it wasn't ready. Two days later the whole thing was in *Newsday*." Lilco had been one of *Suffolk Life*'s largest advertisers, and of course canceled out.

4

What got George Seldes started in his great career of exposing the manipulation of news stories (mostly in his magazine *In Fact*, which was for twenty years *the* underground paper of the news business) was the copy desk's excision from his first story, as a cub on a Pittsburgh paper, of the name of the beer company that owned the truck that had been in an accident. That could still happen, and a weary newspaper proprietor could still object that unless there's a pattern of reckless driving by this company's trucks it's not very important, except to plaintiff's counsel, who owned the truck that hit the lady (and a furious reporter could reply that unless you print the names nobody will know whether there is such a pattern).

"I've always believed in being courageous," says Lowell Blankfort, speaking of the fourteen weeklies and semiweeklies he owns with his partner Rowland Rebele (a Harvard MBA whose newspaper experience was on the college paper at Stanford before he and Blankfort teamed up in 1961), "but even though it's my money and my partner's money, I can't get my local publishers feisty enough. I once wrote a column about the Catholic Church for my papers, and one of them was picketed, lost twelve subscriptions. My publisher was terribly troubled. The fact is that you go to conventions of publishers and it could be a convention of shoe store owners—all they talk about is money."

Of course, money is very important in the lives of the 5,000 or so proprietors of small newspapers around the country. Many have none: Blankfort bought his first paper in Pacifica, California, in 1954, with the $5,000 that was his share when *Quick* magazine, which the Cowles people had given to those who worked on it, was sold to an almost equally short-lived journal named *Tempo*. The previous owner of the Pacifica *Tribune,* Blankfort recalls, "had no books," bartered ad space rather than sold it, and handed over a mostly fictitious subscription list. "I went out to sell ads and left my wife in the office, a man came in and said, 'Would you mind standing up?' and when she did he repossessed the desk and the typewriter and the filing cabinet." For most of the first year, Blankfort wrote the entire paper himself, mostly from information people sent him (he paid a fireman five dollars a week to bring in stories from the police and fire blotter). What got Blankfort started commercially was a builder who was putting up a development with 3,000 homes, who bought a subscription for everyone who bought a house. Then he wanted to incorporate his project as a separate township, and Blankfort decided it was a bad idea and opposed him.

And some are perhaps looking to make more than they ought to make, as Blankfort thinks maybe he did in 1978, when he and Rebele sold Harte-Hanks their twice-a-week Chula Vista *Star-News,* which had 20,000 paid circulation in a well-to-do suburb south of San Diego, for $3.8 million.

The largest of Blankfort's current properties is the Paradise *Post* on the Sierra ridge forty miles or so from Sacramento. As you come up the canyon wall at the city limits, a large sign by the road reads: "May You Find PARADISE to be All its Name Implies," signed by the Elks, the Ridge Quilting Club, the Lions, the Moose, Soroptimist, VASA Order, the Knights of Columbus, and various others. This had been a big apple-growing area in the 1950s, when the Larwin Corp. from Chicago bought up a chunk of it and began developing retirement homes under the name Paradise Pines, flying in people from Los Angeles who wanted a more peaceful old age than they were getting, and feeding them barbecues under the stars. "Our largest industry is social security checks," says editor and publisher Jim Fallbeck, who also owns a piece of the paper (this is common in Blankfort's enterprise). But there is also a somewhat younger group living in Paradise, drawn in the 1960s by the appeal of what Fallbeck politely calls "the pastoral life," now well represented among the community's businessmen. The businesses are retailing, restaurants, health care and some cottage manufacture of antiques (the largest employer in Paradise is the local hospital; the second-largest is the *Post*); most working people in Paradise commute to Chico or Oroville. You may remember Oroville—it's a small world—as the place where the butcher put the strychnine into the Tylenol capsule the same week the still unknown killer was filling capsules with cyanide in Chicago. The town of Paradise was not incorporated until 1979, and the *Post*, interestingly, is not a publisher of record for legal purposes (a major source of income for most rural papers), the Chico paper having grabbed that status some years before with a prehensile grip.

"When I came here in 1973," says Fallbeck, an earnest but not humorless Westerner in black pants, blue shirt, black tie, "this was virtually a shopper, 70 percent ads, 30 percent news, and I've spent my years opening up the news hole. Lowell bought the paper in 1977 and has been very supportive. The first page of each section [the *Post* runs in three sections, full size] is open, no advertising on it." In 1985, paid circulation passed the 9,000 mark, which is about two-thirds of the local households. The paper is mailed under arrangements not unlike those of *Suffolk Life*, with computer-generated labels that put the papers on the stack in "carrier-route sequence." If the *Post* gets the papers to the post office by five in the morning, they will be delivered that day. The remaining 4,500 or so households known to the post office are served once a week with the preprinted shoppers inserted in the paper. "Every one of my papers has these damned shoppers," Blankfort says. "If you've got eighty percent penetration, the supermarkets ask, 'What about the other twenty percent?' "

Many of these inserts the *Post* prints for the advertisers (who also use them elsewhere) on a five-unit Goss Community installation that will do 20 full-size pages at a time and a massive four-unit Goss Urbanite system that prints 64-page papers. Indeed, the largest job on Fallbeck's presses is not his own paper but the San Francisco Bay *Guardian*, one of the larger survivors of the alternative-paper movement, which trucks its plates up four hours from San Francisco and trucks the papers four hours back because the *Post* offers the best price and schedule for the printing job. "We've set ourselves up," Fallbeck says, enjoying victory in a half-million-dollar gamble, "as the K-Mart of the web presses." The presses run virtually all week long, day and night, and require the services of ten pressmen. During the course of a

week, the *Post*'s presses will gobble some twenty-two different kinds of paper, of different widths and qualities. "I'm lucky I discovered the magic of
the truck," Fallbeck says. "We lease a forty-foot trailer truck from Ryder
and keep the paper there."

Working with the presses and the printing jobs now takes most of
Fallbeck's time, and the day-to-day operation of the paper is mostly in the
hands of managing editor Wayne Agner, a hefty, bearded blond young man
who came to the Paradise *Post* in 1982 as a City Hall reporter fresh out of
Fresno State College, left to be assistant managing editor of the Selma *Enterprise* "in the raisin capital of the world," and was hired back by Fallbeck to
be managing editor. His staff consists of a full-time "Skylife" editor for the
entertainment and social section, a thirty-two-hour-a-week sports editor, five
young reporters and a full-time photographer (who takes the police scanner
home with him at night: "He can cover it himself," Agner says, "if it's a
one-structure fire or an injury accident; more than that, he calls me"). Agner tries to lay out the next week's papers at a Tuesday-morning meeting.
The reporters have beats—the town council, police and fire, the water
agency, the parks and recreation district and "any organization or government agency that comes out with regular news for us. Our reporters are in
fairly constant touch with the movers and shakers." Occasionally the planning goes awry—on the day of my visit the front page had a rather dull story
about the town joining a club of towns buying their liability insurance together, because the cops had promised an arrest in a rape case at 5:30 in the
afternoon of a day with a 6:30 deadline, then put off their arrest until
midnight and left a hole on the page. Sometimes the planning pays off
handsomely: the Paradise *Post* did an eight-page special section on the tenth
anniversary of the end of the Vietnam War, entirely pieces about the recollections of veterans of the war living in the area, no advertising whatever in
the section, and it did wonders for the morale of the staff and the reputation
of the paper.

Agner hires two or three new reporters a year, almost always fresh out
of college. "They go on to bigger and hopefully better things. We serve as a
kind of farm club." Agner awards bylines: "We like to give 'em. It helps
reporters in their clip books, and it tells the readers that this is something
produced by the staff locally." It's a good fraction of the reward the kids
get, too. "When I hired people myself," Blankfort says cheerfully, "I would
say, 'You're getting a postgraduate training program here. But instead of
your paying us, we'll pay you. Not very much. Mostly, they stayed eighteen
months, two years." Everybody works in one big L-shaped room, with
graphics people laying out ads and pages in the short part of the L. Behind is
a sort of relaxation room with coffee and soda machines, and a chart for the
year's vacation weeks. There are twenty-nine names on the chart, ranked by
seniority, and only seven of them are of people with the paper more than
two years.

Paradise appears in media history as the home of a violently right-wing radio station, KEWQ, which in the 1960s stood off for almost two years an attempt by the school leadership and various nonpartisan community groups to make the FCC grant a hearing on its license-renewal application. The station reported a listener poll showing 76 percent of the community for George Wallace (as against 22 percent for Nixon and 2 percent for Humphrey) in the 1968 election, and once got sheriff's deputies mobilized along the highway to prevent the immigration of a "nigger" to the ridge.[8] The political views of the town were never that violent (though the fight by right-wingers to prevent incorporation, which meant a layer of government that might actually pay attention to the town, was pretty extreme as late as 1979), but the average age is about fifty, everybody owns land, and the level of Republicanism runs high. Both Blankfort and Fallbeck are on the liberal side of the Democratic Party, and both write columns for the paper (Blankfort writes twelve times a year, a "First Tuesday" column every month, specifically about national and international politics, sometimes discussing things like his trip to Cuba). "The owner of the local shoe store gets furious," Fallbeck says, "when you do a story on the ten pregnant girls at the high school and an editorial calling for sex education. Sometimes my advertising people [whose sales account for 88 percent of the paper's revenue, apart from the job printing] come around and ask if I couldn't ease off for a while. I'm not the most popular person in town. But the circulation of the paper keeps rising."

People don't buy the paper or the ads because they like the management; they buy because the paper does a job for them. Everyone knows it's funny when Reagan's press spokesman Larry Speakes tells a conference of the National Association of Government Communicators that there ought to be "a good-news segment on the nightly news. Let's have Dan and Frank and Roger [Rather and Reynolds and Mudd: this was 1983] turn around in their chair and look dead into the camera and say, 'Now, folks, for some news on the bright side.' "[9] The people who worked for the Huntsville (Tex.) *Item* were not so sure it was funny later that year when a group of local businessmen began printing the Huntsville *Morning News,* based on a principle expressed by the president of the First National Bank of Huntsville: "The news should always be positive. We don't think a newspaper should look under every rock trying to stir up trouble."[10] But a couple of years later, the businessmen's paper went bust, and the *Item* flourished (a property of the Harte-Hanks chain, the one that bought Blankfort's paper and killed his column—he was quite prepared to keep writing it—because he was too liberal), and that story was funny, too.

Part Six

NEW TECHNOLOGIES

15

Is the Future upon Us?

You can argue that printing and publishing is part of the information business. It is, in a way.

–Joseph C. Boyd, chairman
and CEO, Harris Corp.

We made a million dollars last year selling Washington *Post* stories to videotex. I should know the number—I had a fight to keep it for my budget, on the grounds that we earned it, but they said, No, it goes into the general pot.

–Benjamin Bradlee

Who is better able to cover the news in your market than you? Rather than having crews running around the country at great expense, Conus will rely on its owner television stations and subscriber television stations for its news . . . stations equipped with Ku-band send and receive equipment, thus forming the most powerful and flexible news service in America.

–promotional literature
for Conus News Service,
Hubbard Broadcasting Co., Minneapolis

1

"In 1980," said Richard Levine, a casual but neat man in his forties, editor of the Princeton-based Dow Jones News Retrieval service, "I had been fourteen years with *The Wall Street Journal* in Washington. I was chief economics editor, wrote the Monday column on the front page. As you know, this is an organization that's run by ex-reporters—people get tapped to leave the typewriter, which is painful. They offered me a foreign bureau, but I wasn't tempted, would have been ten years earlier, but my kids were of an age where we wanted them in school here. One day Larry O'Donnell, then managing editor, came down and asked me to breakfast at the Hay-

Adams. He said, 'Bill Dunn [then president of the Dow Jones Information Services Group] is looking for editorial brainpower.' My wife said, 'Computers, Dick. That's the future.' "

The history of this was complicated. Dow Jones had been in the business of distributing information electrically for a long time. In 1974, after the stock exchanges had perfected a system of computer storage and retrieval for the flow of bid-and-asked quotes on listed securities, the publisher went into partnership with Bunker-Ramo, one of the early electronics companies, which had designed a terminal with a keyboard through which a fluctuating data base could be queried. The joint venture distributed the broad tape in videotex as well as stock quotes to bankers and brokers who would buy the service wholesale. By then, of course, the copy for the broad tape was being fed through a computer, so the cost of the data base for "news retrieval" was merely a matter of copying blips from one magnetic disk to another. As the home PC loomed on the horizon in the late 1970s, Dow Jones CEO Warren Phillips, a lean and graceful man with a broad black mustache, who seems much too young to have been managing editor of the *Journal* in the 1950s, decided that the future of news retrieval lay in retail distribution. Reorganizing the company, he assigned not only the broad tape but also a new Interactive Information Systems Division to Bill Dunn, a beefy high-voltage Iowa farm boy who had come to publishing originally as a pressman at the Des Moines *Register* and had moved on to supervise the perfection of facsimile transmission by satellite and become chief of production for all Dow Jones. "When I got in trouble with starting the European edition of *The Wall Street Journal,*" managing editor Norman Pearlstine says gratefully, "Dunn came over to Europe and saved it."

"The key moment was in 1977," Dunn recalls, "when Mike Markala walked in here with an Apple computer. We'd never heard of them. It was an interesting machine, you could get it to do simple things like dial a number." Dow Jones technical director Carl Valenti and his people designed software programs for the Apple that would format text material in the ASCII code (American Standard Code for Information Interchange) used in computer-to-computer communications. Valenti also worked out with the telephone company a packet-switching network to permit the service to be offered nationwide for the price of a local call. "Wherever the PC went," Levine says, "we could go with it." At this point the Bunker-Ramo "dumb terminal" became a drag on invention, and Dow Jones bought the computer company out in 1979. (Automatic Data Processing, a technologically sophisticated descendant of the classical service bureau, took over the stock-quote system as part of its expansion from the provision of back-office accounting and executing to the packaging of wall-to-wall operations for broker/dealer firms.)

Even during the retrospectively brief period when it seemed that the PC would join the microwave oven as a necessity of American home life, the correctness of many of these decisions was something less than obvious. Even an Apple costs a lot more than Bunker-Ramo's plain vanilla cathode-ray screen with a formatter and a modem (modulator/demodulator: a contraption that translates the analog signals of telephonics to the digital signals of computers and other text-generating devices, and then translates computer impulses back to analog signals). "We run scared around here," Dunn says. "We looked at Prestel [the British videotex system, struggling along in sidebands of BBC telecasts], we looked at Minitel [the French terminals that do nothing but videotex]. The French were going to throw millions of dedicated terminals at the public, replace the telephone book with videotex; Matra would make them and dump them all over France, and then they'd come here, very cheap. [This may still happen, by the way.] The woods were full of different kinds of dumb terminals that did different things. AT&T was being very aggressive with its dedicated terminal. We thought we'd blown it.

"Then there were all these format things, not ASCII—alpha-mosaic, NAPLP [North American Presentation Level Protocol, an AT&T invention offered to everybody by AT&T without any license fee because it could be used only in conjunction with an AT&T videotex color generator], seventh-generation protocols—and there we were with nothing but old black-and-white ASCII data bases. We felt . . . it was like someone said your sister was a whore." Worse yet, in 1980, when some of these technical doubts had not yet matured, was the fact that the technicians themselves were deciding what Dunn should be sending over the wires to his customers' Apple personal computers. Levine was recruited from Washington because Dunn knew that the broad tape, which is full of statistical compilations of the price of hog bellies for delivery in different months, would not be what the home consumer or even the businessman in his midwestern office would most want. Levine's first question to Dunn was the meaningless "Can you get hard copy?" to which the answer was an impatient "Sure." (Anything that comes up on a computer screen can be printed out by the associated printer.) The second question was "Who decides what goes into this box?" and Dunn exploded. "Goddamnit," he said, "that's what I need you for."

It then turned out that Levine would get more help in that job than anyone has ever had before. "How would you like to run a newspaper stand where people can come up and tear out a story and throw a nickel on the drum?" says Dunn, who is now a vice chairman of Dow Jones though still functionally the maximum leader of the Information Services Group. "You'd have quite a survey, wouldn't you?" For what Dow Jones is delivering to the roughly 200,000 News Retrieval subscribers is something quite unlike a published or broadcast news service; instead, it is, in Levine's words, "information available to the customer on demand." Payment is by use, which creates an entirely different kind of economics for the news business.

"We'd had the luxury of printing a paper," Dunn says. "Our whole business rested on the decision somebody made in 1947 that *The Wall Street Journal,* which had always printed a separate California edition featuring West Coast news, would be a national business newspaper printing the same stories everywhere. Salesman would call on a company in Kansas City, say, 'Why aren't you advertising in the national business newspaper?' Guy would say, 'What national business newspaper?' and the salesman would say, 'Fucking *Wall Street Journal,* you idiot,' and he'd advertise. Then, if people didn't like what they found, tough shitski: we were the only national business paper. Or if people wanted to take six hours with the paper, fine, it cost them the same fifty cents. On News Retrieval, if the menu doesn't show you what you want, you don't pay. Or if you're dumb or a slow reader or have a slow printer, it costs you money." If you're a very fast reader with a very fast printer, however, you can't save as much money as you might like, because DJ News Retrieval charges more for service to a faster modem.

Because different kinds of information may command different prices, and because Dow Jones must pay the providers of the specialized separate data bases on a per-use basis, the computer keeps a record of what each customer demands. Every morning when Levine comes to work he finds a summary of how many customers accessed which stories or services yesterday. These are his sales figures, infinitely more precise in their implications than the word that comes from the newsstands or the subscription department for a printed publication, infinitely more accurate and meaningful than the ratings of television shows. "It raises the same problems for me as polls do for a politician," Levine says. "Am I a leader or a follower? It would be foolish to ignore the information, but in fact I still edit by gut instinct—and over time, I *have* seen some of those judgments confirmed." In a sense, the News Retrieval system places every subscriber in the position of the "gatekeeper" of song and story and sociological jargon, the newspaper editor with stuff from his own reporters and AP and UP and various feature services coming into his newsroom. The difference is, of course, that the editor is paid to choose, has assistants for that purpose and some time to devote to the decisions, while the ultimate news consumer knows only what he likes.

Plus how much he cares, if he does care, about what's going on in the world. Big stories used to boost the newsstand sale of the afternoon papers; now they jump the usage of a videotex news service. The downing of Korean Air Lines Flight 007, Brezhnev's death, the bombing of the American Marine barracks in Lebanon, the arms-to-Iran Nicaraguan flap—such things increase by as much as 50 percent the number of minutes of headline news service the subscribers purchase. (The Beirut bombing moved on the wires at two in the morning, New York time, after East Coast and Midwest papers had gone to bed. "We were," Levine says with some satisfaction, "thirty hours ahead of the morning papers.") And, interestingly, usage does not return all the way down to its previous base when the current emergency ends. A fraction of those who begin watching because today's news grips them decide that their lives require a grip on the news.

News Retrieval is the one moneymaker in this business. By mid-1986, the number of subscribers was above the quarter-million mark, which argues for annual gross revenues of something like $50 million (lots of people subscribe to the service and then don't use it much). In fiscal 1986, Dow Jones reported a 27 percent increase in the profits of the "information services" division. And there is clearly much more to come.

2

News delivery through an interactive videotex system, especially one that has a computing capacity at the receiving end, offers an immense advance over traditional distribution in speed, capacity, selectivity and power.

1. Speed is most important, of course, in dealing with markets. Forty percent of the usage of Dow Jones News Retrieval is for stock market quotes. The technical director for Knight-Ridder's Commodity News Services in Kansas City is Paul Tucker, a computer wonk, mustachioed, prematurely balding, laid back, who fulfills his functions for CNS between weeks of teaching at the University of Illinois. In the nature of the job, he has been thinking about news. "The value of a news item today," Tucker said recently, "is measured in several seconds; the value of a price is measured in tenths of a second." (For most people and most purposes, mind you, seconds are pretty good. Secretary of State George Shultz told William Beecher of the Boston *Globe* in 1983 that he kept a computer on his desk to tie in with the Dow Jones world news service. "From time to time," he said, "I scroll over reports from one part of the world or another and then phone the appropriate official to ask what he makes of this development or that." Not infrequently, Shultz added, he had the news before his desk officers did: "It drives them wild."[1])

The prices the videotex systems distribute come directly out of the computer that feeds the tape at the stock exchanges, registers over-the-counter stock trading, or records the contracts at the Board of Trade or the Mercantile Exchange. In the government bond market, the Telerate information service (which Dow Jones purchased in 1985) *is* the market: that is, the 350 or so market makers worldwide quote the prices at which they are prepared to buy and sell in normal round-lot quantities by calling a Telerate "reporter" or, in some instances, directly keying the information into the Telerate mainframe. Much of it, says Barry Clark, vice president for information services, a faintly professorial middle-aged executive who has established a quiet corner in an aggressive sales office, "goes onto the wire untouched by anybody in-house." There isn't a lot for reporters to do in this context, and reporters in fact occupy a very middling status on the videotex totem pole. A handful of Telerate's people are professionals with sources of their own and judgment of the sources that is worth having (Clark himself, an Englishman, came to Telerate from seven years as a senior commodities editor for Reuters in New York), but most are kids. "The career path," Clark observes, "is from technical to reporting to sales. We're very entrepreneurial around here; when we make a sale to a new customer, bells ring all around the office."

It's some office, too: a giant floor and a half of space more than a hundred stories up, just below the top of the World Trade Center in New York, decorated to fit with tubular chairs and dark walls and posterlike art. The newsroom is something out of *Star Wars,* mostly dark, with three walls of screens and a fourth wall of glass to the hall, so visitors can look in. The location is the result of Telerate's early dependence on the government bonds brokerage house of Cantor, Fitzgerald, which rents the very top floor of the World Trade Center. Cantor alone at the start supplied the quotes (its own and its trading partners') that convinced the banks to subscribe.

Telerate is not for householders: minimum price runs about $7,000 a year and requires a dedicated phone line. (Looking to displace Telerate with customers who have telephone company troubles, Knight-Ridder's CNS has made its Money Center service available via specially jiggered transmissions through a satellite to a dish less than three feet in diameter that can be hung out the window—but this service is not, as we shall see, an interactive service.) Still, there is a pretty obvious symbiosis between the less exotic Telerate "pages" and Dow Jones News Retrieval—indeed, there was a joint Dow Jones–AP–Telerate service offered in Europe and Asia before DJ acquired Telerate—and by the time these paper pages are printed I would expect Levine's "menu" in News Retrieval to include many of Telerate's prices for government securities, large-denomination Certificates of Deposit at the giant banks and foreign exchange. News Retrieval on a per-use charge is not really competition for the Telerate screens. A price transmitted through Telerate is, of course, advertising for the market maker, who may pay Telerate $1,250 a month for his page in the system (or may not: "If you were somebody we really wanted on Telerate we might make a 'source agreement' with you," Clark says).

Reuters in London, which is much larger than Telerate everywhere outside the United States, started computerized reporting of European stock market prices in 1964, a year when its total revenues were about $10 million and its books showed a loss of about $150,000. Twenty-one years later, Reuters' revenue from news products had risen to about $35 million, and the losses were doubtless much greater—but the company's total receipts, driven by its financial market services, had risen to roughly $600 million, with a net profit before tax from all operations of more than $125 million.

Reuters puts real-time prices on the wire from no fewer than 104 exchanges (stocks, bonds, commodities, options), mostly through access to the

exchanges' own computers, though in some smaller cities the news service
has its own reporters on the floor. Even more important, however, are the
almost four hundred thousand "contributed quotes" from market makers
around the world, prices of instruments private and governmental, most of
them traded "upstairs" in broker/dealer offices, rather than on any exchange. The "Reuter Monitor," the company's basic financial service, consists of almost twenty-five thousand separate, constantly updated "pages" of
prices and other market information, plus almost six thousand "pages" of
news and general information, all accessible through a customer's keyboard
and screen. As of late 1986, Reuters was transmitting around the world to
ninety-two thousand terminals, an increasing fraction of them manufactured
by the company's own Rich, Inc., subsidiary in Chicago.

But information per se is only part of what Reuters expects to sell.
"Unlike other vendors," says Andre Villeneuve, a round yet forceful Englishman who went from Oxford to Reuters as a news trainee in the 1960s
and worked his way through administration to be head of the company's
U.S. operation, "we see our terminals as something you do more with than
just retrieve information." Starting with the "Monitor Dealing Service" in
the 1970s, Reuters has made it possible for traders to execute transactions
over its wires. In foreign exchange ("much bigger than these piddling securities markets," says Reuters' managing director, Glen Renfrew), as much as
half the world's spot trading now occurs through Reuters' facilities. This is
done in a "conversational" mode—that is, people make their deals by electronic mail messages back and forth, rather than by simply hitting a bid or
offer shown on the screen—but in its new stock market execution services
(based on the American company Instinet, which Reuters formally acquired
in early 1987), Reuters will offer broker/dealers the opportunity to buy or
sell automatically, untouched by human hand or voice, at the prices and
volumes quoted on the screens. In London, where the London Stock Exchange goofed on its home-designed quotation-cum-transaction service, the
merger between this traditional, provincial securities market and the fully
computerized market administered by the International Securities Self-Reg-
ulatory Organization (ISRO), which has used Reuters from the beginning,
will almost certainly mean that the "news agency" will become the instrument for virtually all trading in private securities in London.

In the United States, these computer-based stock-ordering services
have caught on only in the wholesale over-the-counter stock market. In a
retail basis, the customer's men in the brokerage houses and the institutional
salesmen in the investment banks like to retain their personal telephonic
contact with their customers. (The use of computer-based buying services
by ordinary consumers as distinguished from trading firms, incidentally,
may be costly to the provider: D. C. Anderson of Palo Alto, the first stockbroker to offer order privileges through a PC network at all hours of the
day or night, found that during the first months more than half his orders

arrived in the evening and were revoked late at night: i.e., the subscriber showed off the new toy to his friends before or after dinner and then wiped the slate clean before going to bed.) News services are still news services. But there is handwriting on the tube.

2. Capacity is perhaps the most spectacular aspect of videotex, for on a service like News Retrieval, as Levine puts it, "you have in effect an unlimited news hole." Once the newspaper production process goes directly from the reporters' heads to print through a computer, the text of the *The Wall Street Journal* can simply be put on the wire for use on Dow Jones News Retrieval, as that of the Miami *Herald* went automatically to its affiliate Viewdata for use in the now departed Viewtron, and that of the Los Angeles *Times* went to its videotex subsidiary for use in its Gateway videotex service. Indeed, the newspaper-based videotex projects were the first to become operational, because for newspapers the raw material was cheap and the lure of reusing it was all but irresistible. Little more than announcements have thus far resulted from joint ventures in this area that do *not* include a newspaper or a wire service—and there is no shortage of these, one involving IBM and Sears (CBS dropped out in fall 1986); one with Citicorp and RCA; one with AT&T, Chemical Bank, Bank of America and Time Inc.—because they would incur raw material costs in addition to their system costs. In fall 1986, interestingly, the New York *Times* began offering the front page of tomorrow's paper through the last of these ventures, for transmission after 9 P.M. each night, together with theater listings, restaurant reviews, sports scores, etc.

If videotex becomes more widespread, there will be many arguments in the editors' aeries about which material should be sent out to the home screens and which should be held for the paper. (In Miami, Viewtron editor John Woolley, a go-getter newsman recruited for the videotex project from Knight-Ridder's Detroit *Free Press*, had access to the work of the metro and "Neighbors" desks at the *Herald* before the editors on those desks made their decision on what to use and where to play it.) But the very fact of capacity will tip the scales toward dumping everything on videotex as it comes in. In 1977, David Brinkley wrote a much-criticized article for *TV Guide* arguing that "we should not put a story on the air unless we believe it is interesting to at least 10 percent of the audience. Preferably more. But at least 10 percent."[2] (The subject of the two-minute piece he thought should not have run on his show was, interestingly, the civil war in Lebanon: "Who, in this country, really cared about it? . . . Lebanese living in the United States? Even if they do, they're a tiny fraction of one percent of our population . . .") In videotex, as in pay cable, theory says that usage by only a small minority, 1 or 2 percent of the audience, can generate enough revenue for a program to pay its way.

Videotex, in fact, can cover a very wide spectrum of activities, fishing up its bits with a finer net, because the costs are trivial. The news-gathering organizations already provide enormously more than traditional publishing and broadcasting entities can convey. "There's a hell of a lot we have or can get," Dunn says, speaking of the special situation of a national newspaper, but the point applies only slightly differently to others, "that we can't merchandise because our market is too big. In the future, there will be a category of companies we will report on that will never appear in *The Wall Street Journal,* just on the electronic service. Every reporter will be under orders to do six exclusives a year, for his byline in the electronic service. The world is hearing your words even though they don't see print. Reporters are going to have to learn to accept availability on a videotex menu as a substitute for availability on a printed page. Otherwise it's like you have a painter and there's no room on the wall—or a whore and there's nobody to screw, she'll lose her skills." Dunn, it will be remembered, worked on a newspaper in the pressroom, not in the newsroom.

The contents of U.S. newspapers plus their overset matter, moreover, are only a minor fraction of what can be and already is ready and waiting for customer demand in a videotex service. Dow Jones has a gateway for Kyodo News International, "Today's News from Tokyo Via Satellite," with forty or fifty stories from Japan every day ("We don't edit their material," Levine says; "we've convinced them to get someone with a knowledge of colloquial American English"). On all the existing services, Grolier's Academic American Encyclopedia, updated every six months for this purpose, arrives when the customer hits the code keys to open Grolier's "gateway"; the Official Airlines Guide, updated monthly, lies behind another gateway. (In the mature full videotex service, of course, you not only can get the schedule on your screen, you can order the tickets from a participating travel agent listed on that screen, and pay him immediately or on some future day with a "value-dated" payments order via your home banking facility.)

Oddities do very well. Among the most frequently used gateways in Dow Jones News Retrieval is one that offers short reviews of more than three thousand old movies (Levine thinks people use it to check out what's in the TV listings; Dunn thinks it's people playing some version of Trivial Pursuit). Telerate has a calorie counter and a sports review featuring the soccer scores from Europe. Nor do you have to commit to one thing at a time. All the statistical services have a "window" on the screen for headline news stories that might affect the market (the most important of them generate an audible beep—virtually all PCs will beep—to call the customer's attention to the screen if he is doing something else). A denizen of Shearson Lehman remembers that when the first news of the Mexican earthquake of 1985 flashed onto the screen there was an immediate call across the trading room: "Do we have a position today in Mexican pesos?"

3. Selectivity is the feature that most intrigues the typical subscriber. Virtually all of these services, whether they use a computer or, like the

original Viewtron in Miami, a dumb terminal, permit the user to preprogram the categories of his greatest interest, so that when he walks into his office (or den, or living room—the "he," incidentally, is not chauvinist: 90+ percent of Dow Jones News Retrieval subscribers are men) he can hit a single button and be presented very quickly with what he particularly wants to know: top headlines, stories affecting his own business, action in selected stocks or other markets, up-to-the-minute ball scores for certain teams. And very local matters, too. When I asked chairman Alvah Chapman of Knight-Ridder why he saw so considerable a future for his company's Viewtron videotex service, one of the things he mentioned, pretty high up in the discourse, was the fact that he could push a button and get the box score of his grandson's Little League baseball game that afternoon. Why not? The coaches were more than happy to take a couple of minutes at the local high school, to which Knight-Ridder had given an inexpensive terminal that could be used to originate videotex entries at the computer, and type in that information so the extended families of the performers could see it as news and even, if they received the service through their PC, print it out as a souvenir.

Nevertheless, newspaper-based videotex failed: Knight-Ridder, the Los Angeles *Times,* the Chicago *Sun-Times,* all gave it a shot (the *Sun-Times* with partners who put up most of the money), and all quit. Otis Chandler while chairman of the Los Angeles *Times* spelled out the reasons: "We were misled by the electronic junkies. We thought that once we had the full range of services people would concentrate on the serious stuff, on the late news, the ball scores, that only we could deliver. But the high use was in video games and community bulletins. If you want up-to-the-minute news in this city you don't need videotex, there are three all-news stations and CNN. It gets down to the lifestyle in your home, the allocation of time. The big boom here was in video cassettes, you can rent the tape in Los Angeles for a buck a show, rent the unit overnight for two bucks, and these things compete with videotex. Grassroots [a farmer's statistical, advice and newsletter service in which the L.A. *Times* has a minor interest with Canadian partners] may be marginally successful, things for farmers and commercial fishermen who want to know the price of shrimp and weather conditions, but in terms of the general consumer, no."

The L.A. *Times* wrote off about $10 million; Knight-Ridder, which got Viewtron up to 20,000 subscribers when it went from Miami to national service—and as late as February 28, 1986, two weeks before closing it down, was offering the world an hour a day of free Viewtron for those who would sample the wares—probably blew $30 million. "Although we are disappointed that we were unable to create a viable business," K-R's Jim Batten (not the biggest fan for Viewtron in the company) said in announcing the demise, "we also are heartened by the many valuable lessons we have learned. . . . It is now clear that videotex is not likely to be a threat to either newspaper advertising or readership in the foreseeable future."

Both Viewtron and the Gateway service offered in 1984 by the Los Angeles *Times* counted on revenues from advertising to pay a considerable fraction of the bills, and both were disappointed. Not surprisingly. As a CBS–Automatic Data Processing–AT&T pilot project in Ridgefield, New Jersey, convincingly demonstrated in 1982–83, what subscribers want from a videotex terminal in terms of shopping information is comparative prices (the most popular single item on the Ridgefield menu was a "market basket" service that permitted the subscriber to enter her supermarket list for that day, and then played back the total cost of those purchases at each of half a dozen of the area's markets). And most advertisers advertise because they wish to compete with brand differentiations rather than with prices; indeed, any product line perceived as being purchased for price rather than some other reason is known scornfully to the analysts as a "commodity business," and nobody wants to own stock in companies in a commodity business.

If there is going to be a source of revenue in videotex other than subscriber fees, it will be commissions on actual sales made on this chassis. Dow Jones offers access to Comp-U-Store, and in spring 1985 purchases through that service by subscribers were running over a quarter of a million dollars a month (mostly hard goods like video tape recorders—"You have to remember," says Bill Dunn, referring to New York's most celebrated and zoo-like discount shop for electronics and video, "that most of the country doesn't live near a 47th Street Photo"). Viewtron in Miami had a popular Dutch auction feature called BidQuik, in which some big-ticket item was offered at a price that dropped every fifteen minutes through the day until somebody bought (a "fully loaded" red Corvette started at $27,745 and went for $23,260; a Sony AM/FM microcassette recorder started at $200 and went for $94; a pair of Bruce Springsteen tickets with a Walkman went immediately at the $130 offering price). But that's not enough to support a service. There has to be something people need, like market information, that gets the gimmick in the door; then the subscriber learns to love it.

4. The power these services offer relates to both memory and analysis. News is mostly unmemorable, and not likely to be useful unless it is plugged into its context. One of the earliest uses of videotex was a New York *Times* service that offered a computerized search through specially prepared summaries of the paper, giving researchers something much faster than hunting through the *Times* index year by year and then looking up the relevant items in microfilm rolls. The system was also, the *Times* said, going to replace the morgue at the newspaper. The software for this project was designed by IBM, which also of course supplied the equipment, and it happened to be a year when IBM was experimenting with a new long-text

magazine advertising campaign to explain how its products were helping create a brave new world. I was commissioned to write the ad about the new information service, and fairly quickly found out that it wasn't going to do what the *Times* wanted it to do: even the reporters who were happiest with the terminals that were replacing typewriters in the newsroom were unwilling to give up the batch of clips they ordered from the morgue to give them necessary background on an assignment.

The basic error was that the *Times* was digesting the news stories, which was a service for corporate and scholarly users, but a horror for the reporter who was used to browsing full text. (A Rube Goldberg microfiche system with robot arms was supposed to find full text on demand for the newsroom, but it never worked.) Corporate customers liked the service better, but not enough to pay the costs of building the data base. By the time the paper had moved to computerized "typesetting"—reducing to zero the cost of building the ongoing data base—the *Times* was sufficiently sick of this business to give it to Mead, a paper company with a data products subsidiary that was proprietor of Lexis (the legal search service) and Nexis (a file of 175 magazines and newspapers, full text in memory cores). Knight-Ridder's VU/Text became the contractor for the creation of electronic morgues at other papers, including the Washington *Post,* the Boston *Globe,* the Houston *Post* and the Sacramento *Bee,* as well as the proprietors of the company's established KNT service. As part of the deal, VU/Text will market your morgue to other papers, taking a commission on each use.

Dow Jones News Retrieval started simply with the broad tape, ninety days' worth of it, tacked onto Bunker-Ramo's stock exchange prices, and the tape is still a central feature. That goes out on videotex as it arrives at Dow Jones, because the items are time-stamped and the staff that works the ticker is experienced at concision. And sometime in the next year or so Dow Jones will start offering the full text of the *Journal,* which will in time accumulate a mighty data base that the mainframe will search on request. For now, however, Levine has a staff of almost forty people who rewrite the copy that is in the works at the *Journal* and the material from the wire services. "Wire service copy," says Peter Schuyten, a gaunt and bearded refugee from the New York *Times* who supervises the editorial process for Levine, "tends to be flabby anyway, you can easily boil it down from 700 words to two or three screens, maybe 250, 300 words." This is highly specialized work: the writer sits before two screens and a keyboard, reading the wire service copy on one screen and writing onto the other. (Eventually —it's no big deal but Dow Jones is still paying the penalty of getting there first—the writer will have a split screen that allows him to read the wire copy on one side and what he's writing on the other.) And unlike the rest of the Dow Jones operation, which runs all copy through a continuous rolling mill of heavy editing, News Retrieval allows people to put their own work "in print": as Schuyten puts it: "They push the button and it goes out nationally."

All searching of data bases for memory purposes is managed on a "Key Word in Context" system, which permits the searcher to narrow in on his object (to tell him whether he has narrowed enough, the search report usually starts off by presenting the number of items that will be supplied if no further restrictive terms are entered, and after a few experiences of spewed-out documentation the user tends to acquire expertise at specification). It is also possible in videotex to give the user the suggestion that he might wish some background on this story. Dow Jones's Dunn, Levine and Schuyten all mentioned, separately and proudly, that when Brezhnev died News Retrieval indexed the entry on the Soviet leader in the Academic American Encyclopedia.

What is usually meant by those who talk of the power of these systems, however, is the opportunity for massaging the newest numbers opened up by the combination of instant communication and computing power. With today's PCs, this does not, interestingly, require an interactive system. In fall 1985, the software company Lotus began marketing a floppy disk and an FM radio receiver that could be loaded into and hooked up to a PC and would deliver current information on stock market trading. This information could then be analyzed on Lotus' 1-2-3 spreadsheet program or its Symphony program to give the purchaser the feeling he had high-tech help in making investment decisions.

One of the most ambitious analytical services, Knight-Ridder's Money Center, does not offer the subscriber so much as a chance to query his source. Based on AT&T's fanciest PC, with a gorgeously bright color screen, Money Center simply sends off in a steady stream, twenty-four hours a day, incredible quantities of data about prices and trades of fixed-income securities, financial futures, foreign exchange and some stocks. As many as 150 trades *per second* can be reported to the PC. The information moves through a 4,800-baud communications system, which means that a minute's data in Money Center equals sixteen minutes' data in the normal Dow Jones 300-baud feed, four minutes' in the extra-price 1,200-baud mode. (Reuters in 1986 then trumped that all, offering a service at 19,200 baud, *64 times* as fast as Dow Jones.) Satellite transponders, FM broadcast, microwave relays and leased lines, depending on what's convenient to this location, are used to get the information from Knight-Ridder's computers in Kansas City to the customer. In his PC, a 10-megabyte hard disk retains a year's worth of market information, and the software allows the customer by pushing a button to get instant color charts—long-term as against short-term moving averages (or one-hour moving averages, if you're playing that kind of market); point-and-figure analysis, stochastic analysis, relation of price movements and volume, relative strength charts, etc. The screen can be divided into three separate boxes if desired. "I can do quotes and charts and news, and watch 'em all at the same time," says Sandy Pennington, a young sales-man for Money Center. "And everything updates all the time."

Some things, however, remain too information-rich to be managed even by the most resourceful of personal computers. Telerate, for example, has a service called Telerate II, which takes data from banks and brokers and dealers from all over the world, compares spot prices for currencies, prices in the forward markets and interest rates at different maturities ("not a trivial task," says Phil Ginsburg, one of its two designers, "because there are different holidays in different countries")—and tells traders what sure-thing arbitrage is now available between safe investments in different coun-tries. It takes 800 calculations every one-third of a second to handle this "covered interest arbitrage equation," and that's more than a PC can ac-complish. On the other hand, Telerate did not wish to load all the work onto its mainframes, so Ginsburg and his partner Allen Carsen designed a system that performs some of the calculations centrally and downloads the rest in a continuous stream to a heavily doctored IBM XT the customer must buy before he can use the service.

Ginsburg and Carsen came to financial information through a rather different kind of news-in-depth service. Economists with experience at IBM, the Federal Reserve and the National Aeronautics and Space Administra-tion, they were teaching when they formed Llorex Corp. in 1976. One of their projects was the analysis of "spectral images" in satellite photos of the Soviet Union, to help the U.S. Department of Agriculture forecast that country's grain yield. This was quite a success. In January 1979, wheat prices were $3.50 a bushel, and Ginsburg and Carsen forecast a rise to $4.20 because of problems they could see developing in the Soviet grain crop. The satellite reports to the Department of the Interior, through its Landsat Data bureau in Sioux Falls, Iowa, and this is not a national security facility. The Brazilians got wind of the fact that Llorex was attempting to predict coffee yields ("We weren't very accurate," Ginsburg recalls, "be-cause the bean is under the leaf; it's not like soybeans and wheat, where the payload is exposed"), and presently they filed a Freedom of Information Act request with the Interior Department, which won them free access to the Llorex predictions.

Ginsburg and Carsen sold Llorex to Telerate in 1981, and have moved on to the parent company's projects, but they still cast an occasional eye on their agricultural past. Once the Brazilians had demonstrated that it could be done, it turns out, other countries went after the information the Llorex system was generating. Last time Ginsburg and Carsen looked, the largest consumers of the data their programs developed from the satellite photos were the Russians. They want the news, too. One wonders whether they bought Landsat's photos of their Chernobyl nuclear disaster in April 1986; that was the source of the pictures the television news services showed.

Videotex services to date have been mostly auxiliary to newspapers, but despite Batten's confidence about what Knight-Ridder learned from Viewtron, they may also offer some unexpected challenges. At *The Wall Street Journal,* managing editor Norman Pearlstine is already thinking about what he should do with the eighteen or so pages of yesterday's price quotations on various markets that will be freed up when most of the consumers of such information receive it on their computer screens, long before the newspaper can deliver it. More ominous matters may portend: in Monmouth County, New Jersey, AT&T in 1985 began a service by which realtors can place their listings in videotex for public distribution. For many of the purposes served by classified advertising, videotex is a better distribution system. That was why Knight-Ridder and Times-Mirror gave it a shot themselves; now they will have to find some other defense.

3

"When we merged with Harris Intertype," says Joe Boyd, former chairman of the engineering department at the University of Michigan, a square-shouldered physicist with longish brown-gray hair, originally the proprietor of a company called Radiation that Harris thought it acquired back in 1970, "we sent people around to printing plants. We found they were typing and cutting and pasting. We developed the first electronic editing systems, where after the newspeople keystroked it they could edit it." Harris in those days was a metal-bashing company that made big presses and kept its headquarters in Cleveland; Radiation was in Melbourne, Florida, convenient to Cape Canaveral. Now the Cleveland operation is gone, the printing business has been spun off to be a separate company under the name Harris Graphics (acquired in 1986 by A.M. International, which moved its headquarters back North to Chicago), and Harris Corp. of Melbourne is a $2 billion-a-year inventor and designer and producer of electronic equipment, with more than eleven thousand employees the largest manufacturing employer in the southeastern United States. It is also, in a quiet way, the second-largest producer of "front-end systems"—data banks and terminals for newsroom automation, plus text composition by computer printers, essentially in column format like old-fashioned galley proofs—with about six hundred U.S. newspapers and a number of Australian, Dutch and Finnish papers among the customers.

Harris' first and biggest such job was for the New York *Times* in the late 1970s—"a major undertaking," says Harris spokesman Peter Carney, "a custom job for them." This has been something less than totally satisfactory on both sides, partly because the state of the art has advanced so far that Harris has little interest in simply maintaining and improving the *Times* installation (though the software is updated annually, under pressure from the paper, which has its own resident staff of programmers). Publisher Arthur Ochs Sulzberger considers the text systems at the *Times* irritatingly weak by comparison with the facilities at the Los Angeles *Times* and even (though here it would seem a pure case of the grass looking greener) at the Washington *Post*.

What the *Times* wanted and ultimately got, as the designers perfected the arts of distributed processing, was a network capacious enough to interconnect 500 terminals and give them all access to a single data base. At first, Harris had to limit the different departments to their own data base (i.e., business or Sunday could not access sports), but within a year or two the electronic designers were able to create time-sharing packages, a system they called "copynet," that opened up the entire system to all users with the appropriate keys. Among the values the *Times* especially wanted was complete communications integration of its forty-man Washington bureau, and this has been delivered: in the words of Ed Slattery, manager of Harris' newspaper division, "from inside the system, Washington looks local to New York."

Most reporters resented and resisted the loss of their typewriters; Linotype operators and pressmen who handled the trays of hot-type galleys resented and resisted the loss of their jobs. Where the plant was unionized, which was the case in most cities (the printers' unions are among the oldest, most honest and most democratic in the country, and were among the best established), it was often necessary to buy out the jobs, usually with guarantees that current full-time employees with more than marginal seniority would be kept on the payroll until they retired or voluntarily departed. Even so, it's been very rugged. In 1964, the International Typographical Union had 106,600 members, of whom 92,600 were active and 14,000 were retired; in 1982, there were only 77,100 members, of whom only 50,000 were active; and the number of apprentices was down from 6,200 to 1,100.[3] Toward the end of 1986, the ITV merged itself into the Communications Workers of America.

Reporters, however, with very few exceptions, were quickly won over to automation by the immense improvements in their efficiency that they could *feel* as they worked. Those who sent in their stories from outside the office, and there are such, were charmed by the lightweight portable computer with built-in modem (in 1985, as the original maker of such equipment, Teleram, went bust, Motorola introduced a word processor with a built-in radio transmitter, eliminating even the need to get to a phone line). It was much more satisfying to write out one's story and go home than to call it in or carry it to the office, possibly missing an edition and certainly missing dinner. From the subeditors' and higher editors' point of view, it was useful to be able to see stories much earlier in the process of their creation and development (the editor who used to have to go over to a reporter's desk and sit on it, looking over his shoulder as he wrote, can now punch into any reporter's screen and see how the story is coming along; the reporters, who sometimes feel that they are being spied on and always know that they *can* be spied on without their knowledge, are less enthusiastic about this expansion of journalism's management information system).

The next step, advertised frequently for the better part of a decade, is pagination on the computer. This is a different order of technical problem, for the systems that produce strips like galley proofs to be laid in for photographing are very similar to standard-issue word processing, while making pages takes a lot of software and computer space—something like $250,000 worth in most cases. With laser printers at the other end, pages can be made ready for photographing in a matter of seconds—or stored until wanted (the pagination system *The Wall Street Journal* began to use in 1985 involves twenty-six 300-megabyte disk drives, permitting the operators to jigger new pages to handle changing news, or modify pages according to regional ad sales, at the touch of a button). Four companies are fighting for priority in the pagination business: Harris, Atex (a New England subsidiary of Kodak), System Integrators, Inc. (California proprietors of a text composition system that has replaced Harris as the industry leader; the terminal is named Coyote after the animals that sacrificed their skins to the coat worn by the company's flamboyant designer-salesman-CEO James Lennane), and Information International, Inc. (which did the *Wall Street Journal* system and was the pioneer in the field, supplying pagination equipment to the Pasadena *Call-News* as early as 1981). One of the great achievements of Apple Computer is the new MacIntosh, which does $8^{1}/2 \times 11$ pagination on the memory board of a PC. Several newspapers have been seeking ways to modify this system for much larger-scale use.

Systems Integrators, in an industrial park outside Sacramento, is very much one man's creation. Lennane left IBM in 1966 with ideas for the enhancement of the IBM 1130, which had been selling to newspapers. It was seven years before he had his own product, the System 22, a newspaper front-end system to handle editorial and classified ad copy, which he sold to the San Francisco *Chronicle* and the *Examiner* (who share a mainframe, with rigid separation of access codes so that neither can take out the other's material) and then to the Los Angeles *Herald-Examiner*. In 1979, Lennane ran into a small company called Tandem, which made a "fault-tolerant" or "nonstop" computer with architecture that duplicated processes so that if one part of the system went out another would fill in. Lennane bet his company on Tandem, and won.

The Los Angeles *Times* had gone to Data General for a project that failed, but had fallen in love with a unique keyboard design. Lennane agreed to build his System 55 Coyote around the L.A. *Times* keyboard, and received an initial order for 450 highly intelligent terminals (each, indeed, a PC), now expanded to 700 units (thirty-two of them in Washington, connected by the telephone company's umbilical cord), the largest editorial system in the world. These terminals do little things like automatically reorder the ranking of players in the batting averages as the information arrives. In its end-1985 annual report, SII claimed that three-quarters of all the money spent on large newspaper systems that year had gone for SII systems. Among the foreign purchasers are Reuters ($5.5 million for its British news-gathering operation) and the *Financial Times,* which described SII rather tearfully as "noted for an almost defiant unwillingness to discount its prices."[4]

SII's pagination system, offered in 1986 for the first time, uses a flat-panel plasma display screen instead of the traditional CRT tube, and offers such a mass of memory that entire pages can be blasted in at the push of a button. Sometime in 1987, SII expects to couple these systems with a HAL (shades of *2001)* "laser image setter" being developed by a West German manufacturer, and the electronic path from reporter to press, including the insertion of photos and other art, will be complete. "Ironically," Ithiel de Sola Pool wrote, "the first paperless offices in the world, if there are any, may be in newspapers."[5]

The technical problems III had to manage in paginating *The Wall Street Journal* are of course easier than those that have to be faced down for most papers, because the *Journal* uses no color (and no photographs except—a big except—in advertising). The New York *Times* would be almost as well placed, but the cost of paying people to lay in strips and pictures and headlines for photographic plates turns out to be lower in New York than elsewhere because of the vast oversupply of personnel who have to be paid whether there is work for them or not following the union contracts that permitted the elimination of typesetting. The only place where the *Times* is moving toward computerized pagination is in the classified ad sections, where employment advertising is en route to no-hands automation. The agency placing the ad has its own PC with modem linked to the *Times* and simply types in its ads, in whatever format it chooses, and the *Times* computers automatically slot the ad on a page and send the agency its bill. Quite apart from labor cost savings, pagination on the computer yields benefits in flexibility and control that editors find irresistible.

And there is another market for such equipment, of course, in the advertising agencies. Here the creative types and the account executives both look forward to the day when they can see the result of layout changes without pinning a lot of drawings on the corkboards, and when an ad will be sent out through the satellite this afternoon, with whatever news values may be wanted, to be printed in the newspaper tomorrow. To deal with the agencies placing such advertising, the papers will have to be equipped to receive it. Peter Romano, director of technical services for the American Newspaper Publishers Association, told a meeting in fall 1985 that "by 1990, full-page pagination will be in use in virtually every newspaper with a circulation of over 50,000."[6]

The Wall Street Journal has gone the step beyond pagination, carving a

straight path from the picture on the screen to a laser-cut plate for the press
—absolutely no hands, and only microseconds of time, between the one
stage and the other. Costs here are higher, and the process is problematic,
because making plates for printing without a photo process requires com-
puter-controlled lasers that work more steadily than lasers like to work. At
this writing in early 1986, the *Journal* has installed the process in only two of
its seventeen plants. Gannett tried it in Utica, New York, a few years ago,
but never committed the whole paper to laser-etched plates and did not
expand the experiment to other papers. By mid-1986, however, one of the
most admired of the nation's newspapers—*The Record* of Bergen County,
New Jersey, submerged in the national consciousness, but not in the sensi-
bility of its colleagues, by its metropolitan neighbors in New York—was
printing on computer-generated plates. And the New York *Daily News* has
purchased equipment to make laser plates in its satellite plants around the
city on the receipt of appropriate signals from the home office. The *Journal*
has strong incentives to move, for the new system when fully operational
will allow it to expand its daily editions to 80 pages a day while delaying
deadlines long enough to make the paper fully competitive even on the
West Coast.

What technology has done that matters most to newspaper consumers
is the opportunities it has offered to the makers of the very large and of the
much smaller. Though *The Wall Street Journal* got the two-coast newspaper
started before there were satellite communications, simultaneous distribution of plate material to seventeen plants around the country—and a nationwide circulation of more than two million receiving their paper the same
morning—would have been very difficult without the transponder. Similarly, the satellite and first-class facsimile transmission by digital code made
possible the national edition of the New York *Times* (a two-section version
of what is now a four-section paper, essentially the front part of the paper
plus business, sports and entertainment; significantly, the *Times* distributes
its full-size "regional" edition out into Pittsburgh and up to Maine). And
USA Today is at bottom nothing more than a clever use of Gannett's high-
quality production facilities (to a much lesser degree, its much less costly
reporting facilities) in fourscore American communities, easily linked
through the satellite channel. Meanwhile, computer controls and automated
folding machinery have made it much easier for the metropolitan papers to
zone their circulation and deliver special smaller or larger papers to the
suburbs where the population growth (and especially the income growth)
has been magnetic for advertisers.

In the end, it is not too much to say that technology has saved the
newspapers. Fifteen years ago, I wrote a proposal to the Twentieth Century
Fund for a study aimed at convincing the FCC that the rule prohibiting
newspapers from owning television stations in their own markets was short-
sighted. From the point of view of pure economics, the media for advertis-

ing were pretty much interchangeable. About 1970, the supermarkets and the department stores discovered that television could be used for price advertising. Cigarettes were banned in 1971, opening commercial slots for advertising previously committed to print. The economics of the automobile industry were changing and would soon eliminate the announcement campaign for new models which was the sustenance of the newspapers in the early fall. Two-way cable looked like an imminent danger to the classified sections.

I argued that there was in effect a kind of merchandising fund, like the wages fund of nineteenth-century theory, and as broadcast and point-of-sale became more effective and more flexible in their pricing, as direct merchandisers perfected their use of broadcasting and the mails, marginal moneys would keep leaking away from the newspapers. If you thought newspapers were important to the cohesion of an urban society, as I do (because they are the only way expressions of diversity go routinely to the entire community), then you should make it a goal of public policy to promote the retention of these revenues in the organization that published the newspaper. Not entirely facetiously, I suggested that we might come out with a recommendation turning the FCC rule on its head, requiring that people who had a TV franchise should spend some of those monopoly rents absorbing the losses of a newspaper.

I was not entirely wrong. Two-way cable bombed, but everything else came true. From 1970 to 1985, the newspapers' share of the advertising pot dropped from more than a third to just over a quarter. But I had failed to account for the immense savings that would result from reductions in manning, or the extent to which the shrinkage of the number of directly competing papers would allow the survivors to raise their advertising rates. The importance of the technological change can be seen by comparing the publishing industry in France and England, where the unions virtually prohibited the introduction of computerized composition until 1986, with that in the United States. In 1985, all the papers in France lost money, as did all the better papers in England (some of the girlie papers, like Rupert Murdoch's *Sun,* were profitable), although both French and English consumer expenditure has risen more rapidly than American in the last fifteen years and television commands a lower share of total advertising revenues. But the 1980s have been hog heaven for the owners of American newspapers, because the computer permitted them, at long last, to get their costs under control.

By his own account, Harold Evans when editor of *The Times* of London gave Murdoch, who had just bought the paper, a short lesson in why the British market was so much less profitable. In Britain, he said, physically producing a broadsheet paper like *The Times* or the *Daily Telegraph,* over and above the cost of raw materials and news, cost about 30 percent of revenues; in the United States, such costs ran only 20 percent of receipts.

(Indeed, a visit to a British newspaper plant has been like a trip to a museum. I was privileged to go downstairs at the *Financial Times* in late 1986 and watch several hundred linotypes push out hot lead. Men in printers' caps picked individual headline letters from fonts and inserted them on a stone, and engravers prepared plates without the intervention of a camera— a great paper produced precisely as I had watched Art Hopkins produce the Harvard *Crimson* more than forty years before.) So Murdoch went and built his new plant in Wapping, on the Thames two miles from Fleet Street, arranged to have the electricians rather than the printers man it on the grounds that the whole process was now electronic, and early in 1986 provoked a strike that under British law permitted him to fire all his unionized printers. Now presumably he will make money on his British dailies, too.

4

Radio news mostly had its revolution in the 1950s, when the cheap audio cassette made possible the storage and easy retrieval of telephoned and syndicated reports. All-news radio began not long thereafter, with Gordon McLendon broadcasting a rip-and-read show from Tijuana, then taking the same format to Chicago. That format is still with us, the Westinghouse stations having decided that people want to hear one person reading the news, not a lot of chitchat between anchors. The big change recently has been the introduction of intelligent video display terminals. The person identified as "at the editor's desk" has always been responsible for laying out the fifteen- or twenty- or thirty-minute "segments" for the writers, combining the schedule of events to be covered live by the station's handful of outside reporters and the material arriving through the services (and, sometimes, the television networks, all four of which—including CNN—are displayed without sound on the wall the editor faces). Until recently, the editor started by flipping through the paper coming out of the teletype machines, wrapping it up with whatever cassette material on this subject had come in from the radio news services, and passing it on to a writer with instructions to do seventy seconds' worth. Now all the printed material comes up on half the screen, and the writer makes a script on the other half. Told the name of the anchor who will read this script, the computer, knowing all, will count the anchor's words according to how fast the anchor speaks and compare the timing with the schedule sheet. Then the anchor reads off the computer rather than a sheet of paper, and the screen alerts him if he gets ahead or behind.

Television news, of course, has been the beneficiary of a series of technological revolutions, from the tape recorder to the tape editor to the translator between European 50-cycle, 65-line systems and American 60-cycle, 55-line systems, the minicam that made possible ENG (Electronic News

Gathering), the satellite with C-band transponders and now the satellite with Ku-band transponders. It will soon be impossible for people to realize what a miracle each of these creations was to those who knew the medium before God wrought it. Television news was basically a film medium in its early days, and even after tape "hard" enough to hold the information in a television system had been developed there was no substitute for film because editing videotape was a matter of many minutes per splice. The notion that a CNN could tie into Eurovision and pick up material from the European TV companies ad-lib was just silly as recently as the mid-1970s: there was only one machine in the world that could make that conversion, and it occupied a large room in London and didn't always work. No one could have imagined that the French PTT would ever permit U.S. news bureaus to own and operate their own dishes for satellite communication of pictures, as they have. The only television cameras available into the 1970s could be operated only by strong men whose genetic heritage was free of people who'd ever suffered a hernia. AT&T had never believed that synchronous satellites could be made to work, and placed its bets on the "over the horizon" Telstar that spun around the earth, remaining in sight of the two sides of the Atlantic for perhaps six hours a day.

Domestically, the C-band satellite system was a way to send news from fixed points, not a way to extend coverage. C-band is the part of the radio frequency spectrum that lies between four and six billion cycles per second. Each cycle is thus two to three inches long, crest to crest, and given the diffusion of the beam from the transponder all those miles away, a fairly large dish is needed to be sure that the signal will be caught without too much loss. Moreover, this frequency band is also used for terrestrial microwave, and the placement of a ground-to-satellite link may interfere with microwave transmission. Before the FCC will approve the opening of a new C-band link, then, it must analyze the pattern of radio waves at the site. This may take days or it may take weeks. In any event, it takes too long for C-band to be used as a way to cover a breaking story that was not tipped to the press in advance. And on those terms it isn't worth the hassle to use satellite transmission even when the event is something a network has known for some time it will be covering. The 1984 primaries, for example, and *Monday Night Football* into 1986, were still covered by tying the equipment trucks into the phone lines.

Meanwhile, NBC had grown increasingly disenchanted with its phone bills, and especially with projections of how they were likely to rise (and how service was likely to decline) after the government disassembled AT&T. The network in 1984 was paying $87 a month per mile of coaxial cable to link its affiliates with New York and Burbank, which meant more than a million dollars a month at 12,000 miles—plus 87¢ per minute per mile for occasional use; the total bill for distribution in 1984 ran almost $30 million, and AT&T was proposing a 43 percent increase in 1985. Working with RCA, NBC's engineers had decided that over time the network would spend less for more (including more capacity, to move more than one signal at a time) by developing its own satellite distribution net, renting one or more—in the end, RCA took four, at a price of about $15 million a year— of the rapidly growing number of transponders in the sky. Moreover, they decided that these transponders could work in the 12–14 "gigahertz" or "Ku" band, where the cycles were only about one inch long, crest to crest.

For years, theory had held that radio waves that short could not be counted on to make it through the atmosphere during heavy storms, because they would be deflected or even absorbed by raindrops. AT&T explained the theory to NBC when the network solicited a bid from the telephone company for the construction of a Ku-band distribution system. "They had done monstrous studies of rain attenuation effects on telephone signals," said Mike Sherlock, executive v.p. for operations and technical services, "and they didn't see any need to do anything new on video signals. We'd had it proven to us by lab people that as you increase power in the transponder, and the size of the dish on the satellite, you can contradict the effects of rain, especially as you can distribute the strength of the signal, its footprint on the country, according to weather bureau information." Comsat had been moving along the same lines as the RCA and NBC engineers, especially in its joint-venture Satellite Business Systems project with IBM, jumped for the chance, and guaranteed the network "four nines"—99.99 percent reliability. Once again, Harris Corp. was on the ground floor— almost automatically so this time, having been prime contractor to NASA and to the military for such equipment—with a contract to design and manufacture the ground stations and the Skypath control machinery for the network's 200-odd affiliates.

"The most difficult part of this job," said Harris' Joe Boyd, "is finding out what the customer needs. Technology is not a problem. A customer like NBC—their system just evolved. They don't understand their own system, they've never written it down. One of the first things we saw is that their collecting and distributing systems both involved a lot of switching, and you could use those switches for various purposes." With the radio waves less than an inch in length, a receiving dish for Ku-band except in the rainiest parts of the Southeast had to be only about three feet or so in diameter. To assure four-nines reliability, each station also needed an uplink to tell the satellite and Skypath control whenever anything went wrong. ("In its first message," says Harris project manager Dan Ozley, "the computer says, 'I have a problem and it will take me so many microseconds to tell you about it.' The second message describes and diagnoses the problem. It's so Buck Rogersy it scares you.") And you could put uplinks anywhere, because there was no terrestrial communication in that frequency band.

Part of NBC's order to Harris was for six trucks that could be sent around the country, especially for football games, unfurl their little dish, and establish their own connection to the satellite without the intervention of telephone company wiring. C-band trucks were commonplace, but mounting the big dishes was a problem, and there remained always the need to get an FCC license for carrier microwave at the location. AT&T, ABC and CBS all warned NBC that uplink signals from a Ku-band system would suffer such severe attenuation in a rainstorm that the truck would be useless, but Harris, which had been making these "military mounts" for the Army for some years, gave the network its assurances, and was, of course, right. (The amplifiers on the Harris trucks are equipped to give the signal an extra 3db jolt if a really severe rainstorm strikes.) Harris then went to NBC with the suggestion that the network distribution job and the sports coverage, which was all NBC had in mind, was only part of what the satellite and the ground stations could do for them. This thing could also help you cover the news. Not the least of Reuven Frank's irritations in his last years as president of NBC News was the discovery that this technological planning had been going on and nobody had told him. Eventually, he screamed loud enough to get news vice president Tom Pettit on the committee.

Pettit asked for thirty permanent uplinks from affiliated stations around the country, plus another hundred locations where the power and cables would be in place to plug in a transmitter in less than two hours, permitting origination of news stories in widely scattered places; management eventually offered fourteen, to be expanded in the future. What the news division really wanted, however, was something that could be put in six suitcases and loaded onto a Lear jet, landed at an airport anywhere in the country, set up beside the runway and aimed at the bird. "Now," said Robert Muller, technical v.p. of NBC News, "the limiting factor in getting a story is, how can I get it out of there? You have to find a way to get the tape to a feed point. The problem gets worse every year, because the whole infrastructure of the phone company is changing. The state regulators won't allow the local companies to install a permanent loop and add the capital cost into the rate base in places where you need only an occasional feed. Take West Point: there's a couple of football games a year. The New York State Public Utilities Commission says telco has to expense those lines and charge us full cost. The classic example was the 1976 political convention at Madison Square Garden. The telephone company installed facilities, then had to rip them out—and install again four years later, at horrendous cost."

Management did eventually give NBC News more than twenty uplinks (though not the Lear jet), but the trucks remained committed to sports. And, on Sundays in summer 1984, to a monstrous stupidity called *Summer Sunday*, which opened with Andrea Mitchell and Linda Ellerbee, live from the Mall in Washington on a summer afternoon. "Twenty yards or so behind us was a rope," Linda Ellerbee later recalled, "and behind the rope were people. . . . What could be more real than talking to a camera while people behind you wave to Mom, make faces and shoot you the finger?"[7]

The catalogue of stupidities associated with that show, splendidly described by Ellerbee in her book, tells more than any amount of exposition and argument of why there is no criterion of public interest that can be applied to the argument that the television news division budgets should not be cut.

Meanwhile, someone else has got there first with Ku-band coverage of the news. The winner turns out to be Hubbard Broadcasting, an idiosyncratic right-wing chain based in Minneapolis, which under the leadership of Stanley Hubbard *père* had so little interest in news that its Tampa/St. Petersburg television station, which I visited while writing *About Television,* had neither news show nor news staff. ("Why does everybody feel you've got to have news shows?" said its program director, Loren Mathre, who had been sent down from Minneapolis to run WTOG in Tampa. "It's because of what you promised when you got the license. We are in a market with two stations doing a substantial, good job on news. What's the reason for us to copy? We didn't promise. We're an unaffiliated UHF. We just promised to try to stay alive.")

But Stanley Hubbard *fils* is made of different stuff. Absorbing start-up costs estimated at $10 million, he has rented ten channels on an SBS satellite and on the RCA satellite NBC uses, and has put together a consortium of thirty-six television stations (as of mid-1986) that have bought Ku-band transmitter trucks built by a Hubbard subsidiary and have pledged to feed each other stories from around the country. Hubbard's ten channels permit as many as six simultaneous feeds through the Minneapolis control center, as against the maximum of three for NBC, which permits Hubbard to offer Conus (for "Continental U.S.," the internationally assigned service mark for transmissions within the borders of this country) as an interlink for statewide or regional networks. The cost to stations of participating in these networks is trivial, because RCA to increase transponder use gave any station that asked for it a free receiving dish—and Hubbard then offered to convert that to a sending-and-receiving unit for a single payment of $100,000 or a monthly lease of $1,738 for five years.

There are lots of stories, airplane crashes and hurricanes and forest fires, that the Conus stations as a group now cover faster and better than the networks can. During Hurricane Danny in 1985, three Gulf Coast television stations did live remotes from affected communities that were fed to all the member stations in the group, and the telecast included such spectacular innovations as direct conversation between the reporter getting beaten up by the winds and the director of the National Hurricane Center, appearing together on a split screen. (It should be noted in passing that successful operations through a Gulf Coast hurricane put a final kibosh on the argument that Ku-band signals couldn't get through the raindrops. In early 1987, AT&T itself launched a new Ku-band service.) And it's Hubbard that developed the Video Fly Pac that NBC News asked for and didn't get: seven cases, each weighing seventy pounds, that can be checked as baggage on a commercial flight or carried in a station wagon or loaded onto a Lear Jet, and unpacked by two people, complete with 2.5-kilowatt generator, 275-watt amplifier, cameras, tapes, computer and dish.

Access to feeds from the Conus transponders, said James Coppersmith of WCVB in Boston (not a Hubbard affiliate otherwise), "gives us a tremendous advantage over the competition when things happen. It may be the biggest break-through in news gathering in twenty years." It is through a Conus truck permanently parked outside the White House that Reagan's publicity office offers round-the-clock coverage of news conferences, bill signings, receptions of foreign dignitaries and other such events. "It means that instead of having four or five editors deciding what gets out to the country," said communications director Pat Buchanan, "you've got 900."[8] In 1985, the FCC ruled that television signals are not subject to the restrictive rules of Intelsat, and to the extent that other nations agree, foreign bureaus will be able to open direct satellite links without going through the local telephone companies. Stanley Hubbard himself says gleefully that "the days of network domination of news are over. The day that we got into the satellite news service, that was the end."[9] It may be so.

Part Seven

CONCLUSION

16

Even Paranoids May Have Real Enemies

In the issue of the *Financial Times* on November 13, 1985, we published an article concerning the suspension by Lloyd's of Mr. Colin Edward Davies, a former director of the WMD underwriting agency and former underwriter for Syndicate 174/175. The article stated that Mr. Davies had been found guilty of dishonestly misappropriating syndicate funds.

We are happy to confirm that the disciplinary committee of Lloyd's decision did not include any finding of dishonesty against Mr. Davies and we regret the error in our previous report.

> —"Mr. Colin Davies," *Financial Times,*
> February 14, 1986, p. 9

A famous politician once remarked, on glancing through a copy of *Jo's Boys* by Louisa M. Alcott, that he would rather have written "Three Men in a Boat" than to have dug the Suez Canal. As matter of fact, he never did either, and wasn't quite as famous a politician as I have tried to make out. But he knew what he meant by Success.

> —Robert Benchley, 1931

Abe Rosenthal at the New York *Times* and Ben Bradlee at the Washington *Post* have built their reputations on spotlighting problems—real or imagined; not solutions.

My good friend Tom Brokaw at NBC, despite his South Dakota upbringing; Dan Rather at CBS, despite his Texas background; Peter Jennings at ABC, despite his general sensitivity . . . all leave their viewers more downbeat when they say goodnight to them.

Even Iowa's own lovable Steve Bell on the ABC morning news most often starts our days with alarm after the alarm clock goes off.

Those are the facts about the Eastern media.

> —Al Neuharth, chairman of Gannett Co.,
> introducing Iowa governor Terry Branstad
> at a New York City luncheon
> to introduce a "Discover Iowa" campaign[1]

1

In mid-1985, *The Wall Street Journal* ran an A-head by Bill Richards about Napoleon, North Dakota, noting that "in this age of media conglomerates and high-tech communication, hardly anyone considers the cafe coffee table a news medium, but it is still the primary source of information for many of the nation's 50 million rural residents. Politicians, newspaper reporters, county bureaucrats and travelers through small-town America know that the table at the local cafe is usually the best place to deliver and receive local news. . . . It is usually up front (the better to wave at passers-by), often populated by local movers and shakers, and generally abuzz with horseplay and gossip from 6 A.M. onwards through the morning. 'The smaller the town, the more prominent the table,' says Patrick Smith, a sociologist at North Dakota State University."

Jerome Schwartzenberger, the editor and publisher of the local weekly, called the Napoleon *Homestead,* comes in every morning at about 9:30, Richards continued, and picks up what people remember from earlier conversations, plus what's being said by the midmorning denizens, who tend to be women and the local ministers. " 'You mostly get gossip around the table,' Mr. Schwartzenberger says. 'But in a small town like this, a lot of gossip turns out to be true.' "[2] I myself once had an offer from Lou Dickerson, Otis Dickerson's wife and postmistress at Shelter Island, New York, a woman of mordant wit and sound judgment, to hide me under the counter at the post office for a couple of weeks. The aim here was to help create a piece of fiction, not a news story ("You'd have a novel," Lou said, "would make *Peyton Place* look like *Little Women"),* but the principle was the same. In a small town, or a tribal village, people tend to have a sense of what's going on around them.

And that, of course, is what people want from news: some sense of what's going on around them. In the local context, they can make their own rank order of importance of what they hear (almost all communication at the Table, Richards reported, was by way of wisecracking, except for information about grain prices, which was taken very seriously). When you get beyond the small town, the news consumer needs help in establishing this rank order, and because everybody looks at the world from his own particular place the "media" through which the news is communicated cannot give this help equally well to everyone.

Meanwhile, the subject of the story sees the world from a unique position, and feels bitterly that "they never get it right." Frank Mankiewicz, who ran National Public Radio and left in a flap over cost overruns and revenue shortfalls, told *Time* a few months later that "sooner or later everybody will know the dirty little secret of American journalism, that the reports are wrong. Because sooner or later everybody will have been involved in something that is reported. Whenever you see a news story you were part of, it is always wrong."[3] People who are fighting each other passionately will agree that the story reporting on their fight was wrong. And of course it was. The more you understand the nuance, the more likely you are to know the imperfection of the news.

"Why do they hate us?" Robert MacNeil asked as a running question in his lecture launching the new Gannett Center for Media Studies at the Columbia School of Journalism. He had various suggestions: "We may have been wearing the First Amendment too brazenly, not as a shield but a challenge. . . . Unless our profession redefines fairness and its importance to us, others will increasingly try to define it for us—and perhaps succeed. . . . A reporter or a camera crew acts as though their presence, their action in covering a story, is more important than the event they are covering. . . . We have the media sounding vehement, belligerent, barking at President Reagan, who responds by grinning ruefully. Who is going to win that kind of contest?"[4] A better answer, I suspect, is simpler and a little boring: they hate us because we are outsiders. We don't want to be loved (someone once observed that people who want to be loved don't become reporters, they become ski instructors). We don't understand what it looks like from inside. Or if we do understand, which is worse, we don't care.

Mark Twain wrote a piece in the 1860s about a Washington correspondent for a San Francisco paper, name of Riley, who was asked by his landlady to write an epitaph for a neighbor who had burned to death in an accident with her stove the night before: " 'Not just frizzled up a bit, but literally roasted to a crisp!' . . . 'Put it, *Well done,* good and faithful servant," ' said Riley, and never smiled."[5] One does get jaded, then bored, eventually irritated, with other people's tragedies. The news at the Table in Napoleon, North Dakota, is more satisfying, because its purveyors are insiders, not professionals. (Judy Bachrach has argued, in a funny and nasty piece about Phyllis George while she was trying to anchor the *CBS Morning News,* that "journalism, much like prostitution, is a career in which just one foray makes a professional."[6] But this is not true: in both instances, one becomes a professional only through intent.) For all the wisecracking, the amateurs at the Table do care.

Rage at the press has a grand history, and the more free the press, the more splendid the rage. John Tebbel and Sarah Miles Watts take most of the 550 pages of their book *The Press and the Presidency* to retail the fury of Presidents. The Gannett chain at regular intervals likes to advertise Thomas Jefferson's letter of 1787, with the comment that "were it left to me to decide whether we should have a government without newspapers or newspapers without a government, I should not hesitate to prefer the latter." But Jefferson's own formulation of the First Amendment was chillingly inadequate: "The people shall not be deprived or abridged of their right to speak or write or otherwise to publish anything but false facts affecting injuriously the life, liberty, property or reputation of others or affecting the peace of the confederacy with foreign nations."[7] On another occasion, Jefferson wrote that the only truth one could rely upon in the newspapers was the advertising. When James Monroe was President, Jefferson wrote to him that "from forty years' experience of the wretched guess-work of the newspapers of what is not done in open daylight, and of their falsehood even as to that, I rarely think them worth reading, and almost never worth notice."[8] Richard Nixon himself could not have said it plainer.

Andrew Jackson's Postmaster General specifically permitted the post office at Charleston, South Carolina, to refuse delivery of William Lloyd Garrison's *The Liberator* (interestingly, it was John Calhoun who rose in wrath in the Senate to denounce the action as unconstitutional). Ulysses Grant said of James Gordon Bennett of the *Herald* that he was "ever ready to trade upon the misfortunes of his adopted country. He cares not how terrible a time it is for the country, if it is only a good time for newspapers. He made his paper famous by making it infamous. It mattered nothing to him who was harmed, so that he made money."[9] Theodore Roosevelt while President had his Attorney General secure an indictment of Pulitzer's New York *World* for criminal libel. "It is a high national duty," Roosevelt said, "to bring to justice this vilifier of the American people, this man who wantonly and wickedly seeks to blacken the character and reputation of private citizens and to convict the Government of his own country in the eyes of the civilized world of wrong-doing of the basest and foulest kind."[10] In revenge for a (false) story in the Boston *Herald* about his children tormenting a turkey sent to the White House for the presidential Thanksgiving feast, Roosevelt ordered the weather bureau not to supply the forecasts to that paper.[11] Four years after he left office, when he was again running for the presidency, Roosevelt sued a weekly paper in Iron Ore, Michigan, for libeling him with a statement that "he drinks to excess, lies and curses." He tried his own case before a judge, won, and was awarded 6¢ in damages.[12] Roosevelt's reputation, the judge said, was too substantial to be harmed by such a story.

Of course people try to use news gatherers for their own purposes. Why else would anyone spend the money to prepare and mail press releases, or take his time answering questions for a reporter? If they succeed, they are contemptuous because they have manipulated the press, and if they fail, they are angry (even a partial success leaves a residue of irritation). Those who find the news gatherers used against them are, inevitably, furious. When *The Wall Street Journal* ran stories indicating sympathy with the articles in the Washington *Post* alleging impropriety in the dealings between the Mobil Corporation and the son of its chief executive, p.r. vice president Herbert Schmertz stopped sending the *Journal* his press releases and inviting its reporters to his press conferences. Because those who live by this sword also occasionally die by it, and because everybody remembers what was done to him much more clearly than he remembers what was done for him, the news sources are always wary of their contacts. And if the news gatherers are any good at all, they will necessarily be wary of their sources.

But what can you do when it's the Amal and they hold thirty-nine hostages on a TWA plane—and only they can give the press and the cameras access to the story? It was neither necessary nor wise for the networks to send to Beirut forty (ABC), twenty-five (NBC, but that number included Tom Brokaw hisself) or even twenty (CBS) staffers, clearly foolish for David Hartman of ABC's *Good Morning America* to ask Nabih Berri live on the air whether he had any words for President Reagan, and journalistically improper for ABC to air filmed interviews with the hostages without informing its audience that the Amal had edited and supplied the videotape. No doubt terrorist incidents are staged primarily for the publicity—but so are the summit meetings of "the leaders of the free world." What is new and noteworthy about hostage taking since the Iranian seizure is that the television networks with their philosophy of "moments" have allowed the families of the captives to hold their own government hostage to their grief. Now that President Reagan has personally experienced the harm that can be done when compassion for prisoners and their relatives dicates government policy, this problem will probably take care of itself by normal progression. With budgets being cut, someone at one of the news divisions will realize that it's unnecessarily expensive to send union camera crews to interview the real families of hostages. The daytime department has actors and actresses under contract for the soaps who can do this sort of thing. As the laugh track superseded the studio audience for sitcoms, professionals will replace the real hostage families. One network will try it out first, of course, but as its "docu-moments" begin to draw the best ratings (because, after all, the pros time their responses better), the other networks will follow, and then the public will lose interest. But this may take some time.

In the 1970s, news executives (far more often than reporters) explained the overadvertised hostility of the public with the metaphor of killing the messenger who brought the bad news. And there has certainly never been a shortage of public figures calling upon the press to be more positive. My own favorite example is from Calvin Coolidge, who spoke at the dedication of the National Press Club building in Washington. "Constantly to portray the failures and the delinquents is grossly to mislead the public. It breeds an unwarranted spirit of cynicism. Life is made up of the successful and the worthy. In any candid representation of current conditions they have the first claim to attention. In the effort of the press to destroy vice, it ought not to neglect virtue."[13] But in fact the newspapers and the news broadcasts are full of press handouts that are highly supportive of the virtue of those in whose cause they are issued. (Coolidge himself was the black-belt master of the handout: on August 2, 1927, the fourth anniversary of his presidency, he summoned the White House press corps to a math classroom in a high school in Rapid City, South Dakota, where he had gone on a fishing vacation, and personally delivered to them, one by one, 2-by-9-inch pieces of paper which he himself had cut to size with his own scissors. On each slip was typed ten words: "I do not choose to run for President in 1928." Mr. Coolidge took no questions.) And the surest way to get in the papers is to throw a collie through a hole in the ice and go rescue it. The news loves a hero.

Reporting gets in trouble when people deliberately lie. The damage is done directly when it's Janet Cooke of the Washington *Post* inventing an eight-year-old heroin addict (though far more guilt for the reaction to that not very opaque fiction rests with the management that recommended it for a prize and the Pulitzer committee that awarded one: anyone who knew about urban schools or parents' associations or school boards, which should not be mysteries to the editors of metropolitan papers, should also have known that the legend of the drug pusher in the schoolyard is the most common fairy tale of the slums, as soldiers bayoneting babies is the most common fairy tale of war). Less immediate harm occurs when it's some governmental or private promoter building his importance and the budgets of his organization by dishonestly overestimating the number of missing or sexually abused children, the perils of toluene in the water supply or the significance of illegal immigration, all of which can be personalized by a news operation thirsting for human interest (though here again the greatest blame adheres to the supervisors of the news operations and the collaborating anchors, who are quite willing to run the risks of false witness and inconsequence if that's the price of offering "moments"). But in some ways the worst harm is done when the lies are spoken by a military briefing machine in Vietnam or a President Nixon, because then the news gatherers are compelled to direct confrontation and the news consumers begin to feel itchy about "the arrogance of the media."

In December 1983, *Time* ran a cover story on public disapproval of the news purveyors, noting that "growing numbers of news executives recognize a real problem in the public discontent with the press, especially the perception that journalists are arrogant."[14] The piece was hailed in the "publisher's letter" that leads the table of contents with a comment that *Time*, "of course, is no less fallible than its peers. It is keenly aware that the standards and precepts that are applied to other elements of the press are equally applicable to this magazine." But the piece, though noting the libel suits against CBS by General Westmoreland and against the Washington *Post* by William Tavoulareas of Mobil Oil, somehow failed to mention the suit against *Time* itself by Ariel Sharon. Research must have been asleep at the switch. (Thomas Griffith, *Time*'s admirable media critic, formerly a senior editor of the magazine, suggested in his book *How True* that people especially resent the "news announcer on a local television channel who with resonant voice and unearned air of knowledgeability reads what he had no part in gathering.'') Arrogance is in the eye of the beholder. And, of course, these things don't change much. Michael Robinson of George Washington University examined polls on the accuracy and fairness of "the media" from 1933, 1938 and 1985, and found no change over the years in the proportion who thought they were getting inaccurate (one-third) and occasionally unfair (two-thirds) news reports.[15]

Among the most instructive episodes of the 1980s was the coverage of the space shuttle in the weeks surrounding the *Challenger* disaster. For the better part of January, news reports, especially on television, had been twitting NASA about its inability to hold to its launch schedule; there were even comments about "the little shuttle that couldn't." These were reaching a crescendo just before January 28, which was the day the President was to make his State of the Union address. Though nobody has been able to prove it—every Washington bureau has tried, hard, and Presidential Commission chairman William Rogers says he tried, too, though he didn't go so far as to ask the White House—that speech doubtless contained at least references to and very possibly a gap for live pictures of the teacher the White House publicity machine had put in the capsule to be shot into space. It's impossible to know what role if any publicity pressure played in persuading those in charge of the launch that they had to go on January 28 despite word that the engineers in charge of examining the pigeon entrails had strongly advised against it. Given NASA's immense investments in and faith in publicity, one finds it hard to believe that the stories had no influence at all.

Then there was the "major malfunction," as NASA's play-by-play announcer called it, and seven deaths. And the news-gathering machinery rolled into action. Leslie Gelb of the New York *Times* complained about it in the April 1986 issue of *Washington Journalism Review*. He compared the press and television attention commanded by the *Challenger* disaster to the nine days' wonder of the crash in Newfoundland that had killed 248 American servicemen six weeks before: "Our media and government did not investigate the cause of that tragedy with anything like the attention and diligence they devoted to the *Challenger*. By no account did our Air Force take anywhere near the pains to investigate the safety standards of the air transport companies hired to fly these heroes that NASA did to assure the safety of those on board the *Challenger*. . . . Could it simply be that we in the media and government lost all sense of proportion? Now, in a curious way, this loss of balance continues with the stories about what went wrong, what caused the explosion. Note that the question is often put in terms of what, not who. In the face of such an event, everyone seems determined to keep things impersonal."[16]

In fairness, Gelb pulled himself back from the brink: "It would be in the finest tradition of journalism," he added rather clumsily toward the end of his piece, "if responsibility for the tragedy were clearly fixed, if it can be." But the noises that had offended him were in fact the wheels grinding to achieve that result. For the first two days after the disaster, the news coverage remained in NASA's pocket. NASA employees *and former employees,* current and past executives and employees of companies that did business with the agency, were instructed not to talk to the press. Scattered around the periphery of the launch site on restricted government property were sixty unmanned still cameras owned by the wire services, *Time* and the New York *Times,* placed by prearrangement with NASA. After the accident, the agency refused to permit the owners to gather their film, insisting that NASA itself must open the cameras and develop and print the film, allegedly to make sure its review board would see the pictures. UPI's picture editor Ted Majeski told *Editor & Publisher*'s George Garneau that "NASA employees used the word 'confiscate.'"

Only the *Times* refused to go along, and eventually the paper was permitted to repossess its film, unprocessed. AP and UPI permitted NASA to take the film and give the services copies of the photos. Walter Mears of AP sent a letter of protest to William Graham, acting administrator of NASA, denouncing the seizure of the film as "certainly improper, probably illegal and, ironically, counterproductive." (Everybody stressed the clearly irrelevant point—but it didn't seem irrelevant then—that the news groups would have processed the film faster. NASA may not, in fact, have given back all the shots: new pictures kept surfacing mysteriously from within the agency for the next five months, with nobody proclaiming a provenance.) Several spokesmen for various news groups expressed discomfort with the thought that they might be seen as impeding the inquiry. Even among those paragons of cynicism, the editors, there was at first considerable sympathy for NASA.[17] The fact that the agency had nothing to say for the first six hours was charitably credited to shock. No one objected to the idea that NASA itself would investigate the causes of "the accident" and would be virtually the sole source of information for the Presidential Commission appointed to inquire.

Then an obscure reporter for an obscure organization, Jay Barbree of NBC Radio, who lived near Cape Canaveral and had covered the space program for two decades, heard from some friends at the agency that the problem was in the right booster rocket. He passed the information (but not the names of his sources) to NBC News, and on Thursday night Brokaw led the *Nightly News* with a statement that "NBC News has learned" NASA was concentrating on the right booster. AP and UPI carried word that NBC News had said that. The next day everybody noted that NBC News had hung this piece of wash on the line, except for the *Times,* which claimed to have got the same story from its own anonymous sources. (Among the more unpleasant habits the *Times* acquired under Abe Rosenthal was an all but absolute refusal to credit others for its stories; when ABC-TV put on Pierre

Salinger's three-hour documentary about the negotiations for the release of the Iranian hostages, which was chockablock with stuff nobody had printed or aired before, the *Times* killed a favorable review of the show written by its television critic John O'Connor, planted some of the information with its Bonn bureau and ran the story barefaced as its own, on an inside page.)

Finally, one of the sources surfaced: Richard Cook, a young accountant, not long at NASA, who was willing to be quoted on his strong recollection that several of the engineers had told him one of the cost factors NASA would have to face soon was the need to redesign the seals between the sections of the solid-fuel booster rocket. This young man was called before the Presidential Commission, not as an expert witness, but as a traitor to his class, his employer and his country, and a publicity hound, to boot. As he said immediately after it: "The primary purpose of the Commission hearing was to discredit me." Both the scientists on the Commission and its chairman, William Rogers (Nixon's Secretary of State), were outraged that such a pipsqueak would retail such gossip. But by now the pack was in full cry, and dribble by dribble the story emerged. The cold and windy weather the day of the launch. The recommendation by the engineers from the rocket manufacturer that NASA not attempt a launch in that weather. The insistence by mission controllers at the Marshall Space Center in Huntsville, Alabama, that the *Challenger* should fly that morning despite the engineers' concern. (Only a few of the stories noted that Marshall was a very special place with its own unique culture, having been the creation of Wernher von Braun and the German V-2 crowd spirited to America after the war, including Arthur L. H. Rudolph, who supervised the Saturn V program that put U.S. astronauts on the moon, and then in November 1983, to quote a 1984 AP story, "left the United States forever and renounced his U.S. citizenship rather than face Justice Department charges he 'worked thousands of slave laborers to death' building Nazi V-2 missiles during World War II.") We learned many details about the weaknesses of the "O ring" seals, going all the way back to 1978, and the research showing that the design relying on O rings was not going to work out the way theory had predicted.

While *All the President's Men* was at its zenith, the thoughtful Edward J. Epstein pointed out that it wasn't Woodstein who got to the guts of Watergate but Sam Ervin and his Senate committee with its unrestricted subpoena authority, plus Judge Sirica and his power to vary miscreants' sentences according to their willingness to cooperate. (He also suggested that if the burglary had worked, and the wiretap had produced "material damaging to O'Brien and the Democrats . . . such material would no doubt have found its way into print by being leaked to 'investigative journalists.' "[18] In passing, it should be noted that Jim Hougan in his book *Secret Agent* supplies good reason to doubt that all the guts of Watergate have yet been exposed: his theory, based mostly on some 16,000 documents rescued from FBI files by Freedom of Information Act requests, argues that the CIA itself blew the

White House operation because the agency was illegally monitoring a sex ring to which someone at the Democratic National Committee was sending customers, thereby acquiring lists of important people susceptible to blackmail.[19] Similarly, most of what was truly horrifying about NASA's failure to assure the fundamentals of the safety of the people who climbed into those shuttles was dug out by the Commission's researchers and the Commissioners' own questions, not by the press.

But it is far from clear that the shuttle commission, or the Ervin committee before it, would have looked for the things they found absent steady pressure from an ultimately immense news-gathering operation. When NASA refused to keep the reporters' corps informed of the progress of the underwater salvage operation, six papers (the New York *Times,* the Los Angeles *Times,* the Chicago *Tribune,* the Orlando *Sentinel,* the Philadelphia *Inquirer* and *Newsday)* got together and contracted with a local ham operator to monitor all Navy radio communications to the salvage ship. AP ran its own monitoring system. Walter Mears refused to boast about it: "At any newspaper you use scanners for police news," he commented. "It's not . . . a quantum leap."[20] And, of course, if the Navy had wished to be perfectly tough, it could have coded the transmissions. Still, at the end of the day one must face the fact that the intensity of press attention prevented the Presidential Commission and indeed NASA itself from concealing major information, whether they wished to hide it or not—just as one must face the fact that without Bernstein to note that one of the Watergate burglars had a White House private number in his notebook, and without Woodward to develop the contacts who related the Watergate break-in to Nixon's dirty tricks department, the official investigators would have made less heat and thus probably shed less light than they did.

Three months after the *Challenger* explosion, the *Times* in a splendid demonstration of capability and commitment shattered the NASA myths of efficiency and primary concern for safety with a pair of very long articles based on the contents of more than five hundred previously confidential audits and reports by inspectors and consultants. But at the beginning the story depended upon two of the most despised tactics of modern journalism: the anonymous quote and the formulation "NBC News has learned . . ." Especially since the devotees of the "new journalism" in the 1960s decided that there were higher truths to be served, everyone in and outside the business has believed that some fraction of the quotes in some news stories were just made up by the reporter. (I remember my bemusement reading David Halberstam's *The Best and the Brightest* when I found that the only quotes attributed to anybody in his chapter on McGeorge Bundy were from an article I had written in *The New York Times Magazine,* which was not credited.) "Blind sourcing always outrages me," says John Chancellor. "People have a right to know where you got it."

The Special Committee on Mass Media of the Canadian Senate, itself a creature of the 1960s, gung ho for alternative media and participation, rejected the idea of a reporters' shield law with the savage comment that " 'newsmen's privilege' seems designed primarily for the protection of the reporter."[21] And in a good fraction of the occasions when the protection does benefit the source, the shielding is illegitimate, allowing a President or a Secretary of State or Defense to mislead the public as President Martin Van Buren did ("The President," said that great man Senator John Randolph, "always rows to his objective with muffled oars"). Ben Bradlee wrote in 1972: "A government official—high, low or jack-in-the-game— will generally say one thing if he is sure that his identity will be publicly unknown, and quite another thing if the public can call him on it if he is wrong or misleading."[22] A day before Reagan hit the Libyans, ABC News broadcast a report from anonymous sources that the United States had decided to take no military action against Qaddafi. It would be interesting to know who tipped off the network to that one.

One of the worst moments in the abominable coverage of the attempted assassination of President Reagan in 1981 came when Dan Rather intoned the grieving words: "It is now confirmed that Jim Brady is dead" (it then became necessary to attack political consultant Lyn Nofziger, who had the effrontery to tell CBS reporters that Brady was not dead). One of the few admirable moments in that coverage was ABC's delay in identifying "the suspect" (it would violate the Constitution to describe someone found with a smoking gun in his hand as "the assailant"—Rather himself, *sancta simplicitas,* reminded us that "under our system" this poor flake was entitled to a presumption of innocence), because Frank Reynolds demanded to know the source of the identification before he would put the name on the air.

And yet . . . When the pressure is turned on full, as it was in the Nixon White House and at NASA (or in Franklin Roosevelt's White House, where, Graham White reports, "the President gathered information on the social activities of members of the administration, even down to the lower echelons, especially on their relations with newsmen, and then brought pressure to bear on his subordinates to sever such contacts in order to eliminate the journalists' sources of information"[23]), when people who talk to the news gatherers can expect quick and painful retribution from their bosses and friends, the press may be unable to function unless reporters can promise sources confidentiality. Once that is accepted, and the papers and broadcasters agree that they will permit their reporters to present what they call news without letting the consumers know where it comes from, there is no ducking the question of who watches the watchmen.

2

The one absolute is that anyone must be able to say anything he likes about the government. "The presence or absence in the law of the concept of seditious libel," Chicago University law professor Philip Kurland wrote in the mid-1960s, "defines the society. A society may or may not treat obscenity or contempt by publication as legal offenses without altering its basic nature. If, however, it makes seditious libel an offense, it is not a free society no matter what its other characteristics."[24] This is a very modern notion. Lord Coke in 1606 argued that libel could be prosecuted because it roused desires for revenge and thus led to a breach of the peace, and libel against a government official "concerns not only the breach of the peace but also the scandal of government." Truth is no defense: "a true statement that damages the reputation of the government or an official is the more danger- ous to public peace." Lord Chief Justice John Holt in 1704 ruled that "if people should not be called to account for possessing the people with an ill opinion of the government, no government can subsist."[25]

Such arguments were ultimately rejected in the industrial democracies. Instead, the position adopted was that of John Milton, who argued against any government right to license publication with the words: "This I know, that errors in a good government and in a bad are equally almost incident; for what Magistrate may not be mis-inform'd, and much the sooner, if lib- erty of Printing be reduc't into the power of a few? But to redresse willingly and speedily what hath bin err'd, and in highest authority to esteem a plain advertisement more than others have done a sumptuous bribe, is a vertue (honour'd Lords and Commons) answerable to Your highest actions . . . ."[26] (A quarter of a millennium later, and quite independently, Walter Lippmann came to the same conclusion: "It is because they are compelled to act without a reliable picture of the world, that governments, schools, news- papers and churches make such small headway against the more obvious failings of democracy, against violent prejudice, apathy, preference for the curious trivial as against the dull important, and the hunger for sideshows and three-legged calves."[27]) All that was needed, Milton wrote, was a re- quirement that the publisher and author—at least the publisher, he added, maybe worrying a little—be identified on the item, to take responsibility.

At the other end of the spectrum, there can be no doubt that the state has the right and the power to enact laws that permit ordinary, innocent people to win damages from and take revenge upon those who have sub- jected them to hatred, ridicule and contempt. A cousin of mine was recog- nizable in a picture chosen some years ago by *Ladies' Home Journal* to illus- trate a piece on juvenile gangs, drugs, sodomy, etc. Behind her and her friends, if the full photo had been used, would have been a picture of the

High School of Music and Art, where they were students, and which they were leaving at the close of the school day when this picture was taken. It had wound up in a sort of anonymous file, and then in the magazine. The family wanted only (and got) a nice apology in a prominent place, but if they had wanted some money, I can't see why they should not have had a case. This sort of careless damage to others is as much a negligent tort as dropping a flowerpot from a window onto a passerby, and I cannot imagine that the Founders wished or said it should be constitutionally protected.

Some libels, however, *are* constitutionally protected. Twenty years ago, I noted a case in New Haven where a young black thug was being prosecuted for the rape of a white nurse, and his lady lawyer, a community activist who later went on to great things in Washington, raised a defense of consent with no reason to believe it was true. This got the boy thirty years in jail, while the victim cried and the lawyer walked on to a fine career in foundation work and politics, but that's the way the ball bounces in the courts. The nurse had been deliberately libeled as well as raped, and there was nothing anybody could do about it. We all know about Joe McCarthy, who was extremely careful to accuse individuals only when he was inside the Capitol, on the Senate floor and in the committee rooms, where everything he said was privileged. In addition, libel may be safe for the libeler when the victims are people who just can't subject themselves to the cross-examination that comes with the territory when you sue. Entertainment figures have sometimes fabricated (or had fabricated for them) so much of their public persona that they dare not bring an action, quite apart from the question of what rights they have sacrificed by driving so hard to become public figures.

For the rest, it has been public policy for centuries that the behavior of the press should be controlled by the availability of libel as a cause of action in the courts. Those who seek public office or even leadership in publicized private affairs cannot claim a right to reputation, because they seek to *use* that reputation to govern or otherwise influence the lives of others. Those who come within the searchlight of news without seeking it can claim damages if they are defamed by an untruth. The most dreadful villain in the classic English theater is the fellow who says it, but nobody can quarrel seriously with Iago's complaint about "he who filches from me my good name." One can find some civil libertarians who complain that any successful libel suit has a "chilling effect" on free expression, and surely Lyle Denniston of the Baltimore *Sun* is right to worry about "the awful statistic in libel cases," that "the press has been losing 83 per cent of the libel trials."[28] The cases are then thrown out on appeal, which helps but doesn't entirely cure. Still, even in the business, most practitioners will agree that there are some facets of free expression that ought to be put in the deep freeze.

The rules seem reasonable enough, especially since the Supreme Court in spring 1986 (but only by 5–4) ruled that state laws must leave plaintiffs with the burden of proving that defamatory statements are false and cannot compel libel defendants to prove that their statements are true. This was, incidentally, the most important First Amendment decision of the 1980s, because strong arguments can be and were made on the other side (especially by Justice White, a Kennedy appointment and the greatest skeptic on the bench when it comes to the values of the free press; one notes with amusement that the opinion of the Court was by Justice Sandra Day O'Connor, at that time Ronald Reagan's sole appointee and probably the most conservative judge on that bench). Under the common law, a man damaged by a publication had the right to require that those who had harmed him demonstrate the truth that validated the harm, and Justice Brennan in requiring "actual malice" in *New York Times* v. *Sullivan* had relieved the press of that obligation only when the victim was a public figure. Now, in *Inquirer* v. *Hepps,* the Court decided that when suing a paper that said he had close ties to organized crime a beverage distributor had to prove that the paper had no good reason to believe that, which is a far different matter from making the paper prove that what are alleged to be mere social friendships have business significance. But rules are boundaries, and even good ones may leave room for unreasonable behavior. Like most tort law these days, libel turns out to benefit lawyers rather than to remedy grievances or protect the community.

The reasons are various. The most serious problem is that the cases are expensive to bring and to defend, which means that libel law represents too often an opportunity for the rich to bully the press. Defending cases is so costly (not only in legal fees, but in the time of the staff that will be deposed during pre-trial "discovery" proceedings) that a plausible threat of a suit may discourage publication or broadcast of even a well-researched and significant story. Lawyers' letters, apparently, have prevented medical journals from publishing the results of a study by two doctors at the National Institutes of Health exploring the collaboration of colleagues at Emory University and Harvard with a young medical researcher who later confessed to fraudulently misstating his experiments. The expense of defending suits also, obviously, offers an opportunity for lawyers who keep a portion of the money under contingent-fee arrangements to make cases on behalf of less affluent complainants, if they have reason to hope that the defendants can be blackmailed.

As a result, libel insurance, like other liability insurance, has gone through the roof in price and now covers costs and losses only over a deductible that is painfully high for smaller journalistic enterprises. At most larger newspapers and magazines, lawyers are now asked to provide a *nihil obstat* before important stories are published. This is by no means entirely unfortunate—an outsider asking a writer what he thinks he is saying in a story can, I assure you, avoid a lot of grief; and, of course, the purpose of tort law is to exert a "chilling effect" on behavior that wrongly damages people or organizations—but eventually the steady drip of questions that do not relate well to the point of a story can wear down some foundation stones. And the routine becomes an exercise in self-protection rather than self-examination. And there is a public loss. As Pulitzer put it: "The press may be licentious, but it is the most magnificently repressive moral agent in the world today. More crime, immorality and rascality is prevented by the fear of exposure in the newspapers than by all the laws, morals and statutes ever devised."[29]

In libel as in product liability (which is, after all, a related subject), tort law fails to fulfill its designated function as a way to make people careful because the lawsuits are brought either by the vengeful and the naturally litigious, who are not to be deterred by mere care, or by accident. In forty years of writing for profit-seeking publication, I have been sued exactly once. This was in 1959, but I still want to be pretty careful about how I tell the story. It was in connection with my book *Madison Avenue, USA,* in which I had written: "It was easy enough for Foote, Cone to decide that Colgate had pre-empted the bad-breath business and Gleem the cavities business, so Pepsodent should stick to cleaning the teeth; but without copywriter and jazz hobbyist Don Williams to write 'You'll Wonder Where the Yellow Went' the Pepsodent claim would never have drawn much public attention."[30]

More than a year after the publication of the book (which meant that she had to bring her action against the paperback publisher because the statute of limitations had run against the hard-cover publication), a young lady sued for some hundreds of thousands of dollars on the grounds that while an employee of Foote, Cone, from which she had parted on bad terms before I came around to interview people for my book, she had written the words in question, and that Williams as copy group head had merely written and performed the music for the jingle. Because I had left out her name, which no one at Foote, Cone spoke, she had been libeled by omission. This one got all the way up to the highest court in the state of New York, and was subsequently enshrined in William Prosser's Restatement of Torts (Second) for the American Law Institute. The decision was that libel by omission was indeed an actionable wrong, but only to the extent that pecuniary damages could be proved. At this point, Harper and I each chipped in $100 and settled the case. Incidentally, the case made a difference in authors' contracts with publishers. Harper had been unable to stick me with half the legal bills, though it tried, because I had agreed in my contract only that I would hold the publisher harmless and not that I would reimburse any expenses incurred on behalf of its heirs and assigns. Word of this problem spread quickly through the publishing business, and ever since contracts have required that authors take responsibility for libel suits against paperback reprints, too.

The remedy for abuse of legal process in libel matters (indeed, in tort law generally) is the willingness of judges to penalize frivolous or ill-motivated plaintiffs by compelling them (or their lawyers, if their pockets are insufficiently capacious) to pay the lawyers' fees and court costs incurred by the defendants. This happens every once in a while (*Barron's* collected its costs in defending the suit by a company which had sought to punish the magazine for casting doubt on its reported earnings, and NBC won an award against Lyndon LaRouche after he failed in a suit against the network), but not often enough. If potential plaintiffs knew that their case might cost them not only their own expenses but those of the defendant (and if lawyers who brought such cases on contingency knew that irresponsible suits would cost them not only their time but cash penalties), they would think hard before suing. It should be noted that even a great expansion of the grounds on which costs can be recovered by defendants would not protect CBS, *Time* or the Washington *Post* in incidents like the Westmoreland, Sharon and Tavoulareas cases, for in all of these, whatever the legal liabilities, there was evidence that somebody at the network or publication had been out to "get" the person who sued, so the case could not be called either frivolous or ill-motivated.

What we want is a libel law that makes news purveyors stop and think about what they ought to stop and think about. Given some tolerance for the truth that you can get lucky and you can get unlucky, and some structural adjustment of the relationship of law and social insurance to reduce the number of lawyers who have to be fed by personal-injury cases, this ought not to require much more than jiggling with existing black-letter law. Malice is rare; as noted earlier, the process of socializing reporters (not to mention their professional experience as observers) pretty much beats out of them strong feelings about the outcomes of most of the stories they cover. There are exceptions: Sharon, Westmoreland and Tavoulareas have been noted, and it is generally true that when someone lies to you, you look forward eagerly to the day when the son of a bitch gets his. The reporters who covered the Nixon White House were almost without exception pleased to see that particular President depart it in disgrace.

And inaccuracy is not really a critical failing. "I read the newspapers with lively interest," said Evelyn Waugh's freebooting entrepreneur Mr. Baldwin in *Scoop*. "It is seldom that they are absolutely, point-blank wrong. That is the popular belief, but those who are in the know can usually discern an embryo truth, a little grit of fact, like the core of a pearl, round which have been deposited the delicate layers of ornament."[31] Except in the fantasy press, from *The Sun* to *People*, that's about as bad as it gets. In recent years, I have worked with several more or less eminent figures in the preparation of their memoirs, and have had occasion to compare the contents of the newspapers of the time with their recollections and also with contemporary correspondence and memoranda. It is rare that the papers got the story spot-on right, but even more rare for the recollections of the actors to be better than what was reported contemporaneously.

Of course, it's hard to be certain, even when the contemporary documents are to hand. Inaccuracy develops a constituency, and may have been created by a constituency. On April 26, 1937, German warplanes in the service of the Franco rebellion burned the Basque town of Guernica, thereby stimulating from Pablo Picasso perhaps the most famous piece of political art in this century. Franco's was a sophisticated rebellion, complete to press officers, and even before Picasso had set pencil to sketch pad they were inundating the Western newspapers with stories that the Basques had really burned the town themselves as part of a scorched-earth policy. Among those who contributed to the dissemination of such stories was Kim Philby, later to mount a classic betrayal of the British (and American) secret service in the interests of Moscow, then a correspondent for *The Times* of London. He was already a Soviet agent, but part of his cover was that he was an enthusiast for Hitler, and he was considered highly sympathetic to the Franco cause. In the 1970s, led by Jeffrey Hart, a Dartmouth professor, conservative publications around the world resurrected the dispute over Guernica, insisting that the Picasso painting was a hoax, and in some instances "proving" their case with the argument that the Guernica story had been invented by the notorious Soviet agent Philby, who had in fact been inventing things on Franco's side.[32] Philby was working again as a journalist, by the way, accredited to *The Economist* in Lebanon, when he saw exposure coming and fled to Russia.

Perhaps the most extensive study of the coverage of a recent news story is Peter Braestrup's *Big Story,* which recounts in detail what American broadcast news, newspapers and newsmagazines did with the Tet offensive in Vietnam in early 1968. Braestrup was the chief of the Washington *Post* Saigon bureau at the time. I have read only the abridged, 529-page version, but that's convincing enough: the press got it wrong. The North Vietnamese had expected a much bigger return on their investment than they got; the South Vietnamese Army and militias performed better than had been anticipated in the crisis, and the American public was told more or less the opposite. Especially by television. Braestrup observes that it does not seem to have made much difference in public opinion: "the polls did not show any drastic shifts in mass attitudes toward the war during February–March 1968." It was political Washington that found the news stories devastating Braestrup quotes counterinsurgency expert Robert Komer to the effect that "the U.S. Mission [to Vietnam] lost all 'credibility' in Washington *official* circles in the post-Tet shock. The Pentagon civilians tended to believe the information provided by the media, whether it was firsthand from Vietnam or secondhand from Washington."[33]

Others, notably reporter and novelist Robert Elegant and the people who funded General Westmoreland's case against CBS, have argued that if the news gatherers had got the Tet story straight the war might have been won. Braestrup knows better, and presents his book not as a revisionist history of the war but as part of the ongoing history of journalism. By January 31, 1968, he notes, the country was looking for a way out of a war that had become costly in lives and treasure without becoming comprehensible in the context of national policy. The press on the scene, moreover, had been lied to once too often. Those who contrast the attitude of American reporters in Vietnam with that of those in Normandy in World War II might think of the difference between Westmoreland and Bradley, who came before the press corps the evening after his own high-level bombers had beat up the force he had gathered to sweep the Germans out of the Cotentin Peninsula and said, "I told you a few days ago of what we planned to do in our attack at St. Gilles. We tried it and it didn't work. I am sorry, gentlemen. We shall try it again."[34] The buried story of Vietnam in 1968, the one that would count, was weariness (and fear) of the war back home, and if it hadn't been Tet it would have been something else. In that sense, even Braestrup's catalogue of errors and misanalysis (like the all but universal comparison between the American marines in Khesanh, who could call in B-52 strikes at will, with the truly isolated French forces fourteen years earlier at Dienbienphu) does not deny the "grit of fact" Waugh's Mr. Baldwin found in the news stories.

Not infrequently, there is something to be said for both sides of flatly contradictory stories. On November 27, 1984, the New York *Times* ran a story that began: "Acknowledging that issues of states' rights were involved, the Federal Deposit Insurance Corporation said today that it was moving to restrict banks from going into new lines of business under authority recently granted by some states." The same day, the Washington *Post* ran a story that began: "The Federal Deposit Insurance Corp. yesterday proposed rules that would permit banks to enter the insurance, real estate, data processing and securities and travel agency businesses." Essentially, the *Post* had it right and the *Times* had it wrong—FDIC was in fact proposing to liberalize considerably the established restrictions on what insured banks could do. But the rule would permit the exercise of the new powers only through a separately capitalized and staffed subsidiary, regardless of the provisions of state bank charters, and the *Times* could claim textual validity for its report.

What was wrong with the *Times* story was something more serious. The Reagan administration was committed to liberating businesses from the yoke of regulation, and William Isaac, chairman of the FDIC in 1984, was among those who stood in awe of the magic of the marketplace. One could read the FDIC document either way as an isolated "fact" (indeed, the draftsmanship, with its repeated emphasis on the word "prohibit," was designed to encourage the sort of story the *Times* carried, and the leader of the Conference of State Bank Supervisors agreed with the *Times* reporter that "it's a reregulatory, not a deregulatory, move"), but if you knew what the government was up to you would throw a lot of salt over your shoulder before you went to press with what the *Times* printed.

3

The problem, then, always and everywhere, is context. Among Braestrup's less convincing complaints in his book is that "the tendency of the writer and his editors [on the newsmagazines], in the face of space limitations, was to avoid ambiguities and complexities, to fashion a clear story-line with a beginning, middle, and snappy close. . . . With similar constraints (though of time rather than space), TV correspondents and producers tend to use the same technique."[35] What else is a man to do? Is one to shape a story so that it *doesn't* have a beginning, a middle and an end? Once you get beyond Stephenson's "communications pleasure," the social function of news is to give the world coherence. Where Braestrup is right is that the easiest way to provide coherence is to make the story simple, and the real world is almost never simple. Only individuals—not events, not societies, not political movements—have a beginning, a middle and an end. There are causes behind the causes, and there will be consequences of the consequences. The quantity of related information is endless. The news consumer can't keep all that in mind, and the news producer can't present even a trivial fraction of it; but he must—he really must, it's almost his sole obligation—remain conscious of the great mass of relevant material from which he selects his sample. Only connect.

Braestrup thought better management would improve performance. "In crisis," he wrote, "the major media manager can remind his producers or deskmen—those harassed gatekeepers—of the need for skepticism, of the likelihood that the 'facts' will change and need explicit correction. He can underline the difference between 'drama' and 'significance,' and allocate space or time accordingly. He can discourage instant analysis and prediction. He can order his dispersed reporters to inform one another on the state of current knowledge and to remember the need for a future overview. He can insist on intense questioning of all actors in domestic debate. On television, he can see that a minimum of context is supplied to film reports ('no microcosms' is a good rule). He can order that a running summary be kept of his organization's pertinent news output, in order to detect gaps which need filling in or initial impressions which require fresh investigation. . . . These remedies . . . require something more of managers than visceral reactions to events, 'issues,' and personalities. They require consistent leadership, imagination, some steady intellectual effort, and a strong awareness of the limited capacity of journalism to provide the public with broad knowledge on short notice."[36] Add to this list only an insistence that the morgue be kept in good condition and used—no problem in this age of computer storage and random access—and most failures could indeed be remedied.

Then one asks, how do you do that? Difficulties in maintaining the quality of news services are, as I wrote in 1969 of similar dilemmas in education, "merely a special case of the root problem of politics in a modern society: the control of professional performance."[37] This specification of a root problem was not well received at the time—a reviewer in the New York *Times* worked himself into a lather about the triviality of that concern in an age of racism, sexism, poverty and war—but it was accurate then and is, I think, a little more obvious now. The division of labor in a modern society is such that we rely on supposedly professional skills for an increasing fraction of the services we must consume, and among them is information gathering in a complexly interdependent world.

Ever since the Hutchins Commission on Freedom of the Press reported out in 1947, the preferred remedy for the problems of the press has been self-criticism, peer review and the public acknowledgment of error. Following the Louisville *Courier-Journal* in 1967, a number of papers have employed ombudsmen to monitor and report in print on their own policies and performance, and the New York *Times* has placed bitterly self-critical commentaries in its boxed news index on the split page, one of the most prominent places in the paper. The broadcasters, except to the extent that they are compelled by the personal attack rules of the FCC (written into the Constitution by the Supreme Court in the *Red Lion* case), will give the aggrieved absolutely nothing. The replies to local editorials are a scandal, and the letters to *60 Minutes* are a joke. Michael Kinsley, editor of *The New Republic,* revealed deliciously in a column in *The Wall Street Journal* that his magazine once "enraged ABC President Roone Arledge by refusing to run his letter complaining about an article critical of ABC News. We noted that ABC wouldn't allow us to broadcast our criticism. Why should we publish his answer to it?"[38]

Walter Lippmann in reply to Hutchins argued that peer review was impractical: "They are talking about newspapermen criticizing other newspapermen in their newspapers. We are all tempted, and now and then we indulge, but on the whole we refrain. And the reasons are good reasons. They are the same reasons which make it very rare indeed that a lawyer or a doctor or an actor or a professor will speak out publicly and say how badly the lawyer argued his case, how inexpertly the doctor diagnosed the disease, how lamely the actor performed, how dull was the professor's lecture.

"For there is a fellowship among newspapermen as there is in other crafts and professions. They are not lone wolves. They have to see each other, meet together and work together, and life would become intolerable, as it would in a university faculty or an officers mess, if they practiced vigorous, mutual criticism in public. I may say that I have tried it, and I have had it tried on me, and my conclusion is that the hard feelings it causes are out of all proportion to the public benefit it causes."[39] The short answer to Lippmann is that this "fellowship" is an illegitimate attempt to insulate the business from its true nature. Pulitzer told Alfred Harmsworth, soon to be Lord Northcliffe, of *The Times,* that "I am the loneliest man in the world. People who dine at my table one night might find themselves arraigned in my newspaper the next morning."[40] Why should reporters be able to escape the searchlights they train on everyone else? Nobody in the Chicago school would have tried to claim this benefit of clergy. Writing about Hildy Johnson, Bob Casey noted that he was "an old-school reporter in an era when the motto of the profession was 'All for none and no one for anybody.' "[41]

In point of fact, the news business today is unusually secretive and uncooperative when an outsider wishes information. Though I was able to see most of the editors and publishers and broadcasting executives I wished to see in connection with this book, a surprising number of reporters were shy. Dena Kleiman of the New York *Times,* a superb writer of human interest stories whom I wished to interview out of admiration, turned me down with the comment: "Look, I know how quotes from interviews can be twisted." (In fairness to her, I had warned her I was in Rosenthal's black book for having written critically in the *Columbia Journalism Review* about the way the *Times* had covered the New York City financial crisis. I ran into Rosenthal's sidekick Arthur Gelb at a party a few years after that article appeared, and he said, "It wasn't so much what you said, Martin, *it was your tone of voice that was so unforgivable."*)

"Most influential teacher I ever had was the fellow who taught me accounting," said Albert Hettinger, a lean, Gothic figure who was for years the balance wheel of Lazard Frères. "He used to say, 'Accounting is a way to tell the truth.' " Journalism never was that. It can be a way to convey understanding. That leaves open the interesting question of whether the reporter must understand the story himself, to which the interesting answer is: Sometimes but not always. What makes the news professional is the instinct (training and experience hone it but don't create it) for judging the probity of a participant's or observer's testimony and the relative saliency of its parts. As a normal matter, a reporter is much happier writing well within the limits of what he knows, if only because that margin of knowledge may be called upon when an editor queries, but all of us, I think, have had to live with the knowledge that if a source got it wrong—or our notes got the source wrong—we were in deep shit. Some of the pieces for general magazines about which I was most nervous, however, have been reprinted over and over again, sometimes years later, by technical journals. The rule in such circumstances is to ask the subjects of your interviews for detailed expositions in their own language even in those areas where you think you understand, and to get all the jargon very precisely defined, to avoid the solecism that starts the reader on what is likely to be a fruitful quest for your other inadequacies. This doesn't always work—I have fallen painfully and disgustingly on my face more often than I like to think—but it's always worth trying.

The danger of the dominance of television journalism, to quote Edwin Newman, is that it "tends to turn journalists from outcasts, or at any rate, outsiders, into public figures, heroes, merchants of charm." Television "does not often require the extended exposition of ideas or the elaboration of fairly complicated arguments."[42] Its practitioners, therefore, are not called upon to cultivate instincts of saliency, especially when the news divisions are run by the people who now run them, for whom the question is always "How good is the film and how does it *feel?*" When Diane Sawyer asks Margaret Thatcher whether she makes Dennis' breakfast, when Peter Jennings builds up a child-abuse story because *20/20* has a child-abuse piece that night, they diminish not only themselves but also their occupation. One is comforted, a little, by Tom Griffith's distillation of his experiences on the two magazines, that *"Time* was more about meaning, *Life* about feeling."[43] *Time* for all its faults is still around; *Life* died and could be resurrected only as a shadow in the supermarket racks, between *National Enquirer* and *The Star.*

Robert Casey recalled from his days on the Chicago *Inter-Ocean* a sign pasted on every post in the city room and "bearing the signature of H. H. Kohlsaat, the publisher: 'I can forgive a liar but I hate inaccuracy'—Samuel Butler. 'I concur in this sentiment'—H.H.K."[44] Underpaid and self-important, irritated with sources who try to con him and with editors and producers who get excited only about trivia, envious of the money and recognition that come to lightweights who anchor television shows, pressured by deadlines and now worried about their employers' psychologists who pontificate about stress, reporters retain public sympathy to the extent that they keep pride in themselves and in their work. That pride in the end is the only guarantor of professional performance. Even people who see in print or on the air what they wish to God had not happened or had not got out will be wistful rather than bitter if the information is more or less right and they know they had their say.

"Why do they hate us?" asks Robert MacNeil. Don't worry about it, Robert. A lot of water has gone under the bridge since, and there are lots of new technologies, but we can still live with Joseph Medill's advice to someone who wanted to duplicate the success of the Chicago *Tribune:* "Just print the news." Get the name spelled right, and make sure that what's on the film fairly represents what this fellow wants to say, that the world as you present it is recognizable to the people who live there, and the rest will fall more or less neatly in place. Most of the time.

Notes

CHAPTER ONE

1. Ambrose Bierce quote: Ambrose Bierce, *The Fourth Estate*, in George Barking, ed., *The Sardonic Humor of Ambrose Bierce*, Dover Publications, New York, 1963, pp. 163–64.

2. Twain quote: Edgar M. Branch, *Clemens of the Call: Mark Twain in San Francisco*, University of California Press, Berkeley, 1969, p. 6.

3. Thomson quote: Virgil Thomson, *The State of Music*, William Morrow, New York, 1939, p. 26.

4. Salisbury quote: Harrison Salisbury, *Without Fear or Favor*, Times Books, New York, 1980, p. 426. The phrase is used of Seymour Hersh: "A man whom many of his peers regarded as the best investigative correspondent in the world." This is not, of course, Hersh's fault.

5. One pauses, before beginning, to note the view of Daniel Seligman, executive editor of *Fortune*, that PS 166—of which he, too, is an alumnus—was an extraordinary seedbed of journalists. Seligman reports that he once had occasion to tell Henry Luce that the school that had sent the greatest number of writers to *Fortune*, beginning with the magazine's begetter, Ralph Ingersoll, was not Yale, as Luce had assumed, but PS 166.

"Where," Luce inquired, confused, "is that?"

"Eighty-ninth Street," said Seligman, "between Amsterdam and Columbus avenues."

"Where," asked Luce, now totally bewildered, "are *they?*"

6. Rolly Bales story: Robert J. Casey, *Such Interesting People*, Bobbs-Merrill, Indianapolis, 1943, p. 34.

7. Weaver and Wilhoit: "The Current Journalists," by Debra Gersh, *Editor & Publisher*, April 5, 1986, p. 16.

8. Casey quote: Robert J. Casey, *More Interesting People*, Bobbs-Merrill, Indianapolis, 1947, pp. 88–89.

9. Cahill quote: Robert Schmuhl, ed., *The Responsibilities of Journalism*, University of Notre Dame Press, Notre Dame, Ind., 1984, p. 116.

10. Shaw quote: David Shaw, *Press Watch: A Provocative Look at How Newspapers Report the News*, Macmillan, New York, 1984, p. 210.

11. Geyer quote: Schmuhl, op. cit., p. 70.

12. Northcliffe quote: Harold Evans, *Good Times, Bad Times*, Atheneum, New York, 1983, p. 10.

13. Halberstam quote: David Halberstam, *The Powers That Be,* Alfred A. Knopf, New York, 1979, pp. 563–64.

14. Watergate: ibid., p. 630.

15. Stephen Hess, *The Golden Triangle: Press Relations at the White House, State Department and Department of Defense,* a paper delivered at New York University, March 19, 1983, mimeo, p. 27.

16. Mencken: H. L. Mencken, *Newspaper Days,* Alfred A. Knopf, New York, 1941, p. ix.

17. Herbert G. Klein, *Making It Perfectly Clear,* Doubleday, Garden City, N.Y., 1980, p. 422.

18. Ellerbee quote: Linda Ellerbee, *"And So It Goes": Adventures in Television,* G. P. Putnam's Sons, New York, 1986, p. 16.

19. "Piano playing": "Why Journalism Schools," by Stephen White, *The Public Interest,* Winter 1986, p. 39 @ p. 49.

20. Pulitzer drunk story: W. A. Swanberg, *Pulitzer,* Charles Scribner's Sons, New York, 1967, p. 293. Swanberg completes the story: "Seitz dutifully returned, and in Park Row encountered Esdaile Cohen, a brilliant writer handicapped only by his inability to pass swinging doors. He had once worked for Albert Pulitzer's *Journal* and for almost every newspaper in town. He admitted that he had recently been fired by Hearst's *American* . . . saying, 'I can't let the hard stuff alone.'

" 'I have a life job for you,' Seitz said . . ."

21. Walker quote: Martin Walker, *Powers of the Press,* Pilgrim Press, New York, 1983, p. 13. The [sic] notes that what Walker means is the *Grandes Ecoles.* The *Ecoles Normales,* in which no Frenchman would include the special *Ecole Normale Superieure,* are teachers colleges (like the old American "normal schools") and by no means the sources of national leadership. This sort of error is by no means uncommon when newsmen begin to think of themselves as part of the elite.

22. "Harlots": James Deakin, *Straight Stuff: The Reporters, the White House and the Truth,* William Morrow, New York, 1984, p. 92.

23. Henry Kissinger's birthday: "The ABC's of Sports Broadcasting," by Nancy Collins, *Columbia,* October 1983, p. 24 @ p. 27. The original of the interview appeared in *New York* magazine, August 15, 1983.

24. Abelson quote: "Up and Down Wall Street," by Alan Abelson, *Barron's,* March 7, 1983, p. 1.

25. Rosenbaum quotes: "Battle Tales from Black Rock," by Ron Rosenbaum, *Manhattan, Inc.,* June 1985, p. 64 @ p. 71.

26. Frank quote: Edward Jay Epstein, *News from Nowhere,* Random House, New York, 1973, p. 137.

CHAPTER TWO

1. Pulitzer on news: Swanberg, op. cit., p. 386.

2. Corker: Evelyn Waugh, *Scoop,* Little, Brown, Boston, 1937 (1945 ed.), p. 91.

3. Van Anda's horse: Meyer Berger, *The Story of The New York Times, 1851–1951,* Simon & Schuster, New York, 1952, p. 214.

4. Catholics and Protestants: "Lag by Catholics in Marrying Found," by Kenneth A. Briggs, New York *Times,* March 10, 1985, Section 1, p. 28.

5. "Cissy Patterson," by Lynne Cheney, *Washington Journalism Review,* December 1985, p. 33 @ p. 35.

6. O'Malley story: Casey, *Such Interesting People,* pp. 329–30.

7. Skaggs: "Call Him Mr. Hoax," by Debra Gersh, *Editor & Publisher*, June 14, 1986, p. 48.

8. Harvey Molotch and Marilyn Lester, "Accidental News: The Great Oil Spill as Local Occurrence and National Event," *American Journal of Sociology*, vol. 81 (September 1975), p. 235 @ pp. 235–36, 237.

9. Gitlin quote: Todd Gitlin, *The Whole World Is Watching: Mass Media in the Making and Unmaking of the New Left*, University of California Press, Berkeley, 1980, p. 11.

10. Michael Schudson, *Discovering the News: A Social History of American Newspapers*, Basic Books, New York, 1978, pp. 6, 7.

11. Ibid., p. 4.

12. Pool quote: Ithiel de Sola Pool, *Technologies of Freedom*, Harvard University Press, Cambridge, 1983, p. 77.

13. Arlen quote: Michael Arlen, *The Camera Age: Essays on Television*, Penguin Books edition, New York, 1982, p. 99.

14. Sayle: "Street Blues," by Martin Walker, *Books and Bookmen* (London), January, 1984, p. 10 @ p. 11.

15. Cohen quote: Bernard C. Cohen, *The Press and Foreign Policy*, Princeton University Press, Princeton, N.J., 1963, p. 13.

16. Tocqueville quote: Alexis de Tocqueville, *Democracy in America*, J. P. Mayer, ed., trans. by George Lawrence, Doubleday/Anchor Books, Garden City, N.Y., 1969, pp. 517–20.

17. Johannesburg: "Apartheid Reigns in South African Media," by Steve Mufson, *The Wall Street Journal*, May 8, 1986, p. 34.

18. Competition among papers: The author is Adolf Hitler. In Oron J. Hale, *The Captive Press in the Third Reich*, Princeton University Press, Princeton, N.J., 1973, pp. 45–46.

19. Mickiewicz quote: Ellen Mickiewicz, "Policy Issues in the Soviet Media System," in Erik P. Hoffmann, ed., *The Soviet Union in the 1980s*, Academy of Political Science, New York, 1984, pp. 113–23 @ p. 118.

20. Hart and Wechsler quote: Henry M. Hart and Herbert Wechsler, *The Federal Courts and the Federal System*, Foundation Press, New York, 1973, p. 336.

21. Deakin quote: Deakin, op. cit., p. 23.

22. Hughes quote: Emmet John Hughes, *The Ordeal of Power*, Atheneum, New York, 1963, pp. 78–79.

23. British peer: Leon V. Sigal, *Reporters and Officials: The Organization and Politics of Newsmaking*, D. C. Heath, Lexington, Mass., 1973, p. 131.

24. Percentages: ibid., p. 119.

25. Gallagher quote: Jonathan Fenby, *The International News Services*, a Twentieth Century Fund Report published by Schocken Books, New York, 1986, p. 172.

26. Sperling breakfast: Nora Ephron, *Scribble, Scribble: Notes on the Media*, Alfred A. Knopf, New York, 1978, p. 154.

27. Cronkite quote: "Cronkite Now Critical of CBS News," by Peter Kerr, New York *Times*, December 7, 1983, p. C31.

28. Ethiopia: Fenby, op. cit., p. 258.

CHAPTER THREE

1. Lippmann quote: Walter Lippmann, *Public Opinion*, Harcourt, Brace, New York, 1922, p. 347.

2. *Commercial Appeal* quote: Thomas Harrison Barker, *The Memphis Commercial*

Appeal: The History of a Southern Newspaper, Louisiana State University Press, Baton Rouge, 1971, p. 67.

3. Eastman story: Casey, *Such Interesting People,* pp. 75, 78–79. Casey also tells of a revenge Eastman is purported to have taken on Hearst, who had brought him to the newspaper business originally: "Mr. Eastman's mother died, so the story goes, and her obituary was printed in the *American,* forty-five words on page twenty-six. Old John's pride was hurt. He thought that an old-time friend had intended a personal affront, and the name of Hearst went onto the rapidly lengthening list on the copy desk. Then Mrs. Phoebe Hearst died and Old John adjusted the score.

" 'Mrs. Phoebe Hearst died today,' read Mr. Eastman's contribution to the obit column. 'She was the mother of a newspaper publisher and weighed ninety-five pounds.' " Ibid., p. 77.

4. Zion quote: Sidney Zion, *Read All About It: The Collected Adventures of a Maverick Reporter,* Berkley Books, New York, 1984, p. 344. Dannemora is a prison.

5. Liebling quote: Raymond Sokolov, *Wayward Reporter,* Harper & Row, New York, 1980, p. 3.

6. *Long Island Press:* Richard H. Meeker, *Newspaperman,* Ticknor & Fields, New Haven and New York, 1983, p. 246.

7. Ben H. Bagdikian, *The Media Monopoly,* Beacon Press, Boston, 1983, p. 153.

8. Media Institute: "Turned Off: Why Executives Distrust TV Reporters," by Herbert Schmertz, *Washington Journalism Review,* July/August 1984.

9. Paper Tiger: "State-of-the-Art Criticism," by Laurie Winer, *Columbia Journalism Review,* March/April 1985, p. 18 @ p. 19.

10. Rothman and Lichters material: S. Robert Lichter, Stanley Rothman and Linda S. Lichter, *The Media Elite,* Adler & Adler, Washington, D.C., 1986, pp. 52–72. The quotes are from uncorrected page proof.

11. Franklin quote: cited to *Pennsylvania Gazette,* June 10, 1731, in Stephen Botein, "Printers and the American Revolution," in Bernard Bailyn and John B. Hench, eds., *The Press and the American Revolution,* Northeastern University Press, Stoughton, Mass., 1981, p. 20.

12. Journalistic neuterism: Thomas Griffith, *How True,* Little, Brown, Boston, 1974, pp. 57, 58.

13. Gans quotes: Herbert J. Gans, *Deciding What's News,* Pantheon, New York, 1979, pp. 154, 184, 253–54, 274.

14. Mears quote: John Chancellor and Walter R. Mears, *The News Business,* Harper & Row, New York, 1983, p. 41.

15. Silk quote: Leonard Silk, "The Ethics and Economics of Journalism," in Schmuhl, op. cit., p. 92.

16. Kaltenborn material: Pool, op. cit., p. 121.

17. Glasgow: Greg Philo, John Hewitt, Peter Beharrel and Howard Davis (members of the Glasgow University Media Group), *Really Bad News,* Writers and Readers Cooperative Publishing Society, London, 1982, esp. pp. 113–23.

18. Mencken, op. cit., p. x.

19. Epstein quote: Epstein, op. cit., p. 33.

20. Cokie Roberts quote: "NPR: Low on Money and Morale," by Barbara Matusow, *Washington Journalism Review,* September 1985, p. 29 @ p. 31.

21. Pulitzer quote: Swanberg, op. cit., p. 127.

22. Justice Holmes quote: *Hadley P. Hanson* v. *Globe Newspaper Co.,* 159 Mass. 293.

23. Jody Powell, *The Other Side of the Story,* William Morrow, New York, 1984, pp. 329–30.

24. Mallon story: Hugh Baillie, *High Tension,* Harper & Brothers, New York,

1959, p. 288. It should be noted that while Baillie wrote this book, every word of it ran through my typewriter, with the sole exception of his preface with its acknowledgment to me.

CHAPTER FOUR

1. Liebling quote: A. J. Liebling, *The Wayward Pressman*, Doubleday, Garden City, N.Y., 1948, p. 35.
2. Robert Harris, *Gotcha!: The Media, the Government and the Falklands Crisis,* Faber & Faber, London, 1983, p. 143.
3. A. A. Dornfeld, *Behind the Front Page: The Story of the City News Bureau of Chicago,* Academy Chicago Publishers, Chicago, 1983, p. 49.
4. Ibid., p. 65.
5. Ibid., p. 139.
6. Judge quote: ibid., p. 259.
7. Percentages: The 21 percent figure is a measurement by Johnson & Johnson, which recorded as well as monitored the TV coverage of the Tylenol murders. The statement that this story took more newspaper space than any since the Kennedy assassination was made to Lawrence Foster of J&J by one of the two newspaper clipping firms retained by the corporation. The percentages are from research done for J&J by Young & Rubicam, and were part of J&J's winning entry for a Silver Anvil award from the Public Relations Society of America.
8. Evans, op. cit., p. 251.
9. Self-deprecation: see "Routine Call Provides Tylenol News Tip," by Celeste Huenergard, *Editor & Publisher,* October 9, 1982, p. 33.

CHAPTER FIVE

1. Wainwright: "The Trouble with Blaming Tylenol," by Loudon Wainwright, Jr., *Life,* November 1982.
2. Dana: Swanberg, op. cit., p. 50.

CHAPTER SIX

1. Menninger quote: transcript of remarks, "Tylenol Tragedy" session, APME 1982 convention, mimeo, pp. 22–23. Available from corporate public relations department, Johnson & Johnson, New Brunswick, N.J.

CHAPTER SEVEN

1. Huxley quote: Aldous Huxley, *Jesting Pilate,* George Doran, New York, 1926, pp. 284–87.
2. "Underwoo—ood!": Frederick Lewis Allen, *Only Yesterday,* Bantam Giant edition, New York, 1952, p. 148.
3. Recordings: Federal Radio Commission General Order 32, in *Television Network Program Procurement, Report of the Committee on Interstate and Foreign Commerce,* House of Representatives, U.S. Government Printing Office, Washington, D.C., May 5, 1963, p. 263.

4. White at Dempsey-Charpentier fight: Eugene Lyons, *David Sarnoff*, Harper & Row, New York, 1966, p. 100. This fight, incidentally, was a far bigger news story than any boxing match of the last forty years. The *Times* sent a crew of ten men to New Jersey on the assignment and took twelve pages to tell the story, which began with a three-line headline clear across the top of the front page. See Berger, op. cit., p. 191.

5. Husing as office manager: William S. Paley, *As It Happened*, Doubleday, Garden City, 1979, p. 39.

6. Some of the following material draws on four interviews with Paley in 1975 and on his book. Some of it contradicts Paley's statements in the interviews and in the book. William S. Paley has a safe and highly honorable place in the history of broadcasting, especially news broadcasting, but the fact is that he had an atrociously self-serving selective memory. To take an example that lies in my area of expertise, Paley writes in his memoirs of "my protracted and determined efforts in 1931 to get the Metropolitan Opera on a weekly CBS broadcast. I fought my way through Edward Ziegler, the Met's assistant general manager, who was not enthusiastic, and on to the renowned Otto Kahn, lofty patron of the arts and president and chairman of the Met. I persuaded him to visit my office and to hear the Met's performance as it would be received by a radio listening audience. We put our microphones into the opera house and piped the performance by closed circuit to my office. . . . We heard the overture and several minutes of singing into the first act. Then Kahn leaped to his feet and exclaimed: 'I can't believe it. It's simply marvelous . . . and just imagine, hearing that wonderful music and those marvelous voices and we don't have to look at those ugly faces!'

"With Otto Kahn's zealous go-ahead, I proceeded without any trouble over the next few weeks to arrange broadcasting details with Edward Ziegler. Then one day he came to my office, shaken and white, and announced with some shame that Kahn, while visiting Paris, had met the head of the law firm that handled RCA legal matters, who had convinced him that the Met should broadcast from NBC rather than CBS. It was a callous, dirty trick and I felt terrible about it for weeks." (Paley, op. cit., pp. 71–72.)

As it happens, I have been through the Ziegler correspondence and memo file for 1931. There is no mention of Paley or CBS, though there is an extended discussion of a mock "broadcast" to the offices of Merlin Aylesworth at NBC and a good deal of material about arrangements with Batten, Barton, Durstine and Osborn, which had paid the Met for the right to contract with its singers for broadcasts. One doubts Kahn would be talking about "ugly faces"—a comment revealing the extent of Paley's interests, not Kahn's—in a season that offered performances by authentically sexy ladies like Lily Pons and Grace Moore and Gladys Swarthout (not to mention a Swedish soprano who would presently sue Kahn for winning her intimacy by pledging better roles than she received). What tears it, though, is the reference to the anonymous RCA lawyer Kahn accidentally met in Paris, who arranged the "callous, dirty trick." This was Paul D. Cravath of Cravath, Swaine and Moore, who was Kahn's lawyer, too. Cravath had been on the Met board since 1910, and in fall 1931 would succeed Kahn as its president. It was not until Cravath took over that the Met board discussed broadcasts on any network (I have read the minutes), and then of course it had to be NBC. This sort of thing Paley "forgets."

7. Murrow quote: Alexander Kendrick, *Prime Time: The Life of Edward R. Murrow*, Little, Brown, Boston, 1969, p. 413. The "mortal danger" was the supposed Russian technological advantage—the "missile gap" of which Kennedy was to make so much two years later—and later analysis has argued that there was no such advantage and no such danger.

8. Klauber marching: Gene Fowler, *Skyline*, Viking Press, New York, 1961, p. 292.

9. Bernays story: Edward L. Bernays, *Biography of an Idea*, Simon & Schuster, New York, 1965, pp. 431–32, 434.

10. "Intellectual grasp": ibid., p. 427.

11. White quote: Paul W. White, *News on the Air*, Harcourt, Brace, New York, 1947, p. 39.

12. White quote: ibid.

13. Press-Radio Bureau quote: White, ibid., p. 41.

14. Black quote: *Associated Press* v. *U.S.*, 326 U.S. 1, 20; in Pool, op. cit., p. 211.

15. Murrow quote: Kendrick, op. cit., p. 179.

16. White ad: White, op. cit., p. 201.

17. Advocacy: Mayflower Broadcasting Corp., 8 FCC 333.

18. FCC approval: "Report on Editorializing by Broadcast Licensees," in Part II, *Federal Register*, vol. 29, no. 145, Washington, D.C., July 25, 1964, p. 10424.

19. Justice White quotes: from *Red Lion Broadcasting Corp.* v. *FCC*, 375 U.S. 367, at 398, 398–90. Much of the discussion in these two paragraphs is taken from my previous book *About Television*, Harper & Row, New York, 1972.

20. Sevareid quote: Eric Sevareid, *Not So Wild a Dream*, Atheneum, New York, 1976 edition, p. 111.

21. Sevareid: ibid., p. 196.

22. Murrow on Darlan: Edward R. Murrow, *In Search of Light*, Edward Bliss, Jr., ed., Alfred A. Knopf, New York, 1967, p. 55.

23. Cronkite comment and alleged Johnson reaction: Gary Paul Gates, *Air Time*, Harper & Row, New York, 1978, p. 211.

24. Johnson quote: Lyndon Johnson, *The Vantage Point*, Holt, Rinehart and Winston, New York, 1971, p. 384.

25. Smith quote: Marvin Barrett, *Rich News, Poor News*, the Alfred I. du Pont–Columbia University Survey of Broadcast Journalism for 1977, Thomas Y. Crowell, New York, 1978, p. 57.

26. White quote: Stephen White, *Report on the Chatham Seminar on Television and Society*, mimeo, pp. 147–48.

27. Murrow from Vienna: Bliss, ed., op. cit., p. 4.

28. Praise for Munich coverage: Erik Barnouw, *A History of American Broadcasting*, vol. 2: *The Golden Web*, Oxford University Press, New York, 1968, p. 83.

29. Sulzberger quote: Berger, op. cit., p. 423.

CHAPTER EIGHT

1. Frankel and Hewitt quotes: spoken at a meeting of the Scientists' Institute for Public Information, February 21, 1984; reported in *Columbia Journalism Review* under the title "Why Do People Hate the Press?," May/June 1984, p. 17.

2. "Reality time": David A. Stockman, *The Triumph of Politics*, Harper & Row, New York, 1986, p. 12.

3. Katz quote: Stephen White, op. cit., p. 47.

4. Seldes quote: Gilbert Seldes, *The Great Audience*, Viking, New York, 1951, p. 168.

5. Hewitt quote: Stephen Lesher, *Media Unbound: The Impact of Television Journalism on the Public*, Houghton Mifflin, Boston, 1982, pp. 143–44.

6. Westin quote: Gates, op. cit., p. 59.

7. Gates quote: ibid., p. 61.

8. Friendly quote: Fred W. Friendly, *Due to Circumstances Beyond Our Control,* Random House, New York, 1967, p. 166.

9. Schramm quote: Wilbur Schramm, "Communications in Crisis," in Greenberg and Parker, *The Kennedy Assassination and the American Public: Social Communication in Crisis,* Stanford University Press, Stanford, Calif., 1965, p. 1 @ p. 11.

10. Bagdikian quote: Ben Bagdikian, *The Information Machines,* Harper & Row, New York, 1971, p. 61.

11. Mindak and Hursh: William A. Mindak and Gerald D. Hursh, "Television's Functions on the Assassination Weekend," in Greenberg and Parker, op. cit., p. 130 @ p. 141.

12. White quote: Stephen White, op. cit., pp. 119–22.

13. Black quote: "Al Neuharth's Technicolor Baby, Part II," by Tom McNichol and Margaret Carlson, *Columbia Journalism Review,* May/June 1985, p. 44.

14. Hess quote: Stephen Hess, "Adtech and Washington Reporters," in Gerald Benjamin, ed., *The Communications Revolution in Politics,* Academy of Political Science, New York, 1982, p. 102 @ p. 107.

15. Westin quote: Mayer, *About Television,* p. 192.

16. Stanton quote: Friendly, op. cit., p. 212.

17. These numbers are worth a little analysis. The Nielsen ratings indicated an audience of 12,230,000 households for Rather, 9,850,000 for Brokaw and 9,510,000 for Jennings. Thus the audience for Rather was 29 percent higher than for Jennings, and 24 percent higher than for Brokaw; but the ad rates CBS could charge were only 19 percent higher than NBC's, and 17.3 percent higher than ABC's. The reason for this was demographic: the audience for the *CBS Evening News* is probably the oldest large audience in the world. According to Nielsen, NBC reaches more women under 55 than CBS (almost 20 percent more women 18–34), and ABC reaches more men under 55 than CBS (almost 50 percent more men 18–34).

CHAPTER NINE

1. Boorstin quote: Daniel J. Boorstin, *The Image: Or What Happened to the American Dream,* Atheneum, New York, 1962, pp. 39–40.

2. Haley quote: Marvin Barrett, ed., *Survey of Broadcast Journalism, 1968–69,* Grosset & Dunlap, New York, 1969, pp. 60–61.

3. "Something of quality": Nancy Collins, "The ABCs of Sports Broadcasting," an interview with Roone Arledge in *Columbia,* October 1983, p. 24.

4. Efron quote: Edith Efron, *The News Twisters,* Nash Publishing, Los Angeles, 1971, p. 197 n.; Johnson reference is p. 216 n.

5. "Real people": "How Frank Reynolds Viewed the News, Networks and Notoriety," by Barbara Matusow, *Washington Journalism Review,* September 1983, p. 26 @ p. 27.

6. Brown quote: Les Brown, *Television: The Business Behind the Box,* Harcourt Brace Jovanovich, New York, 1971, pp. 223, 224.

7. Nuclear titles: Dan Nimmo and James E. Combs, *Nightly Horrors: Crisis Coverage by Television Network News,* University of Tennessee Press, Knoxville, 1985, p. 63.

8. Three Mile Island coverage: ibid., pp. 60–86.

9. Weyerhauser: "Aftershocks at Mount St. Helens," by Claudia Morain, *Columbia Journalism Review,* September/October 1983, p. 6.

10. Haley quote: Barrett, *Survey,* p. 61.

11. Ellerbee quotes: Ellerbee, op. cit., pp. 85–86.

12. Belson quote: William A. Belson, *The Impact of Television,* Crosby Lockwood & Son, London, 1967, pp. 145–46.

13. CBS profits: Friendly, op. cit., p. 184.

14. Mickelson quote: "Television's Lords of Creation, II: What Happens to the Talent," by Martin Mayer, *Harper's Magazine,* December 1956, p. 45.

15. Murrow quote: Kendrick, op. cit., p. 318.

CHAPTER TEN

1. Tocqueville, op. cit., pp. 185–86.

2. Frankel quote: *Columbia Journalism Review,* May/June 1984, pp. 18–20.

3. Levy quote: Leonard W. Levy, *Emergence of a Free Press,* Oxford University Press, New York, 1985, p. 86.

4. West quote: "No News Is Bad News: Bored with Campaign '84," by Paul West, *Washington Journalism Review,* November 1984, p. 16.

5. Shields quote: *Mark Shields on the Campaign Trail,* Algonquin Books, Chapel Hill, N.C., 1985, p. 18.

6. Liberal Democrat quote: Haynes Johnson, "The Voters' Mood Is Bad News for Democrats *and* Republicans," Washington *Post,* November 4, 1984, "Outlook," p. 1.

7. Germond and Witcover quote: "Inside Politics," *National Journal,* October 29, 1983, p. 2280; summary quote, of William Schneider, "Divided Electorate," contents page, same issue.

8. Bensley quote: Joan Bieder, "Television Reporting," in Benjamin, op. cit., p. 41.

9. Drew quote: Elizabeth Drew, *Campaign Journal: The Political Events of 1983–84,* Macmillan, New York, 1985, p. 674.

10. Wills quote: "The Networks vs. the Pols: Who Won at San Francisco," by Garry Wills, *Columbia Journalism Review,* September/October 1984, p. 27 @ p. 32.

11. Reedy quote: Martin Linsky, ed., *Television and the Presidential Elections,* Lexington Books, Lexington, Mass., 1983, pp. 122–23.

12. Jefferson quote: Richard Hofstadter, *The Idea of a Party System: The Rise of Legitimate Opposition in the United States, 1780–1840,* University of California Press, Berkeley, 1970, p. 152.

13. Pool quote: Ithiel de Sola Pool, "Citizen Feedback in Political Philosophy," in Pool, ed., *Talking Back: Citizen Feedback and Cable Technology,* MIT Press, Cambridge, 1973, p. 237 @ p. 243.

14. Orren quote: "Pocketbook Politics," by Gary R. Orren, *The Public Interest,* Winter 1979, p. 106 @ p. 107.

15. Shopping carts: "The 90-Second Handicap," by Greg Schneiders, *Washington Journalism Review,* June 1985, p. 44 @ p. 45.

16. Simpson: ibid.

17. Patterson and McClure quotes: "Television and the Less-Interested Voter: The Costs of an Informed Electorate," by Thomas E. Patterson and Robert D. McClure, *The Annals,* vol. cit., p. 88 @ p. 93.

18. Thomas E. Patterson, "Television and Election Strategy," in Benjamin, op. cit., p. 29; the order of the quotes is reversed.

19. Press scores: "General Election Coverage, Part I," by Maura Clancey and

Michael J. Robinson, in Robinson and Austin Ranney, eds., *The Mass Media in Campaign '84*, American Enterprise Institute, Washington, 1985, p. 27 @ p. 29.

20. Al Jolson: "Inside Politics," by Jack W. Germond and Jules Witcover, *National Journal*, November 10, 1984, p. 2176.

21. Minow and Mitchell quotes: Newton Minow and Lee M. Mitchell, "Incumbent Television: A Case of Indecent Exposure," in Herbert E. Alexander, ed., *The Annals*, vol. cit., p. 74 @ pp. 76, 77.

22. Greider quote: Jane Mayer, "How Reagan Staff Manages News," *Wall Street Journal*, October 12, 1984, back page.

23. Robinson and Sheehan quote: Michael J. Robinson and Margaret A. Sheehan, *Over the Wire and on TV: CBS and UPI in Campaign '80*, Russell Sage Foundation, New York, 1983, p. 137.

24. Mondale quote: "Briefing," New York *Times*, September 8, 1984, p. 5.

25. Busby quote: "Strategists Doubt the Nov. Election Will Mark Any Major Changes in Trends," by James M. Perry, *Wall Street Journal*, January 10, 1984, back page.

26. Dr. Hunter S. Thompson, *Fear and Loathing on the Campaign Trail: 1972*, Fawcett Popular Library edition, New York, 1974, p. 432.

CHAPTER ELEVEN

1. *Tribune:* Graham D. White, *FDR and the Press*, University of Chicago Press, Chicago, 1979, p. 107.

2. Wallace quote: Clancey and Robinson, op. cit., p. 33.

3. *Election Call* and comments: "Hot Work for Robin Day," by Richard Last, *Daily Telegraph*, June 4, 1983, p. 11.

4. Self-quote: "Let's Learn from the British," by Martin Mayer, *TV Guide*, September 17, 1983, p. 11 @ p. 15.

5. "Di Is the Spirit of the Night," *The Lens*, June 1, 1983, back page.

6. Cockerell et al. quote: Michael Cockerell, Peter Hennessy and David Walker, *Sources Close to the Prime Minister*, Macmillan, London, 1984, PAPERMAC edition, p. 10.

7. Ibid., pp. 42–43.

8. Underwood quote: ibid., p. 62.

9. Russell quote: Evans, op. cit., p. 191.

10. Agents: Edward Jay Epstein "Journalism and Truth," *Commentary*, April 1974, p. 36 @ p. 39.

11. Isaacs quote: "The Selling of the Candidates," by Bill Hogan, *Washington Journalism Review*, November 1983, p. 16 @ p. 21.

12. Mondale on reporters: "Reporter's Notebook: Mondale on Icy Main Street," by Bernard Weinraub, New York *Times*, January 13, 1984, p. A15.

13. Drew, op. cit., pp. 601–2.

14. Wexler quote: Germond and Witcover, op. cit., p. 447.

15. Blumenthal: "Once Upon a Time in America," by Geraldine Ferraro, *The New Republic*, January 6–13, 1986, p. 28 @ p. 34.

16. Pileggi quote: David Shaw, "The Mafia Dispute: Press and Ferraro: A Case Study," reprint from Los Angeles *Times*, December 5/6, 1984, p. 8.

CHAPTER TWELVE

1. Ross quote: "The Suppression of Important News," *Atlantic Monthly*, March 1910, pp. 303–11; cited in Dan Schiller, *Objectivity and the News*, University of Pennsylvania Press, Philadelphia, 1981, p. 184.

2. Morton quote: "When a Loss Can Mean a Profit," by John Morton, *Washington Journalism Review*, January 1986, p. 56.

3. "The Myth of the Pink Collar Ghetto," by David Lawrence, *Washington Journalism Review*, January 1986, p. 21 @ p. 22. Note that both quotes come from the same issue of the same magazine. Of course, their authors are differently situated.

4. *TV Guide:* "Network News Today: Which Counts More—Journalism or Profits?" by John Weisman, *TV Guide*, October 26–November 1, 1985, p. 7.

5. Scripps quotes: Barker, op. cit., pp. 303, 304.

6. White: (inter alia) Bagdikian, *Information Machine*, p. 75.

7. Liebling to Sulzberger: Liebling, op. cit., p. 165.

8. Laventhol quote: "Hartford *Courant* Is Home to Many Changes," by Bob Davis, *Wall Street Journal*, October 11, 1985.

9. Hanson quote: Richard H. Meeker, *Newspaperman*, Ticknor & Fields, New Haven and New York, 1983, p. 196.

10. Doder quote: "Unusual Activity in Moscow," by Dosko Doder, *Washington Post*, February 10, 1984, p. 1 @ p. 27.

11. "Out the other": "Building a New Plant," by Paul Kruginski, *Presstime*, vol. 5, no. 6 (June 1983), p. 4 @ p. 6.

12. Fenby quote: Fenby, op. cit., p. 124.

13. *Bulletin* and *Press:* "Newspapers in Transition," by Leo Bogart, *The Wilson Quarterly*, special issue, 1982, p. 58 @ p. 68.

14. Sears ads: "Sears Wants to Increase ROP Spending; Asks Newspapers' Help," *Editor & Publisher*, July 5, 1986, p. 19.

15. "Not demanded": "Onward—and Upward?—with the Newhouse Boys," by Michael Hoyt and Mary Ellen Schoonmaker, *Columbia Journalism Review*, July/August 1985, p. 37 @ p. 44. Sorry about the "no one . . . they," but I fear that's how *CJR* is edited.

16. Reynolds comment: "Games Others Play," by Richard Behar, in *Forbes*, May 19, 1986, p. 144 @ p. 151.

17. "Diversity": "The Dulling Sameness of U.S. Newspapers," by Hodding Carter, *Wall Street Journal*, May 1, 1986, p. 33.

18. Jameson quote: Harris, op. cit., p. 43.

19. Brogan quote: Patrick Brogan, *Spiked: The Short Life and Death of the National News Council*, Twentieth Century Fund, New York, 1985, p. 9.

20. "One game": John L. Hulteng, *The Messenger's Motives: Ethical Problems of the News Media*, Prentice-Hall, Englewood Cliffs, N.J., 1976, p. 12. Cited in "Hutchins Revisited," by Elie Abel, in Schmuhl, op. cit., p. 43.

21. Miami *Herald* case: *Miami Herald Publishing Co.* v. *Tornillo*, 418 U.S. 241. In 1986, peculiarly, this case became the leading authority for the opinion in which Justice William Rehnquist ruled that the state Public Utilities Commissions could not constitutionally compel the power-and-light and telephone companies to include in their billing envelopes literature from various Nader types seeking to use this forum.

22. Constitutional right of reply: see *Red Lion Broadcasting Corp.* v. *FCC*, 395

U.S. 367. The argument was that a "licensee . . . has no constitutional right to monopolize a radio frequency to the exclusion of his fellow citizens. The right of the public to receive suitable access to social, political, esthetic, moral, and other ideas and experiences . . . may not constitutionally be abridged either by Congress or by the FCC."

23. *The People and the Press: A Times-Mirror Investigation of Public Attitudes Toward the News Media, Conducted by the Gallup Organization,* Los Angeles, 1986, p. 36.

24. Pool, *Technologies of Freedom,* pp. 238–39.

25. Political endorsements: "Fifty Years in the Doghouse," by Michael J. Robinson, *Washington Journalism Review,* March 1986, p. 44 @ p. 45.

26. Cancer-causing inks: quote from "Technology for Newspapers Continues to Accelerate," *Editor & Publisher,* January 4, 1986, p. 40 @ p. 43.

27. Robinson finding: "Media, Rate Thyselves," by Michael J. Robinson, *Washington Journalism Review,* December 1983, p. 31 @ p. 33.

CHAPTER THIRTEEN

1. Kuttner quote: "Up the Wall Street Journal," by Robert Kuttner, *The New Republic,* April 10, 1984, p. 15 @ p. 16.

2. Rawlings quote: "Burnout in the Newsroom," by Michael Wines, *Washington Journalism Review,* May 1986, p. 35 @ p. 36.

3. Rosenthal-Bradlee story: "Movers and Shakers" column, *Washington Journalism Review,* March 1986, p. 6.

4. Neuharth quote: "Al Neuharth's Technicolor Baby," by Katharine Seelye, *Columbia Journalism Review,* March/April 1983, p. 27.

5. "Statistics junkies": McNichol and Carlson, op. cit., p. 48.

6. "Provincial press": "Fast-Food News: A Week's Diet," by Ben Bagdikian, *Columbia Journalism Review,* March/April 1983, p. 32 @ p. 33.

7. "Simply made up": "Say It Ain't So, Henry," a supposed open letter to Time Inc. editor-in-chief Henry Grunwald by Steven Brill, *American Lawyer,* January/February 1985, p. 1 @ p. 8.

CHAPTER FOURTEEN

1. Bradlee quote: " 'The First Rough Draft of History,' " *American Heritage,* 1982, p. 33 @ p. 42.

2. "Self-serving sensationalism": "Causing a Hoopla in Kentucky," by Michael York, *Washington Journalism Review,* January 1986, p. 46.

3. Clark quotes: from box entitled "Future News" in "Hard News Will Reign," by Dennis Holder, *Washington Journalism Review,* December 1983, p. 25 @ p. 27.

4. Goldstein quote: Tom Goldstein, *The News at Any Cost: How Journalists Compromise Their Ethics to Shape the News,* Simon & Schuster, New York, 1985, p. 62.

5. Benjaminson quote: Peter Benjaminson, *Death in the Afternoon: America's Newspaper Giants Struggle for Survival,* Andrews, McKeel & Parker, Kansas City, 1984, pp. 60–61.

6. "Almost went under": "The Best of Times at *The New York Times,*" *Business Week,* April 28, 1986, p. 46.

7. Ingersoll quotes: "Ingersoll Boasts, Pulitzer Co. Laughs," by Mark Fitzgerald, *Editor & Publisher,* June 14, 1986, p. 14.

8. KEWQ: see "Trouble in Paradise," by Ruth Lieban, Appendix B, in Barrett, *Survey*, pp. 112 et. seq.

9. Speakes: "White House Desire: Upbeat on the News," an AP story in the New York *Times*, January 29, 1983, p. 10.

10. "Trouble": "A Good-News Paper Sparks a Press War in Huntsville, Texas," by Kevin P. Helliker, *Wall Street Journal*, November 4, 1983, p. 1.

CHAPTER FIFTEEN

1. Shultz story: "Shultz Has Fun with Computer," by William Beecher, Boston *Globe*, October 16.

2. Brinkley article: "A Question for Television Newsmen: Does Anyone Care?" in George Rodman, ed., *Mass Media Issues*, Science Research Associates, Chicago, 1981, p. 105.

3. ITU numbers: James N. Dertouzos and Timothy H. Quinn, *Bargaining Responses to the Technology Revolution: The Case of the Newspaper Industry*, Rand Corporation (for the U.S. Department of Labor), January 1985, p. 13.

4. "Discount": "Battle for Spoils of Fleet Street's Revolution," by Raymond Snoddy, *Financial Times*, February 19, 1986, p. 9.

5. "Paperless offices": Pool, op. cit., p. 42.

6. Romano quote: "A Look into Newspapers' Technological Future," by George Garneau, *Editor & Publisher*, October 12, 1985, p. 9.

7. "The finger": Ellerbee, op. cit., p. 199.

8. Buchanan: "White House Aims High for TV Exposure," by George de Lama, Chicago *Tribune*, February 16, 1986.

9. Coppersmith and Hubbard quotes: "The Ambitions of Stanley S. Hubbard," by Lynda McDonnell, *Washington Journalism Review*, October 1985, p. 41 @ pp. 42, 45.

CHAPTER SIXTEEN

1. Neuharth speech: "Touting the 'Discover Iowa' Media Campaign," *Editor & Publisher*, May 24, 1986, p. 44.

2. Richards quotes: "Forget the Newspaper and TV—Local Cafe Is Where the News Is," by Bill Richards, *Wall Street Journal*, June 7, 1985, pp. 1, 13.

3. Manckiewicz quote: *Time*, December 12, 1983, p. 85.

4. Rueful Reagan: "Why Do They Hate Us?" by Robert MacNeil, *Columbia*, June 1985, p. 5 @ pp. 16, 17, 18.

5. "Riley—Newspaper Correspondent," in Mark Twain, *Sketches New and Old*, Harper & Brothers uniform edition, New York, 1903, p. 199 @ p. 204. The sketch itself is from 1867.

6. Bachrach quote: "Television: Gorgeous George," by Judy Bachrach, *The New Republic*, June 10, 1985, p. 28.

7. Jefferson's formulation: Leonard W. Levy, *Emergence of a Free Press*, Oxford University Press, New York, 1985, p. 251.

8. Jefferson quotes: from John Tebbel and Sarah Miles Watts, *The Press and the Presidency*, Oxford U. Press, New York and Oxford, 1985, pp. 39, 40, 41.

9. Ibid., p. 218.

10. Ibid., p. 345.

11. Roosevelt and the weather bureau: Kevin Cash, *Who the Hell Is William*

Loeb?, Amoskeag Press, Manchester, N.H., 1975, pp. 45–46. The presidential secretary who delivered the order, by the way, was the father of the William Loeb, publisher of the Manchester *Union-Leader,* who later terrorized politicians in New Hampshire.

12. Iron Ore, Mich.: "Shop Talk at Thirty," by Jerome H. Walker, Sr., *Editor & Publisher,* March 8, 1986, p. 52.

13. Coolidge quote: Tebble and Watts, op. cit., p. 314.

14. "Journalism under Fire," written by Bill Henry, *Time,* December 12, 1983, p. 76 @ p. 91.

15. Inaccurate or unfair: Robinson, "Fifty Years in the Doghouse," pp. 44–45.

16. Gelb quote: "Was the Tragedy Overplayed?" by Leslie Gelb, *Washington Journalism Review,* April 1986, p. 52.

17. Majeski and Mears: "Protest But No Legal Action," by George Garneau, *Editor & Publisher,* February 8, 1986, p. 7.

18. Leaked material: Epstein, *Commentary,* April 1974, p. 40.

19. Hougan: see "Watergate Revisited," by Phil Stanford, *Columbia Journalism Review,* March/April 1986, p. 46.

20. Mears quote: "NASA's 'Code of Silence,' " by John J. Glisch, *Editor & Publisher,* March 29, 1986, p. 12 @ p. 13.

21. "Newsmen's privilege": *Mass Media, Report of the Special Senate Committee on the Mass Media,* vol. 1: *The Uncertain Mirror,* Ottawa, Canada, 1970, p. 106.

22. Bradlee quote: Laura Longley Babb, ed., *Of the Press, by the Press, for the Press (and Others, Too),* Washington Post Co., 1974, p. 126.

23. Roosevelt: Graham White, op. cit., p. 33.

24. Kurland quote: "The New York Times Case: A Note on the Central Meaning of the First Amendment," *The Supreme Court Review,* 1964, p. 205; cited in Levy, op. cit., p. xvii.

25. Coke and Holt quotes: ibid., pp. 7, 9.

26. Milton quote: *Areopagitica,* in *Complete Poetry and Selected Prose of John Milton,* Modern Library, Random House, New York, 1942, p. 724.

27. "Reliable picture": Lippmann, *Public Opinion,* p. 365.

28. "83 per cent": "Supreme Vindication," by Lyle Denniston, *Washington Journalism Review,* July/August, 1984, p. 14.

29. Pulitzer quote: Swanberg, op. cit., p. 51.

30. Pepsodent: Martin Mayer, *Madison Avenue, USA,* Harper & Brothers, New York, 1958, p. 124.

31. Mr. Baldwin: Waugh, *Scoop,* p. 243.

32. Philby story: Herbert R. Southworth, *Guernica! Guernica!,* University of California Press, Berkeley, 1977.

33. Braestrup book: Peter Braestrup, *Big Story,* Yale University Press, New Haven, 1983 (paperback); pp. xiii, 430.

34. Bradley story: Robert J. Casey, *This Is Where I Came In,* Bobbs-Merrill, Indianapolis, 1945, p. 228.

35. "Story-line": Braestrup, op. cit., p. 40.

36. Ibid., pp. 528–29.

37. "Professional performance": Martin Mayer, *The Teachers Strike, New York, 1968,* Harper & Brothers, New York, 1969, p. 118.

38. Arledge story: "Mobil's Media Master Offers a Corporate Lesson Plan," by Michael Kinsley, *Wall Street Journal,* April 24, 1986, p. 31.

39. Lippmann quote: in Philip Geylin's Introduction to Babb, op. cit., p. ii.

40. Pulitzer quote: Swanberg, op. cit., p. 192.

41. Hildy Johnson: Casey, *More Interesting People,* p. 112.

42. "Merchants of charm": "A Journalist's Responsibility," by Edwin Newman, in Schmuhl, op. cit., p. 31.

43. *Time* and *Life:* Griffith, op. cit., p. 146.

44. Kohlsaat: Casey, *Such Interesting People,* p. 59.

Index